CRIMINAL VIOLENCE

Patterns, Causes, and Prevention

Marc Riedel
Southern Illinois University

Wayne Welsh
Temple University

Roxbury Publishing Company
Los Angeles, California

Library of Congress Cataloging-in-Publication Data

Riedel, Marc
Criminal violence: patterns, causes, and prevention / Marc Riedel,
    Wayne Welsh.
    p. cm.
Includes bibliographical references and index.
ISBN 1-891487-67-1
1. Violence—United States. 2. Violent crimes—United States.
    I. Welsh, Wayne N., 1957– II. Title.
HN90.V5 R54 2002
303.6'0973—dc21   00-045807
                                                            CIP

Criminal Violence: Patterns, Causes, and Prevention

Publisher: Claude Teweles
Managing Editor: Dawn VanDercreek
Production Editor: Jim Ballinger
Copyeditor: Ann West
Proofreaders: David Marion, Scott Oney
Indexing: Rebecca DuBey, Kate Sterner
Typography: Abe Hendin
Cover Design: Marnie Kenney

Printed on acid-free paper in the United States of America. This book
meets the standards for recycling of the Environmental Protection
Agency.

ISBN 1-891487-67-1

Roxbury Publishing Company
P.O. Box 491044
Los Angeles, California 90049-9044
Voice: (310) 473-3312 • Fax: (310) 473-4490
E-mail: roxbury@roxbury.net
Website: www.roxbury.net

Dedication

To Laurine R. Kreipe and Paul Kreipe,
who have provided support and helpful advice
over these many years.
MR

To Dea Silbertrust and Illana Welsh—
It is only with their continued patience, love, and support
that I am able to keep my balance and occasionally strike out
on large projects such as this.
WW

Contents

Preface

We have both taught senior-level undergraduate and graduate courses in criminal violence for many years. During that time, we searched for a text on violence that could satisfy several important criteria. For example, could a single text provide comprehensive coverage of major topics and theories of violence, provide a coherent analytical framework, and yet remain interesting and easy to understand? We were dissatisfied with what we found.

Instead, like many instructors, we used a constantly evolving series of paperbacks, journal articles and book chapters, in addition to drawing upon our own research, expertise, and experience. One of the shortcomings of that approach is that students do not easily acquire an overview of the area from a perspective that provides continuity across different topics. Assigning a book on serial murder, for example, may generate great student interest, but it has a tendency to give students a rather narrow view of criminal violence. It appeared to us that there was a need for a text that would provide a coherent approach to the study of criminal violence without oversimplifying on the one hand and without losing students in specialized terminology and disparate perspectives on the other.

The result, we hope, is a text that provides broad coverage of major topics and controversies in violence, based upon the most current knowledge available. We attempt to provide the "big picture" without oversimplifying. Our approach provides the student with a consistent and coherent framework for analyzing different types of violence, taps the most up-to-date research and knowledge available, employs diverse theoretical perspectives, and examines state-of-the-art prevention and intervention methods. We attempt to communicate to students in a lively, straightforward manner that stimulates critical thinking and interest.

One of the most original features of the book is the use of a consistent and engaging approach to discuss each type of violence.

This framework should help students to understand the important relationship between research, theory and application. Using a tripartite framework, each type of violence is discussed in terms of major patterns, explanations, and interventions:

- *Patterns* include characteristics of victims, offenders and offenses; situational correlates (e.g., places where violence occurs frequently); and trends over time. The search for relevant explanations must be informed by knowledge of major patterns.

- *Explanations* examine major theories that have been used to understand each type of violence. The search for effective interventions must be preceded by the identification of relevant causes.

- *Interventions* represent proposed solutions to each type of violence, including diverse legal and social strategies, both proactive (e.g., prevention) and reactive (e.g., punishment).

Specific subtopics covered include the following:

- Homicide and aggravated assault.
- Urban riots.
- Gang Violence.
- Domestic terrorism.
- Family violence.
- Hate crimes.
- Robbery.
- The role of firearms in violence.
- Rape and sexual assault.
- The role of drugs and alcohol in violence.

The first four chapters provide the building blocks for a systematic study of violence.

The first chapter examines meanings of violence. Definitions, assumptions about causes, and choices of interventions are seen not as simple facts but as the products of social and political processes. We suggest at the outset that violence is not a rare or exotic phenomenon in society, but is expressed in a wide variety of activities such as sports and accidents. The first chapter shows how violence is regulated with criminal law being an important mode of social control. This chapter also discusses the similarities and differences between legal and criminological approaches to violence.

The second chapter examines the challenge of getting reliable and valid information about violence. Three sources of information are examined in detail: Uniform Crime Reports, mortality statistics, and the National Crime Victimization Survey. The Monitoring the Future surveys and General Social Survey are also discussed.

The third chapter provides a historical and comparative perspective on violence in the United States, addressing stereotypes about the current nature and amount of violence in the United States and comparing it with other countries. For example, levels of violence in the United States were much higher in the past century than they are at present.

The fourth chapter introduces students to major theories that are used throughout the rest of the book, providing essential descriptions of each theory and discussion of its major strengths and weaknesses. As we summarize each theory, we indicate the kinds of offenses to which it has been applied. When we discuss explanations in subsequent chapters (5 through 12), we refer back to chapter 4 and show how the general theory is used to explain specific types of violence.

Using the tools and skills developed in the first four chapters, Chapters 5 through 12 then examine specific types of violence using the tripartite perspective.

Chapter 5 discusses criminal homicides and aggravated assaults. Not only are patterns, explanations, and interventions discussed with respect to homicides and assaults generally, but also with stranger violence, serial homicides, and gang violence. Each instance of the latter is prefaced with a discussion of the difficulties or getting an accurate picture of the phenomena. The section on stranger violence describes violent stranger encounters that occur in public settings such as bars. The section on serial homicides or murders describes the myths associated with the phenomena as well as the difficulties of finding and arresting serial killers.

Finally, gang violence is discussed with respect to where it occurs and the amount of violence involved, especially violence related to drugs.

Chapter 6 examines the types of violence occurring between intimate partners and violence by and towards other family members. The many significant changes aimed at reducing violence between intimate partners is discussed in this chapter. Not only do we have a better understanding of the phenomena, but we also have developed a wide variety of interventions for dealing with "people who hit people because they can." The section on violence toward other family members discusses parents killing children as well as children killing parents. Explanations for violence include the role of child abuse.

Chapter 7 discusses one of the most feared crimes in cities, robbery, including its frequency, environmental influences, and the psychological and physical consequences for the victims involved. While persistent robbers are attracted to robbery as a means of getting quick cash, they are also motivated by participation in street culture and a desire to demonstrate physical toughness and even ruthlessness to others. Interventions discussed include targeted law enforcement, mandatory sentencing and Crime Prevention Through Environmental Design (CPTED).

Chapter 8 examines definitions, patterns and trends in rape and sexual assault offenses, as well as characteristics of offenders and victims. Examples illustrate the diversity of rape and sexual assault incidents. We examine causal theories (e.g., psychological theories, feminist theories) and major interventions including rape law reform, victim counseling and assistance and sex offender treatment.

Chapter 9 examines collective and political violence, including the use of power in conflicts between different groups. Detailed examinations of urban riots and domestic terrorism are provided. Explanations of urban riots include social structural conditions (i.e., social conditions such as poverty and inequality), organizational explanations (e.g., police capacity to respond effectively) and social psychological explanations (e.g., diffusion of responsibility in a large mob). Effective interventions must include remedial strategies (e.g., education, job training) and not just social control. Explanations of domestic terrorism focus upon group conflict theory and individual adaptations to social structural conditions (i.e., anomie theory). Interventions include law enforcement strategies (e.g., gathering and disseminating information about terrorists and terrorist groups, formulating effective response strategies to terrorist incidents), but must also include finding ways to reduce alienation among large groups of people (e.g., educational approaches).

In chapter 10, we define the category of hate crimes and the laws behind it, and examine the characteristics of incidents, offenders and victims. We provide examples of how racial tensions can escalate to interpersonal violence. Explanations include social psychological (e.g., group conflict) and social structural (e.g., economic competition) theories. We examine promising intervention strategies including specialized police bias units, hate crime legislation, and educational approaches.

Chapter 11 examines the role of firearms in violence. This chapter illustrates the need to examine situational correlates of violence, including the roles firearms play, the types of crimes involving firearms, what injuries are sustained as a result of firearm use, and various theories explaining the use of firearms (e.g., symbolic interaction theory and the escalation of disputes; routine activities theory and illegal markets). Intervention strategies examined include gun control legislation and targeted law enforcement (e.g., disrupting illegal gun markets).

Chapter 12 examines the evidence linking alcohol and drug use to violence, and provides insight into the claims that drugs are a direct cause of violent behavior. In reality, there are several different types of drug-related violence, and the apparent connections between drug use and violence are considerably more complex than commonly acknowledged. Intervention strategies examined include police-community partnerships (e.g., Weed and Seed), drug courts, and prison-based drug treatment programs.

The final chapter discusses more general types of prevention and intervention that don't fit easily or neatly into any one specific subtopic. We examine criminal justice approaches (e.g., capital punishment, three-strikes laws) as well as public health approaches (e.g., risk-based prevention, community and economic development). We develop two arguments: (1) an effective strategy to reduce violence must balance both preventive and punishment approaches, and (2) public policy must be better informed by valid information regarding violence patterns, causes and interventions.

Criminal violence is a broad, multidimensional topic that has often defied easy categorization or analysis. There are simply a multitude of topics, theories and interventions that cut across many different disciplines and perspectives. No one text can address everything; certainly as authors we had to set some limits for ourselves. For example, some of our reviewers suggested more coverage of international and cross-cultural perspectives on violence. Others wanted more in-depth historical analysis of conditions in the United States. Some wanted more detailed examination of violence measures and statistics, others less. Some wanted more focus on theories of violence, some wanted more attention to public policies and interventions. We suspect that no single text on violence could ever fully satisfy the needs of everyone. However, we firmly believe that the major topics, theories and interventions associated with criminal violence can be usefully and coherently interwoven into a single text that introduces students to one of the most challenging and interesting problems of our time. We hope that we have been moderately successful in our aspirations so far, and we invite our students and colleagues to continue to give us their valuable (and valued) feedback.

We want to acknowledge our debt to the many colleagues who reviewed the manuscript. Their guidance and suggestions proved to be very useful: Jeffrey S. Adler (*University of Florida*), Alex Alvarez (*Northern Arizona University*), Thomas J. Bernard (*Pennsylvania State University*), Derral Cheatwood (*University of Texas at San Antonio*), Scott Decker (*University of Missouri at St. Louis*), Edna Erez (*Kent State University*), Anne Goetting (*Western Kentucky University*), Gary Jensen (*Vanderbilt University*), Steven P. Lab (*Bowling Green State University*), Alex Piquero (*Northeastern University*), Wendy C. Regoeczi (*Cleveland State University*), Dean G. Rojek (*University of Georgia*), Richard Rosenfeld (*University of Missouri at St. Louis*), Frank Scarpitti (*University of Delaware*), Nanci Koser Wilson ((*Indiana University of Pennsylvania*), Richard A. Wright (*Chicago State University*), and Margaret A. Zahn (*North Carolina State University*).

It is somewhat misleading to label authors in a large undertaking of this type as first and second author or senior and junior authors. Both of us have contributed equally to this work and wish to see it regarded as a product of both of us.

We would also like to thank our many students and colleagues who provided constructive feedback on earlier versions of chapters. However we are responsible for any errors in the book or sound advice that was given by others, but not taken! ✦

Chapter 1

Violence and Criminal Violence

Defining Violence

If we pay attention to newspapers, television, and other types of media, violence appears to be a pervasive part of life. Even if we ignore fictional accounts, newspapers, magazines, television, and the World Wide Web provide a plethora of violence both in types and amount. But what is violence? Is there a difference between violence and criminal violence?

Violence is difficult to define because there are so many different kinds. There is violence associated with the *forces of nature*. Tornados, hurricanes, earthquakes, rainstorms, floods, and forest fires are frequently described as violence that results in loss of life and property.

Violence may be the outcome of extreme emotional states such as *rage, anger, or hate*. While rage, anger, or hate may be directed toward people, these emotions may also be directed toward animals or even objects. Kicking the dog after a frustrating day at the office is the most commonly given example, although there are far more serious instances of animals being excessively beaten, starved, or otherwise abused (Newman, 1979).

What comes closest to the definition of violence used in this book is offered by Weiner, Zahn, and Sagi (1990, p. xiii): *Violence* is "the threat, attempt, or use of physical force by one or more persons that results in physical or nonphysical harm to one or more persons." We generally think of violence as actions directed to-

1

ward another in a face-to-face encounter or near-physical contact. Such behavior may be purposeful or motivated by frustration and anger at another.

Violence may be the inevitable accompaniment of socially approved activities. There is an enormous amount of *sports violence* which is not only legal, but acceptable because of the circumstances in which it occurs. Atyeo wrote,

> The thing about sport is that it legitimizes violence, thereby laundering it acceptably clean. Incidents routinely occur in the name of sport which, if they were perpetrated under any other banner short of open warfare, would be roundly condemned as crimes against humanity. The mugger in the parking lot is a villain; the mugger on the playing field is a hero. The pain inflicted in sport is somehow not really pain at all; it is Tom and Jerry pain, cartoon agony which doesn't hurt. We can sit happily at the ringside watching a Chuck Wepner have his face split and torn by a Sonny Liston, yet if we were forced backstage to watch the doctor lace 120 stitches into that same face we would run away in horror. (1979, p. 11)

Because violence is legitimated on the playing field there is a tendency for athletes to be involved in more violence off the field, particularly domestic violence, than nonathletes. According to the National Coalition Against Violent Athletes, male student-athletes constitute 3.3 percent of the population, but they represent 19 percent of sexual assault perpetrators and 35 percent of domestic violence perpetrators (National Coalition Against Violent Athletes, 1997).

What is the source of a far greater number of deaths and injuries than workers assaulting one another in the workplace? It is *corporate violence*. Corporate violence is behavior that produces an unreasonable risk of physical harm to employees, the general public, and consumers resulting from deliberate decisions by corporate managers or executives (Brownstein, 2000; Kramer, 1983).

One of the best-documented examples is the case of the Ford Pinto, which Ford executives knew would burst into flames from a low-speed rear-end collision. The insertion of a plastic shield between the car body and the gas tank would have prevented this, but would have added approximately $11.00 to the manufacturing cost of each of the 11 million cars sold by Ford (Hills, 1987).

Occupationally related deaths also have occurred because the employer did not provide adequate safeguards to prevent contact with toxic substances. For example, people have died from cancer at disproportionate rates because of exposure to high levels of asbestos or vinyl chloride (Swartz, 1975).

In addition to the use of physical force, there is *psychological violence*, which can consist of persistent negative attributions to others, particularly those emotionally close to the speaker. For example, it can be emotionally damaging to one intimate partner if the other persistently threatens, denigrates, or verbally abuses him or her. Other examples include controlling another in a way that provides an opportunity to criticize and denigrate. That is, a husband may allocate too little money to the household food budget and then constantly criticize the wife for the type and quality of food served.

What is notable about the preceding examples is that the violence may or may not be criminal violence. For example, does psychological abuse carry a criminal penalty? While there are numerous instances of sports and corporate violence, few of those responsible for the acts are criminally prosecuted. What is the difference between violence and criminal violence?

Turning Violence Into Criminal Violence

What turns "the threat, attempt, or use of physical force by one or more persons" toward others into criminal violence is *law*. Without law, the violence may be outrageous, immoral, depressing, hurtful, demoralizing, and lamentable, but it is not a crime. There are certain acts of violence that cannot be tolerated in an ordered society so representatives of a government create rules prohibiting some forms of the violent behavior outright and circumscribing their expression in other instances. Sanctions, such as a prison term, are imposed for violations of these laws.

One view of how such laws are created is the **consensus model**, which assumes that members of society by and large agree on what is right and wrong and the law codifies these agreed-upon social values (Adler, Mueller, & Laufer, 1998). The nearest approximation to this view are laws prohibiting homicide, one of the oldest criminal laws. The law of homicide used in the United States developed out of English common law. When the Pilgrims landed at Plymouth Rock, they brought English common law with them. One of the first murders reported in the American colonies occurred in 1630 when John Billington, a part of the original band of 102 Pilgrims to land at Plymouth Rock, fired his blunderbuss at a neighbor from behind a rock and killed him. Billington was charged with murder, tried, convicted, and hung (Nash, 1973).

A second view is a **conflict model** in which power is the key to lawmaking. According to the conflict model, people with political and economic power make laws that protect their interests while using laws to keep the poor at a disadvantage. The conflict model is used to explain why laws governing white-collar and environmental crimes are infrequently and lightly enforced. Those responsible for exposing humans to toxic wastes that shorten lives or those that make unsafe automobiles are rarely prosecuted as violent criminals because of their high social status (Hills, 1987).

Related to the conflict perspective is the view that social reality in general, including criminal laws, is **socially constructed** (Berger & Luckmann, 1967; Spector & Kitsuse, 1987). Brownstein provides a succinct statement of the perspective:

> From the social constructionist perspective, social reality is a product of social interaction in the form of individual decisions, interpretations, and actions. In that individuals act and interact, make decisions, and interpret their experience in the context of their unique social positions and interests, social reality and hence all social phenomena are necessarily constructed in an ideological and political context. That is, the social world in which we live is designed by us in the context of our own values and interests, or, more precisely, by those among us who have the power to design that world in the context of their own values and interests. (2000, p. 4)

Brownstein is suggesting that social problems, such as violence, consist of images and ideas that appear as subjective perceptions to us. But these perceptions are socially constructed, that is, they become social problems as the result of interaction with others, particularly interaction with groups or organizations that have the capacity to socially define a condition as problematic, in a literal sense. These groups and organizations also provide solutions in the form of laws or prevention programs. Among the most powerful of these claims makers are the media, who present constructions of violence that come to be accepted as objectively real even though, in many circumstances, what is uncovered by research shows the constructed reality to be grossly exaggerated or nonexistent. The following are several examples:

- In the mid-1980s, the public was led to believe by media and government officials that we were in the midst of a crack cocaine epidemic that was leading to high levels of violence. At the same time, Henry Brownstein, Paul Goldstein, and Pat Ryan were studying whether crack caused violence. They found a relationship between crack and violence, but 85 percent of the crack-related homicides involved disputes over crack market dealing. Only five of the 414 New York homicides studied were the result of using crack and two of these involved other drugs as well. Clearly, the "drug-crazed killer" was the product of media claims making (Brownstein, 2000).

- The 1970s witnessed the discovery of a new deviant — the Halloween sadist, who gives dangerous and adulterated food to children. For example, the nice lady down the street who gives apples to children may conceal a razor blade inside. Media warnings to parents went out and California and New Jersey legislatures passed laws against Halloween sadism. Best and Horiuchi (1985) searched four major newspapers for all instances of Halloween sadism between 1959 and 1984. Of the 76 instances uncovered, only two resulted in the death of children. In one case, the child ate heroin that was hidden in his uncle's home, not in Halloween candy. In the second case, the child died of cyanide in candy that had been placed there by his father, not some anonymous sadist. The remaining cases had minor injuries.

- The 1980s saw the emergence of a moral panic about serial killings which were, according to widespread accounts, up to 20 percent of all homicides. However, upon investigation, Jenkins (1994) concluded that serial murders were less than 1 percent of all murders. The exaggerated count of serial murderers emerged from dubious statistics presented in Congressional hearings by FBI representatives and were treated as objective fact by the media. Media claims were reinforced and extended by groups such as homosexuals, African Americans, feminists, and various cults who claimed victimization by serial killers.

The focus of the media on drug-crazed killers, Halloween sadists, and serial killers occurs partly because they are associated with unusual forms of violence. The thousands of U.S. murders, sexual assaults, domestic batteries, aggravated assaults, and robberies occur so frequently that they are no longer newsworthy. What we are suggesting is that there must be something unusual about criminal violence to warrant media attention. The issue is captured by the old saying, "It's not news when dog bites man. It's news when man bites dog."

The fact that the media rarely present a representative view of violence in the United States has an important policy implication. The views carried by the media have a profound impact on legislators, policy makers, and the public, and criminal laws can and do result from exaggerated and distorted views of the problem. Perhaps the best example is the severe sanctions imposed for the possession and use of marijuana although the drug has been shown repeatedly to have little or no relationship to violence.

There are a large number of laws governing the expression of criminal violence. We know them under laws prohibiting homicide, assault and battery, robberies, sexual assaults, and laws against collective and political violence, such as terrorism, labor violence, and hate crimes. We will describe these laws in the chapters dealing with the latter forms of violence.

Perspectives on Criminal Violence

The three perspectives of criminology, criminal justice, and public health provide different ways of viewing criminal violence. The similarities and differences of the two most closely related disciplines, criminology and criminal justice, will be discussed in the following section. Although criminological issues overlap with those of criminal justice and public health, we will focus on distinctions between criminal justice and the public health perspective in the second section. All three approaches contribute to policy and practice.

A Criminological Perspective

Criminology in the United States got an important impetus and legitimation from the work of sociologists at the University of Chicago studying crime and social disorganization in the 1920s and 1930s. Criminology is defined as "the scientific study of the making of laws, the breaking of law, and society's reaction to the breaking of laws" (Adler, Mueller, & Laufer, 1998, p. 1).

We have discussed the making of laws in a previous section where we described how criminal law is made through consensus and conflict. For the latter, we discussed the contributions of social constructionists.

The second part of our definition, the breaking of laws, is what is typically thought of as the main concern of criminology. What is important to recognize is the difference between a legal and a criminological approach to crime. Practitioners in the criminal justice system (e.g., law enforcement, prosecutors, judges, probation officers, and correctional personnel) are primarily interested in processing offenders according to criminal law. They are, of course, very interested in any measures that would reduce the appearance or, more likely, the reappearance of offenders, but their job is to work within the limits of law. Criminologists, on the other hand, have the task of explaining why the behavior occurred.

The final component, society's reaction to the breaking of laws, indicates that criminologists are interested in the effect that lawbreaking has on general society. Do people feel that some sanctions are more effective than others? Does the punishment handed out by courts fit the crime in the view of the public?

A Criminal Justice Perspective

Criminal justice achieved its current prominence as a result of legislation funding criminal justice education during the administration of President Lyndon Johnson in the 1960s and 1970s. Although criminology has been heavily influenced by sociology, criminal justice is multidisciplinary, assimilating the insights of a variety of social sciences (e.g., sociology, psychology, economics, history, geography, and political science).

While criminology focuses on why criminal behavior occurred, the focus of criminal justice is the criminal justice system—law enforcement, the criminal courts, and corrections.

Gottfredson (1999) describes four themes that are central to understanding the criminal justice system:

- The conflict between personal liberty and community safety that is reflected in daily criminal justice decisions. While we value liberty, we also recognize that the behavior of some people must be controlled for the safety of others.

- Law enforcement agencies, criminal courts, and correctional agencies are part of an interacting system. What happens in one part affects all the other parts.

- An emphasis in the study of criminal justice is on the quality of decision making by those who work in the system. Decisions should be made in a framework that is legal and ethical.

- The main resource for making decisions and understanding the criminal justice system should be a reliance on scientifically gathered and evaluated information.

The different emphases of criminology and criminal justice are complementary. Criminology focuses on the "front end" of the criminal justice system, criminal justice on the remainder of the system itself. Criminology not only considers the causes of individual crime, but explores the components of a criminogenic society. Criminal justice examines organizations and the impact of decisions on the offender and on other parts of the system.

Both criminology and criminal justice rely on scientific theory and the use of the scientific method to understand and evaluate criminality. Because the public health perspective also relies on the scientific method, we will postpone discussion of how criminal violence is studied until we have described the public health perspective.

Public Health Perspectives

The public health approach views violence as emerging from a complex causal system that includes but is not limited to offender intentions, motivations, and characteristics (Moore, 1995). The public health approach focuses on reducing the probability (risk) of harm. It emphasizes prevention rather than reaction, and reducing risk factors rather than simply incapacitating violent offenders (Prothrow-Stith, 1991). Moore (1995) outlines three key distinctions between public health and criminal justice approaches to violence. Each provides different ideas about (1) the problem, (2) its causes, and (3) effective interventions.

First, each sees the *problem* of violence differently. Criminal justice personnel view *interpersonal attacks* as crimes; public health specialists view them as *intentional injuries*. Intentional injuries are viewed as part of a larger category of health problems that include both disease and injuries; injuries include intentional injuries as well as unintentional injuries, that is, auto accidents, falls, and fires.

Criminal law and public citizens both place greater weight on violent incidents resulting in serious injury or the threat of injury (Moore, 1995). Public health professionals, in contrast, have traditionally focused more on diseases and unintentional injuries. If data show that the death rate due to homicide for young black males is more than ten times the rate for young white males, however, then one must seek to find ways to reduce the level of harm to this population (Mercy & O'Carroll, 1988).

Differences in problem definition also result in different views regarding offenders and victims. In general, the criminal justice system attempts to prevent violent crime through deterrence, rehabilitation, or incapacitation. **Deterrence** refers to the inhibiting effect that punishment has on potential offenders in the public (general deterrence). This may involve increasing the probability of arrest, conviction, and incarceration, or increasing sentence severity. Specific deterrence, in contrast, would seek to prevent future criminal acts only by the individual punished. **Incapacitation** refers to the fact that an offender is restrained from committing any further crimes against the public, at least during the period he or she is confined. **Rehabilitation** refers to any postconviction treatment aimed at reducing an offender's future likelihood of committing crimes. We review some evidence for the effectiveness of each in chapter 13. In reality, though, many criminal justice programs and policies today address multiple goals simultaneously, and traditional distinctions between these goals are less pronounced than they once were (Welsh, 1993).

To public health specialists, the essential task is to repair the damage of the attack and reduce future attacks rather than assign blame. Similarly, the public health community has traditionally been more sensitive to violence occurring between intimates, because much violence unreported to police is likely to turn up in emergency rooms, schools, and other noncriminal justice settings.

Criminal justice also tackles *causes* differently. Criminal justice specialists tend to focus on the individual offender's intentions, motivations, and background. Indeed, violence would be treated as accidental rather than criminal, were not some level of intention on the part of the offender present. The criminal justice system's emphases on deterrence, incapacitation, and rehabilitation flow naturally from its focus on the intentions and motivations of individual offenders (Moore, 1995).

Public health tends to see violence as emerging from complex causes, including but not limited to the individual offender. **Risk factors** can be defined as statistical or conditional probabilities that elevate the likelihood of violent victimization. **Protection** is indicated when certain factors, such as being raised in a two-parent rather than a single-parent family, lower the statistical likelihood of violent victimization.

A four-step "risk-based" approach guides prevention and intervention efforts (Mercy & O'Carroll, 1988): (1) surveillance (collect, analyze, interpret, and report health data); (2) risk group identification (identify persons at greatest risk of disease or injury, and the places, times, and circumstances associated with increased risk); (3) risk factor exploration (analyze data to explore potentially causative factors); and (4) program implementation and evaluation (design, implement, and evaluate preventive interventions based on understanding of risk factors and the population at risk). This approach is thus highly empirical and pragmatic, rather than theoretical in nature. Public health specialists are informed by theoretical research, although they are more directly concerned with identifying risk factors that are malleable or changeable through ethical and humane methods. Part of the test for a useful theory or a useful risk factor is whether interventions based on its logic will work or not (Moore, 1995).

Public health perspectives focus on at least three broad classes of risk factors: (1) structural and cultural; (2) criminogenic commodities; and (3) situational (Moore, 1995). Poverty, for example,

is a structural risk factor. Poverty exposes children to highe ___
of trauma, victimization, and poor health, with the result that the
likelihood of future success is lowered and the likelihood of future
victimization and/or offending is increased. Criminogenic commodities refer to items that increase both the likelihood of violence
and the seriousness of injury: guns, alcohol, and drugs (see chapters 11 and 12). Situational risk factors refer to specific types of interactions and settings where the risk of violence is elevated. The
notion of *dangerous offenders*, central to criminal justice, is conspicuously missing from the public health perspective (Moore, 1995, p.
246).

As Moore suggests, the public health perspective complements (not replaces) criminal justice. It widens strategies for prevention and intervention. It identifies important opportunities for
preventing and controlling violence that go beyond deterrence, incapacitation, and rehabilitation. It also challenges our moral values about who should be blamed for violent incidents. At least
some interpersonal violence may be seen as heavily influenced by
structural, cultural, and situational factors, rather than the moral
depravity of offenders. If the causes of violence go beyond the individual, then so must solutions.

Indeed, the different foci of *intervention* for criminal justice and
public health advocates is the third key distinction between the
two approaches (Moore, 1995). Traditionally, criminal justice is
more *reactive* while public health is more *proactive*, attempting to
intervene before violence occurs. As a result, three types of prevention are distinguished by public health.

Primary prevention attempts to prevent the occurrence of disease, injury, or death entirely, by targeting and altering one or more
critical risk factors. One might seek to prevent, for example, the
initial occurrence of child physical or sexual abuse. Public health
strategies typically emphasize the importance of primary prevention. **Secondary prevention** attempts to identify and change key
stages in the development of disease, death, or injury that, if left
unaltered, are likely to lead to more serious physical or mental
health consequences. Secondary prevention programs often target
individuals who have already begun to experience some negative
health consequences as a result of their exposure to certain risk factors, but have not yet progressed to serious illness or injury. **Tertiary prevention** attempts to intervene after an illness has been

contracted or an injury inflicted. It seeks to minimize the long-term consequences of the disease or injury, and reduce the likelihood of its reoccurrence. Tertiary prevention programs tend to focus on targets who have already suffered serious, negative consequences (e.g., serious injury, physical or mental disability, and/or criminal justice involvement) as a result of their exposure to certain risk factors.

Preferred interventions are at the level of primary prevention, the prevention of harm before it occurs. The public health perspective complements criminal justice efforts, which mostly take place at secondary and tertiary levels when the risk of violence has been identified and when violence has already occurred. The public health approach brings a different set of strategies for observation and intervention, additional resources for developing and using data, and a broader constituency. The public health approach is not limited to reducing victimization; it extends to reducing violent offending. To reduce harm, public health specialists are equally interested in interrupting the processes that produce violent offenders (Moore, 1995).

For example, a primary prevention approach attempting to reduce drug abuse by adolescents would seek to reduce the likelihood of initial experimentation. Secondary prevention programs target users who have tried drugs, but not yet experienced serious physical or mental health consequences. Tertiary prevention programs target users who have already experienced serious, negative health or behavioral effects (Greenwood, 1992). The extension to violent offending is clear: Public health specialists prefer primary prevention, wherever possible, and thus emphasize the desirability of trying to prevent *first offenses,* or initial occurrences of violent behavior (Moore, 1995). Public health specialists, in contrast to criminal justice professionals, also tend to target structural, cultural, environmental, and situational risk factors much more than individual characteristics. When behavioral approaches are considered (e.g., altering adolescent attitudes and behavior regarding drug use), educational approaches rather than legal interventions (e.g., massive mobilization of police resources to combat drug sales in high crime neighborhoods) are emphasized.

How Is Criminal Violence Studied?

Theoretical perspectives. The study of criminal violence is anchored in criminal law; without criminal law, as we said at the beginning of the chapter, the behavior may be violent, but it is not criminally violent. However, criminology, criminal justice, and public health perspectives are not compelled to view criminal violence through the lens of criminal law. The essential characteristic of a discipline is that it contributes its unique view to an understanding of a phenomenon. The three perspectives discussed in the preceding pages may each view the same phenomenon differently from the way it is viewed by criminal lawyers and other practitioners.

To use an example from criminology, the major legal difference between aggravated assault and criminal homicide is the existence of a dead body. Thus, if an offender robs and beats a victim, leaving him or her in a coma, the offender can be charged with aggravated assault and robbery. However, if the victim dies, the charge is changed to criminal homicide.

Viewing criminal homicide and aggravated assault as separate categories of violence may not be the most useful way of looking at it from the aspect of developing a scientific theory to understand this type of violence. The two crimes are legally distinct, and are processed differently because the homicide ends in death and the assault does not. However, an analysis of police records indicates that the two types of crimes have very similar characteristics (Block, 1977; Pittman & Handy, 1964; Pokorny, 1965). In a more recent comparison of assaults and homicides in Dallas, Harries (1989) found results similar to earlier studies. Homicides are similar to assaults with respect to socioeconomic status, temporal patterns, and racial, age, and gender distributions. Homicides differ from assaults primarily in the more frequent use of firearms.

From the viewpoint of understanding the causes of criminal homicides and assaults, does it make sense to have a theory of homicides and a theory of assaults because they represent different legal categories? A more useful approach is to assume that because they share many characteristics, criminal homicides and assaults may be subsets of one general theoretical category of violence. From this perspective, the causes of both crimes are similar. The differences between the two crimes are the result of factors related to the situation (i.e., differential availability of firearms) or the process of the violent event. In other words, a scientific explanation of criminal violence may call upon criminologists to conceptualize violent behavior in ways that are substantially different from the goals of criminal law and criminal justice processing. In chapter 4, we will examine some of these scientific explanations of violence.

*Research methods.*The preceding discussion on theoretical perspectives was meant to illustrate how researchers can view violence using their particular perspectives. In many instances, research is carried out to answer policy or practice questions using legal categories. For example, homicide has been declining in the United States since the mid-nineties. Using the criminal law definition of homicide, researchers continue to explore the reasons for the decline (Blumstein & Rosenfeld, 1998).

What does bind the three perspectives together is that they use scientific methods to acquire information about criminal violence. For example, Sherman, Shaw, and Rogan (1995) did an **experiment** in which police intensified their efforts to enforce existing gun laws on an experimental patrol beat in Kansas City. The results of their effort were compared to another patrol beat (control beat), in which no increased effort was made to enforce gun laws. The results show that gun-related crimes in the target beat decreased from 37 per 1,000 persons to 18.9, while gun crimes in the control beat showed little change. Other positive findings included a decline in homicides and less citizen fear in the experimental area as compared to the control area.

The National Crime Victimization Survey (NCVS), discussed in detail in the next chapter, is an example of how a **survey** is used to study violence. In addition to questions on violence, the NCVS asks a nationally representative sample a series of questions about how often they have been victimized and the nature of their victimizations.

Researchers use **interviews** as a method of learning about violence. Giordano, Millhollin, Cernkovich, Pugh, and Rudolph (1999) interviewed a representative sample of 12- to 19-year-old males and females in 1982 in Toledo and again in 1992. The authors wanted to know if prior delinquency involvement and self-concept played a role in relationship violence, particularly among females. The results of their analysis supported the view that prior delinquency involvement and a self-concept of angry adult did, indeed, increase relationship violence among females.

Participant observation is one of a number of qualitative research techniques used to study violence. For example, Jankowski (1991) conducted studies of 37 gangs in Boston, New York, and Los Angeles. The gangs were African American, Jamaican, Puerto Rican, Dominican, Chicano, Central American, Irish, and gangs of mixed ethnic membership. He studied these gangs by participating in their daily activities, even to the extent of fighting with them when it became impossible to do otherwise. He became accepted by the gangs and took notes and made tape recordings of their activities.

Secondary data and content analysis, as will be seen in the next section, is frequently used because violent phenomena are statistically rare (Riedel, 2000b). Somewhat less frequently used is content analysis to determine the kinds of information that are available—and presumably read—by selected audiences. Social constructionists who study the impact of media interpretations of public opinion and legislation use content analysis of television, magazines, the World Wide Web, and newspapers. Best and Horiuchi's (1985) study of Halloween sadism is an example of how content analysis of newspapers is used to study violence.

Challenges of Violence Research

The challenge in doing research on violence has little to do with method and everything to do with content because it is criminal violence that is being studied rather than violence.

Because it is *criminal* violence, the research has to be anchored in some fashion in a legal concept of crime. This fact alone shapes and limits the kind of information that is available for research purposes. For example, there are relatively few studies of violent offenders who are not incarcerated, and studies of these offenders indicate awareness that they are committing a violent crime. Although such research is enormously useful, it is clear that offenders interviewed may or may not be a representative sample of offenders.

Much research on violent crime draws upon secondary data, that is, information gathered for another purpose. Most of this research draws upon official records (e.g., police department records or official statistics, such as the Uniform Crime Reports, an annual summary of crime in the United States published by the FBI). We will discuss the latter and other sources of data in the next chapter. The following section considers some characteristics of crime that make access to reliable and valid data on violent crime difficult.

The first obstacle to obtaining valid and reliable data is the rarity of the event. As a rule, the more serious the crime, the less frequently it occurs and the less likely it can be observed directly. For example, in 1999, there were only 2,006 murders and nonnegligent manslaughters in a California population of 34,036,000, which is .0059 percent of the population (Riedel, 2000a; 2001). Given its rarity and generally unannounced occurrence, information about criminal homicides is obtained as a byproduct of police investigation and apprehension of offenders.

The reader may be puzzled by the opening pages of this chapter, in which numerous examples of violence and criminal violence are given. Yet, in the preceding paragraph, it is said that violent crime is statistically rare. In one sense, both statements are true, depending on what is being compared. When we consider 2,006 murders and nonnegligent manslaughters in a population of over 34 million people, they are, indeed, rare events. However, when we consider violent crime in comparison to other technologically advanced nations, criminal violence is extremely high in the United States. We consider these issues in chapter 3.

Second, there are violent crimes more prevalent than criminal homicides, but they cannot be observed easily for other reasons. For example, Harries (1989) found that aggravated assaults (N = 32,096) occurred 27 times more frequently than criminal homicide (N = 1,228) in Dallas from 1981 through 1985. However, aggravated assaults occur in settings that are not routinely subject to surveillance. Thus, robberies and rapes, as well as crimes like burglaries, occur in locations and in ways that reduce the possibility of the offender being identified and apprehended.

Violent assaults also occur in settings that are legally protected from outsiders. Thus, the study of domestic violence must be limited to voluntary reports of violence by the victims or offenders because of the protected privacy of the settings (Gelles & Straus, 1988).

Third, a major premise of the criminal justice system is that victims or bystanders will report crimes. In many instances, victims have a clear interest in reporting crimes because they seek justice, retribution, or restitution for an injury suffered. However, crimes go unreported because victims may be legally implicated in offenses like prostitution, gambling, or possession of controlled substances. Aside from legal accountability, victims may not report crime because they fear humiliation, embarrassment, or offenders. For this reason, spousal and child abuse, sexual assaults, and rapes are underreported.

Generally, violence involving family members and relatives is less frequently reported than violence involving strangers for several reasons. There is a tendency to "normalize" violent attacks by people known to the victim, which does not occur for attacks by strangers. A violent attack is "normalized" by a victim's effort to attribute a socially acceptable and benign meaning to it. The *older* literature on violence between spouses is replete with examples of normalizing: The wife believes that a beating by her husband has to be forgiven and understood in the context of his fears and insecurities over losing his job.

In addition, the criminal justice system is less willing to deal with violent offenses involving people known to one another in comparison to offenses involving strangers, although recent legislation has compelled more attention by law enforcement to domestic violence. Gottfredson and Gottfredson summarize the impact of strangers on discretionary decisions:

> The major pattern may be stated succinctly: It is preferred that the criminal justice process not deal with criminal acts between nonstrangers. Nearly every decision maker in the process seeks alternatives for criminal acts between relatives, friends, and acquaintances. The gravest dispositions are reserved continuously for events between strangers. Victims report nonstranger events less frequently, police arrest less frequently, prosecutors charge less frequently, and so on through the system. (1988, p. 259)

Fourth, victims may respond differently depending on what is considered "normal" in their particular environments. For example, victimization surveys find that victimization by assault is positively correlated with education despite the fact that police files indicate that most victims of assault are lower class. It may be that better-educated persons are better respondents and give more information. However, it is also likely that lower-class persons may see certain types of violence as a normal part of life, whereas better-educated persons have had very little contact with physically assaultive behavior and see such acts as criminal violence (Skogan, 1982).

Fifth, because crime is stigmatizing and carries with it penal sanctions, large portions of the record may be missing, even though the crime is reported. Obviously, offenders have the greatest interest in concealing events. Except for observations supplied by the victim, information about the offender depends on "clearing" an offense by the arrest of one or more offenders. But clearance percentages are very low; the clearance percentage for the most serious crime, homicide, was 69 percent in 1999 (Federal Bureau of Investigation, 1999). If the offender is not known and the victim is dead, police records are missing information about an important participant in the crime for almost 30 percent of these cases.

What Lies Ahead?

The first four chapters of this book provide a background for understanding subsequent chapters on specific forms of violence. The following chapter reviews and discusses the strengths and limitations of different measures of violence. These include data available from police and medical professionals at the local and national levels and the National Crime Victimization Survey.

Chapter 3 focuses on historical and comparative perspectives. Was the United States always a violent society or is it more violent now than in previous historical periods? How does the rate of criminal violence in the United States compare to other technologically advanced and third-world countries?

Chapter 4 is a review of some major theories of violence. Clearly, there are many more theories than we discuss in chapter 4. We have been selective and describe those theories which we draw on in later chapters to explain specific forms of violence.

A Tripartite Approach to Understanding Violence

Following Welsh and Harris (1999), we adopt a **tripartite approach** to violence in chapters 5 through 12. For any specific type of violence, we should first examine **patterns** of violence (who is involved, where, how much, how often, and so on). Second, we attempt to understand or **explain** violence based on those observed patterns. Third, we need to explore **solutions** (interventions) to specific types of violence that are consistent with *both* observed patterns and explanations. Failure to do so increases the likelihood of failed interventions.

Accordingly, each of the chapters on specific forms of violence is divided into three main sections. First, we examine general patterns of specific types of violence. Then, we briefly review major explanations, setting the stage for an examination of promising prevention and intervention strategies. Although our responses to violence have become more punitive over the past few years, new and promising prevention strategies are being developed and tested. *Arguably, the best responses to violence can, must, and will include a balance of both punishment and prevention.* Chapter 13 will examine promising prevention and intervention strategies in more detail.

Patterns. We begin analysis of any specific type of violent behavior by examining information about it. We are interested in questions like the following: How do we define a specific behavior (e.g., homicide, robbery)? How prevalent is it, and where is it? Who are the offenders, and who are the victims? How long has the problem existed? How has it changed over time? We need to be careful, because problems are often socially constructed by the media, politicians, or even criminal justice officials. In other words, certain problems are perceived, and decisions are made to focus attention and resources on a particular situation (Welsh & Harris, 1999). However, perceptions of a problem and reactions to it may be quite different than the actual size or distribution of a problem (Spector & Kitsuse, 1987; Walker, 1998). We need methods to document, describe, and analyze patterns for any specific type of violence.

We also need to look at some kind of data to estimate the degree and seriousness of a problem. Wherever time and resources allow, it is always desirable to use as many techniques as possible to analyze a specific issue. Social indicators, such as police and National Criminal Victimization Survey data, are perhaps the most accessible and widely used information for analyzing criminal justice problems. Other types of data include interview and participant observation.

Examine potential causes of the problem. What causes any specific type of violence? How can we explain why people commit particular acts of violence? This is a critical stage of analysis, because different causes imply different solutions. If we choose a solution (e.g., changing existing laws) before examining causes, it is likely that the solution will be ineffective. Any intervention should be aimed at a specific cause or causes. Causes may be identified at different levels of analysis ranging from individual to social structural:

- *Individual:* Presumed causes lie within individuals (e.g., personality traits such as "aggressiveness").

- *Group:* Presumed causes lie within the dynamics of particular groups to which a person belongs (e.g., patterns of roles and relationships within a family or a gang).

- *Organizational:* Presumed causes lie within the particular culture and procedures of a specific organization such as the police, courts, or prisons (e.g., how police officers are recruited, selected, or trained; how criminal justice officials use their discretion in case processing).

- *Community:* Presumed causes lie within the behavioral patterns and dynamics existing within a specific community (e.g., community "cohesiveness" or the degree of involvement in community organizations, such as churches and community associations; attitudes toward deviance; supervision of juveniles).

- *Social Structural or Cultural:* Presumed causes lie within the underlying social structure of society (e.g., the unequal distribution of wealth and power engendered by the economic system of capitalism) or its cultural attitudes regarding behaviors, such as drug use, sexuality, education, crime, and so on.

We must explicitly examine what our causal assumptions about a specific type of violence are, and we must examine empirical evidence for any cause or theory. One should look at journal articles, books, and government and agency reports (e.g., numerous branches of the U.S. Department of Justice, including the National

Institute of Justice). Although we have tried to provide a useful summary of theories in chapter 4, theories are constantly being refined and tested. We highly recommend reading one of several excellent books on criminological theory (Akers, 1997; Vold, Bernard, & Snipes, 1998).

Interventions. We usually need to discover what types of previous interventions have been attempted to reduce a specific type of violence. The analyst must attempt to find out what major interventions have addressed specific types of violence, and he or she should identify which specific causes the intervention was attempting to modify. Excellent sources of information about interventions are officials working in justice-related positions, criminal justice journals and books, and government reports. Numerous data bases can be searched by key words and terms. Criminal justice literature searches can be conducted on-line, via computer software (disk or CD-ROM), and in printed index format. These include the National Criminal Justice Reference Service (NCJRS) Abstracts sponsored by the U.S. Department of Justice (<www.ncjrs.org>).

Conclusions

This chapter has been concerned with introducing the topic of violence and criminal violence. Violence may be legally neutral. We gave examples of violence in nature and instances of sports violence. In the case of violence in sports, it is looked upon as part of the sport, regrettable as it may be.

What turns violence into criminal violence is law. Laws are constructed by consensus or conflict. We discussed how laws are socially constructed and the powerful effect media claims have on shaping our image of violence and shaping the laws that define criminal violence.

In the third part of the chapter, we discussed criminology, criminal justice, and public health perspectives that will inform the discussion of criminal violence in this book. The final pages of that section described the difficulties of doing research on criminal violence because of the limitations of data. Hopefully, we have left the reader with the curiosity to read the next chapter, in which we describe sources of data about criminal violence and how some of the shortcomings are addressed.

The final section discussed how the remainder of the book is organized. In the first four chapters, we provide a background describing data sources, historical and comparative perspectives, and a summary of the theories we used to explain violence. Chapters 5 through 12 approach specific forms of violence through the tripartite approach of patterns, explanations, and solutions. Chapter 13, the final chapter, examines several broad approaches to punishment and prevention, with a goal of developing a more multifaceted strategy to reduce violence.

References

Adler, F., Mueller, G. O. W., & Laufer, W. S. (1998). *Criminology* (3rd ed.). Boston: McGraw-Hill.

Akers, R. L. (1997). *Criminological theories: Introduction and evaluation* (2nd ed.). Los Angeles: Roxbury.

Atyeo, D. (1979). *Blood and guts: Violence in sports.* New York: Paddington.

Berger, P. L., & Luckmann, T. (1967). *The social construction of reality: A treatise in the sociology of knowledge.* Garden City, NY: Doubleday.

Best, J., & Horiuchi, G. T. (1985). The razor blade in the apple: The social construction of urban legends. *Social Problems, 32,* 188–499.

Block, R. (1977). *Violent crime: Environment, interaction and death.* Lexington, MA: Lexington Books.

Blumstein, A., & Rosenfeld, R. (1998). Explaining recent trends in U.S. homicide rates. *Journal of Criminal Law and Criminology, 88,* 1175–1216.

Brownstein, H. H. (2000). *The social reality of violence and violent crime.* Boston: Allyn & Bacon.

Federal Bureau of Investigation. (1999). *Uniform crime reports for the United States, 1997.* Available: <http://www.fbi.gov/ucr/Cius_97/97crime/97crime.pdf> [June 23, 2001].

Gelles, R. J., & Straus, M. A. (1988). *Intimate violence.* New York: Simon & Schuster.

Giordano, P. C., Millhollin, T. J., Cernkovich, S. A., Pugh, M. D., & Rudolph, J. L. (1999). Delinquency, identity, and women's involvement in relationship violence. *Criminology, 37,* 17–40.

Gottfredson, D. M. (1999). *Exploring criminal justice: An introduction.* Los Angeles: Roxbury Publishing.

Gottfredson, M. R., & Gottfredson, D. M. (1988). *Decision making in criminal justice: Toward the rational exercise of discretion.* New York: Plenum.

Greenwood, P. W. (1992). Substance abuse problems among high-risk youth and potential interventions. *Crime and Delinquency, 38,* 444–458.

Harries, K. D. (1989). Homicide and assault: A comparative analysis of attributes in Dallas neighborhoods, 1981–1985. *The Professional Geographer, 41,* 29–38.

Hills, S. L. (Ed.). (1987). *Corporate violence: Injury and death for profit.* Totowa, NJ: Rowman & Littlefield.

Jankowski, M. S. (1991). *Islands in the streets.* Berkeley: University of California Press.

Jenkins, P. (1994). *Using murder: The social construction of serial homicide.* New York: Aldine de Gruyter.

Kramer, R. C. (1983). A prolegomena to the study of corporate violence. *Humanity and Society, 7,* 149–178.

Mercy, J. A., & O'Carroll, P. W. (1988). New directions in violence prevention: The public health arena. *Violence and Victims, 3,* 285–301.

Moore, M. (1995). Public health and criminal justice approaches to prevention. In M. Tonry & D. F. Farrington (Eds.), *Building a safer society: Strategic approaches to crime prevention* (Vol. 19, pp. 237–262). Chicago: University of Chicago Press.

Nash, J. R. (1973). *Bloodletters and badmen: A narrative encyclopedia of American criminals from the Pilgrims to the present.* Philadelphia: Lippencott.

National Coalition Against Violent Athletes. (1997). Available: <http://campussafety.org/NCAVA/> [May 25, 1999].

Newman, G. (1979). *Understanding violence.* New York: Lippencott.

Pittman, D., & Handy, W. (1964). Patterns in criminal aggravated assault. *Journal of Criminal Law, Criminology, and Police Science, 55,* 462–470.

Pokorny, A. D. (1965). A comparison of homicide in two cities. *Journal of Criminal Law, Criminology, and Police Science, 56,* 479–487.

Prothrow-Stith, D. (1991). *Deadly consequences.* New York: Harper Collins.

Riedel, M. (2000a). *California homicides data file.* Carbondale: Southern Illinois University.

———. (2000b). *Research strategies for secondary data: A perspective for criminology and criminal justice.* Thousand Oaks, CA: Sage.

———. (2001). *California population by counties, 1970–2040.* Carbondale: Southern Illinois University.

Sherman, L. W., Shaw, J. W., & Rogan, D. P. (1995). *The Kansas City gun experiment (Research in brief).* Washington, DC: National Institute of Justice.

Skogan, W. G. (1982). *Issues in the measurement of victimization* (NCJ-74682). Washington, DC: Government Printing Office.

Spector, M., & Kitsuse, J. I. (1987). *Constructing social problems*. New York: Aldine de Gruyter.

Swartz, J. (1975). Silent killers at work. *Crime and Social Justice*, (Spring-Summer), 15–20.

Vold, G. B., Bernard, T. J., & Snipes, J. B. (1998). *Theoretical criminology*. New York: Oxford University Press.

Walker, S. (1998). *Sense and nonsense about crime*. Belmont, CA: Wadsworth.

Weiner, N. A., Zahn, M. A., & Sagi, R. J. (Eds.). (1990). *Violence: Patterns, causes, public policy*. San Diego, CA: Harcourt, Brace, Jovanovich.

Welsh, W. N. (1993). Ideologies and incarceration: Legislator attitudes toward jail overcrowding. *Prison Journal, 73*, 46–71.

Welsh, W. N., & Harris, P. W. (1999). *Criminal justice policy and planning*. Cincinatti, OH: Anderson. ✦

Chapter 2

Measures of Violence

A s the final section of the preceding chapter made clear, getting information or data on the amounts and kinds of criminal violence is a challenging task. Criminologists deal with the problem by using different methods of collecting information in a way that the strengths of one data source are the weaknesses of another and vice versa, that is, the different measures of violence *complement* one another. For example, because we know that victims do not report all crimes to the police, the Bureau of Justice Statistics and the U.S. Census Bureau regularly conduct crime victimization surveys to get information on victimizations that may not be reported to the police. By comparing results of the two data sources, we get a more complete and rounded picture of criminal violence.

The following section describes crime rates. Rates are used so frequently that most people fail to recognize important differences between rates and amounts. The section distinguishes the two and discusses the strengths and limitations of rates.

There are three measures of violence discussed in this chapter. The first two are official statistics compiled by law enforcement and medical people. The third measure is the National Crime Victimization Surveys. Two other measures of violence are discussed briefly: the General Social Survey, and Monitoring the Future surveys.

The first official statistics source is the Uniform Crime Reporting program administered by the Federal Bureau of Investigation (FBI). *Crime in the United States*, more commonly known as the *Uniform Crime Reports* (UCR), is an annual publication that sum-

marizes and synthesizes information on crimes reported by the
police.

The second official statistics source is information published
by the National Center for Health Statistics (NCHS) as *Vital Statistics of the United States*. Information on homicide is obtained from a
death certificate completed by medical personnel.

The best known survey is the National Crime Victimization
Survey (NCVS) administered by the Bureau of Justice Statistics
and U.S. Census Bureau. The Bureau of Justice Statistics issues regular reports on criminal victimization in the United States as well
as reports on specialized topics.

Crime Rates

In 1999, according to police reports, Dallas, Texas, had 191 murders in a population of 1,091,386. By comparison, Chicago, Illinois,
had 642 murders in a population of 2,821,032 (FBI, 1999). Which
city had the greater risk of murder victimization?

Obviously, Chicago had over three times more murders, but on
the other hand, the city has slightly more than 2.5 times the population of Dallas. Other things being equal, the larger the population,
the more murders. In order to compare the two cities, we need a
method that takes account of the differences in population and
that is the purpose of rates.

It is also important to distinguish between rates and what are
variously called raw numbers, amount, volume, incidence, and
prevalence. The latter (we use the term *amount*) is how much violent behavior there is of whatever type defined by location and
time span. Thus, in terms of amount, there were 642 murders in
Chicago and 191 murders in Dallas in 1999.

Rates are a measure of the amount of change in relation to some
basis of calculation such as a population at risk. Crime rates have
five components: (1) amount of the crime in question; (2) population at risk for that crime; (3) a constant multiplier such as 100,000;
(4) location; and (5) time span. Diagrammatically, the following are
the components for a given jurisdiction and time:

Crime Rate = (Amount / Population at Risk) x 100,000

If we "plug in" the numbers for Dallas and Chicago, we have the
following 1999 murder victim rates:

(Dallas) 17.5 = (191 / 1,091,386) x 100,000
(Chicago) 22.7 = (642 / 2,821,032) x 100,000

Because Chicago has the higher rate of 22.7 murders per 100,000, persons living in that city have a higher risk of being a murder victim than those living in Dallas, where the murder rate is 17.5 per 100,000. It is worth noting that while the amount of murder in Chicago is more than three times that of Dallas, the murder victim rate is less than twice the rate for Dallas when the size of the population is taken into account. Thus, relying only on the amount of murder without taking into account population differences can be misleading.

In addition to specifying risk for defined populations, crime rates are useful for comparing the same population groups at different times or different population groups at the same time. Thus, we can compare how murder victim rates have changed in Dallas over a period of years or we can compare Dallas rates to those of other cities with smaller or larger populations.

To get an idea of how crime rates can vary, the murder victimization rate for the United States in 1999 was 5.7 per 100,000 (FBI, 1999). Although this is considerably lower than either Dallas or Chicago, it is important to keep in mind that crime rates are generally lower in rural areas and small towns than in large cities; hence, the murder rate is going to be lower for the entire country than for specific cities. At the other extreme is Cali, Colombia, famous for drug-related violence; in 1993, it had 1,829 homicides for a crude rate of 104 per 100,000. For males, ages 25 to 29, the rate was 450 per 100,000 (Centers for Disease Control, 1995).

Two other features of crime rates deserve mention. First, the constant multiplier of 100,000 is a number conventionally used to convert a decimal to a whole number. In some measures, such as the NCVS, the constant multiplier is 1,000. Beyond making certain that all comparisons of rates use the same multiplier, the number has no significance. Second, while there is generally a question about the extent to which a violent offense is reported accurately, the greatest problem resides in specifying the denominator, the population at risk. In order for a crime rate to be useful, there must be a match between the characteristics of the entities in the numerator and denominator. Thus, we can argue that all citizens of Chicago and Dallas are at risk of being homicide victims, although the level of risk obviously varies.

But what about offender rates? How many newborn babies can manage to fire a handgun with felonious intent? How about hospitalized people in a coma? Strictly speaking, a murder offender rate would have to exclude the latter from the population at risk.

If rates are being computed for approximate comparisons between two cities, for example, offender rates might use the total population even though it is not completely accurate. In using the total populations, the person computing the rates has to assume the two populations are similar along dimensions that would affect the rate. In other words, if it can be assumed that the two populations have about the same proportion of people unable to offend for one reason or another, the crude rate can lead to meaningful comparisons.

But that is frequently not a valid assumption. For example, African-American and white homicide victimization rates for Los Angeles cannot be usefully compared to the same two groups in Chicago even if the proportion of African Americans is the same in both cities. The reason is that there are many more Latinos in Los Angeles than in Chicago; they are an ethnic, not a racial group, and are frequently classified as white. Nevertheless, Latino homicide rates and patterns are distinct from both racial groups (Riedel, 2000a). What is required is that the amount or number of homicides for each racial or ethnic group be divided by the appropriate racial or ethnic population before multiplying by 100,000. This gives us a race/ethnic-specific homicide victimization rate.

Obviously, crime rates can be refined even further by age and gender groups. Thus, we can have race/ethnic-age-gender-specific rates or any combination of the four categories, depending on the purpose of the comparisons. The rate given earlier for 25- to 29-year-old males in Cali, Colombia (450 per 100,000), is an instance of an age-gender-specific homicide rate. The extent to which rates can be refined is determined by the availability of data that can be used to construct a population at risk. Although population data are generally available for age, race, ethnicity, and gender, there are no population data available, for example, on the number of strangers in a population.

Crime rates have been criticized because city population data are not sufficiently accurate to support the kinds of rates needed.

Block (1987), in her study of Chicago homicides, avoided the use of rates because the city population base is not appropriate when substantial numbers of homicide victims are nonresidents. In addition, the use of interpolation for population numbers between census years may not correspond to actual changes in the population. Finally, young black and Latino men are undercounted in the Census, yet they represent a large number of homicide victims and offenders. For many of her comparisons, Block (1987) relied on percentages where the denominator was the total number of homicides.

Uniform Crime Reports

The Uniform Crime Reports (UCR) began in the late 1920s when J. Edgar Hoover, with the support of the International Association of Chiefs of Police, began a program to collect national crime data. In 1930, the U.S. House of Representatives passed a bill authorizing the FBI to be the official national clearinghouse for information on crime obtained from the nation's police departments.

Initially, the UCR program cooperated with police departments on a voluntary individual basis. But as the number of law enforcement agencies grew, the UCR program supported the development of state-level mandatory reporting systems. A state-level system, created by legislation, designates an official crime reporting agency in that state and mandates reporting by all law enforcement agencies within that state.

In 1999, there were over 17,000 city, county, and state law enforcement agencies reporting to the UCR program either directly or through state agencies. This coverage represents 95 percent of the total population or nearly 260 million people (FBI, 1999).

The UCR divides offenses into Part I and Part II offenses. Part I offenses are further divided into crimes against the person (criminal homicide, forcible rape, robbery, aggravated assault, and arson) and crimes against property (burglary, larceny-theft, and motor vehicle theft). Part I offenses are called index offenses; arson was added to the list by congressional mandate in 1979. All other crimes, except traffic violations, are Part II offenses. Part II offenses include 21 other offenses, such as fraud, embezzlement, weapons offenses, and simple assault.

Collecting Violent Crime Data

The process of collecting information about violent crime begins most often with a complaint to law enforcement officials who investigate and determine whether a criminal offense has occurred. The process of compiling records, what records are compiled, and how they are transmitted to the UCR program is illustrated in Figure 2-1.

As Figure 2-1 indicates, states with mandatory reporting programs collect information consistent with UCR requirements. They may collect additional information from local law enforcement agencies, but minimally, they collect information needed by the UCR. The state UCR agency issues its own report; for example, the UCR agency in Illinois is the Department of State Police, and they publish an annual report, *Crime in Illinois*. States without a mandatory reporting system and some large cities, such as Chicago, report directly to the UCR program.

Although the UCR program requires a number of forms, three have the most relevance to violent crime: Return A; Age, Sex, Race, and Ethnic Origin of Arrested Offenders; and the Supplementary Homicide Report. Information from these three forms is the primary source for the annual UCR report.

Return A: Crimes known to the police. As the name implies, this form contains the following information:

1. Offenses reported or known.

2. Founded or unfounded complaints.

3. Number of actual offenses (founded complaints).

4. Total number cleared by arrest or exceptionally cleared (described below).

5. Number of clearances for persons under 18.

A number of features of this form need to be noted. First, because not all jurisdictions report, the numbers of crimes given in annual editions of Uniform Crime Reports are *estimates* based on Return A reports. An "imputation methodology" used to arrive at the estimates is described in detail in Schneider and Wiersema (1990).

Figure 2-1
Uniform Crime Reporting Program

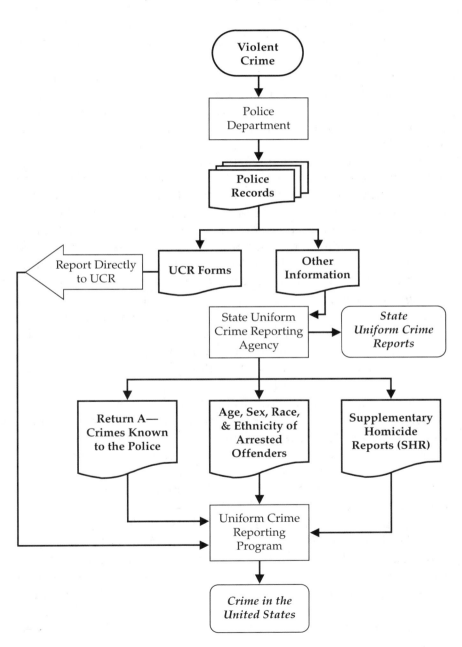

Second, there is no information on specific cases. The published numbers are aggregated and reported monthly. In other words, the annual number of forcible rapes reported in the UCR is a 12-month summary of Return A reports. Indeed, the only case-level information available in the UCR is found in the Supplementary Homicide Reports.

Third, the number of *arrest clearances* refers to the number of offenses for which an arrest was made, not the number of offenders arrested. One arrest can clear many crimes and the arrest of many people may clear only one crime. *Exceptional clearances* refer to the administrative closing of cases for a variety of circumstances beyond the control of police departments. When cases have been adequately investigated, some of the reasons for not effecting an arrest include offenders who committed suicide, died from accidents or natural causes before being arrested, made deathbed confessions, or were killed by police or citizens. Other reasons include confessions by offenders prosecuted for other crimes in other jurisdictions, denial of extradition to the jurisdiction where the crime occurred, or the refusal of the district attorney to prosecute.

Age, sex, race, and ethnic origin of persons arrested. There is one paper form of this type for adults and another for persons under age 18. The two forms are the same except that the juvenile form requests information about curfew violations and runaways. Unlike the clearance measure for offenses, this form asks for the number of arrested offenders.

Offenders are classified into four racial groups: white, black, American Indian, and Asian or Pacific Islander. Ethnicity is coded as Hispanic or Not Hispanic. *Hispanic* refers to Mexicans, Puerto Ricans, Cubans, Central or South Americans, or any persons of "Spanish culture or origin, regardless of race" (FBI, 1984, p. 58). In practice, ethnicity of offenders is determined by investigating officers who may use a variety of definitions.

Supplementary Homicide Reports (SHR). While Return A and Age, Sex, Race, and Ethnic Origin of Persons Arrested forms represent aggregated monthly and annual information, the SHR provides information on each recorded case of murder and nonnegligent manslaughter. From 1962 through 1975, the SHR was primarily a record of the age, race, and gender of victims, weapon used, and circumstances of the offense. Readers interested in the history of the SHR as well as research on the current version are referred to Riedel (1990; 1999).

Beginning with information reported in 1976, the SHR underwent a major revision that substantially improved its usefulness as a data source. The current version of the SHR contains the following information:

1. A situation code indicating combinations of single or multiple victims and single, multiple, or unknown offenders.

2. Age, sex, race, and ethnicity of all victims and offenders involved in the event.

3. Weapons used.

4. Victim/offender relationships.

5. Circumstances, including type of involvement in other felony crimes associated with the homicide.

National Incident-Based Reporting System (NIBRS)

The UCR has been subject to severe criticism for its shortcomings from the 1950s onward (Beattie, 1962; Robison, 1966; Sellin, 1951; Wolfgang, 1963). Two events have reduced the amount of criticism directed toward the UCR program. First, the appearance of the National Crime Victimization Survey in the late 1960s and early 1970s provided information about violent crime that was not available from the UCR. In addition, because of their experience with victimization surveys, criminologists began to appreciate some of the difficulties involved in collecting valid and reliable data about violence (Gove, Hughes, & Geerken, 1985).

Second, although there were some modifications and improvement of the UCR in 1976, a major evaluation and redesign began in 1982 as the result of an FBI/Bureau of Justice Statistics task force (Akiyama & Rosenthal, 1990; Poggio, Kennedy, Chaiken, & Carlson, 1985). The resulting system, the National Incident-Based Reporting System (NIBRS), was based on reporting major characteristics of serious crimes rather than aggregate counts of incidents and arrests. In a word, the kind of detail that was requested for the Supplementary Homicide Reports in the traditional UCR system was also being requested for a large number of serious offenses in NIBRS.

NIBRS is designed to gather detailed information on 46 Group A offenses in 22 categories, such as robbery, types of homicides, assaults, sex offenses, fraud, and stolen property offenses. Group A offenses were selected, in part, because of their seriousness, frequency, prevalence, and visibility to law enforcement. Group B offenses consist of 11 less serious offense categories, including bad check offenses, curfew violations, disorderly conduct, and drunkenness. For Group A crimes, a detailed incident report is filed, but only an arrest report is filed for Group B crimes (FBI, 1992).

When fully implemented, NIBRS will provide much more data and in greater detail than is currently available. First, as noted, the UCR provides little or no detailed information on serious offenses other than homicide. NIBRS would collect information for Group A offenses on type of victim, victim characteristics, victim-offender relationship, use of force or weapon, type and nature of injury, time, type of location, and residence status of victim.

Second, one of the major problems with the traditional UCR system is that, except for homicide, it is impossible to link together victims and offenders for a given incident. In other words, there is no way of connecting a robbery reported on Return A with an arrest reported on the Age, Sex, Race, and Ethnic Origin of Arrested Offenders. In the NIBRS system, however, all segments of an incident will be linked together with originating agency numbers, incident numbers, and sequence numbers when multiple victims and offenders are involved (Jarvis, 1992).

Third, one of the most persistent criticisms of the traditional UCR system is the use of the Hierarchy Rule. The Hierarchy Rule requires that in an incident in which several crimes are committed, only the most serious crime is counted and the remaining offenses are ignored. Thus, if there is an incident in which a female victim is robbed, beaten, raped, and murdered, the traditional UCR system counts that as one murder or, to use UCR terminology, a murder and nonnegligent manslaughter. The Hierarchy Rule applies to all index offenses except arson, which if committed concomitantly with another offense, is counted in addition to the other offense. In the NIBRS system, the Hierarchy Rule is no longer used. Information on up to 10 offenses, 99 victims, and 99 offenders will be gathered (Biderman & Lynch, 1991).

Fourth, in the UCR system, Return A reports whether the offense is cleared, that is, whether an offender or offenders are arrested on the charge. Beyond that, there is no information that can be linked directly to the offender. In the NIBRS system, information will be available on many more items, such as whether offenses are cleared or exceptionally cleared; data about age, race, ethnicity, and gender of arrestees; dates of arrests; codes to distinguish arrests for each offense; whether arrestees were armed; what weapon was used; and disposition of arrestees under age 18. Fifth, in contrast to the UCR system, the NIBRS system will provide information on offenses attempted and completed, drug and alcohol use, bias crime involvement, type of premise entry, and property crime characteristics.

Finally, the UCR program accepts reports from agencies up to one year after the UCR is published. Thereafter, unless there is a major change, such as a large city turning in a missing month of data, the master files are unchanged. Although this policy leads to a comprehensive data set, it means that available totals are characterized by small shifts in numbers, depending on sources and times they were obtained (Cantor & Cohen, 1980). The NIBRS system, on the other hand, provides information about updating by requiring notification as to whether an incident report is an initial or a supplemental report (FBI, 1992).

Converting crime reporting throughout the nation from the traditional UCR format to the NIBRS system is a massive undertaking, although substantial progress is being made. The FBI was able to accept data in the NIBRS format beginning in January 1989. According to the 1999 UCR, 19 state-level programs had been certified for NIBRS participation. Additionally, 14 state agencies, several law enforcement agencies in two states not having state-level programs, and five federal agencies have submitted test tapes containing NIBRS data. Examples of the kind of detailed analysis that can be done with NIBRS data can be found at the UCR website (<http://www.fbi.gov/ucr/ucr.htm>).

National Center for Health Statistics (NCHS)

Homicide is the only offense for which there are two local and national reporting systems that gather detailed information on the entire population of events. Both police (or an appropriate law enforcement agency) and county medical examiners or coroners begin an investigation when a suspected homicide is reported. Even though police and medical examiners cooperate, they operate independently and have separate responsibilities. In the course of determining whether a homicide has occurred, files are generated concerning identification of the victim, relatives, family members, medical cause of death, circumstances, and possible offenders. Medical examiners are charged with assigning a cause of death and judging whether medical evidence indicates that the death occurred by the actions of another person. The records they produce include death certificates, autopsy results, and related materials. Although limited to victim characteristics, medical examiner records are especially useful to answer questions about, for example, the presence of drugs or alcohol in the victim's body at the time of the killing.

Police, on the other hand, have different legal responsibilities. They conclude whether a criminal homicide has occurred and, if so, develop records to facilitate the investigation, arrest, and prosecution of offenders (Riedel, 1999).

The NCHS system for reporting homicides as part of mortality data covers the 50 states, the District of Columbia, New York City (with its own registration system), Puerto Rico, the U.S. Virgin Islands, Guam, American Samoa, and the Trust Territory of the Pacific Islands (NCHS, 1996). Information on homicide is collected through the use of standardized death certificates that are completed by some designated official (such as a medical examiner) in the case of violent deaths. When completed, death certificates are given to local registrars who are usually county health officers; they verify the certificates' completeness and accuracy, make records of them, and forward copies to state registrars. Personnel at state vital statistics offices check death certificates for incomplete or inconsistent information, then send them to the National Center for Health Statistics. Cause of death is classified according to categories in the *International Classification of Diseases* (ICD) and ultimately entered into the national mortality data set.

The death certificates received by NCHS are sent by states which are members of death registration areas and can demonstrate that the data submitted include at least 90 percent of all events that occurred. NCHS assumes complete coverage since 1933; no estimates are used, and all published data are considered final and not subject to revision (Cantor & Cohen, 1980). By 1985, national officials concluded "that over 99 percent of the birth and deaths occurring in this country are registered" (NCHS, 1985, p. 15).

The ICD, published by the World Health Organization (WHO), is an elaborate cause-of-death classification system. Using this classification, the WHO has collected information on mortality from national health organizations since 1948. Further, the WHO publishes amounts and rates for victims of homicide classified by age and gender. Because data are available for between 40 and 55 nations each year, it is a source for studies comparing homicide in different countries discussed in chapter 3.

The participating nations, including the United States, meet approximately once every 10 years to review and update the classification system. The ninth edition classification, used by NCHS, will be described briefly, although a tenth edition classification is beginning to be implemented. The various ICD causes of death used in homicide are prefixed with the letter *E* for "External Causes" and have three-digit codes. The homicide codes and the corresponding categories are given in Table 2-1.

Table 2-1
Homicide Cause of Death ICD Codes: E960-E969

E-Code	Cause of Death
E960	Fight, Brawl, or Rape
E961	Corrosive or Caustic Substances
E962	Poisoning
E963	Hanging and Strangulation
E964	Submersion (Drowning)
E965	Firearms and Explosives
E966	Cutting and Piercing Instruments
E967	Pushing From a High Place
E968	Other and Unspecified Means
E969	Late Effect of Injury

Source: U.S. Department of Health and Human Services. October, 1991, *International Classification of Diseases* (9th revision, 4th edition, volume 1). (DHHS Publication No. PHS 91-1260). Washington, DC: Government Printing Office.

Beginning in 1949, criminal homicides (E960-E969) were distinguished from legal intervention homicides, such as lawful executions and police shootings (E970-E978).

What has made ICD classification very useful for violence researchers is the addition of a fourth digit in 1979 for more detail. For example, under the three-digit code of E965—firearms and explosives—we have E965.0, which are handguns, E965.1, shotguns, to E965.9, which includes unspecified explosives.

Strengths and Limitations

The mortality reporting system of NCHS is clearly much simpler than the system used by the UCR program. It relies on one form (i.e., the death certificate) and claims complete reporting since 1933. For the NCHS, the most important source of information—a dead victim—is at hand, so it is not plagued with the unknown information problem in regard to offenders found with the UCR program. However, complete vital statistics reports are released two or three years (or even longer in recent years) after the reporting year; in contrast, the UCR program has no more than a one-year lag in releasing its information.

The addition of four-digit codes in the 9th revision of the ICD contributes much to the utility of NCHS data. Homicide researchers can manipulate three- and four-digit codes to create a variety of data sets. In addition, in recent decades, NCHS has added a number of variables to the death certificate that are very useful to homicide researchers, especially information concerning ethnicity, location, occupation, and education.

Although NCHS endeavors to create and maintain complete data sets, omissions and underreporting inevitably occur. Not all death certificates sent to NCHS are received; further, not all that are received find their way into reported mortality figures. As a case in point, the 1964 deaths for Massachusetts were never received by NCHS, affecting figures for the United States and the New England region. Also, records of deaths in Alabama, Alaska, and New Jersey for 1992 were amended because of errors, but NCHS did not receive copies of the amended records (NCHS, 1996).

Because the International Classification of Diseases (ICD) is revised approximately every 10 years, a question arises about the comparability between classifications. To determine the effect of classification revisions, NCHS uses comparability ratios based on dual codings of a single set of death certificates. A comparability analysis indicated a ratio of 0.9969 for the category of homicide between the 7th and 8th revisions (Klebba & Dolman, 1975), a very high level of agreement.

In a sharp critique of NCHS data, Sherman and Langworthy (1979) contend that there

> [is] . . . apparently widespread lack of the coroners' awareness of, support for, and legal obligation to comply with the system's request for the full information necessary to code the causes of death according to ICD categories. (p. 548)

One problem noted by Sherman and Langworthy is that the instructions for completing the death certificate are vague. Very small spaces are available on the form to describe how the injury occurred and respondents are encouraged to be complete while "using as few words as possible" (p. 549).

Comparing UCR and NCHS Data

We noted at the beginning of the chapter that although it is difficult to get valid measures of violence, researchers use a number of different approaches so that the weaknesses of one measure of violence will be balanced against the strengths of another. The use of homicide data offers the best opportunity to test validity because this is thought to be the best reported offense and because data are collected locally and nationally by two agencies. We proceed by assuming that if two measures of the same phenomenon show a high degree of convergence, our confidence in the validity of the measure is increased. If, on the other hand, there are variations in the amount of agreement, we must then consider where the sources of invalidity might be found.

Previous research suggests there is considerable agreement when UCR and NCHS homicide data are compared nationally. The agreement is progressively less when specific characteristics of the homicide are examined, smaller geographic areas (e.g., states) are considered, or both. If smaller units show less agreement, then how much agreement between UCR and NCHS data exist when the smallest available units, counties, are examined?

Wiersema, Loftin, and McDowall (2000) undertook to answer this question using county data because medical examiners and coroners are county officials and report data at that level. Wiersema and colleagues obtained the number of homicides by county compiled by the UCR on the Supplementary Homicide Report (SHR) forms and NCHS for years 1980 through 1988. The data covered 3,111 counties or county equivalents in 49 states and the District of Columbia.

The two systems agree exactly in their counts of homicide in only 22 percent of the counties. If the agreement is defined as no more than a difference of four homicides, the agreement percentage increases to 68 percent.

It is disturbing that the greatest discrepancies occur in some of the largest counties, as Table 2-2 indicates.

Earlier research has shown that the NCHS frequently reports more homicides than the SHRs of the UCR. But there are two surprising facts in Table 2-2. First, the discrepancies between the two data sources occur in very large counties. Given the difference in resources available to counties with large and small populations, we might expect small counties to show the greatest discrepancies. Second, the differences in the number of homicides reported are very large. For example, the office of the Cook County medical examiner shows almost twice as many homicides as are reported by police jurisdictions in that county.

What accounts for these discrepancies? Unfortunately, very little is known about why UCR and NCHS data disagree. Wiersema et al. (2000) suggest two general factors: differences in case definition and ambiguous or failed procedures.

In attempting to understand why the two data sources are not more comparable, the cogent summary by Rand (1993) is worth noting. In attempting to match death certificates to SHR, Rand concluded that

> differences between cases in the files are to a great degree the result of differences in the two programs' purposes and procedures. Basically, the UCR measures crimes, of which death is one outcome. The Mortality System measures deaths, of which crime is one cause. (p. 112)

For example, NCHS classifies homicides by the county in which death occurred, whereas the UCR classifies homicides by county in which the event occurred. Thus, victims could be shot in one county and transported to the hospital in another county, where death occurred.

Table 2-2
Counties With the Largest Differences Between NCHS and SHR Homicides

Five Counties With Largest Difference Where NCHS Is Larger Than SHR:

County	NCHS	SHR	Difference	Percentage of Total Positive Difference
Cook (Chicago)	8,089	4,968	3,121	11.3
Harris (Houston)	6,002	4,455	1,547	5.6
New York City	15,023	14,008	1,015	3.7
Los Angeles	13,531	12,543	988	3.6
Dade (Miami)	4,344	3,457	887	3.2

Five Counties With Largest Difference Where SHR Is Larger Than NCHS:

County	NCHS	SHR	Difference	Percentage of Total Negative Difference
Franklin (Columbus, OH)	314	789	-475	11.8
Alameda (Oakland)	1,164	1,385	-221	5.5
Summit (Akron)	70	226	-156	3.9
San Joaquin (Stockton)	403	510	-107	2.6
Baltimore (Baltimore suburbs)	202	266	-64	1.6

Source: Modified from Wiersama, B., Loftin, C., & McDowall, D. (2000). A comparision of supplementary homicide reports and national vital statistics system homicide estimates for U.S. counties. *Homicide Studies, 4*, pp. 322, 324. Copyright © 2000 by Sage Publications. Reprinted by permission of Sage Publications.

With respect to procedures, the UCR program does not adjust SHR data for underreporting, and some jurisdictions do not report all their homicides. Federal law enforcement agencies do not participate in the UCR program, so homicides in national parks, federal prisons, and Indian reservations are reported by NCHS but not UCR. However, none of the preceding satisfactorily accounts for the large discrepancies found.

The point of the preceding discussion is not merely to discuss differences in homicide statistics. Homicide is the best reported crime and if the amount of agreement between these two data sources can be questioned, it is reasonable to suppose that statistics on other violent crimes are even less accurate. While the validity of violence statistics raises serious issues for researchers, it raises far more consequential issues for policies and programs that rely on this data. The latter becomes a critical issue particularly when small units of analysis, such as counties, are used.

National Crime Victimization Survey

The other major source of information about violent crime is the National Crime Victimization Survey (NCVS). Crime surveys, unlike information collected from police or medical examiners, rely on interviews with victims. One purpose of crime surveys is to get an idea of how much crime occurs that is not reported to or by the police. The first crime surveys of victims were conducted in the mid-1960s and were sponsored by the President's Commission on Law Enforcement and Administration of Justice. In addition to a national survey, surveys were conducted in Washington, DC, Boston, and Chicago. One of the most surprising findings of these studies was that crime rates reported by the UCR were only one-half to one-third of those based on victim reports (O'Brien, 1985).

After a few years of preliminary research to determine questions of reliability and validity, the National Crime Survey was started in 1972. Questions of reliability included such issues as how likely respondents were to answer questions, how far back victim's memories were reliable in reporting victimization, and how questions should be worded. Victimization surveys of large cities were done from 1972 to 1975, then dropped. What remained is the nationwide survey and, since 1991, the National Crime Survey has been known as the National Crime Victimization Survey (NCVS).

The Redesign of the NCVS

The NCVS began a major redesign in 1989 that incorporated several needed changes. A new screening questionnaire (to determine whether the respondent has been the victim of any crime within the scope of the survey) uses extensive, detailed cues to help respondents recall and report incidents. These new questions and cues jog memories of the respondents and let them know that the survey is interested in a broad spectrum of incidents, not just those involving weapons, severe violence, or strangers. Because of these changes, substantial increases occur in the extent to which victims tell the interviewers about simple assault (i.e., assault without a weapon, resulting in minor injury) and sexual crimes.

Because of the original National Crime Surveys' limited capacity, the redesign included more and better questions about domestic violence and sexual assaults. For example, multiple questions and cues on crimes committed by family members, intimates, and acquaintances have been added. The survey also encourages respondents to report incidents even if they are not sure whether a crime has been committed. The survey staff review these reported incidents using standardized definitions of crimes.

The NCVS also broadens the scope of covered sexual incidents beyond the categories of rape and attempted rape. These include the following:

- Sexual assault (other than rape).

- Verbal threats of rape or sexual assault.

- Unwanted sexual contact without force, but involving threats or other harm to the victim.

One of the reasons for the redesign and the addition of more questions about sexual violence is that public attitudes about sexual violence have changed since the inception of the National Crime Survey in the 1970s. At that time, it was deemed inappropriate for a government-sponsored survey to ask respondents directly about rape. Reports of rape and attempted rape were obtained only if the respondent volunteered this information in response to questions about assault and attacks. The new survey asks directly about rape and attempted rape. It also distinguishes among sex crimes by asking directly about sexual attack, coerced and unwanted sexual activity (with and without force), and verbal threats of rape or sexual attack.

These new categories, broadened coverage, and more extensive questions on sexual victimizations have elicited information on about three to four times as many sexual crime victimizations as in the past. The redesign changes made were done in such a way as to maintain continuity between the older and newer versions of the NCVS; results from the redesign began to be available October 1994 (Bureau of Justice Statistics, 1994; 1995).

What is collected? There are two steps in interviewing victims. In the first stage, screening questions are asked to determine whether the respondent has been the victim of a crime in the past four months. If the respondent indicates that someone in the household has been a victim, then an individual victimization report is completed for each incident mentioned in response to the screen questions.

The survey categorizes crimes as personal or property. Personal victimizations include rape and sexual assault, robbery, simple and aggravated assault, and purse snatching or pocket picking. Property victimizations include burglary, theft, and motor vehicle theft. Unlike the UCR, the NCVS does not collect information about homicide or arson.

In addition to estimating the number of victimizations, the NCVS gathers details on each incident. These include such information as:

- Characteristics of the victim (age, sex, race, ethnicity, marital status, income, and educational level).

- Characteristics of the offender (sex, race, and approximate age).

- The relationship between victim and offender.

- The month, time, and location of the crime.

- Self-protective actions taken by the victim during an incident.

- Results of those actions.

- Consequences of the victimization, including any injury or property loss.

- Whether the crime was reported to police and reasons for reporting or not reporting.

- Offender use of weapons, drugs, and alcohol.

How are incidents collected? The NCVS collects victimization data from a nationally representative sample of about 100,000 individuals age 12 or older living in about 50,000 U.S. households. Basic demographic information (e.g., age, race, sex, and income) is collected to enable analysis of victimizations of various subpopulations. Interviews are translated for non-English–speaking respondents. The NCVS does not cover individuals living in institutions.

Each month the U.S. Bureau of the Census selects respondents for the NCVS using a panel design. Panel designs mean that the same household is randomly selected and interviewed every 6 months for a total of seven interviews over a 3-year period. At the conclusion of this 3-year period, a new household is selected. Once in the sample, all age-eligible individuals in the household become part of the panel.

The first and fifth interviews are face-to-face; the remainder are by telephone from a central location. What has helped to reduce the cost of interviewing such a large number of people has been the use of CATI, Computer Assisted Telephone Interviewing. When CATI is used, interviewers read questions from a computer screen and enter responses directly into the computer. The computer then automatically presents the interviewer with the appropriate next question. The use of CATI allows for automated internal consistency checks and fewer transcribing errors. CATI's centralization also improves data quality because interviewers can be monitored, fostering adherence to standardized techniques. Under the redesigned NCVS, about 30 percent of interviews are completed with CATI. The interview takes about one-half hour and the NCVS consistently records a response rate of 95 percent (Biderman & Lynch, 1991; Bureau of Justice Statistics, 1994).

Limitations of the NCVS

Cost of large samples. Probability samples are used to achieve representativeness and avoid the unacceptable costs of interviewing a population. Done within the rules of scientific sampling, we can obtain information on a population of millions by correctly sampling a few thousand. If that is the case, why does the Bureau of the Census sample 50,000 households when doing the NCVS?

Although everyone agrees there is too much crime, from a sampling and statistical point of view it is a rare event, particularly violent crime. Therefore, to capture a substantial number, a large sample must be taken. For example, suppose we knew that 10 percent of the population was a victim of crime X and the victims were distributed more or less randomly throughout the population. Therefore, if we took a representative sample of 100, we would, on average, get only 10 victims. On the other hand, if we took a sample that is 10 times larger, 1,000, we would get 100 victims, which would better meet requirements for statistical validity and reliability. Thus, to get a reliable number of victimizations, a very large number of people must be sampled. Because of the enormous cost of sampling, only organizations that have access to the economic resources of a nation can afford to carry out national victimization surveys (Glaser, 1978; Hagan, 1997).

The preceding characteristic of victim surveys also serves to explain why homicide is not part of the NCVS. It is true, as many writers point out, that a dead homicide victim cannot be interviewed. But the survey unit in the NCVS is a household, not an individual. It seems likely to us that if a homicide occurred in a household in recent months, someone in that household would be inclined to remember and report it to an NCVS interviewer.

The real reasons for the exclusion of homicide from the NCVS are twofold. First, among the violent crimes of homicide, robbery, rape, and aggravated assault, homicide is, by far, the most rare offense. For example, in 1999, in a population of more than 268 million people, there were 89,109 forcible rapes, 409,670 robberies, and 916,383 aggravated assaults reported in the UCR, but only 15,533 reported homicides (FBI, 1999). To draw and interview a national sample large enough to obtain reports on, for example, 100 homicides would be prohibitively expensive and time-consuming.

Second, there are two reporting systems for homicide already in existence, the UCR and the NCHS. It makes greater economic sense to take the additional funds needed to include homicide in the NCVS and give them to the Uniform Crime Reporting program and the National Center for Health Statistics to improve their own reporting of homicides.

Poor memory and telescoping. As a rule, the longer the time between the actual victimization and the interview, the greater the likelihood of memory failure. To minimize recall decay, the NCVS requests that respondents recall victimization that occurred within the previous 6 months.

The difficulty with that approach is what is called telescoping, that is, a victimization that occurred a year ago is recalled as occurring within the last 6 months. The NCVS controls for this problem by using the first interview as a bounding interview. In other words, the actual amount of victimization reported in the first interview is not published because of uncertainty over when this occurred. However, by comparing later interviews with the first, NCVS interviewers and analysts can determine whether telescoping has occurred.

Errors in reporting. There are several types of errors in reporting. Mistaken reporting occurs when the respondent believes he or she was the victim of a crime and was not. A person who reports that his lawnmower was stolen neglected to check with his unreliable brother-in-law who borrowed it without informing the owner. Persons may report that others are trying to break into their homes when no such incident took place. Most of these kinds of events would be treated as *unfounded* crimes by police, but may end up being published in victimization surveys.

Thus, there is also a tendency for overreporting in NCVS surveys. Persons may report crimes to NCVS interviewers that, indeed, occurred, but victims regarded them as too trivial or unimportant to report to the police. One reason the NCVS reports a greater volume of crime than the UCR is that it reports many more minor property crimes which would have been labelled unfounded by the police (Gove et al., 1985).

Sampling bias. NCVS surveys fall victim to the same problems that affect census surveys of the population: the undercounting of young people, males, and members of minority groups. This poses a problem not only for crime rates, noted earlier, but also for a lack of responses in the NCVS (Hagan, 1997).

Comparisons Between the NCVS and the UCR

It is important to recognize that the NCVS as a reporting system is not in competition with the UCR program; it is not a matter of NCVS *versus* UCR. Rather, the two reporting systems are an instance of *complementarity*, that is, the strengths of one system compensate for the weakness of the other system, and vice versa, to provide a well-rounded picture of violence in the United States (FBI, 1999). The following are some of the ways that the two systems complement one another:

- The NCVS measures both reported and unreported crime. The UCR focuses only on reported crimes. Hence, the NCVS is not affected by the extent to which people report crime to the police or improvements in police record-keeping technology.

- The NCVS provides information on a national sample. The UCR provides police department data on cities, towns, counties, and states.

- The NCVS does not interview children under 12 while the UCR measures crime affecting young children. Survey experts do not agree that children under 12 can be reliably interviewed.

- The NCVS does not collect information on homicide or arson, but the UCR does collect that information.

- The UCR collects only summary information about violent offenses other than homicide. The NCVS collects detailed information about each offense.

- Except for homicides, the UCR provides only aggregated and summary information about offenders and arrests. NCVS collects detailed information on victims' perceptions of offenders and relates it to victimizations.

- Preceding comparisons between the traditional UCR and NCVS do not take into account changes that will occur as the National Incident-Based Reporting System (NIBRS) becomes fully implemented. As the latter happens, there will be a greater similarity between police-based reporting and victimization surveys.

Other Measures of Violence

General Social Survey

The General Social Survey (GSS) has been conducted by the National Opinion Research Center at the University of Chicago since 1974. Except for 1979, 1981, and 1992, it has collected information annually on a representative sample of the U.S. adult population. The GSS collects information on a wide range of attitudes and behavior. A small core of questions is repeated each year to facilitate research on social trends (Singleton & Straits, 1999).

Questions about the fear of crime are regularly included in the survey. There are also questions on robbery, the death penalty, the use of guns, and the use of violence (Maxfield & Babbie, 1998). For example, in one series of items, the interviewers ask whether the respondent approves of one man hitting another if (a) the victim is in a protest march; (b) the victim is drunk; (c) the victim hit the man's child; (d) the victim is beating a woman; and (e) the victim broke into the man's house (National Opinion Research Center, 2001).

Monitoring the Future

Monitoring the Future surveys began in 1975 and are carried out by the University of Michigan Survey Research Center. Among their many purposes is to study changes in the beliefs, attitudes, and behavior of young people in the United States. These surveys are most frequently used to study trends in the use of tobacco, alcohol, and controlled substances (<http://monitoringthefuture. org/purpose.html>). Although the relationship of drugs to violence is a complex issue, the use of alcohol is not. A well-known expert on the effect of drugs, Erich Goode, puts it in unequivocal terms:

> Of all drugs, nationally, internationally, and cross-culturally, alcohol is *by far* the one most likely to be implicated in violent

crimes. The empirical evidence linking alcohol and violence is overwhelming. More individuals who commit violent offenses are under the influence of alcohol than of any other single drug. (1993, p. 130)

The survey is administered annually to about 50,000 eighth-, ninth-, and twelfth-grade students in about 420 public and private schools. Beginning with the class of 1976, a randomly selected sample of each senior class is followed bi-annually after high school. In addition to tobacco and alcohol, questions are asked about drug use, including ecstasy, cocaine, heroin, amphetamines, methamphetamines, marijuana, inhalants, LSD, other hallucinogens, PCP, barbiturates, tranquilizers, steroids, and rohypnol (date rape drug). The year 2000 results indicate that the use of ecstasy has increased sharply from 1991 (Monitoring the Future, 2001).

Conclusions: Violence Statistics, Policy, and Practice

Although violence statistics from various sources are used in policy decisions, because of its long history, the UCR illustrates some of the risks and dangers of unreliable data.

UCR data are being used to allocate federal funds. In reauthorizing the Ominibus Crime Control and Safe Streets Act of 1968, additional anticrime funding was appropriated for qualifying jurisdictions. The amount of funds was to be based on the number of violent crimes in the three most recent years. According to the legislation, the UCR was to be the source of data (Maltz, 1999).

Many of the violence statistics discussed in this chapter are instantly available on the Internet. The actual data can be downloaded as entire files, but because of their large size in many instances, websites are now making it possible to construct a smaller desired data set on-line, which then can be downloaded (Riedel, 2000b). While this increases convenience, unwary or unsophisticated users may reach conclusions that attract the attention of media, but cannot be substantiated.

Because of the greater accessibility, researchers are more frequently using UCR data at the subnational level, particularly at the county level. Maltz (1999) gives the instance of a 1983 Bureau of Justice Statistics Report, *Report to the Nation on Crime and Justice,* which was updated in 1988. This report showed county-by-county changes in violent crime rates using untested imputation proce-dures for missing data. Perhaps the most controversial analysis of county data was done by Lott (1998), who concluded that liberal use of concealed firearms laws reduced violent crime. Even though these results were contested on other methodological grounds, the analysis by Wiersema and colleagues (2000) strongly suggests caution in using county-level data.

The single greatest problem in the use of violence data for pol-icy and practice decisions is missing data. We have noted previ-ously that almost 30 percent of offender data are missing in homicide sources because of uncleared offenses. The percentages are much higher for other violent crimes. In addition to declining clearances, unknown amounts of error are introduced at recording and reporting levels.

The implementation of the NIBRS promises much more de-tailed information on violent crime than was available with the UCR. However, there is a major problem that cannot be addressed by more elaborate data collection systems.

None of the forms used by the NCHS or the UCR is going to be any more valid than the quality of decisions by police and medical examiners. In the case of death certificates, no matter how sophisti-cated the data collection *after* the death certificate is completed, ac-curacy in making initial classification decisions is crucial to the value of the information provided by this source. Research on this issue regarding NCHS data is sparse (NCHS, 1982) and that on the UCR program is simply nonexistent. Until some system of quality control can be implemented for police and medical examiner deci-sions and records, information on crime and violence will continue to suffer from limitations that will inevitably hamper policy, prac-tice, and research.

References

Akiyama, Y., & Rosenthal, H. M. (1990). The future of the Uniform Crime Reporting program: Its scope and promise. In D. L. MacKenzie, P. J. Baunach, & R. R. Roberg (Eds.), *Measuring crime: Large-scale, long-range efforts* (pp. 49–74). Albany: State University of New York Press.

Beattie, R. (1962). Problems of criminal statistics in the United States. In M. E. Wolfgang, L. Savitz, & N. Johnston (Eds.), *The sociology of crime and delinquency* (pp. 37–43). New York: John Wiley.

Biderman, A. D., & Lynch, J. P. (1991). *Understanding crime incidence statistics: Why the UCR diverges from the NCS.* New York: Springer-Verlag.

Block, C. R. (1987). *Homicide in Chicago: Aggregate and time series perspectives on victim, offender, and circumstances (1965–1981).* Chicago: Loyola University of Chicago.

Bureau of Justice Statistics. (1994). *Questions and answers about the redesign* (NCJ-151171). Washington, DC: Government Printing Office.

———. (1995). *National crime victimization survery redesign.* Washington, DC: Government Printing Office.

Cantor, D., & Cohen, L. E. (1980). Comparing measures of homicide trends: Methodological and substantive differences in the vital statistics and Uniform Crime Report time series (1933–1975). *Social Science Research, 9,* 121–145.

Centers for Disease Control. (1995). Patterns of homicide—Cali, Colombia, 1993–1994. *MMWR Morbidity and Mortality Weekly Report, 44* (39), 734–737.

Elliott, D. S. (1994). Serious violent offenders: Onset, developmental course, and termination. *Criminology, 32,* 1–21.

Federal Bureau of Investigation (FBI). (1984). *Uniform crime reporting handbook.* Washington, DC: Government Printing Office.

———. (1992). *Uniform crime reporting handbook (National incident-based reporting system edition).* Washington, DC: Federal Bureau of Investigation.

———. (1999). *Uniform crime reports for the United States 1999.* Available: <http://www.fbi.gov/ucr/Cius_99/99crime/99cius.pdf> [April 16, 2001]. Washington, DC: Government Printing Office.

Glaser, D. (1978). *Crime in our changing society.* New York: Holt.

Goode, E. (1999). *Drugs in American society* (5th ed.). New York: McGraw-Hill.

Gove, W. R., Hughes, M., & Geerken, M. (1985). Are Uniform Crime Reports a valid indicator of index crimes? An affirmative answer with some minor qualifications. *Criminology, 23,* 451–501.

Hagan, F. E. (1997). *Research methods in criminal justice and criminology* (4th ed.). Boston: Allyn & Bacon.

Jarvis, J. P. (1992). The National Incident-Based Reporting System and its application to homicide research. In C. R. Block & R. Block (Eds.), *Questions and answers in lethal and non-lethal violence* (pp. 81–85). Washington, DC: Government Printing Office.

Klebba, A. J., & Dolman, A. B. (1975). *Comparability of mortality statistics for the seventh and eighth revision of the International Classification of Diseases,*

United States (Vital Health Statistics, Data Evaluation and Methods Research Series 2, Number 66 DHEW Publication No. (HRA) 76-13540). Rockville, MD: National Center for Health Statistics.

Lott, J. R., Jr. (1998). *More guns, less crime*. Chicago: University of Chicago Press.

Maltz, M. D. (1999). *Bridging gaps in police crime data* (NCJ 176365). Washington, DC: U.S. Bureau of Justice Statistics.

Maxfield, M. G., & Babbie, E. (1998). *Research methods for criminal justice and criminology* (3rd ed.) Belmont, CA: Wadsworth/Thomson Learning.

Monitoring the Future. (2001). *Purpose and design*. (<http://www.monitoringthefuture.org/purpose.html>) [June, 2001].

National Center for Health Statistics (NCHS). (1982). *Annotated bibliography of cause-of-death validation studies: 1958–1980* (Series 2, No. 89, DHHS Publication No. PHS 82-1363). Washington, DC: Government Printing Office.

———. (1985). *Vital statistics of the United States 1980* (Vol. II, Mortality, Part A, Technical Appendix). Washington, DC: Government Printing Office.

———. (1996). *Vital statistics of the United States 1992* (Vol. II, Mortality, Technical Appendix). Washington, DC: Government Printing Office.

National Opinion Research Center. (2001). *General Social Survey 1972–1998 Codebook*. (<http://www.icpsr.umich.edu/GSS/title.htm>) [May, 2001].

O'Brien, R. M. (1985). *Crime and victimization data*. Beverly Hills, CA: Sage.

Poggio, E. C., Kennedy, S. D., Chaiken, J. M., & Carlson, K. E. (1985). *Blueprint for the future of the Uniform Crime Reporting program: Final report of the UCR study*. Boston: Abt Associates.

Rand, M. R. (1993). *The study of homicide caseflow: Creating a comprehensive homicide dataset, questions and answers in lethal and non-lethal violence: Proceedings of the Second Annual Workshop of the Homicide Research Working Group* (pp. 103–118). Washington, DC: Government Printing Office.

Riedel, M. (1990). Nationwide homicide datasets: An evaluation of UCR and NCHS data. In D. L. MacKenzie, P. J. Baunach, & R. R. Roberg (Eds.), *Measuring crime: Large-scale, long-range efforts* (pp. 175–205). Albany: State University of New York Press.

———. (1999). Sources of homicide data: A review and comparison. In M. D. Smith & M. A. Zahn (Eds.), *Homicide: A sourcebook of social research* (pp. 75–95). Thousand Oaks, CA: Sage.

————. (2000a). Homicide in Los Angeles County: A study of racial and ethnic victimization. In D. Hawkins (Ed.), *Crime control and social justice: The delicate balance*. New York: Greenwood.

————. (2000b). *Research strategies for secondary data: A perspective for criminology and criminal justice*. Thousand Oaks, CA: Sage.

Robison, S. M. (1966). A critical review of the Uniform Crime Reports. *University of Michigan Law Review, 64*, 1031–1054.

Schneider, V. W., & Wiersema, B. (1990). Limits and use of the Uniform Crime Reports. In D. L. MacKenzie, P. J. Baunach, & R. R. Roberg (Eds.), *Measuring crime: Large-scale, long-range efforts* (pp. 21–48). Albany: State University of New York Press.

Sellin, T. (1951). The significance of records of crime. *The Law Quarterly Review, 67*, 489–504.

Sherman, L. W., & Langworthy, R. H. (1979). Measuring homicide by police officers. *Journal of Criminal Law and Criminology, 70*, 546–560.

Singleton, R. A., & Straits, B. C. (1999). *Approaches to social research*. New York: Oxford University Press.

Wiersema, B., Loftin, C., & McDowall, D. (2000). A comparison of Supplementary Homicide Reports and national vital statistics system homicide estimates for U.S. counties. *Homicide Studies, 4*, 317–340.

Wolfgang, M. E. (1963). Uniform Crime Reports: A critical appraisal. *University of Pennsylvania Law Review, 111*, 708–738. ✦

Chapter 3

Violence in Other Times and Places

To understand our present beliefs, attitudes, and behavior, it is important to understand our country's history of violence—both that of the United States and that of the United States compared with other countries. In his historical review of violence, Richard Maxwell Brown stated that "historically, American life has been characterized by continuous and often intensive violence" (1979, p. 48). Criminal activity, political assassination, and racial conflict are part of this picture of profound violence.

Noncriminal violence has also been prevalent, Brown suggested. Violence has formed a "seamless web" (Brown, 1979, p. 40) incorporating some of the most positive accomplishments of U.S. history: independence from Britain; freedom for the slaves in the Civil War; stabilization of the frontier through vigilante initiative; and the social elevation of farmers and laborers through agrarian and labor conflict.

> Thus, as our nation approaches the twenty-first century, historical patterns of violence survive and are deeply embedded in our heritage and habits. Violence is strongly rejected for inclusion in the American creed, but so great has been our involvement with [this behavior] over the long sweep of American history that violence has become a compelling, although unacknowledged, element in our values and in our culture. (Brown, 1989, pp. 50–51)

As Brown has proposed, violence is the instrument not merely of the criminal disorderly, but of the most upright and honorable.

Prior to the American Revolution, mob protest and violence against British rule were common, usually involving young males loosely organized into gangs. Roger Lane, a leading historian of violence, gives an instance:

> On the cold winter night of March 5, 1770, following several days of tense encounters, a big crowd, mostly young men and boys, pinned eight redcoats and their Irish captain, Thomas Preston, against the wall of the Customs House, center and symbol of imperial rule. Yelling insults and waving sticks, throwing stones and snowballs, they dared the Brits to shoot. One threw a club; it hit a soldier. A single shot rang out immediately; then, after a pause of about six seconds, a whole round of shots—without Preston's order. A number of townsmen were hit in this Boston Massacre, five of them mortally, including the escaped slave Crispus Attucks, traditionally counted the first victim of the American Revolution. The crowd fell silent; Preston screamed at his panicked troops, lined them up, and marched them off, without pursuit or retaliation. The royal governor quieted the city with the promise that the troopers would stand trial for murder. (1997, p. 70)

John Adams, revolutionary radical and later U.S. president, orchestrated the trial carefully, eliminating jurors with strong anti-British feelings to demonstrate the importance of lawful proceedings. Adams argued that the soldiers were endangered and fired in self-defense. Some were provoked into firing which was, at worst, manslaughter. None of the soldiers was sentenced to death; Preston and six soldiers were acquitted, and two were found guilty of manslaughter and branded on the thumbs.

Feuds and dueling were other forms of early American killing. Dueling was used to settle insults to one's or another person's honor, probably the most famous duel being the one between Alexander Hamilton and Aaron Burr. Less well-known were two pre-presidential duels by Andrew Jackson and a duel by Senator Thomas Hart Benton, a famous antebellum leader, who killed a man early in his career. Dueling as a practice faded after the Civil War.

In the decades after the Civil War and before World War I, feuds became a popular and violent way of settling matters. In addition to the famous Hatfield-McCoy feud of the Kentucky-West Virginia border, there were the Martin-Tolliver and Hargis-Cockrell feuds of eastern Kentucky and the Allen family feud in the Virginia Blue Ridge country.

The feuds of Texas and the Southwest were as bloody as any found in Appalachia, however. The most deadly was the "Pleasant Valley War" in Arizona between the Graham family (cattle ranchers) and the Tewksbury family (sheep ranchers), which finally ended with only one survivor (a Tewksbury) (Brown, 1989).

Before proceeding further, it is worth noting that the study of violence is plagued by myths and outright fabrications that characterize historical events in general and violence in particular. Perhaps the cruelest blow to mythology was struck recently by Lane:

> And it is a historian's unpleasant duty to inform readers steeped in Hollywood legend that nowhere in the Wild West, nor ever, did any two cowboys or anyone else stand in the middle of a street, revolvers strapped to their sides, and challenge each other to a fatal 'quick-draw' contest. (1997, p. 171)

It is also important to understand that information about interpersonal violence in the United States prior to the twentieth century is fragmentary, unreliable, and practically nonexistent. The information that exists from that time is based on coroners' reports, indictments, and convictions rather than on arrests or incidents. By relying on information at later stages of the criminal justice process, cases that dropped out at earlier stages, such as arrest, are not available. Further, no accurate crime information was kept in the unsettled areas of the middle and far western parts of the United States. Finally, given popular prejudice, few records were kept if the victim of violence was a Native American or African American.

The next two sections of this chapter focus on violence involving Native Americans and African Americans. Conflicts between these two nonwhite groups and whites have had a long-term impact on our history and society. Partly due to popular interest, a third section deals with a group of offenders sometimes characterized as "social bandits," such as Jesse James, Billy the Kid, Bonnie and Clyde, and Al Capone. The final sections of the chapter examine current trends in violence, primarily homicide, and compare them to trends in other countries.

White–Native-American Warfare

The earliest contacts between European settlers and Native Americans were generally peaceful. What is regarded as the first Thanksgiving in the United States occurred in 1621 after the completion of the harvest. Governor William Bradford proclaimed a day of thanksgiving and prayer for the Plymouth colonists and neighboring Native Americans.

In a similar but rare moment of cooperation between whites and Native Americans, in 1681 William Penn, a Quaker, obtained from the British king a grant of territory in North America in payment for a debt owed to his father. In 1682, Penn sailed for the United States, planned and named the city of Philadelphia, established peaceful relations with the local Native American tribes, and ruled the colony for two years.

The usual history of the relationship between whites and Native Americans is as follows: treaties made, treaties broken, warfare resulting in Native Americans losing and being pushed westward off their land. For example, encounters between whites and Cherokee Indians ended in the Trail of Tears, a typical, yet one of the saddest, episodes in the history of conflicts between whites and Native Americans.

The Trail of Tears

Although the Cherokee initially sided with the British during the American Revolution, they negotiated a peace treaty with the United States in 1785. Because Cherokee resistance had continued for a decade, a new treaty was signed in 1791 giving the Cherokee land in parts of Georgia, Tennessee, and North Carolina. By 1820, the tribe had established a governmental system similar to the United States with a principal chief, a senate, and a house of representatives. In 1827, this group drafted a constitution and incorporated as a Cherokee nation.

Problems started for the United States when valuable gold deposits were discovered on tribal lands. In 1819, Georgia appealed to the U.S. government to remove the Cherokee from Georgia lands. This failed, so attempts were made to purchase the territory. The Cherokee nation retaliated by enacting a law prohibiting any sale of lands under penalty of death. In 1828, the Georgia legislature outlawed the Cherokee government and confiscated their land.

The Cherokee nation appealed for federal protection and the request was rejected by President Andrew Jackson, who used the Indian Removal Act of 1830 to force Cherokee from their land. In 1832, the U.S. Supreme Court ruled the Georgia legislation was unconstitutional, but federal authorities, following Jackson's policies, ignored the decision.

In 1835, 500 Cherokee agreed to cede territory for $5,700,000 and land in Oklahoma, which was then called Indian Territory. However, this action was repudiated by 90 percent of the tribe, and several dissenters among the Cherokee nation were assassinated by tribal members. When federal troops began to forcibly evict the Cherokee, about 1,000 of the tribe escaped to the North Carolina mountains and purchased land there. The remaining 18,000 to 20,000 people were force-marched about 800 miles to Indian Territory. Because about 4,000 perished in the march from hunger, disease, and exposure to the elements, this exodus became known as the Trail of Tears (Microsoft, 1998a).

In the process of removal, the U.S. Army divided the large number of people into 13 detachments. The Army commanded some of the detachments while others were directed by contractors, who were paid $65 for each person in their care—money that did not always go for its intended purpose. Two of the detachments traveled by river and the others traveled overland. Of those traveling by water, 311 people drowned when an overloaded flatboat capsized. Among those traveling by land, cholera broke out and, of 800 in one detachment, only 489 survived (Mulligan, 1970).

Other tribes were similarly offered treaties, which were also broken as European settlers wanted more of their land; and like the Cherokee, other tribes were herded into reservations. By the 1850s, only scattered groups of Native Americans remained in the eastern half of the United States.

Much the same fate awaited plains and western Native Americans, even though history acknowledges the combat expertise of the First Peoples. For example, on a one-on-one basis, Native-American warriors were better fighters than U.S. cavalrymen. Moreover, without Native-American scouts from enemy tribes, the army was helpless. However, given better tactics, artillery, and no women or children to slow them down, the army eventually could not lose. George Armstrong Custer's famous 1876 loss at the Little Big Horn was more of an exception than the rule.

What really defeated Native Americans was loss of habitat and attrition. By the early 1880s, white hunters with repeating rifles had reduced the buffalo herds, central to Native-American lifestyle and survival, to a few hundred. Hemmed in by miners and farmers, decimated by European diseases, exhausted by cold and hunger, the last of the Native Americans were pushed onto reservations by the 1890s (Lane, 1997).

Slavery, African Americans, and Violence

Slavery got its start with the rise of tobacco farming, the first commercially viable crop that was grown in the early settlement of Jamestown, Virginia. But tobacco is a very labor-intensive business. Initially, Native Americans were tried as a labor source, but they either ran away or had to be coerced to the point of death.

Another approach to the labor shortage used indentured servants. Under England's new Poor Laws, people could sell themselves and their labor for a period of 4 to 7 years. They received no pay, the master provided for their keep, and they were given 50 acres of land when their indenture ended. Often, the 50 acres of "free land" were swampy plots that could not sustain a livelihood.

There were two problems with this indentured servitude. First, the death rate among these young men was appalling. In about 1620, for instance, the annual death rate among indentured servants was 80 percent, the result of malaria, typhoid, overwork, malnutrition, and general ill-treatment. Although the men could be replaced free of charge, communities faced a bigger challenge. Once free of their masters' control, a class of discontented young men who typically had guns often played a role in local power struggles (Lane, 1997).

The first Africans were purchased as early as 1619 in Jamestown. Initially, Africans were treated as indentured servants, but they spoke no English, knew no law, and frequently had no idea when their term of indenture was up. Thus, they could be kept in bondage for long years, even for life. Lane (1997) stated it well:

> Over the years practice became custom, and custom law. In 1664 the legislature of Maryland took the final step, decreeing not only that all "negroes" were to be slaves for life but that the children of

all female slaves were also to be slaves, ensuring that those with known African ancestry were doomed to serve forever. (p. 43)

Meanwhile, due to improved conditions in England, the number of people available for indenture declined toward the end of the seventeenth century. To meet the increasing demand for labor in the colonies, larger and larger numbers of slaves were imported. In Virginia, for example, slaves were about 7 percent of the population in 1680 and were more than 40 percent by the middle of the eighteenth century (Microsoft, 1998b).

Slavery was a system to meet the labor demands of the South, first, with respect to growing tobacco and, subsequently, cotton. Because of the religious origins of such states as Massachusetts, and because there was no need there for unskilled labor to grow labor-intensive crops like tobacco, neither indentured servants nor slaves played a large role in northern states (Lane, 1997). Hence, by the middle of the eighteenth century, 90 percent of slaves lived in southern states (Microsoft, 1998b).

But, historians concede, even in the South slavery was an unstable system. First, in a country in which the rhetoric of equality was part of the ideology that supported the American Revolution, it was difficult to justify the obvious inequality represented by slavery. Indeed, there was a persistent fear and sense of uneasiness among southerners that their slaves would one day rise up and kill them. Second, slave productivity was very inefficient, that is, plantation owners had daily evidence that their slaves were not happy with their lot. There was a constant problem with foot-dragging and deliberate slowdowns by slaves who pretended to be sick, feigned difficulty understanding instructions, or "accidentally" misused tools and animals.

There were constant plots, real and imagined, but the best known was the Nat Turner Rebellion. Nat Turner was born a slave in Southhampton County, Virginia, in 1800. Turner was a popular religious leader among his fellow slaves. In 1831, he believed that he had received a sign from God by means of the color of the sun, indicating that he should lead his people to freedom.

In August of that year, Turner and five other slaves killed their master and his family. Over the next 40 hours, they were joined by about 60 other slaves from neighboring plantations. They then moved about the county, murdering about 50 whites. Consequently, an unknown number of blacks were lynched in reprisal by white mobs. The revolt lasted until August 24 when it was put down by federal and state troops and associated volunteers, but Turner was not captured for another 6 weeks. After his capture, Turner and 15 of his companions were tried, convicted, and hung.

As a result of the Nat Turner Rebellion, the movement to abolish slavery, which had enjoyed some support in the South, became a northern phenomenon. In contrast, southern legislatures used the enormous level of white fear generated by the revolt to impose even greater restrictions on slaves (Lane, 1997).

Lynching

There is good reason to agree with Lane that, in comparison to previous centuries, the nineteenth was the most violent. As the conflicts over slavery became more intense, they not only ended more often in violent death, but also in the Civil War. Of the 2,500,000 who served during this war in either the southern or northern armies, 620,000 people, or one in four, died.

The amount of race hatred expressed on both sides led to unbelievable atrocities—gross exceptions to the rules of combat. After Lincoln's Emancipation Proclamation in 1863, for example, black soldiers began to serve in Union units. In April 1864, after his Confederate troops overran Fort Pillow, Mississippi, General Nathan Bedford Forrest refused to accept the surrender of the many black soldiers in the Union garrison. With hands up, they were methodically bayoneted to death. Forrest later stated the river ran red for nearly 200 yards downstream (Lane, 1997).

The most murderous outbursts of the Civil War accompanied the New York City Draft Riots of 1863. During the early stages of the war, the government had relied on voluntary enlistment to obtain recruits for the Union armies. Because of pressing need, however, Congress passed the Enrollment Act in 1863 that imposed liability for military duty on every able-bodied male between the ages of 20 and 45. There were draft riots in several cities but none as bad as in New York City, with its heavy concentration of Irish immigrants who were highly antagonistic toward African Americans. Irish immigrants did not believe the Civil War was their war and were further angered by the Emancipation Proclamation that gave freedom to African Americans. In addition, critics of President Lincoln's administration objected to policies exempting potential draftees who could supply a substitute or $300.

The Monday after the law became effective, a crowd gathered and set ablaze the draft headquarters and prevented the efforts of firefighters. As a result, the flames spread and destroyed a city block. Rioters roamed freely throughout the city attacking, murdering, and lynching many black men, whom they blamed for the war. The mob attacked and burned the Colored Orphan Asylum, and only the courageous intervention by one Paddy McCaffrey and several firemen kept the children from being killed as well. The riot lasted from July 13th to July 16th, when troops returning from the Battle of Gettysburg dispersed the rioters. Fatalities from the four days of havoc were estimated at more than 1,000.

Violence toward African Americans in the form of lynching became especially pronounced after the Civil War. Although the South had formally lost the war, between 1865 and 1877 they informally won back much of what they had lost by using murder, in effect, as an instrument of social policy (Lane, 1997). Lynching, hanging, or other forms of execution carried out by self-appointed commissions or mobs without due process of law have occurred at some time in every state. For instance, these methods were used for punishing Tories during the American Revolution. Likewise, more than 3,700 lynchings occurred between 1889 and 1930, and well over 80 percent took place in the South.

What have fascinated and occupied scholars over the decades are the sheer cruelty and savageness of many such incidents.

> The results included the most barbaric episodes in the history of American homicide: special excursion trains took passengers to Paris, Texas, in 1893, to watch a retarded black man die, over the course of an hour, of red-hot irons thrust into his body and down his throat; in 1911 an accused rapist was tied to a stake on the opera house stage in Livermore, Kentucky, and tickets bought the privilege of shooting at him from the seats. (Lane, 1997, p. 151)

Lynching finally declined because white fears had been put to rest by U.S. Supreme Court decisions that all but excluded African Americans from the political process through poll taxes and literacy requirements. When these barriers were coupled with practices of legal segregation, African Americans found themselves economically dependent and politically powerless. Nothing more was required to hold them down, so the practice of lynching declined for the simple reason that it was no longer needed.

Social Banditry

The period after the Civil War was one of enormous industrial growth in the United States, particularly in the North. It was also a period of unrestrained capitalism. While the Rockefellers, Carnegies, and Morgans grew wealthy, however, sharecroppers, farmers, ranchers, and small merchants were caught by economic cycles that left them in poverty. Further, in the South and in Civil War border states, many men who had been sympathetic to the Confederacy were left to find their own way after the war, which meant an increase in gangs organized for robbery and murder. But rather than being appalled by the violence of people like Wild Bill Hickock, Jesse James, Billy the Kid, the Daltons, the Younger brothers, and a host of others, we turned them into romantic figures. Thus were influenced contemporary notions of "real men," heros who supposedly "fight and die for the things that make America great."

There are several reasons this particular group of "Wild West" killers became romantic figures. First, in addition to weak law enforcement in border and western regions, a great many Confederate sympathizers admired outlaws who were former Confederate soldiers. Nash (1973, p. 275) related the story of Cole Younger, a member of the James-Younger gang. In the course of a stagecoach robbery, a passenger with a southern accent turned over a gold watch. Younger asked him if he had served in the Confederate Army and, if so, to name his rank, regiment, and commanding officer. After doing so, Younger gave back the watch to the startled passenger and said, "We are all Confederate soldiers. We don't rob Southerners, especially Confederate soldiers."

Second, in the latter half of the nineteenth century, many small landowners and merchants suffered economically and blamed their troubles on eastern banks and the growth of railroads. Thus, a kind of vicarious revenge grew in these people who rejoiced to hear of outlaws who had come from the same humble backgrounds and were inflicting damage on banks and railroads by robbery and murder of their agents (Brown, 1969).

Finally, it is difficult to underestimate the impact of favorable publicity from eastern newspapers, pamphlets, and dime novels.[1] New York detective magazines churned out dozens of pamphlet-sized stories that portrayed outlaws of the time as simple farmers driven to violence by unscrupulous and vindictive lawmen serving the interests of greedy railroad owners and bankers.

Nowhere was the outlaw as social bandit cultivated more carefully than with Jesse Woodson James, his brother Frank, and the Younger brothers, Cole, James, John, and Robert. Frank was born in 1843 and Jesse in 1847 to Robert James, a minister, and his wife, Zerelda. The Younger brothers were cousins of the James boys and lived a few miles from the James Homestead in Clay County, Missouri.

Although the James and Younger boys were neighborhood troublemakers, the pivotal event in their lives was the Civil War. Frank James and Cole Younger rode with the southern guerrilla leader William Clarke Quantrill, and Jesse, when he got old enough, joined "Bloody Bill" Anderson's gang. Both the Quantrill and Anderson gangs were exceptionally violent and brutal toward Union soldiers and sympathizers. Quantrill's Raiders burned the town of Lawrence, Kansas, and killed all its male inhabitants in 1863; Anderson and his gang massacred 75 unarmed Union soldiers in Centralia, Missouri, in 1864.

The Civil War provided an education in violence and, after the war, the James and Young boys turned to robbing trains and banks. If they managed to escape to their home territory on the Missouri-Kansas border, they were safe because of strong sympathies for the Southern Cause and because local people thought that the James and Younger brothers were being victimized by the same railroads and banks that were also victimizing them.

The Robin Hood image of robbing from the rich and giving to the poor was cultivated assiduously by the James gang. Whenever they visited friends and neighbors in the western wilds of Missouri while on the run from lawmen, they paid handsomely for their board and room. One story, more myth than fact, illustrates the heroic legend of Jesse James. Jesse and his gang reportedly stopped at the cabin of a lonely widow woman. Although impoverished, she feeds the gang. Upon seeing tears in the woman's eyes, Jesse inquires about the problem. She tells him that a banker is coming that very day to foreclose on her small farm unless she can produce $3,000 to cover the mortgage. Jesse gives her the money before riding away with his gang.

> A few hours later the banker arrives and is astounded when he receives the amount due him. The widow woman demands her note and mortgage (remembering Jesse's warning to do exactly that) and these are handed over to her by the startled banker. Fondling his money, the greedy banker leaves in his buckboard. Three miles from the cabin, Jesse James emerges from the brush, pistol in hand and leveled at the banker, he recoups his $3,000, plus the banker's watch for his trouble, and rides away chuckling. (Nash, 1973, p. 268)

The James-Younger gang continued to rob banks and trains and to kill uncooperative employees. Even though they could be identified by living victims and pursued by posses, they would always manage to escape back to their home territories, where they were protected by local people who would not cooperate with law enforcement. Victims who did identify one of the gang would, within a short period of time, become unwilling to testify because of threats from supporters of the gang.

Things changed when the gang attempted to rob the First National Bank of Northfield, Minnesota. One of the Northfield citizens was alerted to the robbery and the local citizens, rather than running and hiding, grabbed guns and started shooting. Cole and Jim Younger both were shot, but not fatally. They survived and were sentenced to life imprisonment at the Minnesota State Penitentiary.

Jesse and Frank James escaped the Northfield debacle, moved to Tennessee, and went into hiding as farmers for 3 years. Then, in 1879, they organized a new gang and robbed a bank in Riverton, Iowa, as well as a train 5 days later, during which a passenger and the engineer were killed. Responding to the public outcry over the brutal murders, the governor of Missouri offered a reward of $10,000 for the capture and conviction of the James brothers.

The promise of the reward was sufficient incentive for Robert Ford to kill Jesse James. Robert Ford had never been a full-fledged member of the gang, but had moved about the periphery along with others who helped the outlaws escape after a robbery. While visiting Jesse and talking about the dissolution of the gang, Jesse got up, unbuckled his gun belt, picked up a chair, and got up to adjust a picture on the wall. Seeing his unprotected back, Ford drew his pistol and fired several shots, killing Jesse. He then proceeded to collect the reward.

Subsequently, Frank James turned himself in to the governor for a promise of protection and a fair trial. The unscrupulous shooting of Jesse James aroused and upset the nation, especially Missouri, which improved Frank's chances of acquittal. After a series of trials, Frank James was freed and returned to his farm to die a natural death in 1915.

Prohibition

The Eighteenth Amendment to the Constitution prohibited the sale, manufacture, distribution, and importation of intoxicating liquors in the United States. The Prohibition Amendment became effective in 1920 and was repealed in 1933. Most people have been taught that this 13-year period resulted in wholesale violation of Prohibition laws in the form of illicit drinking, violence in the face of legal efforts to enforce the laws, and the appearance of organized crime.

The latter is somewhat of an oversimplification. Accurately, Prohibition did produce a switch from low potency drinks, such as beer, to distilled spirits, a high-potency source of alcohol. This occurred for two reasons. First, distilled spirits are much easier and cheaper to transport than beer, which is bulky. Second, prior to refrigeration, beer would spoil whereas distilled spirits would not. Thus, one unanticipated result of Prohibition was that people began consuming a higher volume of a more dangerous beverage.

Another impact of Prohibition was that more people, desperate to get their hands on an alcoholic drink, ended up consuming toxic forms of alcohol, such as methyl alcohol, which caused blindness, paralysis, and death. Of course, organized crime came to assume the organizational shape we know today because illicit alcohol was a major source of revenue for high-level gangsters. But it is not correct to believe that Prohibition increased the amount of alcohol consumption. The available evidence indicates that alcohol consumption declined with Prohibition and increased once the Eighteenth Amendment was repealed.

Although there is no hard data on alcohol consumption because it officially no longer existed, other indicators were used. For

68 *Criminal Violence*

example, the rate of death from cirrhosis of the liver is closely correlated with alcohol consumption in the population. Between 1900
and 1919, the death rate was between 12 and 17 per 100,000 individuals; during Prohibition, the rate dropped to between seven
and nine per 100,000. By the mid-1930s, however, the rate of death
from cirrhosis of the liver began to increase again (Goode, 1999).

The message to be drawn from the preceding is that "there is no
free lunch." True, alcohol consumption declined, but at what cost
to other important social values? Prohibition encouraged disrespect for the law, increased consumption of distilled spirits, increased the general risk of consuming toxic substances, corrupted
law enforcement, and increased organized crime. We leave it to our
readers to determine whether similar arguments might be used
with respect to contemporary laws against the use of marijuana.

The Role of Organized Crime

It is important to recognize that the production, distribution,
and sale of alcohol is like the production, distribution, and sale of a
loaf of bread: Both require a complex organization to move from
raw material to a finished product. When the product is legal, a
large variety of laws govern relationships between employers, employees, and the public. Labor unions, for example, are monu-
ments to the types of relationships that prevail between workers
and managers.

The situation becomes dramatically different when the product carries criminal penalties. Assuming there is a market for the illegal product, the objective tasks of production, distribution, and
sale remain the same with respect to needing a complex bureaucracy to accomplish the task. But these interrelated series of tasks
must be accomplished without alerting law enforcement, and discipline must be maintained in the ranks of illegal workers.

Moreover, several consequences accompany the production of
our illegal product, alcohol. Costs will increase because of the necessity of concealment. These costs include higher pay for workers
because they are taking greater risks, the expense of using more
circuitous routes and means of transportation and distribution,
and bribes for police, lawyers, and court officials. Such costs can, of
course, be passed on to consumers because they are willing to pay
more for the forbidden substance.

Above all, there is the necessity for maintaining discipline within the ranks. Large amounts of money will be changing hands at various levels and the manager of an organized bootlegging operation must make certain that he is not cheated. The difficulty is that he has no recourse to law if his employees are dishonest; he must enforce his own rules, which means injury or death to anyone who betrays him.

Finally, it is a simple fact that organizations become larger and more profitable if they have no competition. In the violent world of Prohibition, there was a constant struggle to eliminate the competition.

No one illustrates these characteristics better than "Scarface" Al Capone. Capone was originally from New York and spent his formative years as a member of the Five Points gang in Brooklyn. He was someone who beat up on union leaders unwilling to kick money back to the gang and acted as a bouncer and bartender in a brothel-saloon, the Harvard Inn, owned by "Big Jim" Colosimo. Capone moved to Chicago to work for Colosimo's immense brothel empire, but kept in touch with Johnny Torrio, who was the leader of the Five Points gang.

When Prohibition became law in 1920, Torrio and Capone saw a chance to make a fortune in bootlegging. Unfortunately, Colosimo did not agree and wanted nothing to do with it, so Capone killed him. The next day, Torrio took over Big Jim's empire with Capone as his right-hand man.

Competition was fierce in the bootlegging business in Chicago. The main rivalry was between Dion O'Bannion's North Side gang and Torrio-Capone's gang on the South Side. So long as each gang stayed on its agreed-upon territory, there was peace.

Of course, gang members occasionally needed discipline. A hood named Joe Howard spent some time bragging about how easy it was for him to hijack beer trucks, particularly those belonging to Torrio. But he made his big mistake when he slapped around and insulted Capone's financial wizard, Jake "Greasy Thumb" Guzik. Guzik complained to Capone, who, minutes after the event, went into the bar where Howard was, stuck a gun to his temple, and emptied all six bullets. Loyalty was important to Capone and those who were loyal to him could expect to be repaid.

On another occasion, Capone heard that three of his associates—John Scalise, Albert Anselmi, and Joseph Giunta—were planning to kill him. The three had been loyal Capone gunsels and had killed numerous rival gangsters and uncooperative politicians over the years. Capone invited them to an elaborate dinner along with his usual collection of associates. At the conclusion of the meal, he praised the work of the three men, grabbed a baseball bat concealed under the banquet table, and beat each one to death.

The peace between the rival O'Bannion and Capone-Torrio gangs did not last. Capone and Torrio gunned down O'Bannion. Hymie Weiss, an infuriated O'Bannion supporter, almost killed Torrio and made an attempt on Capone's life. Torrio had had enough. After he recovered from his wounds, he turned everything over to Capone. Capone was now number one man in Chicago's gangland with an annual income of $5,000,000, but he had a war on his hands. Capone managed to kill Weiss and most of the remainder of the O'Bannion gang, with the exception of George "Bugs" Moran.

Capone, now living in Miami, arranged for the St. Valentine's Day Massacre by phone. Capone's men, dressed as police, raided the garage that was Moran's bootleg headquarters. They lined up seven of the mobsters and machine-gunned all of them on February 14, 1929. At last, Capone completely controlled bootlegging in Chicago, but he forgot one thing—to pay his taxes. Capone was finally brought to his knees by the federal government on a charge of income tax evasion. He served 8 years at Leavenworth and Alcatraz and was paroled in 1939.

By this time, his lifestyle had turned his life to shambles. He had contacted syphilis years before from a prostitute in Colosimo's brothels. Left untreated, the spirochete that causes syphilis travels up the spinal cord and destroys the brain. The organisim, in other words, ate Capone alive and he died at his Palm Island mansion near Miami in 1947.

What can be concluded from this brief survey of violence? We are forced to agree with Brown that violence is a persistent feature of our historical landscape: "We have resorted so often to violence that we have long since become a 'trigger-happy' people" (Brown, 1969, p. 56).

Americans also express a curious ambivalence about violence. Although we oppose violence, there is a tradition of admiration for figures like Frank and Jesse James and John Dillinger, whose robberies of banks and the railroads made them popular among poor people. Billy the Kid retained the respect and admiration of Mexicans and poor people in villages of the Southwest. Pretty Boy Floyd was admired by sharecroppers from whose stock he came.

Ambivalence toward violence is also expressed in television programs and movies:

> Hollywood has made no fewer than 21 movies about Billy the Kid: in one version, the hero was played by Paul Newman, and in another, by Kris Kristofferson, although in real life Billy was described as a 'slight, short, buck-toothed, narrow-shouldered youth' who 'looks like a cretin.' (Silberman, 1978, p. 33)

Contemporary Trends in Violence

Current Rates Compared to the Past

Lane (1997) points out that historians of criminal violence are frequently asked how current rates compare to homicide in the past. By and large, any answer to that question would involve focusing on homicides because those are the records that are most available. Even then, comparing rates involves a large amount of guesswork.

Before the 1900s, there was no national data of any kind. Lane's (1979) Philadelphia research from 1839 through 1901 could only suggest that the murder rate, based on indictments, was down from the period before the Civil War. Lane also suggested that murder rates in rural areas were higher than in cities.

But what makes the count of homicides impossible to ascertain with any degree of accuracy is the number of infanticides (the killing of newborns). Lane reported that in the middle of the 19th century in Philadelphia, dead infants were often found in gutters and privies several times a week. What further complicates any accurate estimate of homicide is the absence of a system for counting the number of black-on-black or white-on-black killings, which must have been substantial, particularly in the South. Finally, at least until the 1880s when the last Native Americans were herded onto reservations, the killing of Native Americans was rarely subject to counting or legal action by either tribal or white authority (Lane, 1997). Taking these kinds of homicides into account may mean that the homicide rate was higher than it is today, but it is really impossible to tell.

History is useful in providing a perspective and, in that context, it is worth considering some of Lane's suggestions about how contemporary homicide has changed or might change in comparison to the past.

Impersonalization of Homicide

The overriding image that Lane conveys is the growing impersonal nature of homicide. Frightening forms of homicide have emerged in recent decades, such as serial murder and domestic terrorism. We would like to point to the close links between terrorism and serial murder. The Unabomber, Theodore Kaczynski, represents an instance of this new and frightening combination.

Both serial killing and terrorism undermine the legitimacy of the existing legal, political, and cultural order by generating an enormous amount of fear and suspicion within a community. Second, serial offenders and terrorists operate in very small groups, either one or two individuals. Third, both types of killers select their victims carefully to maximize media attention and are successful at eluding law enforcement. Finally, on the surface, the acts of serial killers and terrorists appear to be incomprehensible and irrational, the acts of a maniac. Although serial killers seem to retain this characteristic, terrorists are believed to be committed to a rational ideology in irrevocable conflict with the existing order. But distinctions about rational behavior are highly relative; after all, one group's "terrorist" is another group's "freedom fighter" (Riedel, 1998).

A different side of the impersonal nature of homicide is given by Lane in explaining contemporary homicide:

> The bad news that more Americans are being killed by strangers, criminals, and teenagers has been balanced by good news, in that lower percentages are being killed by family, friends, and acquaintances. (1997, p. 326)

Within recent history, there is little doubt that family killings, particularly spousal homicides, have declined. This issue is explored in chapter 6. The question of an increase in stranger homicides is more difficult to evaluate. The difficulty is one that has been discussed in a previous chapter: the precipitous decline in arrests for homicide from 93 percent in 1960 to 66 percent in 1997.

Therefore, it has been suggested that many of the homicides for which no offender has been arrested involved stranger offenders.

It is likely that the future will consist of a greater number of stranger homicides if, for no other reason, there will be more strangers. As is indicated in chapter 5, urban areas are the domain of strangers and it appears that the United States will continue to become more urbanized.

Violence in Other Places

It is also important to know how violence in the United States compares with violence in comparable countries. Archer and Gartner (1984, p. 4) indicate that without an understanding of violence in other societies, our knowledge "remains provincial at best and at worst, simply wrong." If knowledge of violence is based on a single society, the United States, we have no way of generalizing about the size of the problem.

For example, are homicide rates higher in the United States than in comparable countries? Transnational comparison allows researchers not only to determine the relative amount of violence, but to explore the generalizability of causes. Such research allows us to understand whether a specified cause is peculiar to the social structure and culture of one society or is more generally important. Likewise, cross-cultural research helps to explore and understand a variety of treatment and prevention programs. If a specific program is successful in another country, policy makers may be willing to consider its application in the United States (Archer & Gartner, 1984).

Even though it is difficult to determine whether the United States is more violent today than in previous centuries, it is clear that in this century, the United States is more violent than comparable technologically developed countries. Unfortunately, international data sources did not begin until the 1950s and are still limited to reports of homicide and involve only a limited number of countries. International sources of crime data can be divided into data sets collected by private researchers and those collected on a regular basis by the International Police Organization (INTERPOL) and the United Nations, which includes the World Health Organization (WHO).

The best-known privately collected data comprise the 110-nation Comparative Crime Data File, compiled by Dane Archer and Rosemary Gartner (1984). The Comparative Crime Data File contains annual frequencies on crime for 110 nations and 44 cities from 1900 through 1970. A second privately collected source is the Human Relations Area Files that contain data on homicides from a sample of small nonindustrial societies that are representative of major world cultural regions (LaFree, 1999).

INTERPOL has collected and published crime data from national police forces since 1950. It collects data on homicide, which it defines as "any act performed with the purpose of taking human life, no matter under what circumstances." This definition excludes manslaughter and abortion, but includes infanticide, sex offenses, larceny, fraud, counterfeiting, and drug offenses. The data are presented by yearly quarters, and statistics are given on the number of crimes solved by police. Each category of offense is broken down by gender and specifies whether the offenders are adults or minors. The number of nations reporting vary. For example, from 1980 to 1984, 145 countries were listed as members of INTERPOL, but no more than 85 countries reported crime data in a single year.

Beginning in 1974, the United Nations began a series of surveys covering crime trends and operations of criminal justice systems. The first survey covered the years 1970 through 1974, with 56 member and nonmember states responding. The most recent, the fifth, covers the years 1990 through 1994; 65 nations provided information on homicides in 1994. The surveys are collections of data on officially reported crimes, such as intentional homicides (death purposely inflicted by another including infanticide and attempts), assaults, sex crimes, robberies, and kidnappings, with the data broken down by age and gender. They also provide information on prosecutions, convictions, and penal sanctions.

By far, the best-known and generally believed to be the most valid international source of information comes from the World Health Organization of the United Nations. The WHO has collected mortality statistics, categorized by cause of death, from national health organizations since 1951. The definition of homicide used by the WHO ("death due to injuries purposely inflicted by others") has varied, at times including deaths due to legal intervention and war. Raw data and rates are provided only on victims of homicide. Classifications are given for age and gender. Data are available for between 40 and 55 nations each year (Riedel, 1999).

Generally, cross-national data on homicide are more reliable than data on other crimes, such as rape, robbery, and assault. Limitations on cross-national homicide research are design specific: Time-series studies of homicide are more reliable than cross-sectional comparisons of national rates. Ultimately, however, researchers that rely on official statistics of national agencies must use what is available; there are few opportunities to adjust information for over- or underreporting or misclassification of events.

Cross-national homicide statistics provide few variables and limited detail: The data consist of total homicides and are classified by age and gender. Data on whether the homicide involved robbery, originated in domestic conflict, or involved weapons are absent, as is race and ethnicity information. While such information would provide valuable insights, variations in cultural definitions make it difficult to collect this kind of cross-national data.

Finally, available cross-national data are biased toward more developed countries that have sufficient resources and political stability to develop an adequate reporting system. Some countries are involved in devastating civil wars and civil unrest, which provides little opportunity for governments to function, control crime, or count it. Afghanistan, Croatia, Bosnia-Herzegovina, and Somalia fall into this category. Other countries, such as Zaire (Democratic Republic of Congo) and Albania, have had, or are undergoing, profound political changes in which the government's capacity to report crime is nonexistent.

Transnational comparisons. Although we may question whether homicide rates were higher in previous centuries, there is little doubt that homicide rates in the United States are substantially higher than homicide rates in comparably developed countries. Figure 3-1 shows that U.S. homicide rates range from more than seven times (1976) to more than 26 times higher (1980) than homicide rates for England. Homicide rates in the United States are two (1984) to three times (1974) higher than in Finland.

It is important to recognize that trends for Finland and England in Figure 3-1 "bracket" the trends for 13 other countries. Mean rates were obtained for all countries for which data were relatively complete from 1965 through 1995. Excluding the United States, the highest mean rate was Finland and the lowest was England and

Wales. The mean rates of the remaining 13 countries (Australia, Austria, Canada, Denmark, France, Italy, Ireland, Japan, Netherlands, New Zealand, Norway, Sweden, and Switzerland) generally fell somewhere between Finland and England. These countries were chosen because they are economically and socially developed democracies with well-developed statistical reporting systems.

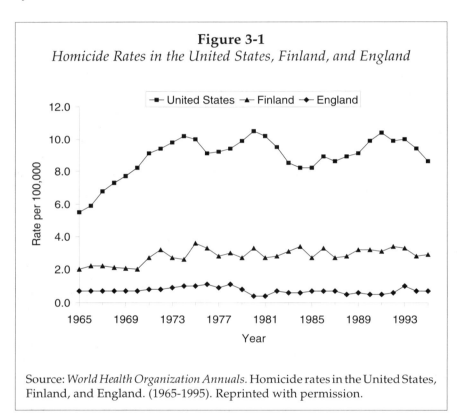

Figure 3-1
Homicide Rates in the United States, Finland, and England

Source: *World Health Organization Annuals*. Homicide rates in the United States, Finland, and England. (1965-1995). Reprinted with permission.

On the basis of social, economic, and political factors, it is certainly appropriate to include the United States in the above group of countries. Unfortunately, the generally high rates of homicide in the United States are actually more comparable to those of some of the poorest and least economically developed countries in the world. Homicide rates for 77 countries were taken from the 1998 United Nations Demographic Yearbook and ranked. Table 3-1 indicates that, among the countries reporting homicide victimization rates to the United Nations, the United States ranked 19th among the top 25.

Table 3-1
Homicide Rates in Selected Countries

Rank	Year	Country	Rate per 100,000
1	1994	Colombia	80.0
2	1993	El Salvador	45.7
3	1992	Puerto Rico	23.8
4	1997	Russian Federation	23.8
5	1998	Estonia	18.3
6	1998	Kazakhstan	18.1
7	1998	Albania	17.4
8	1995	Mexico	17.2
9	1994	Venezuela	15.7
10	1995	Bahamas	15.1
11	1995	Ecuador	13.4
12	1998	Latvia	12.9
13	1998	Belarus	12.1
14	1998	Ukraine	12.1
15	1994	Trinidad and Tobago	11.7
16	1998	Rep. of Moldova	11.3
17	1992	Tajikistan	10.4
18	1998	Lithuania	8.2
19	1997	United States	7.3
20	1998	Kyrgyzstan	7.3
21	1996	Cuba	6.6
22	1955	Barbados	6.4
23	1997	Azerbaijan	6.0
24	1994	Nicaragua	5.5
25	1995	Costa Rica	5.4

Source: United Nations. (2000). Table 21: Homicide rates in selected countries. *Demographic yearbook 1998*. New York: United Nations. Reprinted with permission. The United Nations is the author of the original material.

In reality, the United States probably would rank lower in this list if accurate homicide rates were available from developing countries. It is likely that homicide rates for countries like El Salvador, Colombia, and the Russian Federation reported in Table 3-1 are minimal estimates. Given the unsophisticated and haphazard system of law enforcement, minimal systems of communication and transportation, and a poorly developed system of criminal statistics, it is likely that many homicides in developing countries go unreported, particularly in rural areas (Clinard & Abbott, 1973).

One perspective explains transnational homicide rates by suggesting that societies at different stages of modernization will show different crime patterns, reflecting differences in criminal motivations, controls, and opportunities. A major prediction of modernization theory is that property crimes will be higher and violent crimes lower in modernized societies, with the reverse true for developing countries. Although modernization and social disorganization theories have been the most generally explored, research has shown that economic development has no effect or a negative effect on national homicide rates (LaFree, 1999).

Another perspective is that crime results from economic hardship, such as economic inequality, poverty, and unemployment. Studies examining the cross-national impact of unemployment rates on homicide have been largely negative. However, a number of studies support the view that there is a relationship between levels of economic inequality and homicide rates (LaFree, 1999).

Conclusions

The first part of this chapter provided a brief review of the history of violence in the United States. We have shown that violence is not only a persistent feature of our past, but it has served both positive and negative goals. Violence was a prominent part of our historical development from the Revolutionary period to Prohibition and the appearance of organized crime.

The second part of the chapter examined current trends in violence. We focused on homicide because that is the most reliable information available—yet this is of limited value before the twentieth century. There are two major conclusions.

First, violence will become more anonymous as Americans become more urbanized and come to rely more heavily on technological forms of protection. Second, although violence rates have declined since the mid-1990s, homicide rates in the United States are much higher than in comparable technologically developed countries. Our excessively high homicide rates are, therefore, more comparable to those that are found in less developed societies.

Endnote

1. Dime novels were so-called because of their cost—one dime. The University of Minnesota has a collection of over 3,000 titles published from 1840 to the early 1900s. These popular books revealed the ideals of the time and, to some extent, our own. The colorful characters—frequently outlaws—display American virtues of patriotism, rugged individualism, frontier virtues, and faith in hard work as the road to success (University of Minnesota Research Collections, 2000).

References

Archer, D., & Gartner, R. (1984). *Violence and crime in cross-national perspective.* New Haven, CT: Yale University Press.

Brown, R. M. (1979). Historical patterns of violence. In H. D. Graham & T. R. Gurr (Eds.), *Violence in America: Historical and comparative perspectives* (Vol. 1, pp. 35–64). Washington, DC: Government Printing Office.

Brown, R. M. (1989). Historical patterns of violence. In T. R. Gurr (Ed.), *Violence in American: Protest, rebellion, reform* (Vol. 2, pp. 23–61). Newbury Park, CA: Sage.

Clinard, M. B., & Abbott, D. J. (1973). *Crime in developing countries: A comparative perspective.* New York: John Wiley & Sons.

Goode, E. (1999). *Drugs in American society* (5th ed.). New York: McGraw-Hill.

LaFree, G. (1999). A summary and review of cross-national comparative studies of homicide. In M. D. Smith & M. A. Zahn (Eds.), *Homicide: A sourcebook of social research* (pp. 125–145). Thousand Oaks, CA: Sage.

Lane, R. (1979). *Violent death in the city: Suicide, accident, and murder in 19th century Philadelphia.* Cambridge, MA: Harvard University Press.

———. (1997). *Murder in America: A history.* Columbus: Ohio State University Press.

Microsoft. (1998a). *Cherokee, Encarta Encyclopedia.* Redman, WA: Microsoft Corporation.

————. (1998b). *Slavery, Encarta Encyclopedia*. Redman, WA: Microsoft Corporation.

Mulligan, E. (1970). Accounts of the 'Cherokee Trail of Tears' with reference to 'Princess Otahki.' *St. Louis Post Dispatch*. Available: <http://www.ywiiusdinvnnohii.net/articles/princes.html> [May 16, 2000].

Nash, J. R. (1973). *Bloodletters and badmen: A narrative encyclopedia of American criminals from the Pilgrims to the present*. Philadelphia: Lippincott.

Riedel, M. (1998). Serial murder, communities, and evil: A review essay. *Criminal Justice Review, 23*, 220–232.

————. (1999). Homicide. In L. Kurtz (Ed.), *Encyclopedia of violence, peace, and conflict* (pp. 123–138). San Diego, CA: Academic Press.

Silberman, C. E. (1978). *Criminal Violence, Criminal Justice*. New York: Random House.

United Nations. (2000). *Demographic Yearbook 1998*. New York: Author.

University of Minnesota Research Collections. (2000). Dime Novels. Available: <http://www.umi.com/hp/Support/Research/Files/57.html> [May 19, 2000]. ✦

Chapter 4

Theories of Violence

Is Theory Important?

There is a saying that "facts speak for themselves." This is probably one of the most intellectually dishonest statements foisted on an unsuspecting public. All people, including researchers, make observations of the world around them. How they *interpret* these observations, that is, how they attribute organization and meaning to what they are seeing, draw upon cultural belief—a kind of implicit theory that is part of how we were socialized. Whether we are talking about cultural belief systems or scientific theory, however, it is certain that observations are processed through an affective and cognitive framework in ways that permit observers to understand events; facts, in short, never speak for themselves.

Scientific theory shares with cultural beliefs the purpose of organizing and giving meaning to our observations, whether it involves someone driving down a road or an act of violence. Scientific theory differs from the cultural beliefs with which we grow up by being explicit and testable. A theory is explicit when all parts of the theory—assumptions, propositions, consequences—are available for everyone's review and examination. A scientific theory is testable when it allows the collection of observations to test its falsity.

Criminology is interested in explanation. Why did the offender commit this act? Is there some behavior that the offender learned as a child that caused him or her to commit this violent act? Was the event caused by a quarrel between victim and offender that escalated into fatal violence? Did alcohol and drugs play a role? Whether we are discussing homicide, aggravated assault, rape, or robbery, the role of theory is to offer testable explanations of how and why violent events occur.

Because of the success of the physical sciences beginning in the sixteenth century, it was just a question of time until the same type of rational thinking and scientific method would be applied to the study of crime. In the eighteenth century, Beccaria's (1963) treatise, *On Crimes and Punishments*, originally published in 1764, became the most prominent instance of a rational analysis of the crime problem. Meanwhile, scientific methods were illustrated by the work of Adolphe Quetelet and Andre Guerry in France and Lombroso in Italy in the nineteenth century (Vold & Bernard, 1986).

Prior to the emergence of rational and scientific explanations, violent events and violent offenders were explained by invoking moral or religious explanations. Current reactions of the community and the continued use of explanations based on religious and supernatural causes attest to a continuing and pervasive interest in understanding violence.

A chapter on theories of violence presents a challenge for two reasons. First, there are few theories of violence because theorists have generally tended instead to explain delinquency and crime, of which violent crime is a part. One reason for doing so is that offenders rarely specialize in violent crimes like homicide, assault, and robbery. As Blumstein, Cohen, Das, and Moitra (1988, p. 342) have noted, "the more impulsive violent crimes of homicide, rape, and weapons violations were among the least specialized." Although the latter does not preclude a theory of violence, a general theory of crime is seen as more useful.

Second, if there are too few theories of violence there are too many theories of crime and delinquency. A comprehensive review of crime theories constitutes a book in itself. Readers interested in the large variety of theories available should consult Curran and Renzetti (2001), Shoemaker (1996), and Vold, Bernard, and Snipes (1998). The practice followed here is to review the theories that will be applied in the discussion of violence in subsequent chapters. In this chapter, we describe specific theories and provide a brief overview of their strengths and limitations.

The next section examines Freud and psychoanalytic explanations of crime. This is followed by one of the earliest sociological theories, social disorganization. Social disorganization theory was formulated at the University of Chicago early in the twentieth century by people who left a lasting impression on criminology. One of the most famous graduates of the University of Chicago was Edwin Sutherland, who formulated differential association theory. A more recent formulation of differential association theory was proposed by Burgess and Akers (1968).

Following that section, we examine strain and subcultural theories. These theories include Merton's strain theory, subcultural theories by Cohen, Cloward, and Ohlin, and Agnew. A variant of subcultural theories, cultural deviance theories, are represented by the theories of Miller and Wolfgang and of Ferracuti.

The third group of theories focuses on why people do not commit crime, that is, how social control works. These include theories by Hirschi and Matza. The final two sections discuss routine activities theory and symbolic interaction theory.

Freud and Psychoanalysis

Sigmund Freud was a physician who lived most of his life in Vienna and published most of his important ideas in the first 40 years of the twentieth century. Freud divided the human personalty into three parts: id, ego, and superego. The id is the reservoir of biological and psychological drives; it is permanently unconscious, and is governed exclusively by the pleasure principle, that is, "If it feels good, do it."

The superego is the voice of self-criticism and conscience. The superego contains all the cultural prohibitions and religious taboos and may be partly conscious. We learn these moral prohibitions through moral attachments to our parents.

Finally, there is the ego, which is called by Freud the "reality principle." The ego is the conscious part of the personality and is oriented toward the world in which the person lives. It is constantly mediating between the demands of the id and the superego (Freud, 1920).

According to the psychoanalytic theory of criminality, crime occurs for three reasons: The offender has a conscience so overbearing that it arouses feeling of guilt, his or her conscience is so weak that it cannot control personal impulses, or there is a need for immediate gratification. Behavior, Freud believed, was "overdetermined," that is, there was typically more than one reason for the behavior. Hence, a violent act could encompass one or more of the three reasons given.

Psychoanalytic theory is used to explain the bizarre character of serial homicide, which is discussed in chapter 5. Similarly, rape and sexual assaults are sometimes explained by psychoanalytic theory, as described in chapter 8.

Although listed among the great thinkers of the twentieth century, the contribution of Freud to understanding violence has been small and psychoanalytic explanations are used infrequently. Partly, this is the result of the growth of sociological theories and partly the result of better theories developed in the psychoanalytic tradition. The lasting contribution of psychoanalytic theory is threefold: (1) actions and behavior of adults need to be understood in terms of childhood development; (2) behavior and unconscious motives are intertwined and their effect needs to be distinguished if criminality is to be understood; and (3) criminality is a representation of psychological conflict (Adler, Mueller, & Laufer, 1998).

Social Disorganization Theory

The earliest attempt to apply a sociological perspective to the study of crime and violence occurred at the University of Chicago. Researchers in one of the first sociology departments in the United States laid the foundation for social disorganization theory (Harris, Welsh, & Butler, 2000).

Burgess (1925) compared urban growth to the metabolic processes of the body: Many different processes interact to keep the body in a "steady state"; anything that disturbs that steady state (e.g., a virus) results in attempts to readjust and adapt. Researchers asked to what degree rapid urban expansion occurring in Chicago necessitated readjustment in the social organization of communities. Temporary disorganization was to be expected to some extent, given the large numbers of immigrants to the city and the loss of former social ties and norms. However, to the degree that disorganization became permanent, rather than temporary, it was "pathological," not "progressive." In areas of high mobility, the social control of the *primary group* was weakest, contributing to social disorganization and delinquency.

Shaw and McKay (1942) developed quantitative measures to test these ideas. Their theory had two main components. First, people compete for desirable space in a city. There is an economic advantage associated with being near the marketplace, and most cities have grown around the marketplace. Second, levels of social organization and integration varied in different communities. For example, they found that crime rates were highest near the center of the city, and decreased as one moved outward. Their explanation centered on changes in the physical environment and resultant impacts on the social behavior of residents. As the central city became too crowded and too expensive, stable businesses and residents moved out. The resulting area around the central city became a *zone in transition*, characterized by high mobility, *social disorganization*, and high rates of delinquency and violence.

Shaw and McKay (1942) replicated their findings in several large American cities. In Philadelphia, for example, they examined delinquency rates over a three-year period. Three structural factors (low economic status, ethnic heterogeneity, and residential mobility) accounted for most of the community variation in delinquency rates, ostensibly by disrupting local community social organization. Various community factors were all highly interrelated, however, making causal interpretations ambiguous until many years later when more sophisticated statistical techniques became available. Shaw and McKay carefully noted exceptions to these general patterns, including "pockets" of minority communities characterized by high stability and low crime rates. Shaw and McKay were once again struck by the stability of crime rates in particular communities over time, even after considerable population turnover.

There were two important implications of the Shaw and McKay research. First, it demonstrated that social structure and change had more to do with delinquency and violence than individual motivation. Second, their research showed that no specific race or ethnic group had a monopoly on crime and violence. As various race and ethnic groups immigrated to Chicago and moved into the zone of transition because it was the only housing they could afford, the violence and delinquency rates of their children began to increase. However, as succeeding generations moved out of this area their crime rates declined, only to be replaced by the high rates of an incoming migrant group. At a time when the popular theories of crime were based in biology that later supported racist ideologies, the Shaw and McKay research provided an important antidote (Faris, 1967).

Two important criticisms are discussed by Harris et al. (2000). First, juvenile justice statistics are generally biased because juveniles of lower socioeconomic status are arrested more frequently. Second, Shaw and McKay made inappropriate assumptions about individual-level behavior from aggregate, neighborhood-level data. What is called the "ecological fallacy" occurs when conclusions are made about individuals on the basis of group data (Robinson, 1950).

Few works in criminology have had greater influence than Shaw and McKay's (1942) *Juvenile Delinquency and Urban Areas* (Bursik, 1988). Finestone (1976) illustrates how virtually all theoretical and empirical work in the field of criminology since 1929, including subcultural theories, learning theories (e.g., differential association), labeling theories, and social process theories, can be seen as extensions of or reactions to the research conducted by Shaw and McKay.

Crime as Learned Behavior

Differential Association

The simple idea that criminal behavior is learned just like any other kind of behavior represents an important change in thinking about criminality. First, treating criminality as learned behavior means that what is learned can be replaced with more useful learning. Changing criminal behavior is a matter of providing criminals with noncriminal learning patterns that will not lead to conflicts with the law.

Second, conceiving of criminality as learned behavior removes some of the stigma from criminals. Criminals are no longer intrinsically evil people; they are the products of the same process that characterizes every person who learns the innumerable tasks that people use throughout life.

Finally, criminality as learned behavior reduces the moral chasm between "law-abiding" people and criminals. It is part of the general historical movement from the pitiless and horrible violence imposed on criminals in the Middle Ages to a view of punishment that recognizes a common humanity in even the most violent of criminals.

This is not to suggest that Sutherland's (1947) differential association theory was the first to recognize that criminality is learned behavior. The notion of learned behavior was implicit in a wide variety of theories prior to Sutherland. Beccaria's (1963) view in 1764 that the purpose of punishment was deterrence implies that this result teaches offenders and others not to commit crime. Gabriel Tarde (1907) argued that people became criminals because they were brought up in an environment in which they learned criminality from others as a way of life.

Sutherland did, however, place criminality as learned behavior at the center of his differential association theory. The nine propositions of differential association theory are given below.

1. Criminal behavior is learned.

2. Criminal behavior is learned in interaction with other persons in a process of communication.

3. The principal part of the learning of criminal behavior occurs within intimate personal groups.

4. When criminal behavior is learned, the learning includes: (a) techniques of committing the crime, which are sometimes very complicated, sometimes very simple, and (b) the specific direction of motives, drives, rationalizations, and attitudes.

5. The specific direction of motives and drives is learned from definitions of legal codes as favorable or unfavorable.

6. A person becomes delinquent because of an excess of definitions favorable to violation of the law over definitions unfavorable to violation of the law.

7. Differential associations may vary in frequency, duration, priority, and intensity.

8. The process of learning criminal behavior with criminal and anticriminal patterns involves all of the mechanisms that are involved in any other learning.

9. Although criminal behavior is an expression of general needs and values, it is not explained by those general needs and values, since noncriminal behavior is an expression of the same needs and values. (Sutherland, 1947, pp. 6–7)

One way of viewing the theory is to divide it into *what* is learned and *how* it is learned. People learn to be criminals by learning from other criminals. They learn not only the skills required to shoplift, pick a lock, or roll a joint, but also how to rationalize and defend their actions.

As used by Sutherland, definitions have nothing to do with dictionaries! Social definitions of law-abiding behavior have to do with general attitudes toward law. For example, young middle-class persons acquire a definition of the Internal Revenue Service (IRS) from the kinds of views expressed by parents. Does the parent take a questionable deduction because "the government just wastes my money anyway and buys $700 hammers" or does the parent forego the deduction until he or she can check with the IRS? In the former case, the child learns a definition favorable to the violation of the law (i.e., I should keep my money because the government wastes it). In the latter case, the parent conveys a definition unfavorable to the violation of the law (i.e., the IRS code is a fair and equitable way of raising revenue needed for public services). It is those kinds of views toward laws that constitute social definitions favorable or unfavorable to violation of laws.

It is the *definitions* that are important here. It is a key principle of differential association that it is a social definition, not people. Rather, it is a question of definitions learned through interaction. Prison guards do not become criminals because they associate with criminals, they become criminals by an excess of definitions favorable to violation of law that can be acquired from a number of sources.

Likewise, the extent to which associations and definitions result in criminality depends upon the frequency, duration, priority, and intensity (Proposition 7) of definitions favorable and unfavorable to violation of law. In other words, the content and the extent of contact with favorable and unfavorable definitions have an impact on criminality. Obviously, then, social definitions learned through interaction with intimate personal groups like family and friends are going to have the greatest impact.

The last proposition states that the same needs and values underlie both criminal and noncriminal behavior. What Sutherland is saying is that individual goals can be achieved either through criminality (i.e., an excess of definitions favorable to violation of the law over definitions unfavorable to violation of law) or the reverse (i.e., an excess of social definitions unfavorable to violation of law over social definitions favorable to violation of law). Put another way, a person can obtain money either through theft or hard work (Lilly, Cullen, & Ball, 1994).

As Vold et al. (1998) have noted, differential association has had a massive impact on criminology. As we noted earlier, the Chicago school of sociology, of which Sutherland was a prominent member, played a prominent role in reorienting criminology away from biological explanations and toward criminality as learned behavior (Faris, 1967). As differential association has changed and learning theory components have become more important, it has proven to be a useful theory; it is discussed further in chapter 7.

Social Learning Theory

Other theorists have looked more carefully at the process of learning. As far back as Aristotle, learning was viewed as a matter of association: Sensory experiences became associated with one another because they occur in certain ways as we interact with the object. For example, we learn that houses have doors because all the houses we have been acquainted with had doors. There are three perspectives to learning by association.

First, there is the classical conditioning described by Pavlov. This is a passive method, in which a conditioned stimulus is paired with the unconditioned stimulus, as when a bell is rung each time meat is presented to a dog who salivates at the appearance of meat. Soon, even without the appearance of meat the dog will salivate at the sound of the bell, the conditioned response.

Second, there is modeling or social learning theory, which emphasizes that behavior is shaped not only by rewards and punishments, but also by expectations acquired by watching what happens to other people. Albert Bandura (1973), a leading proponent of behavioral modeling, argues that children learn to be violent adults by watching the violence on television or in their families.

Finally, operant conditioning is different from classical conditioning. In classical conditioning the organism is passive, but in operant conditioning the organism is expected to do something to get what it wants from the environment. Thus, pigeons learn to peck at a bar that releases food. Receiving the food for pecking at the bar is rewarding or reinforcing.

Robert Burgess and Ron Akers (1968) improved upon differential association by combining it with operant conditioning and modeling. By incorporating the principles of modern learning theory, Burgess and Akers strengthened differential association theory because although Sutherland wrote that social definitions were learned in intimate settings, he provided little indication of how such learning occurred.

One factor added by Burgess and Akers was that nonsocial situations could also be discriminative in producing criminality; that is, the environment itself can reinforce criminality. In a later revision, Akers moved in the direction of incorporating more social learning principles. In other words, people learn criminality by watching others (Akers, 1997).

One of the positive features of the Burgess and Akers formulation is that it has been praised as being very practical. Correctional facilities have adopted a variety of behavior modification principles that incorporate elements of social learning theory. However, one of the difficulties with the theory is that it does not address the question of how criminal and deviant definitions originate, nor how reinforcement schedules come into existence.

Strain and Subcultural Theories

Merton's Strain Theory

Strain theory argues that most people are law-abiding, but they become criminal under pressure. The task is to explain what is meant by pressure or strain. Robert Merton (1957b) believes that the disparity between cultural goals and institutionalized means leads to a number of adaptations.

Merton first distinguished between cultural goals and institutionalized means. Every culture has goals that are considered desirable and important. In the United States, a major cultural goal is success, primarily economic success or wealth. Because it is an egalitarian society, the United States encourages everyone to pursue this goal and praises the few who reach it. Those who do succeed become the stuff of legend, the Horatio Alger story of "poor boy makes it big," but those who do not even try are characterized as "lazy" or "unambitious."

In a well-integrated society, people also prescribe institutionalized means to reach these goals. In U.S. society, the institutionalized means to reach the success goal consist of such elements as the willingness to work hard, be honest, get an education, and defer gratification, such as purchasing an expensive automobile, buying an expensive house, taking expensive vacations, and so forth.

Where these two components are well integrated, the mode of adaptation is described as *conformity*. But there are several other adaptations that have implications for crime and violence, as can be seen in Table 4-1.

When there is a disjunction between goals and means, it gives rise to *anomie*, which is most closely translated as "normlessness."

Table 4-1
Typology of Individual Adaptations

Modes of Adaptation	Cultural Goals	Institutionalized Means
I. Conformity	+	+
II. Innovation	+	−
III. Ritualism	−	+
IV. Retreatism	−	−
V. Rebellion	±	±

+ Accepts cultural goals or institutionalized means
− Rejects cultural goals or institutionalized means
± Rejects cultural goals and institutionalized means but wishes to replace with new goals and means

Source: Reprinted and adapted with the permission of The Free Press, a Division of Simon & Schuster, Inc., from *Social Theory and Social Structure*, Revised & Enlarged Edition (p. 194) by Robert K. Merton. Copyright © 1967, 1968 by Robert K. Merton.

In short, Merton thought that without the guidelines provided by culture, behavior would arise that culture was designed to prevent—like crime.

Criminological theorists interested in explaining crime and violence drew upon the second adaptation—innovation. In this adaptation, the cultural goal of success is accepted, but criminal and deviant means are used to reach it.

Innovation occurs when the goal is emphasized at the expense of the institutionalized means. The culturally approved version of institutionalized means states that "It's not whether you win or lose, it's how you play the game." Merton claims that the goal has become more important than the means: "It's not how you play the game, its whether you win." With an undue emphasis on the goal, we realize that institutionalized means have little intrinsic satisfaction.

Consider two types of individuals. Individual A has been hard working, is honest, has struggled to get an education, and has saved his money. He receives little social reward for his efforts and, unless he was prudent in providing for himself, may well have financial difficulties when he retires.

Individual B does none of these things. She has been a gambler, moved from job to job, and has a reputation for legal and moral "corner cutting," but is wealthy. Individual B is going to receive more rewards of prestige and social status than Individual A, even though her wealth may not have been achieved by approved means. Individual B is rich and, according to Merton, that is really what counts when the innovation adaptation is used. Consequently, crime is another way of being successful.

This strain or disparity tends to be concentrated on the lower class because the ability to achieve wealth is limited by the social structure itself. Because of income and education differentials, it is the lower class that does the worst job of preparing children to achieve success goals. On the other hand, strain is least apparent in the upper and middle classes because members of these strata can achieve wealth with only a reasonable effort.

Consider the third adaptation—*ritualism*—which does not generate criminality. In this adaptation, the cultural goals are rejected while the institutionalized means are accepted. This is demonstrated by people who "go through the motions," but feel there is little hope of achieving higher goals; they are satisfied with a modest level of achievement (see Table 4-1).

A variant of this adaptation is the *bureaucratic personality* (Merton, 1957a). This is seen in people who insist that the "rules are the rules" that must be followed regardless of whether they correspond to the goal for which they were intended. Generally, these are people who are unable or unwilling to exercise the discretion that would result in a more flexible application of rules.

Retreatism is noted in people who reject both means and goals. They are best described as dropouts from society, which include drug addicts, alcoholics, and vagrants. *Rebellion*, the last of the adaptations, is what the name implies: It is an adaptation by those who reject the current culture and structure and want to replace it with something new (see Table 4-1). This is discussed in chapter 9.

Clinard (1964, p. 10) states that Merton's theory has been the "most influential single formulation in the sociology of deviance in the last twenty-five years. . . ." But this does not mean it has been without criticism.

Critics have pointed out that Merton's description of alcoholics and drug addicts is something of an oversimplification. Rather than the disjunction between goals and means being the cause of drug addiction, retreatism may be the result of drug use (Lindesmith & Gagnon, 1964). Similarly, rather than crime and deviance being the outcome of anomie, following a labeling perspective, crime and deviance may be the outcome of social control efforts (Curran & Renzetti, 2001).

The emphasis on the blockage of legitimate opportunities because of the disparity between cultural goals and institutionalized means was adopted and expressed in different ways by Albert Cohen, Robert Agnew, and coauthors Cloward and Ohlin. Cultural deviance theory represents yet another variation on social class differentials and is represented here by Miller and coauthors Wolfgang and Ferracuti.

Albert Cohen and Delinquent Boys

Subcultures are a subdivision within a dominant culture. Subcultures emerge when groups in similar circumstances face a problem that will isolate them from the mainstream. These groups band together for mutual support and can be found among racial and ethnic minorities, occupational groups, or ghetto dwellers. Subcultural members are part of the larger society, but have a life-style that distinguishes them from members of the dominant culture.

The formation of subcultures represents a step forward in the specificity of criminological theory. The difficulty with strain theories is that they explained the conditions under which criminality would emerge, but did not explain what groups would become criminal. It is not enough to say that lower-class members are predisposed toward crime; a good theory must say *which* groups are predisposed and to *what* kinds of crime.

Unlike Merton, Albert Cohen did not believe most crime was an illegitimate, but purposeful, path to wealth. Cohen believed that the purpose of delinquent acts was to achieve status, not any kind of monetary success. From his work with delinquent gangs, Cohen (1955) thought that most crime was committed by gangs and that most of it was "nonutilitarian, malicious, and negativistic."

When Cohen set out to explain gang delinquency, he noted that most delinquents came from lower-class homes. He suggested that lower-class children were not prepared to succeed in school, a solidly middle-class institution run by middle-class teachers and middle-class administrators. Status in school was achieved by showing ambition, responsibility, achievement, deferred gratification, rationality, courtesy, ability to control aggression, constructive use of time, and respect for property. While these are virtues taught from early childhood in middle-class homes, they are less common in lower-class homes. Hence, the lower-class adolescent is at a competitive disadvantage and is placed under severe strain.

One alternative for the lower-class adolescent is to rebel against middle-class values and set up a new value structure that will confirm his status and self-worth. Because other juveniles have the same low-status problems, they tend to band together, which is the origin of the delinquent gang.

But these juveniles have a problem. They have internalized to some extent the norms and values of the dominant class and feel anxiety about violating these norms. To deal with this anxiety, members of the delinquent gang develop *reaction formation*. Reaction formation is a psychological mechanism that rejects that which is causing the anxiety by doing the opposite. Hence, juveniles stand middle-class virtues on their heads by behavior that is the opposite: nonutilitarian, malicious, and negativistic. They steal things, then discard or destroy them rather than using or selling them; they get involved in gang fights over trivial matters, and they vandalize property in an apparent random fashion.

The problems of lower-class males that lead to status frustration have to do with values and behavior that are traditionally masculine: comparisons with other males with respect to fighting, stealing, athletic contests, and work. In what is now a quaint turn of events, Cohen believes it is a masculine problem. Girls, he notes, are more interested in developing relationships with the opposite sex:

> We do not suggest that girls are in any sense 'naturally' more interested in boys than boys are in girls. We mean that the female's station in society, the admiration, respect and property that she commands, depends to a much greater degree on the kinds of relationships that she establishes with members of the opposite sex. (1955a, pp. 140–141)

Cohen's theory has been criticized for its portrayal of delinquency as malicious and nonutilitarian. His delinquents are annoying, but most of their crimes are trivial and redundant. Although this may be true for a number of delinquents, many gangs now engage in serious and utilitarian crimes. Drive-by shootings cannot be classified as minor forms of violence (Sanders, 1994). Perhaps because of the time in which he wrote, Cohen does not deny female offending, but he treats it as a minor problem.

Delinquency and Opportunity: Richard Cloward and Lloyd Ohlin

Differential opportunity theory, developed by Cloward and Ohlin (1960), relies on Merton's basic concept that crime occurs because legitimate opportunities are blocked. What makes differential opportunity theory different is that previous theories explain why juveniles become criminal, but they do not explain the kinds of offenses chosen. In other words, in addition to the legitimate opportunity structure, there is an illegitimate opportunity structure that determines the kinds of crimes that occur.

Cloward and Ohlin suggested that the type of gang that a juvenile joins is not determined by personal preference; a juvenile cannot just decide to join a theft-oriented or a violence-oriented gang. The type of gang available to join depends upon the type of neighborhood in which the juvenile lives.

In areas where legitimate and illegitimate opportunities are integrated and closely connected, *criminal gangs* emerge. Older criminals can serve as role models. Juveniles cannot help but be impressed by the drug dealer, for example, who always has money to burn, drives an expensive automobile, dresses well, and is usually found in the company of beautiful women. To juveniles in poor neighborhoods, such people look impressive and worthy of emulation.

In addition, where there is a criminal subculture, older criminals teach juveniles criminal skills, and how to exploit people and the system. They also introduce young people to relationships with other criminals, and the way to make the right connections with corrupt criminal justice personnel.

A second type of subculture adaptation to the illegitimate opportunity structure is found in neighborhoods characterized by transience and instability. Neighborhoods in which high turnover of residence, high unemployment, and low home ownership are prevalent have few organized criminal activities to learn. In these areas *conflict gangs* emerge, which are out to gain status for their toughness and destructive violence. Members of these gangs belong to the world of the warrior, in which violence is valued as a means of showing courage, defending the honor of the gang, and never showing fear.

The third type of subculture is the *retreatist subculture*. Members of this subculture are what Cloward and Ohlin called double failures. They have failed to succeed in both the legitimate and illegitimate opportunity structure. They have retreated into a world in which the most important feature is getting high through drugs, alcohol, atypical sexual experiences, or a combination of all three. Members of a retreatist subculture may sell drugs, but do so to acquire money to buy drugs for themselves. For these individuals, membership in retreatist gangs offers a sense of belonging and well-being that cannot be found elsewhere.

One of the positive features of the Cloward and Ohlin formulation is showing not only what causes crime and deviance, but also what kinds of crimes are chosen. Not only do they make use of strain theory, but they incorporate social learning in describing how criminal behavior and careers are chosen.

Researchers have not been able to find support for the three distinct subcultures posited by Cloward and Ohlin. Studies find that lower-class gangs use drugs, fight, and vandalize property, but do not specialize and continually engage in violence, for example (Brunson & Miller, 2000). Cloward and Ohlin are subject to the same criticism as are proponents of other subcultural and cultural deviance theories: Crime is a lower-class phenomenon. An abundance of crime, albeit crimes related to trust violation, are committed by the middle and upper classes as well (Friedrichs, 1996).

The General Strain Theory of Robert Agnew

Robert Agnew (1992) pointed out that strain theory was popular in the 1960s, but that its influence was diminished by the emergence of social control and learning theory. Explanations based on strain, the discrepancy between cultural goals and institutionalized means, highlight the anger and related emotions that lead to delinquency because of negative relationships with others.

> Social control theory, by contrast, focuses on the *absence of significant relationships with conventional others and institutions.* . . . In differential association/social learning theory, the adolescent commits delinquent acts because group forces lead the adolescent to view *delinquency as a desirable or at least justifiable form of behavior* under certain circumstances. (1992, p. 49)

There is more than one type of strain that can lead to delinquency. Agnew (1992) agrees with Merton, Cohen, and Cloward and Ohlin that strain can arise in the disjunction between aspirations and expectations (expected levels of achievements). For lower-class adolescents, middle-class monetary success is expected, but not achieved. This leads to anger and frustration that drives delinquent behavior. There are *two other subtypes* of strain resulting from the disjunction between means and ends plus *two other major types.*

In addition to the subtype discussed by Merton, a second subtype of strain is the disjunction between expectations and actual achievement. One response to the failure to achieve expectations may be to reduce the gap between expectations and achievements. Delinquency then is not so much a "striking out" at blocked opportunities, but more a recognition that crime is a kind of achievement that is realistic, particularly when adolescents compare themselves to others like themselves.

A third subtype is the strain between what individuals see as a just and fair outcome and actual outcomes. In their interactions with others, individuals expect that outcomes will be dictated by equity or rules of fair play in how resources should be allocated. Where rules of fair play do not prevail, adolescents experience distress. Inequity leads adolescents to behavior to restore equity.

> Individuals in inequitable relationships may engage in delinquency in order to (1) increase their outcomes (e.g., by theft); (2) lower their inputs (e.g., truancy from school); (3) lower the outcomes of others (e.g., vandalism, theft, assault); and/or (4) increase the inputs of others (e.g., by being incorrigible or disorderly). (Agnew, 1992, p. 54)

In addition to the former and its subtypes, another major type of strain for individuals is the *removal of stimuli they positively value*, including positively valued achievements or relationships: the loss of a boyfriend or girlfriend, death of a friend, moving to a new school, divorce of parents, or a combination of these. Although the research is sparse, it does support the view that such adolescent loss leads to anger, frustration, and delinquency.

The third major type of strain is the *presentation of negative stimuli*. Agnew refers here to the kind of negative relationships from which adolescents cannot easily escape. Child abuse/neglect, excessive physical punishment, negative relations with peers, and negative school experiences are examples of events that can lead to aggression and delinquency.

Not all adolescents who experience strain respond to it with crime and deviance; strain represents *pressure* or predispositions to commit delinquent acts. Individuals may respond to strain in a number of ways. The coping strategies may include minimizing the importance of the stressor, engaging in vengeful behavior, or temporally using drugs or alcohol excessively.

Agnew (1992) also suggests there are conditioning factors that influence how people respond to strain. The individual may embrace other goals or values unless the ones subject to strain receive a high level of support. Coping strategies are also affected by individual levels of self-esteem; persons with high levels of self-esteem are less likely to respond to strain with delinquency.

Agnew's theory is multifaceted and complex and introduces a variety of concepts from social psychology. Because of the recency of the theory, it has not been thoroughly tested. The research that has been done supports the view that strain has an impact on delinquency and that delinquency reduces negative emotional consequences. The empirical support for conditioning factors, however, is limited (Curran & Renzetti, 2001).

Cultural Deviance Theory

Cultural deviance theory makes use of subcultures, but theorists in this tradition do not believe that delinquency results from a failure to reach middle-class goals. Cultural deviance theory is rooted in culture conflict, that is, the fact that different social groups have values that conflict with the dominant culture. But the nature of the conflict is different from subcultural theories. In subcultural theories, delinquency represents a reaction and a rejection of middle-class values; in cultural deviance theories, delinquency is simply an expression of subcultural values that, *coincidentally*, are in conflict with middle-class values. In other words, in cultural deviance theories, my subcultural values may call for violence in certain situations; that this violence is wrong from a middle-class perspective is a matter that is either unknown to me or one about which I do not care.

Cultural Deviance: Walter Miller

Walter Miller (1958) believed that lower-class culture is a separate identifiable culture that has traditions as old as middle-class culture. In a very important sense, Miller's need to emphasize the integrity of lower-class communities is extremely important in countering a middle-class view that lower-class people are "all criminals and dope addicts," in general, a disreputable lot. A large variety of social and emotional problems certainly do exist in lower-class culture, but not *all* lower-class persons are criminals and deviants; merely being poor is not criminal. Thus, more current theories have moved away from class-based theories, recognizing the possibility that they can lead to a biased picture of the lower class.

Miller (1958) advanced the view that the lower class have "focal concerns," very similar to social values. He suggested that these shape the behavior of young people in ways that lead to delinquent behavior. The focal concerns he mentioned are the following:

> 1. **Trouble.** This relates to getting into and out of trouble—lower-class involvement in such activities as fighting, drinking, and sexual misbehavior is a daily part of lower-class life.
>
> 2. **Toughness.** This focal concern refers to a show of masculinity and a denial of sentimentality. Miller argued that this results from many lower-class males growing up in female-dominated households.
>
> 3. **Smartness.** Street smarts is the ability to get something by outwitting or conning another person.
>
> 4. **Excitement.** This is expressed by fighting, getting drunk, or using drugs, anything to break up a monotonous existence.
>
> 5. **Luck.** People believe that life is subject to forces over which they have little control. The focal concern of luck expresses itself in a belief in lucky numbers, whether the cards are right, or whether the dice are good to them.
>
> 6. **Autonomy.** This is expressed in the lower-class person's resentment of authority and its rules.

The focal concerns are the generating conditions, and juveniles who behave in accordance with these concerns are likely to engage in behavior that is delinquent and criminal.

On a positive note, Miller provided a compelling picture of the culture of poverty: the belief in fate or luck, the ability to handle oneself and outwit others, and masculine toughness. However, Miller does emphasize that female-dominated households play a causative role in delinquency. Partly because the relative proportion of female-dominated households is greater among African Americans than whites, what was a class-based theory has become a race-based theory. Attempts to test the effect of female-dominated households have generated contradictory results (Shoemaker, 1996).

Cultural Deviance: Marvin Wolfgang and Franco Ferracuti

One of the difficulties with the theories we have considered thus far is that they aimed to explain the enormous variety of delinquent and criminal behavior. Wolfgang and Ferracuti's (1967) theory of the subculture of violence, however, was limited to an explanation of violent behavior.

Wolfgang (1958) noted that many homicides occurring in the lower class seemed to result from very trivial events that became very important because of expectations held by the participants.

> The subject of stimuli, such as a jostle, a slightly derogatory remark, or the appearance of a weapon in the hands of an adversary is differentially perceived and interpreted by Negroes and whites, males and females. Social expectations of response in particular types of social interaction result in differential "definitions of the situation." A male is usually expected to defend the name and honor of his mother, the virtue of womanhood . . . and to accept no derogation about his race (even from a member of his own race), his age, or his masculinity. (pp. 188–189)

Wolfgang and Ferracuti (1967) generalized the findings from Wolfgang's homicide research as well as other studies into an overall theory that explains violence, particularly the unplanned kind that erupts in a variety of social and recreational settings. Hence, the content of the subculture of violence consists of norms, values, and behavioral expectations that define the behavior of lower-class individuals with regard to the expression of violence. That is, violence is seen by subcultural members as problem-solving behavior.

For example, in a social situation, another person makes a negative comment about my mother, which I interpret as an attempt to disrespect me. I am expected to indicate that the other person's behavior is unacceptable in a number of normatively acceptable ways. I can insult him by making derogatory remarks about his mother, I can demand an instant apology, or I can simply engage in violence immediately. Because the former two are also avenues that will probably result in a violent encounter, the occurrence of a violent event may be just a matter of time. Subcultural theories of violence are also applied to the explanation of gang violence (chapter 5) and robbery (chapter 7).

Wolfgang and Ferracuti's overall subculture of violence theory is similar to Miller's theory in that it postulates cultural beliefs that justify the use of violence. What makes this theory different is that Wolfgang and Ferracuti specified one class of crimes—violence—and attempted to locate it among lower-class males. Shoemaker and Williams (1987) found inconsistent support for the theory, however.

Social Control Theory

Many of the theories considered thus far have explained criminality by relying on special forces (whether biological, psychological, or sociological) that drive offenders to commit crime. Social control theories begin with a different assumption; they assume that criminality is part of human nature and all individuals would commit crime if left to their own devices. The problem then becomes one of explaining why most people do not commit crimes.

Put another way, what are the social and psychological forces that "keep people in line," that is, keep them from committing crimes. When these forces are weakened or break down, crime is the result. It is from this perspective that social control theories are often described as theories that explain why people *do not* commit crime.

Social Control Theory: Travis Hirschi

In order to explain criminality, social control theorists must first explain conformity, then show how people become nonconforming. The person most closely associated with control theory is Travis Hirschi (1969). He explained conformity and socialization by attachment to four types of social bonds.

- **Attachment.** Attachment is the most important bond and takes three forms: attachment to parents, teachers and school, and peers. An indication of the intensity of attachment is measured by how much time the child spends with parents, the intimacy of communication, and the amount of affection the child has for the parent. Where this social bond is weak, delinquency results.

- **Commitment.** This social bond refers to what can best be described as a stake in conformity. Commitment is the extent to which the juvenile makes a rational investment in conventional society and recognizes the risk of committing deviant behavior. In other words, what does a juvenile jeopardize in his or her future by delinquent activity?

- **Involvement.** The more juveniles are involved in conventional lines of action, the less involved they are in delinquency. What Hirschi was driving at is expressed in the old adage, "Idle hands are the devil's workshop." Juveniles who strive to be successful academically and who are involved in school activities are less likely to be delinquent.

- **Belief.** This social bond has to do with the extent to which juveniles believe in the laws, norms, and values of conventional society. Do juveniles believe norms and laws are fair? When they do not believe the rules are equitable, deviance results.

Although Hirschi's social control theory has attracted a great deal of attention, a review of the research by Curran and Renzetti (2001) found that control theory was most successful at explaining minor forms of delinquency. One of the positive features of the theory is that it can be used to explain white-collar crime.

Social Control Theory: David Matza

In *Delinquency and Drift*, David Matza (1964) took issue with the traditional theories of delinquency by claiming that they unduly emphasized differentiation and constraint. Traditional theories, Matza thought, placed too great an emphasis on showing how different delinquents are and how much they are involved in delinquency. For the most part, delinquents are engaged in routine, everyday activities. They do not spend all their time committing delinquent acts as traditional theories tend to assume. Further, the majority of delinquents "age out" of their delinquency so that by late adolescence or early adulthood, many delinquents have adopted a conventional lifestyle, a fact that is not explained by traditional theories.

Matza proposed the concept of *drift*. Rather than deterministic forces that drive juveniles to delinquency, Matza suggested that juveniles may or may not be delinquent in a given set of circumstances, but in areas of the social structure where social control is loosened, drift is more likely. Matza did not deny there are committed and compulsive delinquents, but he suggested that the vast majority of delinquents are not; they are drifters.

Consistent with the notion of drift is how delinquents view law and its violation. Matza found that delinquents do not value delinquent behavior and view violations as morally wrong, but they describe their behavior as involving extenuating circumstances. In other words, juveniles develop techniques to rationalize their actions, which neutralizes and releases youths from the guilt and constraints of a moral order. Rationalizations include the following:

- **Denial of Responsibility.** This is the familiar claim by the delinquent that it was not his or her fault; someone else is responsible and the delinquent is the victim of circumstances.

- **Denial of Injury.** This technique of neutralization is accomplished by claiming that the delinquent act did not result in any real injury. Thus, claims are made that "No one was hurt," "They have so much they will never miss it," or "It is insured."

- **Denial of the Victim.** This is the rationalization that "Anyone would have done the same thing in my position." Alternatively, there is a selective denigration of certain types of victims; it is acceptable to steal from drunks or beat up homosexuals.

- **Condemnation of the Condemner.** This neutralization technique rationalizes misbehavior because "Those who are condemning me have done much worse, so why am I being arrested?"

- **Appeal to Higher Loyalities.** Deviant behavior is justified by arguing that it is behavior consistent with more important values such as loyalty to friends or protection of gang "turf."

Hamlin (1988) raises an interesting issue about the nature of neutralization. One question raised by critics is whether neutralization occurs before the act or following the act. In other words, do techniques of neutralization play a causative role or do they simply make the offender feel better?

Support for the theory has been inconsistent. Giordano (1976) surveyed public school students and juveniles who had been in various stages of contact with the justice system. She could find no important differences between the students and official delinquents. On the other hand, Landsheer, Hart, and Kox (1994) found support for neutralization techniques among youth in the Netherlands. Techniques of neutralization are discussed further in chapter 7.

Routine Activities

There are two components of routine activity theory that make it different from preceding social control theories. First, it is a theory of victimization in that it describes the conditions of victimization. Second, it avoids any assumptions about the psychological behavior of offenders.

As might be expected from the name, routine activity assumes a routine range of behavior that is followed by everyone. People get up, have breakfast, and usually go to work during the early morning hours. In most cases, children go to school while both parents head off to work. In the evening, the house and the neighborhood are populated once more as parents and children return for the round of evening routine activities.

Three components are essential to a crime being committed. First, there is what Cohen and Felson (1979; Felson & Cohen, 1980) called a suitable target. Suitable targets can include human beings, but they also include objects that can be easily stolen and resold illegally. For example, it is unlikely that refrigerators would be stolen in a burglary, but laptop computers, VCR equipment, and CD players would be stolen for three reasons: (1) they are light in weight and easily carried; (2) they are easily concealed; and (3) a market exists for these types of stolen goods.

The second component is the absence of a capable guardian. Although police officers are not excluded as capable guardians, Cohen and Felson (1979) attach a much broader meaning to the term. A capable guardian is basically anyone who is present to prevent a crime. Suppose you are waiting in the ticket line at an airport with a friend and a suitcase. You want to go to the bathroom so you ask your friend to watch your suitcase in your absence. In that instance, your friend is acting as a capable guardian.

The third component in routine activity theory is a likely offender. This means that an offender is available to exploit the situation of a suitable target and the absence of a capable guardian.

For a crime to occur, the three components must coexist in space and time as shown in Figure 4-1.

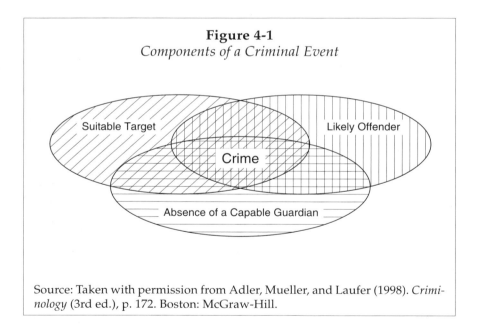

Figure 4-1
Components of a Criminal Event

Source: Taken with permission from Adler, Mueller, and Laufer (1998). *Criminology* (3rd ed.), p. 172. Boston: McGraw-Hill.

As Figure 4-1 indicates, where the three circles overlap indicating simultaneity, a crime occurs. For example, after World War II, socioeconomic conditions improved; rather than crime rates declining as would be expected from a better economy, they increased. But there was also a change in routine activities: an increase in the amount of female participation in the workplace and more out-of-town travel. Cohen and Felson (1979) interpreted this as an absence of capable guardians in the home, which would cause an increase in the number of residential burglaries.

Likewise, technological changes provided more suitable targets. Television sets became much smaller and lighter, which made them more suitable targets. As noted earlier, technology has moved increasingly in the direction of making valuable objects smaller, lighter, and ever more suitable targets. The addition of likely offenders in conjunction with suitable targets and absence of capable guardians meant an increase in crime, which is what routine activity theory would predict.

Routine activities theory is not a causal theory: *If* certain conditions occur simultaneously (suitable targets, likely offenders, and absence of capable guardians), a crime may occur. *Why* it occurs in this particular time and place, however, is not explained further. What is needed, and supplied recently by rational choice theory, is an understanding of offenders (Clarke & Felson, 1993). Hence, rational choice theory posits a calculating offender who determines that the rewards for committing this offense outweigh the risks.

Finally, the policy orientation of routine activity theory is implicit. Cohen and Felson (1979) describe the conditions under which crime occurs without offering any explicit policy suggestions. Routine activities theory is used to explain robbery, stranger violence, and the role of firearms.

Symbolic Interaction Theories

Symbolic interaction is a variety of sociological theory that emphasizes the capacity of humans to use and be motivated by symbols and language. In this sense, behavior is determined by meanings and symbols through interaction with others in social situations (Ritzer, 2000), a theoretical assumption similar to one used by Sutherland.

Symbolic interactionists draw upon the writings of Erving Goffman (1959). A fundamental concept in Goffman's theory is the concept of the self. Goffman was impressed by the fact that the self was divided into two components: (1) the *spontaneous self* (i.e., the part that on any morning might decide we do not want to go to class or work and, instead, want to go to a Carribean island and do nothing until we get tired of it), and (2) the *socialized self* (i.e., the part that ultimately convinces us to go to work and further portray ourselves as hardworking, dedicated students or employees). We might, as part of our spontaneous self, convince ourselves that we really do not need to "break our backs" making money and impressing the boss—we can live on the beach instead. If we follow our socialized selves, we will put extra effort into a project that, if done well, will dispose the boss favorably toward us.

Two features of Goffman's theory need to be kept in mind. First, both selves are extremely important. Although it is obvious that the spontaneous self is, as we say, "really us," the socialized self is equally important because it is our public identity, the view of ourselves that we offer others. We work very hard at making sure that the image of ourselves, our "face" according to Goffman, is credible and acceptable to others.

Second, there is a continuous tension between the two selves. As we indicated in previous paragraphs, many times we struggle between what we would like to do and what, in the name of our public image, we find that we have to do.

The tension between the two components of selves can be illustrated in numerous ways in everyday life. Observe the initial encounter between a single college-age male and a single college-age female attracted to one another. Let us assume this initial interaction occurs in a recreational setting, such as a bar, where each has the opportunity to interact freely with the other.

Much of their interaction time is spent convincing each other of their respective attractiveness. The male will put forth the image he believes will make him attractive to her, and she does the same to him. If both participants are sufficiently skillful to put forth a "face" that the other finds pleasing, the relationship will continue. If not, unless one or the other senses what is wrong with his or her face presentation and corrects it, the initial attraction will disappear.

As indicated previously, we have a substantial emotional investment in our socialized selves, our public face. When that image is challenged or threatened, there is anger and conflict on the part of the person challenged. This tension between the spontaneous and the socialized self is the focus of a theory of violence by David Luckenbill (1977).

Luckenbill's theory is used in the chapters on homicides (chapter 5), robbery (chapter 7), and the chapter on firearms (chapter 11), but the foundations of these chapters draw upon Goffman's (1959) general theory of how the self is presented in everyday life. An insult, in both Goffman and Luckenbill's theories, is a threat or a challenge to one's public face. Not to respond is to acknowledge that it is true. One possible response is to present a challenge to the face of the person making the insult. Insults and counter-insults continue and escalate until violence occurs or one of the participants leaves the setting.

Nonlethal violence occurs between the participants that remain, but it can escalate, in a small number of instances, to homicide. Where physical violence is employed, one participant may inflict an injury that ultimately proves fatal, even though this was not his or her intent. In other cases, a firearm is used and one of the participants dies of a gunshot wound.

Most of these "face" violations occur among working-class individuals over issues that would not drive a middle-class person to violence. Triggering issues might include "disrespecting" a participant's gang or his mother.

Middle-class males are driven to violence because of different kinds of challenges to their "face." For example, in an instance related to the first author, Person A had purchased $450,000 worth of stock at $5 per share in a large corporation. Unfortunately, a few weeks after his purchase the company declared bankruptcy and the stock dropped to 35 cents a share and finally was no longer traded.

Person A happened to be drinking subsequently with four individuals whom he knew socially. The topic of conversation turned to the general decline in the stock market that began in the early to middle months of 2000. He related his losses to the other four and they ridiculed his initial judgement in purchasing the stock in a corporation they regarded as of dubious value in the first place. Person A, of course, could not tolerate an attack on his financial judgement, a very important component of his public face. Insults led to counter-insults and finally to violence with flying fists and empty beer bottles as weapons. The outcome was several injuries, including a couple of broken noses.

Conclusions: Which Theory Is True?

In this chapter, we have reviewed a large number of theories that are used in later chapters to explain violence. Certainly, understanding violence would be much simpler if there was one theory that would explain the enormous variety of violence. As a step in this direction, a common question is, "Which theory is 'true'?"

The short answer is all, none, or some, depending on what you mean by the word *true*. To begin with, a theory is a creative endeavor as surely as is a novel, painting, or sculpture. It is the vision of a theorist who believes that he or she has an explanation of why and how certain phenomena work. At that level, to ask whether the theory is true is like asking whether Leonardo Da Vinci believed that the painting of the Mona Lisa was true. It was his vision of what the woman looked like just as it is the vision of Sutherland that crime is learned in intimate groups. Truth or falsity at this level is meaningless.

But if that is the case, why cannot just anyone develop a theory of criminality? If all views are equally legitimate, why can I not credibly publish a theory that crime is caused by aliens—little green men with evil powers? There are two answers.

First, although truth or falsity of a theory *per se* may be irrelevant, the consequences of theory are testable by observation. What differentiates the world of art and Da Vinci from science and Sutherland is that researchers are able to falsify hypotheses drawn from the latter—differential association theory. No such process is relevant with the vision that is the art of Da Vinci.

Consequently, this process of testing and verification is continuous. Not only does it occur in as many different ways as researchers can conceive, but while it is occurring, other people are also generating new theories, which also require testing. There is, in other words, a continuous ferment among criminologists and violence researchers trying to determine whether a given theoretical hypothesis is supported by research, whether other theoretical hypotheses are supported better, or whether it might be a better idea to consider how two or more theories can be integrated. In this highly competitive milieu, it seems unlikely that any theory suggesting that crime is caused by little green men would long survive.

The second answer is prompted by a question: Why is it that specific theories become popular, whether they be learning, subcultural, social control, or symbolic interactionist theories? It is certainly true that theories require extensive testing, but what is there about a theory that attracts the attention of criminologists in the first place? Why is it that a theory suggesting that crime is caused by little green men would be ignored while one suggesting that victimization is the result of suitable targets, absence of capable guardians, and likely offenders stimulates a great deal of interest?

The answer is that the latter is *heuristic* while the former, to put it mildly, is not. If a theory is heuristic, it means it stimulates interest, it causes the reader to ask questions that he or she may never have asked about the phenomenon. For example, in the initial statement of routine activities, Cohen and Felson (1979) asked why crime rates should be going up after World War II even though the economy was strong and employment was high. It was precisely because of greater involvement in work-related activities (more women in the workplace) that the home was left unguarded and became a target for burglars. In addition, of course, there was miniaturization of expensive consumer goods, which were described as suitable targets.

Even though it was novel to ask why crime rates should be going up during a period of prosperity, it was intellectually stimulating to suggest that everyday activities play a role in whether persons are victimized. In other words, it is heuristic to incorporate the observation that one person's routine activities are another person's criminal opportunities.

Whether a theory is heuristic is, in many ways, an individual preference. There are very few theories in the history of science that have simply swept the population and achieved wide acceptance. In the social sciences, perhaps Marxism in the nineteenth and early twentieth century is an example. Certainly, the writings of Sigmund Freud during the 1920s achieved that level of popularity in the United States.

Except for those few examples, what seems to be true is that some individuals are attracted to some theories while ignoring or actively disliking others for mostly personal reasons. No doubt the readers of this volume will be particularly interested in certain types of violence over others. Equally certain is the fact that users will find some explanations of violence compelling and others bordering on the irrelevant!

References

Adler, F., Mueller, G. O. W., & Laufer, W. S. (1998). *Criminology* (3rd ed.). Boston: McGraw-Hill.

Agnew, R. (1992). Foundation for a general strain theory of crime and delinquency. *Criminology, 30,* 47–87.

Akers, R. L. (1997). *Criminological theories: Introduction and evaluation* (2nd ed.). Los Angeles: Roxbury.

Bandura, A. (1973). *Aggression: A social learning analysis.* Englewood Cliffs, NJ: Prentice-Hall.

Beccaria, C. (1963). *On crimes and punishments.* Indianapolis, IN: Bobbs-Merrill.

Blumstein, A., Cohen, J., Das, S., & Moitra, S. (1988). Specialization and seriousness during adult criminal careers. *Journal of Quantitative Criminology, 4,* 303–346.

Brunson, R. K., & Miller, J. (2000). Girls and gangs. In C. M. Renzetti & L. I. Goodstein (Eds.), *Gender, crime and criminal justice* (pp. 44–59). Los Angeles: Roxbury Publishing.

Burgess, E. W. (1925). The growth of the city: An introduction to a research project. In R. E. Park, E. W. Burgess, & R. D. McKenzie (Eds.), *The city* (pp. 47–62). Chicago: University of Chicago Press.

Burgess, R. L., & Akers, R. L. (1968). A differential association-reinforcement theory of criminal behavior. *Social Problems, 14,* 128–147.

Bursik, R. J. J. (1988). Social disorganization and theories of crime and delinquency: Problems and prospects. *Criminology, 26,* 519–552.

Clarke, R. V., & Felson, M. (Eds.). (1993). *Routine activity and rational choice.* (Vol. 5). New Brunswick, NJ: Transaction Publishers.

Clinard, M. B. (1964). The theoretical implications of anomie and deviant behavior. In M. B. Clinard (Ed.), *Anomie and deviant behavior* (pp. 1–56). New York: Free Press.

Cloward, R. A., & Ohlin, L. A. (1960). *Delinquency and opportunity: A theory of delinquent gangs.* New York: Free Press.

Cohen, A. K. (1955). *Delinquent boys: The culture of the gang.* Glencoe, IL: Free Press of Glencoe.

Cohen, L. E., & Felson, M. (1979). Social change and crime rate trends: A routine activity approach. *American Sociological Review, 44,* 588–608.

Curran, D. J., & Renzetti, C. (2001). *Theories of crime.* Boston: Allyn and Bacon.

Faris, R. E. L. (1967). *Chicago sociology: 1920–1932.* San Francisco: Chandler.

Felson, M., & Cohen, L. E. (1980). Human ecology and crime: A routine activity approach. *Human Ecology, 8,* 389–406.

Finestone, H. (1976). The delinquent and society: The Shaw and McKay tradition. In J. F. Short (Ed.), *Delinquency, crime, and society* (pp. 23–49). Chicago: University of Chicago Press.

Freud, S. (1920). *A general introduction to psychoanalysis.* New York: Liveright.

Friedrichs, D. O. (1996). *Trusted criminals: White collar crime in contemporary society.* Belmont: Wadsworth.

Giordano, P. (1976). The sense of injustice? An analysis of juveniles' reactions to the justice system. *Criminology, 14,* 93–112.

Goffman, E. (1959). *The presentation of self in everyday life.* Garden City, NY: Doubleday.

Hamlin, J. E. (1988). The misplaced role of rational choice in neutralization theory. *Criminology, 26,* 425–438.

Harris, P. W., Welsh, W. N., & Butler, F. (2000). A century of juvenile justice. In G. LaFree (Ed.), *Criminal justice 2000* (Vol. 1, pp. 359–426). Washington: National Institute of Justice.

Hirschi, T. (1969). *Causes of delinquency.* Berkeley: University of California Press.

Landsheer, J. A., Hart, H. T., & Kox, W. (1994). Delinquent values and victim damage: Exploring the limits of neutralization theory. *British Journal of Crimnology, 34,* 44–53.

Lilly, J. R., Cullen, F. T., & Ball, R. A. (1994). *Criminological theory: Context and consequences* (2nd ed.). Thousand Oaks, CA: Sage.

Lindesmith, A. R., & Gagnon, J. (1964). Anomie and drug addiction. In M. B. Clinard (Ed.), *Anomie and deviant behavior* (pp. 158–188). New York: Free Press.

Luckenbill, D. F. (1977). Criminal homicide as a situated transaction. *Social Problems, 25,* 176–186.

Matza, D. (1964). *Delinquency and drift.* New York: John Wiley.

Merton, R. K. (1957a). Bureaucratic structure and personality. In R. K. Merton (Ed.), *Social theory and social structure* (pp. 195–206). New York: Free Press.

———. (1957b). Social structure and anomie. In R. K. Merton (Ed.), *Social theory and social structure* (pp. 121–160). New York: Free Press.

Miller, W. B. (1958). Lower class culture as a generating milieu of gang delinquency. *Journal of Social Issues, 14,* 5–19.

Ritzer, G. (2000). *Modern sociological theory* (5th ed.). Boston: McGraw-Hill.

Robinson, W. S. (1950). Ecological correlation and the behavior of individuals. *American Sociological Review, 15,* 351–357.

Sanders, W. B. (1994). *Gangbangs and drive-bys: Grounded culture and juvenile gang violence.* New York: Aldine de Gruyter.

Shaw, C. R., & McKay, H. D. (1942). *Juvenile delinquency and urban areas.* Chicago: University of Chicago Press.

Shoemaker, D. J. (1996). *Theories of delinquency.* New York: Oxford University Press.

Shoemaker, D. J., & Williams, J. S. (1987). The subculture of violence and ethnicity. *Journal of Criminal Justice, 15,* 461–472.

Sutherland, E. H. (1947). *Criminology.* Philadelphia: Lippincott.

Tarde, G. (1907). *Social laws: An outline of sociology.* New York: Macmillan.

Vold, G. B., & Bernard, T. J. (1986). *Theoretical criminology.* New York: Oxford University Press.

Vold, G. B., Bernard, T. J., & Snipes, J. B. (1998). *Theoretical criminology* (4th ed.). New York: Oxford University Press.

Wolfgang, M. E. (1958). *Patterns in criminal homicide.* Philadelphia: University of Pennsylvania Press.

Wolfgang, M. E., & Ferracuti, F. (1967). *The subculture of violence: Towards an integrated theory in criminology.* London: Tavistock Publications. ✦

Chapter 5

Homicides and Assaults

The first major section of this chapter provides an overview of homicides and assaults in the United States. Because aggravated assaults are closely related to, and sometimes precede, homicides, we discuss the two offenses together.

As was pointed out in chapter 1, the two offenses share behavioral similarities. However, we have drawn upon two different data sources to describe patterns and trends, explanations, and interventions. For homicides, the most reliable sources of information are police reports and their representation in the *Uniform Crime Reports* (UCR) of the FBI. Although the UCR does present information about aggravated assaults, we believe that data from the National Crime Victimization Survey (NCVS) provide a more detailed picture of such offenses. Hence, we have used the NCVS in describing aggravated assaults.

The remaining sections of this chapter describe specialized types of violence that occur in public space. For example, confrontational stranger violence, serial homicides, and gang violence are fear-provoking because they appear to represent unprovoked attacks on urban dwellers as they go about their routine activities. In addition, probably more than other kinds of violence, it is difficult to determine the amounts of each. When this fact is combined with the fear-provoking quality of the offenses, serial homicides, stranger violence, and gang violence become subjects of media presentations that further combine myths and facts.

Homicides and Assaults in the United States

The Uniform Crime Reporting Program of the FBI divides criminal homicide into murder, nonnegligent manslaughter, and manslaughter by negligence. *Murder* and *nonnegligent manslaughter* are "the willful (nonnegligent) killing of one human being by another." Only murder and nonnegligent manslaughters are discussed here (FBI, 1999, p. 409).

According to nationwide FBI statistics for 1999, there were 15,533 murders and nonnegligent manslaughters in the United States, a rate of 5.7 per 100,000 inhabitants.

Although this is seen as a large number of preventable deaths, the rate is actually 8 percent lower than the rate for 1998 and is part of a continuing decline in violence in the United States (FBI, 1999). We will return to this issue in a later section.

The National Crime Victimization Survey defines *aggravated assault* as "an attack or attempted attack with a weapon, regardless of whether or not an injury occurred and attack without a weapon as when serious injury resulted." *Simple assault* is an

> attack without a weapon resulting either in no injury, minor injury (for example, bruises, black eyes, cuts, scratches, or swelling) or in undetermined injury requiring less than two days of hospitalization. Also includes attempted assault without a weapon. (Bureau of Justice Statistics, 1999, p. 1)

For 1998, the NCVS reported 1,674,000 aggravated assaults, a rate of 7.5 per 1,000. Among aggravated assaults, the rate of 7.5 represents a 12.8 percent decline from 1999 (Rennison, 1999). Aggravated assaults are much more common than murders. For example, in Dallas, Texas, Harries (1989) found that aggravated assaults reported to the police (32,096) were 27 times more frequent than homicides (1,228).

Patterns

Table 5-1 gives the age, gender, and race of murder victims and offenders.

Perhaps the most persistent finding reflected in Table 5-1 is the predominance of males as both murder victims and offenders. For males, 75.5 percent were murder victims and 64.8 percent were offenders. Females were more frequently victims (24.4 percent) than offenders (7.4 percent), a fact reflected in their higher level of victimization in intimate partner murders.

Table 5-1
*Percent of Murder Victims and Offenders by
Age, Gender, and Race (1999)*

Characteristic		Victims	Offenders
	Total	12,658	14,112
Age	Under 18	11.5%	6.7%
	18 and Over	86.9%	59.0%
	Unknown	1.7%	34.3%
Gender	Males	75.5%	64.8%
	Females	24.4%	7.4%
	Unknown	0.1%	27.8%
Race	White	49.8%	33.2%
	Black	46.3%	35.7%
	Other	2.9%	2.2%
	Unknown	1.0%	28.9%

Source: Federal Bureau of Investigation (1999). *Uniform crime reports for the United States, 1997* (<http://www.fbi.gov/ucr/Cius_99/ w99tbl2-5.xls>). [April 23, 2001].

Generally, most murder victims and offenders are found in the over-18 age group; 86.9 percent of the victims and 59.0 percent of the offenders are over 18. Because of media coverage and the sensational nature of murders involving very young victims or offenders, or both, it is easy to believe the number of such crimes is large. In fact, there are relatively few murders involving young people.

Likewise, the percentages for crimes involving race given in Table 5-1 do not take into account differences in the size of the black and the white population. Table 5-1 would lead the reader to believe slightly larger proportions of murder victims (46.3) and of-fenders (35.7) are black. However, using rates rather than percent-ages leads to extraordinarily high rates of homicide victimization for blacks in comparison to whites, because blacks are only 13 per-cent of the population. For example, in 1994, in the highest victim-ization age range (15 to 24), the homicide victimization rate for blacks is 87.4 per 100,000, which is more than eight times higher than the white rate (10.6) for the same age range (Riedel, 1999a, p. 128).

The UCR program requests information from police depart-ments on whether murder victims and offenders are of Latino ori-gin, but the amount of missing information is so large as to render the available data unreliable. Therefore, age, gender, and race com-parisons of aggravated assault and murder must be made with caution. To make matters even more complex, the NCVS uses rates rather than percentages, and a rate base of 1,000 rather than 100,000. Also it gives a different classification of ages, and reports only on victimization of persons age 12 or older.

Table 5-2 provides detail on the amount of aggravated assault victimizations. Table 5-2 affirms the involvement of males in vio-lent crime found in Table 5-1. Males predominate as murder vic-tims and offenders; they also have much higher rates (10.5 versus 4.7) as victims of aggravated assaults. Similarly, young people are more involved in serious assaults just as they are more involved in murders. Table 5-2 indicates that the age ranges of 16 to 19 and 20 to 24 have the highest rates of serious assault victimization. For the 16-to-19 age group, the victimization rate per 1,000 is 19.0, and for the 20-to-24 age group, it is 16.0.

Table 5-1 and Table 5-2 also agree on the large amount of minor-ity involvement in violent crime. Black murder victim and of-fender rates are very high; black aggravated assault victimization rates are also much higher than white rates. Moreover, Table 5-2 in-dicates that serious assault rates for Latinos are higher than for whites. For homicide Latinos occupy a generally intermediate po-sition between blacks and whites, a finding that is paralleled in a study of Latino homicide in California (Riedel, 2000). Hence, we can succinctly summarize the research to date on the demographic characteristics of victims and offenders: Murders and aggravated assaults predominantly involve young black males.

Table 5-2
Rates of Aggravated Assault Victimization by
Gender, Age, Race, and Ethnicity (1998)

Victim Characteristic		Aggravated Assault Rates per 1,000
Gender	Male	10.5
	Female	4.7
Age	12–15	12.2
	16–19	19.0
	20–24	16.0
	25–34	8.4
	35–49	6.8
	50–64	3.3
	65 plus	0.5
Race	White	7.0
	Black	11.9
	Other	6.6
Hispanic Origin	Hispanic	6.1
	Non-Hispanic	7.6

Source: Bureau of Justice Statistics (1999). *Criminal Victimization, 1998* (NCJ-176353), p. 4. Washington, DC: U.S. Department of Justice.

Table 5-3 is a description of other characteristics of murder victims. With respect to victim-offender relationships, intimate partner murders accounted for 10.1 percent of 12,658 murders in 1999. "Other family" relationships are somewhat less (8.2 percent), other murders in which the offender is known to the victim make up the largest proportion (29.4 percent), and strangers are 11.9 percent of murders on which there is information about victim-offender relationships.

It is worth noting that no relationship information is given for 40.4 percent of murders, and no circumstance information for

29.9 percent of murders. In both instances, the information is missing because no offender has been arrested. Slightly more information is available in the case of circumstances because the

Table 5-3
Victim/Offender Relationships, Weapons, and Circumstances of Murder Victims (1999)

Characteristic		Percent
	Total	12,658
Victim/Offender Relationship	Intimate Partner	10.1
	Other Family	8.2
	Other, Known	29.4
	Stranger	11.9
	Unknown	40.4
Weapon	Handguns	51.3
	Other Firearms	13.9
	Knives, Blunt Objects	19.0
	Other Weapons	15.8
Circumstances	Robbery	8.0
	Rape	0.3
	Property & Sex Crimes	1.7
	Drugs	4.4
	Brawls & Arguments	32.1
	Gang Related	5.5
	Other	18.1
	Unknown	29.9

Source: Federal Bureau of Investigation (1999). *Uniform crime reports for the United States, 1999*, pp. 19, 21 (<http://www.fbi.gov/ucr/Cius_99/99crime/99c2_03.pdf>). [June 23, 1999].

type of crime, such as robbery, can be inferred from events surrounding the victim.

It is probably no surprise to most readers that over half (51 percent) of the murders in 1999 were committed with handguns. If we include the 14 percent of murders attributed to other types of firearms, 65 percent of murders involve the use of firearms of one type or other. The remaining 35 percent involve other types of weapons, as Table 5-3 indicates.

The crimes listed as *circumstances* are sometimes referred to as *motives*. They are events, such as robbery or rape, that occur in the course of a murder. As Table 5-3 indicates, the most frequent circumstances or motives are brawls and arguments. These are typically conflicts with persons known to the victim and they escalate to combat and lethal outcomes. The following case, drawn from the first author's files, illustrates how a conflict escalates to murder:

> Dallas Akins, a 69-year-old black man, was in his house when he heard a commotion. He went downstairs to find 14-year-old Roger Baker in the living room. Akins' grandson had admitted Baker to the house, where Baker began arguing with Akins' daughter. Akins told Baker to leave, at which time Baker produced a handgun. The two men struggled; the gun discharged, striking Akins in the back and entering a lung. Akins died at the hospital a few hours later.

The total rate for aggravated assaults in 1998 was 7.5 per 1,000 persons age 12 or older. The threat of a weapon constituted a frequent accompaniment to assaults, with a rate of 5.1 per 1,000. Aggravated assaults with injury were at the rate of 2.5 per 1,000.

NCVS respondents who acknowledge being victims of aggravated assaults are attacked about as often by people they know (50 percent) as by strangers (48 percent). Among nonstrangers, aggravated assault victimization occurs most frequently with friends and acquaintances (33 percent), followed by intimate partners (10 percent), and, lastly, by other relatives (7 percent) (Rennison, 1999).

The NCVS collects information on household income and marital status for households reporting violent victimizations. Rates for aggravated assaults are highest for households with an income of less than $7,500 (19.6); the lowest rates are for households with incomes of $75,000 or more (6.2). Part of the difference in rates may be affected by the number of income producers in the household. However, victims who report never having been married or who are divorced or separated report aggravated assault victimizations that are similar to persons with the lowest incomes. That is, the aggravated assault rate for those never married in 1998 was 12.9, and the rate for those divorced or separated was 12.8 per 1,000.

One of the more surprising recent events in the study of violence has been the decline of violence in the United States, especially murders, as Figure 5-1 indicates.

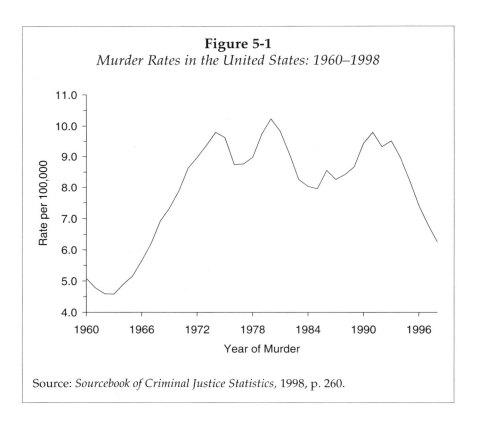

Figure 5-1
Murder Rates in the United States: 1960–1998

Source: *Sourcebook of Criminal Justice Statistics,* 1998, p. 260.

Beginning in 1991, murder rates took a downturn that continued through 1999. In 1991, the murder rate was 9.8 per 100,000 population; by 1999, the murder rate was 5.7 per 100,000, a 41.8 percent decrease.

Aggravated assaults have likewise declined, according to the NCVS. In 1993, the aggravated assault rate was 12.0 per 1,000; by 1998, the rate was 7.5, a 37.5 percent decrease (Rennison, 1999).

Explanations

Symbolic interaction. Although a large number of theories are described in chapter 4 that would be applicable to explaining homicides and aggravated assaults, one characteristic makes interactional theories particularly appropriate: Few murders or assaults are planned. Murders planned to the last intricate detail and unraveled by a master sleuth happen in fiction, but almost never in reality. Murders and assaults typically evolve in social situations and begin with a conflict.

One of the more amazing characteristics of assaults and homicides is the wide range of motives that compel people to injure or kill others. There are some conflicts that we understand, and even sympathize with, such as the battered wife who finally kills her tormentor after years of abuse. There are others that defy understanding, such as the instance of one person killing another because he allegedly stole the offender's beer and refused to buy him another (Athens, 1980).

Trying to understand homicide and aggravated assault by determining the "reality" or "importance" of causes is a futile endeavor. Instead, we take the view that violence is goal-oriented or instrumental behavior that results from aggressive attempts to achieve what people value. "Aggressive actions seek to compel and deter others, to achieve a favorable social identity, and to obtain justice, as defined by the actor" (Felson, 1993, p. 104). In other words, the validity of motives for the killing has to be examined from the perspective of what the offender hoped to achieve. On the one hand, it may be that the battered wife has decided that she will not be beaten again; on the other hand, the offender perceives the stolen beer as an insult to his ego that he cannot or will not tolerate. The latter will be become clearer when we discuss confrontational stranger violence.

As the conflict becomes an effort to frustrate or "put the other down," the interaction escalates with insults and counterinsults. At some point, either one of the participants withdraws or violence occurs. The violence may take the form of pushing, shoving, or hitting, and it may result in one or the other's death from injuries.

It is also important to recognize that not all ego insults result in escalation and violence. It takes two to play the escalation game, which raises the question of what conflict may possibly occur when one party simply gets up at the first sign of trouble and leaves the setting.

Subcultural theories. As chapter 4 explains, Wolfgang and Ferracuti (1967) would agree that violence happens as the result of what participants perceive as insults to their self-image. However, they carried the analysis one step further in positing a subculture of violence: norms, values, and behavioral expectations that violence is problem-solving behavior. In addition, values and beliefs that sanction violence as problem-solving behavior are differentially distributed. Lower-class youth are more likely to express these beliefs than middle-class youth. Moreover, when other males with the same beliefs are present, a violent response is reinforced, as the following case illustrates.

> The offender and his friend were sitting in a booth at a tavern drinking beer. The offender's friend told him that the offender's girlfriend was 'playing' with another man (victim) at the other end of the bar. The offender looked at them and asked his friend if he thought something was going on. The friend responded, 'I would not let that guy fool around with [her] if she was mine.' The offender agreed, and suggested to his friend that his girlfriend and the victim be shot for their actions. His friend said that only the victim should be shot, not the girlfriend. (Luckenbill, 1977, p. 171)

But since there are more flirtations than assaults and homicides, we can only conclude than many encounters of the type described above end without violence. It is consistent with the subculture of violence theory that if one of the parties does not regard the behavior of the other as a threat to his or her self-image, there will be no violence. The insulted party may respond by simply leaving the setting.

Interventions

Because crime rates follow a fluctuating pattern, it is not always clear whether a decline (or increase) signals a trend or is merely an annual fluctuation. There are people, including politicians, who attribute any positive fluctuation, however minor, to the effect of their pet programs; criminologists recognize that understanding trends, much less forecasting them, is a challenging enterprise.

According to research findings, homicides have been declining because of social changes and criminal justice interventions. With respect to social changes, Blumstein and Rosenfeld (1998) show support for the following causes of the decline in nationwide homicide.

- The growth of homicide during the 1980s was largely due to the 15-to-24 age group. The decline, beginning about 1992, was partly accounted for by a decline in arrests in the 15-to-24 age group.

- Beginning about 1993, there was a decline in handgun homicide among both white and Latino youth, but greatest among black youth.

- Blumstein and Rosenfeld hypothesize that drug markets have matured and stabilized and other dispute resolution mechanisms have emerged, such as negotiation over sharing of markets.

- Economic expansion has increased the number of legitimate job opportunities and increased the amount of interaction between legal and illegal opportunities to earn money.

With respect to interventions, an increased use of incarceration may have contributed to a decline in violence. Spelman (2000) found that since the 1970s, the prison population has expanded fourfold. Although it might be suspected that this is due to increased incarceration, especially for repeat offenders, it must be remembered that violence increased substantially during the 1980s while incarceration was also increasing.

Spelman draws upon a wide variety of studies and derives statistical estimates of the impact of incarceration. He suggests that only about 25 percent of the drop in crime is attributable to incarceration. The question that Spelman (2000) and Rosenfeld (2000) propose in their essays is whether the massive social and financial cost of prisons is worth the benefits derived. The nation's corrections budget is approaching $40 billion annually, money that could conceivably be spent on other crime reduction endeavors, such as welfare, education, and health.

It is also possible that programs to control the use of guns have played a role in reducing homicides. Wintemute (2000) presents evidence on the role of guns from studies of changing police practices of stopping and frisking gang members, increasing criminal justice sanctions, tracing guns used in crime, limiting the number of dealers, and restrictions on buyers. With respect to the latter, passage of the Brady bill into law has prevented over 400,000 handgun purchases. Sheley and Wright (1995) suggest that handguns are carried by young males for self-protection in high-crime areas and dispute the effectiveness of gun legislation (see chapter 11).

As will be seen in chapter 6, other successful interventions involve legislation and social policies that have led to a decline in intimate partner homicides. In 1976, for example, there were over 2,000 intimate partner murders, but by 1996, the number had declined to 987. Unfortunately, legislation, programs, and policies have had the effect of reducing the number of male intimate partners killed by females, but not the reverse (see chapter 6).

Eck and McGuire (2000) assessed the effect of different types of policing on violence and found weak effects. They examined increasing the number of police, community policing, firearms enforcement, and problem-oriented policing programs and found them to have little or no effect on violence rates. Directed patrols in "hot spots," that is, increasing police patrols in small areas with very high rates of violence, had reasonably strong support and may have contributed to a reduction in homicide rates.

Violence in Public Places

When people think of violence, they are more likely to think of being victimized in public places than in their homes, and public places are populated by strangers. According to the 1990 census, about 75 percent of the U.S. population lives in urban areas, which means that we interact on a daily basis with a large number of people about whom we know almost nothing—that is, strangers (World Almanac, 1998). The dilemma faced by the typical urban dweller is summarized by what Silberman (1978) calls "a startling paradox":

> Life in metropolitan areas . . . involves a startling paradox: we fear strangers more than anything else, and yet we live our lives among strangers. Every time we take a walk, ride a subway or bus, shop in a supermarket or department store, enter an office building lobby or elevator, work in a factory or large office, or attend a ball game or the movies, we are surrounded by strangers. The potential for fear is as immense as it is unavoidable. (p. 11)

Thus, for some kinds of violence, "location" is more than another variable to describe patterns. Citizens must feel free to move about in public space in comparative safety if a society is to continue to exist. A very important task of a government is to maintain public order; where that fails, or appears to be failing (as in terrorism), chaos may follow. This is one reason governments place a premium on responding quickly to collective violence (see chapter 9).

The three types of violence discussed here—stranger violence, serial homicides, and gang violence—pose real and perceived dangers to public order. For example, serial homicides represent unpredictable attacks on citizens as they go about their routine activities. Because, as we will see, serial killers are not readily distinguishable from the multitude of strangers we encounter every day, their activity undermines the tenuous trust we have as we interact with strangers. Fisher (1997) explores how members of an entire community come to regard one another with doubt, mistrust, and suspicion until the serial homicide offender is arrested.

In addition to real and perceived dangers of the three types of violence, they share one other problem: We have no reliable and valid indicator of how many instances there are of stranger violence, serial homicides, and gang violence. The policy implications are obvious. Without an accurate indicator of the size of the problem, policies, practices, and resources may not be effective. Thus, we will preface each section with a discussion of the problems of obtaining a reliable and valid count.

Stranger Violence

Counting Stranger Violence

With respect to counting the number of homicides in the United States, probably the most accurate count is for intimate partner and family murders. It is less accurate for relationships outside the family and relatively inaccurate for stranger murders (Riedel, 1993; 1999b).

Why is it difficult to obtain an accurate count of the number of stranger murders in this country? In Table 5-3, we provided the percentages of intimate partner, other family, other known, and stranger victim/offender relationships for 1999. Table 5-3 also indicated that 11.9 percent of murder victims involved strangers, but that 40.4 percent of the relationships were unknown mostly because no offenders were arrested. If the victim is dead and the offender is not available, there is little the police can do to identify the prior relationship between victims and offenders.

Some writers have assumed that the missing victim/offender relationships were stranger homicides and have added that percentage to those identified as stranger homicides by police. Stranger homicides, under such assumptions, would be in excess of 50 percent (Federal Bureau of Investigation, 1993; Walinsky, 1995). It is certain that this estimate is incorrect (Riedel, 1998a). As a rule in the study of crime, when validity and reliability on crime data are weak, a variety of special interest groups use concocted numbers to promote their agendas (Riedel, 1998a). We will return to this issue when we discuss serial murders.

Data on victim/offender relationships for both the UCR and NCVS have to be interpreted with caution. *In the case of the NCVS*, it is likely that aggravated assaults among people who know one another are underreported. The reason for this was discussed in chapter 2: Conflicts between friends and family tend to be forgotten, forgiven, or overlooked and are not remembered or reported to NCVS interviewers. Thus, although the estimated *frequencies* of stranger assaults may be accurate, the *percentages* are meaningless because of the underreporting of assaults among victims and offenders known to each other.

In dealing with murder victim/offender relationships, stranger homicides may be the most difficult to clear by arrest, although this is not known with certainty. If that is the case, then stranger homicides will be underreported. Hence, in percentage calculations, nonstranger homicides will assume undue prominence by comparison (Riedel, 1993).

Patterns

Confrontational violence involving strangers is characterized by conflict that proceeds from verbal disagreements, to the display of weapons, to death, with sometimes great rapidity. This kind of violence involves assault rather than robbery; the latter is discussed in chapter 7. The following case from the first author's files is an example.

> Dan Smith, a female friend, and her 3-year-old son were in a truck leaving an apartment complex when another car attempting to enter the parking lot could not pass. The vehicles apparently stopped facing each other, with the driver of the other car jumping out and saying to Smith, 'You motherfucker, you need to learn how to drive.' Smith reached for a pool cue behind him in the gun rack in the window, while the man approached the truck on Smith's side. Smith said, 'You're the one who needs to learn how to drive.' The other driver then pulled a pistol out of his front pocket and fired three times at Smith, hitting him in the neck, chest, and abdomen. The murderer was apprehended within moments of the incident.

One of the few studies done on stranger homicides originating in assaults compared them to stranger homicides during which a felony, such as robbery or rape, occurred; the former are called felony homicides and the latter are nonfelony homicides or confontational stranger homcides (Zahn & Sagi, 1987). The authors found that 16 percent of homicides in nine American cities in 1978 involved strangers and felonies; 12 percent were stranger nonfelony homicides.

Approximately 86 percent of homicides studied in the nine cities were intraracial or intraethnic, that is, victims and offenders were of the same race or ethnic group. Forty percent of stranger felony and 21 percent of stranger nonfelony homicides were interracial with blacks killing whites; white strangers, on the other hand, seldom crossed racial lines in a nonfelony killing.

Comparing the mean ages of victims and offenders, we note a much larger spread between ages of victims and offenders in stranger felony than in stranger nonfelony homicides. For stranger felony homicides, the mean age of victims is 40 while that of offenders is 26. By contrast, stranger nonfelony homicide victims have a mean age of 30 while the offenders are only 1 year younger at a mean age of 29 (Zahn & Sagi, 1987).

These differences reflect the differences in circumstances. For example, a prominent type of felony homicide is robbery-murder. Robberies and robbery-murders occur in commercial locations where, until comparatively recently, white persons were more likely to be employed than blacks. Further, it is also likely that given the responsibilities of full-time employment, the clerk, manager, or store owner who becomes the victim is likely to be older than the murderer.

Nonfelony stranger homicides, on the other hand, are more likely to occur in bars or other recreational settings in which the participants are similar in age. Hence, in these two settings, a violent conflict involving a felony homicide is more likely to involve older victims and younger offenders but a nonfelony homicide there is more likely to involve victims and offenders of similar ages.

Perhaps the best indicator that stranger nonfelony homicides are the outcome of emotional confrontations is the number of eyewitnesses for each type of homicide studied by Zahn and Sagi. In stranger felony murders, 68.1 percent had one or more eyewitnesses, and almost 90 percent (88.6 percent) of stranger nonfelony homicides had one or more eyewitnesses. In other words, in the grip of an emotional conflict in a public setting, the participants apparently care little about whether other people are watching them engage in lethal violence.

Trends

In contrast to some popular accounts, Figure 5-2 indicates that the percentage of stranger murders has remained largely unchanged. The percentages in Figure 5-2 included both felony and nonfelony stranger murders taken from annual editions of the UCR. Except for small increases in 1984 and again in 1995 and 1996, there has been little change in stranger murders that have been labeled as such by police officers. To what extent these reported trends would change with accurate information about missing victim/offender relationships on cases not cleared by arrest is unknown.

Figure 5-2 indicates a slight decline in aggravated assaults by strangers from 1977 to 1998. Given the difficulties of measuring stranger violence, it is difficult to know whether the decline represents fewer stranger-aggravated assaults or whether aggravated assaults involving nonstrangers are being better reported in the NCVS.

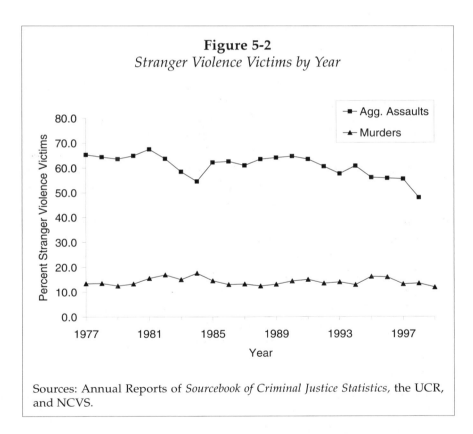

Figure 5-2
Stranger Violence Victims by Year

Sources: Annual Reports of *Sourcebook of Criminal Justice Statistics,* the UCR, and NCVS.

Explanations

For intimate and family violence, the immediate social situation is typically the final act in a homicidal drama preceded by months and even years of abuse. Stranger violence, however, is at the other end of the continuum; the social situation is the beginning and end of interaction between victims and offenders. The circumscription in the space and time of the encounter serves to explain why these murders and assaults seem to turn on such trivial causes. The reason is simple: By definition, victims and offenders do not share a past that would lend plausibility to reasons for violence. Such causes of violence between intimates as infidelity or quarrels over money, therefore, do not exist for strangers.

If prior relationships are not relevant, what are the causes of confrontational violence? A hint is given by Lofland's (1969) suggestion that people impute an identity to places independent of the people who frequent them: "Nice places are frequented by that kind of people; crummy places are frequented by their kind of people" (p. 168). In short, to understand this type of violence, we need to look at the places where it occurs.

Routine activities theory (described in chapter 4) has been important in explaining stranger violence. For example, young males, particularly if they are unmarried, spend more time in public locations where the risk of stranger victimizations is higher (Sampson, 1987). Researchers have focused on bars and taverns as high-risk places for stranger violence (Roncek & Maier, 1991; Sherman, Gartin, & Buerger, 1989). This research has shown that strangers looking for a fight are likely to go to places where they can find one. To depict the effect of proximity on offenders and victims, Sherman et al. developed the concept of *hot spots* of crime. They plotted the calls for police assistance for a year in Minneapolis, Minnesota, and found that 3 percent of the locations accounted for 50 percent of the calls received. Roncek and Maier (1991) found that more violence was committed in blocks that contained bars and taverns.

The fact that some bars and taverns are gathering places for young males has another implication for violence. In the event of a conflict, both males have a self-image at stake: They do not want to be seen as backing down, particularly by their friends. Research confirms that the presence of aggressive third parties increases the aggressiveness of offenders, particularly when third parties are young males or significant others (Felson, 1982; Felson, Ribner, & Siegel, 1984; Felson & Steadman, 1983). The latter research helps to explain the earlier finding that almost 90 percent of nonfelony stranger murders are witnessed by more than one person.

Interventions

Of course, one implication of the "hot spots" perspective is greater police surveillance and quicker response time for those locations where the probability of violence is greater. Another implication for intervention follows closely from the concept of "guardians" in the routine activities perspective. Felson (1998) points out that people who reside in a location for a long time assume crime prevention responsibilities. Both renters and homeowners come to know their neighbors and have a stake in the appearance of their neighborhood; conversely, neighborhoods with a highly transient population have higher crime rates.

Felson suggests that *place managers* are persons who have a stake in maintaining law-abiding behavior in the locations where they work. Felson gives the example of receptionists, apartment managers, store clerks, and gas station attendants.

Homel, Tomsen, and Thommeny (1992) found that levels of violence could be moderated by the behavior of place managers in the role of doorpersons or bouncers. The authors state that many

> bouncers seem poorly trained, obsessed with their own machismo (relating badly to groups of male strangers), and some of them appear to regard their employment as giving them a licence to assault people.

The authors conclude that the confrontational violence in bars is less a matter of the relationship between the physiology of alcohol and violence than a matter of good management, effective legislation, and police surveillance.

Serial Homicides

Counting Serial Homicides

During the 1980s, the term *serial murder* or *serial homicide* was coined by the media. Serial homicides are distinguished from mass murders, which are multiple murders committed in a brief period of time, and spree killings, which are carried out over a few days or weeks. Serial murder or homicide implies that the killings are spread out over months or years, with a cooling-off period between (Jenkins, 1994).

Prior to the 1980s, most experts believed that serial homicides constituted 1 or 2 percent of total homicides. But during the 1980s, the most widely quoted claims were that serial homicides were 20 to 25 percent of all homicides rather than less than 1 percent, which is regarded as accurate. How did this enormous, and largely false, estimate gain credence among otherwise rational and thoughtful people?

The distortion of statistics can occur in the three following circumstances: (1) the rise of an issue of public concern that can be shaped into a major social problem with the help of media; (2) the lack of valid and reliable statistics or the ignoring of the existence of pertinent statistics; and (3) the presence of constituencies organized to use statistics to promote specific agendas.

Gang-violence, stranger, and serial homicides are issues of public concern. Citizens, practitioners, and policy makers have an interest in knowing the size of the problem as a first step in devising solutions. Where there is a lack of valid, reliable, or pertinent statistics to describe the problem, the door is open for a variety of agencies to advance numerical claims to promote their own agendas. For example, if child welfare agencies can convince a large segment of the public that child abductions are the work of serial killers, they are in a position to ask for large sums of public money for education, prevention, and treatment—all of which fall within their purview.

Joel Best (1988) described the importance of statistics in discussing child abductions: "Three principles seem clear: big numbers are better than small numbers; official numbers are better than unofficial numbers; and big, official numbers are best of all" (p. 90). With respect to serial homicides, however, it was the Behavioral Sciences Unit of the FBI that in 1984 came prepared to provide "big official numbers."

A number of events propelled the popularity of serial homicide in the 1980s, but the preposterous belief that serial homicides made up a fifth of all homicides received an enormous amount of legitimation from the Behavioral Sciences Unit in congressional hearings. It was in these hearings that William Webster, FBI director, described "patterns of murders committed by one person in large numbers with no apparent rhyme, reason or motivation." (U.S. Senate, 1984, cited in Jenkins, 1994, p. 59).

As nearly as can be determined, cases with unknown relationships were factored into the serial-killings estimate. *Unknown* was interpreted to mean "no apparent motive," which, in turn, was taken to mean "motiveless." If it was motiveless, it was then classified by the Director of the FBI in congressional hearings to be "patterns of murders committed by one person in large numbers with no apparent rhyme, reasons, or motivations." This represented an enormous inflation of serial homicide numbers because it included a larger number of homicides committed by solitary offenders regardless of whether they were serial offenders. In fact, "unknown" in homicide data simply means that the police did not know the the circumstances: It is a confession of ignorance rather than an affirmation of serial homicide (Jenkins, 1994). This attempt at manipulating statistics is very similar to an effort mentioned in the previous section to use missing data or "unknowns" for victim/offender relationships to conclude that the number of stranger homicides was in excess of 50 percent.

Patterns

It is important to recognize that serial homicides are an extremely rare offense. If we assume that serial killings are 1 percent of all recorded homicides, there would have been 127 serial homicide victims among the 12,658 victims of murders and nonnegligent homicides reported to the FBI in 1999 in a U.S. population of over 270 million people. If we assume that each serial offender had killed two victims, we would be left with 64 offenders. Fisher (1997), on the other hand, estimates that there are ten serial killers operating in the United States every year—which is an even smaller percentage of offenders. Even though serial homicide is a frightening phenomenon, the small number of offenders makes the study of serial homicides very difficult.

In addition to their rarity, the traditional image of serial killers has been shaped by media presentation and by case studies of offenders by forensic psychiatrists. In more recent decades, criminologists using a social science perspective have examined social and cultural forces underlying serial killings. In addition, law enforcement operatives have shown greater sophistication in using research-based techniques to track and apprehend serial killers (Fox & Levin, 1999).

Given their late start, criminologists have labored to correct many of the myths and misconceptions concerning serial offenders. These can be divided into (1) myths about their psychological characteristics and (2) social and demographic myths.

One of the myths discussed by Fox and Levin (1999, p. 167) is that serial killers are unusual in appearance and lifestyle. Virtually all researchers on the subject agree that serial killers are "extraordinarily ordinary" (Egger, 1998; Fisher, 1997; Hickey, 1997; Holmes & Holmes, 1998; Jenkins, 1994). Indeed, one reason serial killers are difficult to identify and apprehend is that they do an excellent job of blending in with the crowd and not drawing attention to themselves. They frequently hold full-time jobs, are involved in stable relationships, and are members of various community groups.

Fox and Levin (1999) enumerate several other psychological myths about serial killers. They list and describe beliefs that serial killers are all insane, sociopaths, products of bad childhoods, and sexual sadists, selecting victims who somehow resemble their mothers, and really wanting to get caught—none of which is generally true.

The most popular social and demographic myth is the image of the serial killer as a lone white male. In actual fact, from 10 percent to 20 percent of serial killings can be attributed to two or more individuals working together (Jenkins, 1994).

Neither is it true that all serial killers are males. Hickey (1997) studied 337 male and 67 female serial killers who were responsible for a minimum of 2,526 homicides between 1800 and 1995. The 67 female killers were 16 percent of the total pool of offenders. The 67 female killers represent *known* cases. Both Jenkins (1994) and Hickey (1997) point out that the number of female offenders may be underrepresented because they have been more likely to use asphyxiation or poisoning, which were less likely to be noticed before the emergence of modern forensic medicine.

Not all serial killers are white. Until the arrest of Wayne Williams, claims were made that no serial killers were African Americans. However, Hickey (1997) found that African Americans constitute 20 percent of the offenders in his study.

Finally, serial killers do not generally move about the country. The claims in the 1980s that the typical killer moved around within

10 to 20 states was made to justify increased federal involvement. Although a minority of serial offenders do move about, the majority tend to operate in one city or even in one neighborhood (Jenkins, 1994).

Trends

There is no doubt that serial murder offenders have increased in recorded number. Hickey (1997) found that of the 337 serial homicide cases studied, approximately 94 percent began their killing since the year 1900. Between 1900 and 1924, 7 percent of the cases were reported; 10 percent between 1925 and 1949; 32 percent between 1950 and 1974; and 45 percent between 1975 and 1995. More cases were identified in just the 20-year time frame between 1975 and 1995 than during any previous 25-year span. However, the central question is whether the increase is the result of better reporting or a genuine increase in the number of serial killers (Fox & Levin, 1999).

Three problems have an impact on the recording of serial homicides. First, there is no publicly available source of homicide data that records serial homicides. Neither the Uniform Crime Reports nor the National Center for Health Statistics (see chapter 2) maintains a separate category for recording serial homicides. Rather, the estimates given are drawn from stranger homicide records and newspaper accounts, which are useful but of unknown validity and reliability.

Second, until recently it has been possible for a serial offender to move among jurisdictions, killing one or two victims in each place without law enforcement suspecting that a serial offender was active. That serial offenders could be mobile and kill with impunity has been possible because of linkage blindness, that is, the "nearly total lack of sharing or coordinating of investigative information and the lack of adequate networking by law enforcement agencies" (Egger, 1998, p. 180).

Finally, even if communication between law enforcement agencies has improved, serial killers can and do alter their mode of operation. What connects seemingly unrelated killings to one offender is the *modus operandi*; such things as the same type of victim, the same method of killing and disposing of the remains, and so forth link the offender to the event. If the serial offender decides to change his or her mode of operation, then the offense will not be linked to this individual.

Explanations

The difficulty in explaining serial homicides is not a shortage of explanations, but an abundance of them. Among the biological factors implicated in serial homicide are the XYY chromosome, blood levels of neurotransmitters, and types and levels of hormones. Psychological factors include psychosis, dissociative disorders, psychoanalytic factors, personality disorders, and psychopathy. Among the more sociologically inclined theories are those relating to urbanization, aggression, child abuse, neutralization, labeling, and social control theory.

Explanations after the fact and an excess of false positives are two major problems with explanations of serial murderers. False positives occur when a person is predicted to have a condition, but does not, although he or she may share characteristics used to predict the condition with those who actually turn out to have it. False positives are illustrated in Egger's (1998) discussion of the diagnosis of Kenneth Bianchi, the Hillside Strangler, as having "antisocial personality disorder 301.70" according to the *Diagnostic and Statistical Manual* (DSM). Yet, Egger points out that many of his own students had demonstrated an inability to maintain consistent work behavior and a failure to accept social norms with respect to lawful behavior during periods of their lives. The latter were two of the four characteristics attributed to Bianchi's official diagnosis of antisocial personality disorder.

After the fact occurs and once the offender is identified, hindsight makes possible a description of some negative trait or flaw that is supposed to have caused the killing. Postdicting, in contrast to predicting, is the theoretical analogue to Monday morning quarterbacking.

In sum, serial homicide is a rare event and the theories of crime and violence used have little applicability to rare events. When physical theories attempt to explain a rare event, such as a large asteroid hitting the earth, they make use of general laws. But sociological and psychological theories have ill-defined boundaries, are imprecise, and are largely untested. They provide few insights and no predictions when applied to serial killers, who are extremely rare and remarkably diverse.

Interventions

One of the greatest investigative challenges for law enforcement is apprehending a serial killer. As we have discussed, serial killers are nondescript, have conventional lifestyles, and are exceptionally skilled in their presentation of self so that they appear beyond suspicion. These are the major reasons they are difficult to apprehend.

Egger (1998) discusses the wide variety of police strategies used in investigating serial murders and how some of them can be used to reduce linkage blindness. He discusses in detail each of the following (see Riedel, 1998b):

a. Interagency conferences.

b. Information clearinghouses.

c. Task forces.

d. Central coordination efforts.

e. Profiling.

f. Investigative consultants.

g. Forensic consultants.

h. Major incident room procedures.

i. Solicitation from public.

j. Computer analysis systems.

k. Offender rewards.

l. Psychics.

m. Rapid response teams.

n. Centralized investigative networks.

The approach that receives the most public attention is investigative profiling. Three types of investigative profiling have emerged in the past 20 years. The first investigative model was developed by the Behavioral Sciences Unit of the FBI and depends heavily on the intuition and experience of the profiler. The experienced profiler studies the crime scene carefully and attempts to construct a psychological profile of the offender. The FBI type of profiling is usually productive in crimes in which there is evidence of psychopathology, such as sadistic torture, lust and mutilation murders, and evisceration.

This kind of profiling has been evaluated and the results are inconclusive (Godwin, 1978; Levin & Fox, 1985). A more useful approach is being pursued at the University of Liverpool by David Canter, who is building an empirical base in which he considers victim information and relies on statistical analysis and the generation of probabilities from continuously updated information (Egger, 1998).

The third approach is geographic profiling, which is based on the criminal geography research of Brantingham and Brantingham (1978). More recent research by D. Kim Rossmo has led to the use of spatial data to generate a three-dimensional probability map that indicates areas (e.g., home, work site, travel routes) most likely to be associated with the offender (Egger, 1998).

There has been relatively little variation on what is done with serial offenders once they are apprehended. Clearly, they will be sentenced to long prison terms with essentially no chance of release.

In many instances, these offenders are sentenced to death and executed. Although this may feed the public's need for vengeance and retribution, it may be more useful to keep them incarcerated, for purposes of research. Given the phenomenal advances that are occurring in research on the human genome, for example, serial killers would offer an opportunity to resolve some long-standing questions about biology and crime.

Gang Violence

Counting Gangs and Gang Violence

The question of being able to count gangs and incidents of gang violence involve different dimensions of the same question about strangers and serial homicides. Although official statistics record fewer stranger murders than actually exist because fewer stranger offenders than known offenders are arrested, the most difficult issue facing gang researchers relates to the very definitions of *gangs*, *gang members*, and *gang-related crime* (Huff, 1990). Thus, it is standard practice for gang researchers to caution their audiences about definitional issues; typically, these are directed to what is meant by *gang, gang members,* and *gang crime* (Maxson, 1999).

Maxson and Klein (1995, p. 26) compared definitions of gangs and gang violence in Los Angeles County and Chicago. In Los Angeles County, the police's and the sheriff's department follow a *gang member* definition: "[I]n a criminal or a violent event, evidence that either the victims or the offenders are gang members makes the event gang-related." Chicago, on the other hand, follows a *gang motive* definition: A "killing is considered gang-related only if it occurs in the course of an explicitly defined collective encounter between two or more gangs." Using this definition, a gang killing would involve conflicts over territory, retaliation, or "representing" (wearing gang colors, shouting gang slogans, graffiti, etc.). Thus, the robbery of a jewelry store by a gang member would not be considered a gang crime in Chicago, but it would be in Los Angeles.

To determine whether different definitions make a difference, Maxson and Klein recoded Los Angeles County gang homicides using the Chicago gang motive definition. When these recoded cases were compared with Los Angeles County homicides using their gang member definition, differences in *patterns* were small. For example, there was no difference is the number of drive-by shootings between the two cities with different definitions.

However, it should not be surprising that motive-based definitions overall result in a smaller number of recorded gang homicides. The National Youth Gang Survey (National Youth Gang Center, 1999) assessed gangs and gang activities using a nationally representative sample of 3,018 law enforcement agencies. Using survey results, the total number of member-based gang homicides in 1997 was 3,341, but the total number of motive-based homicides was 1,880.

The question of the number of gangs and gang killings has important political and economic implications for a city. For example, the size of the gang problem determines what kind of resources are made available to combat the problem. In one case, the fact that a major city industry would have economic implications led authorities to a denial that there was a local gang problem.

At the beginning of his study of gangs in San Diego, Sanders (1994) found that the police department denied that there were gangs. The official policy that San Diego had no gangs may have been a way of protecting the multimillion-dollar tourist industry. Further, city officials believed that any publicity about gangs would encourage gang activity. Partly as a result of media accounts of gang violence, the city police department formed a gang detail unit a few years later.

Patterns

Cities with a population over 25,000 have the most gangs (12,831). Small cities (2,500 to 25,000) and suburban and rural counties have progressively smaller numbers of juvenile gangs. Large cities also have the largest number of jurisdictions reporting gang homicides (11 or more) and the highest involvement in aggravated assaults. Seventy-four percent of the jurisdictions in the western United States report youth gangs, followed by the Midwest (52 percent), the South (49 percent), and the Northeast (31 percent) (National Youth Gang Center, 1999).

More detailed information on gang and nongang characteristics in Los Angeles County is given in Table 5-4. Table 5-4 shows that gang homicides occur predominantly in public settings like streets, involve firearms, have a larger number of participants than nongang killings, and involve young male offenders and victims. Given the sensationalistic treatment by the media of violent gang events involving minorities, the research by Maxson and Klein in Los Angeles County shows relatively small differences in the proportion of minorities in gang and nongang homicides. The proportion of black gang victims and offenders was only slightly larger (.05) than the proportion of black nongang victims and offenders. Among Hispanics, the difference between the proportion of gang and nongang victims was small (.05), and even smaller (.03) for offenders. In both cases, the proportion of Hispanic gang killings was smaller than the proportion of Hispanic nongang killings (Maxson, 1999).

One of the more common portrayals of gangs is that they are involved with drugs. According to the 1997 National Youth Gang Center (NYGC, 1999), large cities had the highest percentage (49 percent) of youth gangs involved in drug sales, followed by suburban counties (43 percent), rural counties (35 percent), and small cities (31 percent).

Table 5-4

Incident and Participant Characteristics in Gang and Nongang Homicides: Los Angeles County, 1988–1989

Category	Characteristic	Gang (N = 201)	Nongang (N = 201)
Incident Characteristics	Street Location	57%	34%
	Residence Location	30%	50%
	Other Location	13%	16%
	Firearms Present	98%	75%
	Participants on Suspect Side	2.75	1.71
Homicide Victims	All Male	90%	77%
	Mean Age	24.2	34.4%
	Proportion Black	.80	.75
	Proportion Hispanic	.18	.23
Homicide Suspects	All Male	93%	83%
	Mean Age	20.5	31.3
	Proportion Black	.86	.81
	Proportion Hispanic	.14	.17

Source: Maxson, C. L. (1999). Gang homicide: A review and extension of the literature. In M. D. Smith and M. A. Zahn (Eds.), *Homicide: A sourcebook of social research*, p. 248. Copyright © 1999 by Sage Publications. Reprinted by permission of Sage Publications.

Respondents (law enforcement agencies) were asked to indicate the percentage of sales by youth gangs for several types of drugs. The highest percentage for youth gang street sales was for crack cocaine (33 percent) and for marijuana (32 percent). In addition, youth gang members were thought to be involved in 16 percent of powder cocaine sales, 12 percent of methamphetamine sales, and 9 percent of heroin sales (NYGC, 1999).

Even though the National Gang Youth Survey shows a high degree of involvement of youth gangs with drugs, it does not report on the relationship between drug involvement and violence. Maxson (1999) found that drug involvement is more likely to be a nongang characteristic, as Table 5-5 shows.

Table 5-5
Drug Characteristics in Gang and Nongang Homicides:
Los Angeles County, 1988–1989

Category	Characteristic	Gang (N = 201)	Nongang (N = 201)
All Homicides	Drug Mention	62%	66%
	Crack Mention	19	30
	Cocaine Mention	34	48
	Sales Mention	40	33
	Drug Motive Mention	17	27
Drug Homicides	Crack Mention	31	45
	Cocaine Mention	55	73
	Sales Mention	65	50
	Drug Motive Mention	27	41

Source: Maxson, C. L. (1999). Gang homicide: A review and extension of the literature. In M. D. Smith and M. A. Zahn (Eds.), *Homicide: A sourcebook of social research*, pp. 239–254. Copyright © 1999 by Sage Publications. Reprinted by permission of Sage Publications.

What is initially noteworthy in Table 5-5 is the very high frequency of mentioning drugs in law enforcement records for all homicides of both gangs and nongangs. Drugs were mentioned in 66 percent of the nongang homicide records and 62 percent of the gang records. Crack (30 percent) and cocaine (48 percent) were mentioned in the records more frequently for nongang homicides, as was the mention of a drug motive for the homicide (27 percent). Not unexpectedly, the mention of drug sales was more common among gangs, but the difference did not meet the criteria of a statistically important difference.

Similar results are found when the records for drug-related homicides are examined. The mention of crack, cocaine, and drugs as a motive for killing was more common among nongangs than gangs. Considering only drug-related killings, the mention of drug sales as an important component in the homicide was more common among gangs than nongangs. Similar findings are reported by Meehan and O'Carroll (1992). Goldstein, Brownstein, Ryan, and Belluci (1989) also found that the greatest amount of violence with respect to drugs occurred in connection with the manufacture, distribution, and sale of crack.

Trends

Because of variation in definitions and implementation of definitions of gangs, there is little reliable nationwide information about trends in gang violence. In the National Youth Gang Survey, law enforcement agencies were asked about the severity of the gang problem in their jurisdictions. Forty-nine percent of the jurisdictions believed the problem was getting worse, 41 percent believed the problem was staying the same, and 10 percent believed it was getting better. Possibly because it is a more recent problem for them, more suburban and rural areas (43 percent) than urban areas believed the problem was getting worse.

Maxson (1999) provides a discussion of trends in Los Angeles County and Chicago. Examining the trends for gang-related homicides in Los Angeles County, she indicated a decline from 19 percent in 1980 to 15 percent in 1984. From 1985 through 1991, there was an increase in total homicides, but gang-related homicides also increased from 2 percent to 5 percent each year through 1991. Gang-related homicides were 37 percent in 1991, and dipped slightly in 1992 and 1993 before ending at 43 percent and 45 percent in 1994 and 1995.

In Chicago, the trends from 1965 through 1995 have shown peaks and troughs depending on the level of gang activity. During the 1970s, gang homicides averaged 5 percent; were just under 9 percent in the 1980s; and then nearly doubled to 17 percent during the first half of the 1990s. The trend for Chicago shows that gang homicides constitute an increasing share of all homicides, more than one-fourth in 1994 and 1995.

Explanations

Until comparatively recently, the most popular explanations of gang delinquency were subcultural theories. These subcultural theories include the work of Albert Cohen (1955), Walter Miller (1958), Richard Cloward and Lloyd Ohlin (1960), and Marvin Wolfgang and Franco Ferracuti (1967).

Wolfgang and Ferracuti's theory holds that subcultural members have *some* different beliefs from mainstream culture. In the case of the subculture of violence, members hold different beliefs about the use of violence in interpersonal relationships. As mentioned earlier, violence is seen as a way of solving interpersonal conflicts. This subculture also plays a role in drive-by shootings.

Drive-by shootings. Although hit-and-run attacks were carried out in traditional East Coast cities, they were limited to attacks on foot or bicycle because of dense populations, narrow streets, and congested traffic. Drive-by shooting became popular in California because of neighborhoods spread out on ground level, an excellent road system, and relatively little public transportation.

In neighborhoods where gangs are common, gang members are socialized in a particular way to respond to a drive-by shooting in which they or someone in their neighborhood is a target. In his explanation of San Diego gangs, Sanders (1994) points out that middle-class youths subject to victimization will conclude that they were in the wrong place and avoid that location in the future. In contrast, nongang lower-class youths, who cannot escape the neighborhood, learn to manage times, places, and people to avoid becoming a target. Gang youths subject to a near-hit, on the other hand, are provided with a very different perspective. They hear about the weakness of their enemy from others, the revenge that should be exacted, and the courage of those who attack another gang.

What is heard at the individual level is built upon at the level of the gang. Emerging over a period of time, sometimes over generations, are accounts of rival gangs in which they are portrayed as murderous, cowardly, venal, and dangerous. With those kinds of justifications and accounts, hit-and-run attacks or drive-by shootings are not difficult to comprehend (Sanders, 1994).

Interventions

Because of the proliferation of gangs, the most recent National Youth Gang Survey, the 1997 survey (NYG, 1999), included a question to determine the extent to which law enforcement agencies had created specialized response units. Among those jurisdictions with active youth gangs, 66 percent reported they had some type of specialized response unit. Large cities were the most likely (77 percent) and rural counties the least likely (34 percent). The most common type of specialized-response unit was a youth-street gang unit or officer(s) (35 percent). Eighteen percent of the respondents had gang prevention units or officer(s) and 29 percent had one unit that combined both of these.

In an earlier study, Spergel and Curry (1995) surveyed the views of a wide range of criminal justice personnel in 45 cities. They asked their respondents to list and rank the five most important causes of the gang problem. The most highly ranked response pointed to social system failures, such as poverty and unemployment, criminal opportunity, and drug phenomena. The second highest cause was targeted as institutional failure, such as defective families and schools.

What is interesting about the survey results is that the primary causes mentioned bear no relationship to the primary strategies cities had chosen for dealing with the problem. Among all agencies, the most frequently chosen (44.9 percent) tack was suppression, which refers to formal and informal social control processes such as agency supervision, arrest, incarceration, and other criminal justice actions.

Conclusions

The first section of this chapter examined national patterns of homicide and aggravated assaults. Because both offenses share a large number of characteristics, we described risks, patterns, trends, explanations, and interventions in the same section.

Subsequent sections focused on confrontational stranger violence, serial homicides, and gang violence. They were discussed together because they represent real or perceived danger to urban dwellers going about their public activities; it is difficult to obtain an accurate count of the amount of these types of crime; and, partly because it is difficult to obtain reliable information, knowledge about them is a combination of facts and myths.

The kinds of confrontational violence with strangers discussed here is strongly bound to the social situation. Prototypically, two strangers engage in conflict over issues that may appear trivial on the surface, but represent a challenge to the egos of the participants. Because confrontational stranger violence emerges in what appears a spontaneous fashion, increased police surveillance and response to locations that account for a large amount of violence, "hot spots," is one promising intervention. Another useful intervention emerges from the routine activities perspective: "Place managers" can play an important role in reducing these types of violence.

Serial killers are the most puzzling of violent offenders. They are extremely rare and the cruelty and brutality of their murders exceeds anything found in other arenas of violence. What is most amazing about these people is their ability to conceal themselves and their ability to commit offenses over a long period of time. Although modern law enforcement makes it more difficult to continue offending without discovery, serial killers remain the most difficult type of violent offender to describe, explain, and apprehend.

Successful arrest of serial homicide offenders depends as much on luck as on skill. As Egger (1998) has indicated, law enforcement agencies are encouraged to practice an enhanced degree of cooperation; they need to avoid "linkage blindness."

Gang violence is a serious form of violence in large cities and has been studied most extensively in Los Angeles County and the city of Chicago. The gang's most important role is to provide a source of identity for young males and, to a lesser extent, females. Trapped in high-crime neighborhoods, attending poor schools, victims of racial and ethnic discrimination, gangs provide a source of identity and pride to young people who believe they have few other alternatives. What is probably the greatest future problem is the spread of gangs and gang violence to small towns.

References

Athens, L. H. (1980). *Violent criminal acts and actors.* Boston: Routledge & Kegan Paul.

Best, J. (1988). Missing children: Misleading statistics. *The Public Interest, 92,* 84–92.

Blumstein, A., & Rosenfeld, R. (1998). Explaining recent trends in U.S. homicide rates. *Journal of Criminal Law and Criminology, 88,* 1175–1216.

Brantingham, P. J., & Brantingham, P. L. (1978). A theoretical model of crime site selection. In M. Krohn & R. Akers (Eds.), *Theoretical perspectives* (pp. 105–118). Thousand Oaks, CA: Sage.

Bureau of Justice Statistics. (2001). *Assault rates have declined since 1994.* Available: <http://www.ojp.usdoj.gov/bjs/glance/aslt.htn> [July, 2001].

Cloward, R. A., & Ohlin, L. E. (1960). *Delinquency and opportunity: A theory of delinquency gangs.* New York: Free Press.

Cohen, A. K. (1955). *Delinquent boys: The culture of the gang.* Glencoe, IL: Free Press of Glencoe.

Eck, J., & McGuire, E. (2000). Have changes in policing reduced violent crime? In A. Blumstein & J. Wallman (Eds.), *The crime drop in America* (pp. 207–265). Cambridge: Cambridge University Press.

Egger, S. A. (1998). *The killers among us.* Upper Saddle River, NJ: Prentice-Hall.

Federal Bureau of Investigation. (1993). *Crime in the United States, 1992 Uniform Crime Reports.* Washington, DC: Government Printing Office.

———. (1999). *Uniform crime reports for the United States, 1997.* Available: <http://www.fbi.gov/ucr/Cius_99/w99tbl2-5.xls> [April 23, 2001].

Felson, M. (1998). *Crime and everyday life.* (2nd ed.). Thousand Oaks, CA: Pine Forge.

Felson, R. B. (1982). Impression management and the escalation of aggression and violence. *Social Psychology Quarterly, 45,* 245–254.

———. (1993). Predatory and dispute-related violence: A social interactionist approach. In R. V. Clarke & M. Felson (Eds.), *Routine activity and rational choice* (Vol. 5, pp. 103–125). New Brunswick, CT: Transaction.

Felson, R. B., Ribner, S. A., & Siegel, M. S. (1984). Age and the effect of third parties during criminal violence. *Sociology and Social Research, 68,* 452–462.

Felson, R. B., & Steadman, H. J. (1983). Situational factors in disputes leading to criminal violence. *Criminology: An Interdisciplinary Journal, 21,* 59–74.

Fisher, J. C. (1997). *Killer among us: Public reactions to serial murder*. Westport, CT: Praeger.

Fox, J. A., & Levin, J. (1999). Serial murder. In M. D. Smith & M. A. Zahn (Eds.), *Homicide: A sourcebook of social research* (pp. 165–175). Thousand Oaks, CA: Sage.

Godwin, J. (1978). *Murder USA: The ways we kill each other*. New York: Ballantine Books.

Goldstein, P. J., Brownstein, H. H., Ryan, P. J., & Bellucci, P. A. (1989). Crack and homicide in New York City, 1988: A conceptually based event analysis. *Contemporary Drug Problems, 16*, 651–687.

Harries, K. D. (1989). Homicide and assault: A comparative analysis of attributes in Dallas neighborhoods, 1981–1985. *The Professional Geographer, 41*, 29–38.

Hickey, E. W. (1997). *Serial murderers and their victims* (2nd ed.). Belmont, CA: Wadsworth.

Holmes, R. M., & Holmes, S. T. (1998). *Serial murder*. Thousand Oaks, CA: Sage.

Homel, R., Tomsen, S., & Thommeny, J. (1992). Public drinking and violence: Not just an alcohol problem. *Journal of Drug Issues, 22*, 679–697.

Huff, C. R. (1990). Introduction. In C. R. Huff (Ed.), *Gangs in America* (2nd ed., pp. xxi–xxvii). Thousand Oaks, CA: Sage.

Jenkins, P. (1994). *Using murder: The social construction of serial homicide*. New York: Aldine de Gruyter.

Levin, J., & Fox, J. A. (1985). *Mass murder*. New York: Plenum.

Lofland, J. (1969). *Deviance and identity*. Englewood Cliffs, NJ: Prentice-Hall.

Luckenbill, D. F. (1977). Criminal homicide as a situated transaction. *Social Problems, 25*, 176–186.

Maxson, C. L. (1999). Gang homicide: A review and extension of the literature. In M. D. Smith & M. A. Zahn (Eds.), *Homicide: A sourcebook of social research* (pp. 239–254). Thousand Oaks, CA: Sage.

Maxson, C. L., & Klein, M. W. (1995). Street gang violence: Twice as great, or half as great. In M. W. Klein, C. L. Maxson, & J. Miller (Eds.), *The modern gang reader* (pp. 24–32). Los Angeles: Roxbury Publishing.

Meehan, P. J., & O'Carroll, P. W. (1992). Gangs, drugs, and homicide in Los Angeles. *America Journal of Disease Control, 146*, 683–687.

Miller, W. (1958). Lower-class culture as a generating milieu of gang delinquency. *Journal of Social Issues, 14*, 5–19.

National Youth Gang Center. (1999). *1997 National youth gang survey*. Washington, DC: Office of Juvenile Justice and Delinquency Prevention.

Rennison, C. M. (1999). *Criminal victimization 1998* (National Crime Victimization Survey NCJ 176353). Washington, DC: Government Printing Office.

Riedel, M. (1993). *Stranger violence: A theoretical inquiry.* New York: Garland.

———. (1998a). Counting stranger homicides: A case study of statistical prestidigitation. *Homicide Studies, 2,* 206–219.

———. (1998b). Serial murder, communities, and evil: A review essay. *Criminal Justice Review, 23,* 220–232.

———. (1999a). Homicide. In L. Kurtz (Ed.), *Encyclopedia of violence, peace, and conflict* (pp. 123–138). San Diego, CA: Academic Press.

———. (1999b). Sources of homicide data: A review and comparison. In M. D. Smith & M. A. Zahn (Eds.), *Homicide: A sourcebook of social research* (pp. 75–95). Thousand Oaks, CA: Sage.

———. (2000). Homicide in Los Angeles County: A study of racial and ethnic victimization. In D. Hawkins (Ed.), *Crime control and social justice: The delicate balance.* (In Press). New York: Greenwood.

Roncek, D. W., & Maier, P. A. (1991). Bars, blocks, and crimes revisited: Linking the theory of routine activities to the empiricism of 'hot spots.' *Criminology, 29,* 751–753.

Rosenfeld, R. (2000). Patterns in adult homicide: 1980–1995. In A. Blumstein & J. Wallman (Eds.), *The crime drop in America* (pp. 130–163). Cambridge, MA: Cambridge University Press.

Sampson, R. J. (1987). Personal violence by strangers: An extension and test of predatory victimization. *Journal of Criminal Law and Criminology, 78,* 327–356.

Sanders, W. B. (1994). *Gangbangs and drive-bys: Grounded culture and juvenile gang violence.* New York: Aldine de Gruyter.

Sheley, J. F., & Wright, J. D. (1995). *In the line of fire: Youth, guns, and violence in urban America.* New York: Aldine de Gruyter.

Sherman, L. W., Gartin, P. R., & Buerger, M. E. (1989). Hot spots of predatory crime: Routine activities and the criminology of place. *Criminology, 27,* 27–55.

Silberman, C. E. (1978). *Criminal violence, criminal justice.* New York: Random House.

Spelman, W. (2000). The limited importance of prison expansion. In A. Blumstein & J. Wallman (Eds.), *The crime drop in America* (pp. 97–130). Cambridge, MA: Cambridge University Press.

Spergel, I. A., & Curry, G. D. (1995). The national youth gang survey: A research and development process. In M. W. Klein, C. L. Maxson, & J.

Miller (Eds.), *The modern gang reader* (pp. 254–265). Los Angeles: Roxbury Publishing.

U.S. Senate. (1984). *Serial murders: Hearings before the subcommittee on juvenile justice of the committee of the judiciary. On patterns of murders committed by one person in large numbers with no apparent rhyme, reasons, or motivation.* Washington, DC: U.S. Senate, 98th Congress, 1st Session.

Walinsky, A. (1995, July). The crisis of public order. *Atlantic Monthly, 276,* 39–54.

Wintemute, G. (2000). Guns and gun violence. In A. Blumstein & J. Wallman (Eds.), *The crime drop in America* (pp. 45–96). Cambridge, MA: Cambridge University Press.

Wolfgang, M. E., & Ferracuti, F. (1967). *The subculture of violence: Towards an integrated theory in criminology.* London: Tavistock.

World Almanac. (1998). *The world almanac and book of facts 1998.* Mahwah, NJ: K-III Reference Corporation.

Zahn, M. A., & Sagi, P. C. (1987). Stranger homicides in nine American cities. *Journal of Criminal Law and Criminology, 78,* 377–397. ✦

Chapter 6

Intimate Partner and Family Violence

'People Hit Family Members Because They Can'

Gelles and Straus (1988, p. 20), from whom this quotation was taken, describe the 10-year marriage of Chet and Margorie, in which Chet beats his wife once every couple of months because he thinks she does a poor job of keeping the house neat. The other case described concerns David, Marie, and their 3-year-old son, Peter, who was being x-rayed for a possible skull fracture given to him by his father because he knocked over the new television set and shattered the picture tube.

In the next paragraph, the authors ask whether Chet would feel free to beat up the janitor if he failed to keep Chet's office clean. What would happen to David if he had a new television in his automobile showroom and a 3-year-old son of a customer overturned it? Obviously, the outcomes would be quite different if Chet and David behaved toward strangers as they had behaved toward their wife and son. If they attacked the janitor and the 3-year-old, both would be facing arrest and prosecution for assault and battery. Why should hitting loved ones be any different?

This chapter is an examination of how attitudes toward hitting or expressing other kinds of violence toward loved ones has changed. When Gelles and Straus (1988) wrote their book, widespread changes in the treatment of intimate partner and family violence were occurring in the form of legislation, criminal justice practices, and treatment of victims and perpetrators. This chapter looks not only at violence between intimate partners, but also at violence between parents and children. As the following pages will make clear, while the changes have been enormous, the results have been less effective than hoped. In short, people still hit family members because they can.

Violence Between Intimate Partners

Until the 1970s, assaults against wives were considered misdemeanors in most states even if the severity of the attack would be considered a felony if perpetrated on an acquaintance or stranger. Emergency orders of protection were unavailable and carried no penalties or provisions for enforcement. Pleas of self-defense in spousal abuse cases were not effective (Browne, Williams, & Dutton, 1999).

The dark side of the traditional *Leave It To Beaver* family was that males were dominant and women subordinate; the woman's responsibilities were to bear and raise children, cook meals, clean house, and generally keep a tidy domicile. If she were fortunate enough to have a husband that treated her well and appreciated her domestic efforts, she were very lucky. If her husband belittled her and beat her regularly, there was relatively little she could do to change her unfortunate situation. There were substantial numbers of the latter type of marriage: The "first national survey conducted in 1975 found that 28 percent of all married couples reported at least one physical assault occurring in their relationship" (Browne et al., 1999, p. 149). Put simply, the only widely recognized intimate relation was marriage, and men were recognized as master of their castle with almost no limits to the kind of treatment they could hand out to wives and children.

All this changed in the next decade with sweeping changes in law, police practices, social resources, and public awareness. By 1980, 47 states had passed some type of domestic violence legislation. One of the most important legal reforms was legislation that requires police to make an arrest on the basis of probable cause in domestic violence cases. Formerly, when domestic violence cases were treated as misdemeanors, the officer was required to witness the crime or secure a warrant to effect an arrest (Caringella-Mac-Donald, 1997).

The phenomenal growth of women's shelters from 20 in 1975 to 1,200 in 1995 was testimony to the impact of the women's movement to advocate and galvanize public opinion and support. Finally, the self-defense plea for battered wives who killed their tormentors became more widely accepted by courts (Cardarelli, 1997).

Patterns of Intimate Violence

In addition to the changes mentioned above, there is now a recognition that the range of intimate relationships extends beyond heterosexual marriage. The term *intimate partner* now includes former and current dates, spouses, boyfriends, girlfriends, cohabiting couples, and members of common-law relationships. For the most part, the term *intimate partners* is applied to heterosexual couples, although it is equally applicable to gay and lesbian couples (Browne et al., 1999; Renzetti, 1997; Tjaden & Thoennes, 2000; Zawitz, 1994).

One of the most current sources of information about intimate violence is the National Survey of Violence Against Women (NSVAW). Consisting of interviews with a random sample of 8,000 men and 8,000 women, this survey provides detailed information about rape, physical assault, and stalking victimization (Tjaden & Thoennes, 2000). Rape and sexual assaults are also discussed in chapter 8. Discussions of homicide will rely on police and FBI information.

We noted earlier that men, for the most part, make up the ranks of murder victims and offenders. By contrast, what is most characteristic of intimate violence is that males remain the predominant offenders while women are the majority of victims. Among recent intimate partner homicide victims, almost 75 percent of the 1,368 victims were female while only 25.1 percent were male. Among offenders, the percentages were reversed; 75 percent of the offenders were male and 25 percent were female (FBI, 1999).

There are two types of intimate relationships that account for the largest percentage of female murders. For the 2,361 women victims for which 1997 relationship information was available, 20.7 percent were wives and 18.3 percent were girlfriends. The combined category of wives and girlfriends (39.0 percent) was the single largest group of female victims. With the addition of the small percentage of other intimate victims (4.3 percent), over 40 percent of all women killed are victims of intimate murders (FBI, 1999).

Intimate partner violence is not limited to homicide. According to the NSVAW, 7.7 percent of the women surveyed were rape victims at some time during their life. By contrast, only 0.3 percent of males were rape victims during their lifetime. Slightly over 22 percent of the women surveyed were the victims of physical assaults while only 7.4 percent of men surveyed were victims of intimate partner assaults during their lifetimes.

Of course, queries about victimizations in the past 12 months resulted in much lower percentages, although there were gender differences. For incidents in the past 12 months, 0.2 percent of women and none of the men were rape victims. Of women surveyed, 1.3 percent were victims of physical assault, but this was true for only 0.9 percent of men.

While women were more frequently victims of assault, the type of assault for both genders was relatively minor and consisted of pushing, grabbing, shoving, slapping, and hitting. Less than 1 percent for either gender used a gun or a knife.

The difference is not so much the type of assault as the effects. Browne (1997) pointed out that women are just as verbally and physically aggressive as men. What is different is that men who punch, choke, or beat up women, or do all of these things, are simply going to inflict more severe injuries than the same series of actions employed by a woman against a man. The similarity between the genders begins and ends with a *willingness and desire* to employ violence, not the amount of injury inflicted.

Thus, 41.5 percent of women assault victims surveyed claimed they were injured in comparison to 19.9 percent of the men. But there are relatively small differences between men and women as to whether medical care was received. Of those injured, 28.1 percent of the women received medical care compared to 21.5 percent of the men. While over one-third of women rape victims (36.2 percent) were injured, 79.1 percent received hospital care and 51.3 percent were given emergency room treatment. Almost 60 percent (59.2 percent) were treated by a physician.

The NSVAW also asked their respondents about stalking. *Stalking* is defined as

a course of conduct directed at a specific person involving repeated visual or physical proximity; nonconsensual communication; verbal, written, or implied threats; or a combination thereof
that would cause fear in a reasonable person, with 'repeated'
meaning on two or more occasions. (Tjaden & Thoennes, 2000, p.
5)

Among women surveyed, 4.8 percent had been stalked by intimate partners in their lifetimes and 0.5 percent in the last 12
months. Among men, the figures were much lower: 0.6 percent in
their lifetime and 0.2 percent in the last 12 months.

Race and ethnicity. A useful way of describing murder among
different race and ethnic groups, as well as different types of intimate relationships is by examining sex ratios of killing or SROK
(Wilson & Daly, 1992). Sex ratios of killing are the number of homicides perpetrated by women per 100 perpetrated by men. Let us
examine Table 6-1, which shows SROK taken from a study of 2,686
intimate criminal homicides in California from 1987 through 1996
(Riedel & Best, 1998).

Table 6-1
SROK for Relationships by Race/Ethnicity

	Race/Ethnicity							
	White		Latino		African American		Asian/ Pacific Islander	
Relationship	N	SROK	N	SROK	N	SROK	N	SROK
Husband/ Wife	140/ 547	26	34/ 223	15	88/ 119	74	7/ 45	16
CL Husband/ CL Wife	9/ 29	31	17/ 19	89	41/ 31	132	0/ 2	--
Boyfriend/ Girlfriend	86/ 133	65	86/ 353	28	111/ 199	56	2/ 44	5

Source: M. Riedel and J. Best (1998). Patterns in intimate partner homicide:
California, 1987–1996. *Homicide Studies, 2,* 305–320. Copyright © 1998 by Sage
Publications. Reprinted by permission of Sage Publications.

One way of interpreting SROK is that the lower the number, the more women are being killed in relation to men, while the higher the number, the more men are being killed in relation to women. Thus, Table 6-1 shows that for every 100 white wives killed by husbands, 26 white husbands were killed by wives. On the other hand, for African-American common-law (CL) husbands and wives, the SROK is 132, which indicates that for every 100 CL African-American wives killed by CL husbands, 132 CL African-American husbands were killed by wives—a substantial increase in violence parity for women.

For marriage partners, the lowest SROK are for Latinos (15) and the Asian/Pacific Islander category (16). By contrast, the highest husband/wife SROK are for whites (26) and African Americans (74). Research supports the view that the greater the inequality between intimate partners, the greater the risk of violence. Because Latinos and Asian Americans have strong family traditions and, in the case of Latinos, patriarchal family traditions, the wife may be in a subordinate positions and at greater risk (Martinez-Garcia, 1988).

Except for Latinos, Table 6-1 indicates that the boyfriend/girlfriend relationship presents the greatest risk for lethal intimate victimization for females. Asian Americans (5) and whites (24) have the lowest SROK while African Americans have the highest (55).

Table 6-1 shows that CL marriages have the highest SROK of any of the intimate relationships shown. Thus, for every 100 white CL wives killed by CL husbands, 31 CL husbands are killed by wives. Likewise, for Latinos, the SROK is 35; and for African Americans, in fact, more CL husbands are killed by CL wives than the reverse.

Common-law marriages may be a greater source of frustration and conflict than other intimate relationships. Makepeace (1997) states that cohabitation is noted for its normative ambivalence. For example, he cites research indicating that participants disagree about sexual meanings, and when and if they will marry, as well as express concerns about the stability of their relationships.

The NSVAW survey also examined intimate partner violence among race and ethnic groups. Comparing white with nonwhite groups, nonwhite groups have a higher percentage of intimate partner violence over a lifetime. What is most interesting is the nature of similarities and differences among groups.

Excluding the mixed-race group, the largest percentage of rape victims is found among American Indian/Alaska Natives (15.9 percent), and the smallest percentage is found in Asian/Pacific Islander women (3.8 percent). White (7.7 percent) and African-American women (7.4 percent) have similar victimization percentages. Less than 1 percent of males of any race or ethnic group reported being rape victims.

The largest percentage of physical assault victims was the group American Indian/Alaska Natives (30.7 percent). Excluding the mixed-race group (27.0 percent), the next highest percentage was African-American women (26.3 percent), followed by whites (21.3 percent) and Asian/Pacific Islander women (12.8 percent). Tjaden and Thoennes (2000) suggest that traditional Asian values emphasizing close family ties may possibly discourage Asian respondents from disclosing physical and emotional abuse. Moreover, a leading authority on intimate violence, Browne (1997), suggests that many Asian Americans consider marital problems highly private matters that must remain in the family.

Among males, American Indian/Alaska Natives reported the largest percentage of assault victimization (11.4 percent), followed by African Americans (10.8 percent) and whites (7.2 percent). The mixed-race category was 8.6 percent. The number of Asian/Pacific-Islander male victims was less than 5 and was not included in the tables.

No substantively important differences were reported in intimate partner violence between Latino and non-Latino respondents. These results need to be viewed with caution, however, because of the very small number of Latino respondents.

However, the number of Latino respondents was too small to compare where they were born, which may make a difference. In a study of the Los Angeles area, Mexico-born Mexican Americans reported a 12.1 percent lifetime prevalence rate for spousal abuse. However, the rate for U.S.-born Mexican Americans was 30.3 percent. The difference in rates between Mexico-born and U.S.-born Mexican Americans raises the possibility that early socialization in the United States plays an important role in teaching children aggressive patterns toward family members (Sorenson, Richardson, & Peterson, 1993).

Although women are more likely to be stalked than men, there is very little difference among percentages of white and nonwhite women victims. Among white men, 0.6 percent were the victims of stalking 1.1 percent of nonwhite men.

Among women, 10.2 percent of American Indian/Alaska Natives were stalked in their lifetimes; there were too few to tabulate among Asian/Pacific Islander women, and white and African-American women had very similar percentages (4.2 percent versus 4.7 percent, respectively). Among men, 1.1 percent of African-American males and 0.6 percent of white males were stalked during their lifetimes. Latino victims were very similar to non-Latino victims with respect to stalking.

Prior to the NSVAW, research on violence in same-sex relationships was limited to small, nonrepresentative samples of gay and lesbian couples. Although the NSVAW survey did not ask sexual orientation, it did ask whether respondents had ever lived with same-sex partners as part of a couple. Examining lifetime victimization, it appears that same-sex relationships are more violent than opposite-sex relationships.

Among women surveyed, 35.5 percent reported physical assaults in same-sex cohabitation in comparison with 20.4 percent in opposite-sex cohabitation. Among men, 21.5 percent in same-sex cohabitation reported assaults compared with 7.1 percent in opposite-sex cohabitation. None of the women or men in same-sex cohabitation reported stalking by an intimate partner (Tjaden & Thoennes, 2000).

The preceding patterns must be viewed with caution. The NSVAW authors discuss differences between their results and those from the National Crime Victimization Survey. In addition to learning more about why these differences occur, more research needs to be done on race and ethnic differences. For example, little is known about why intimate partner violence is high among American Indians/Alaska Natives. Similarly, this survey is one of few instances of research that has explored intimate partner violence among same-sex couples.

Trends

Using data on the most reliably recorded offense, Figure 6-1 gives the number of murders involving intimate partners from

1976 through 1996. The number of spouse murders has dropped dramatically in the 20-year period studied. In 1976, there were over 2,000 intimate murders, but by 1996, the number of spouse murders had declined to 987. The number of murders involving boy- and girlfriends increased slightly from 662 in 1976 to 749 in 1996. Ex-spouse murders declined slightly from 123 in 1976 to 73 in 1996. Overall, the number of intimate murders decreased by 36 percent and spouse murders decreased by 52 percent between 1976 and 1996 (Greenfeld, 1998).

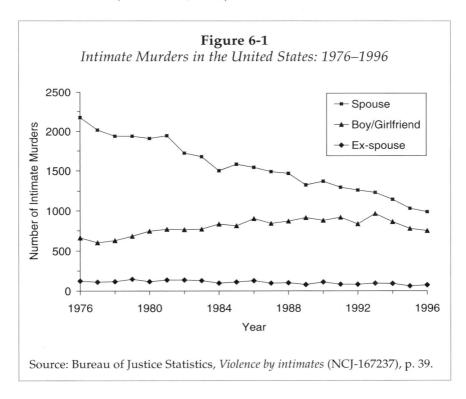

Figure 6-1
Intimate Murders in the United States: 1976–1996

Source: Bureau of Justice Statistics, *Violence by intimates* (NCJ-167237), p. 39.

That was the good news! The bad news is that the decline is lopsided; far more women are being killed in intimate relationships than men, as Figure 6-2 shows. While male murder victims declined from 1,357 cases to 516, female victims declined only from 1,600 to 1,326.

Another way of looking at it is to consider the changes in percentages of male and female intimate partner victims in relation to

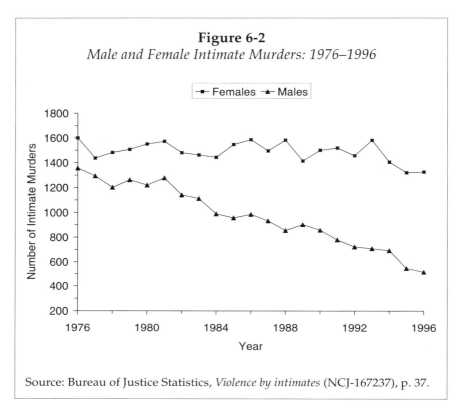

Figure 6-2
Male and Female Intimate Murders: 1976–1996

Source: Bureau of Justice Statistics, *Violence by intimates* (NCJ-167237), p. 37.

total male and female victimization. From that perspective, female intimate victimization declined only from 31.3 percent to 29.0 percent of all female homicides. Male murders declined from 11.2 percent to only 5.4 percent of all male victimizations. The reasons for this differential decline will be discussed in a later section.

Figure 6-3 shows murder rates among intimates broken down by race and sex. It is apparent that much of the decline in men's rates is happening among black males.

During the 20-year period, the intimate murder rate declined an average of 8 percent among black males, 4 percent among white males, 5 percent among black females, and 1 percent among white females. An examination of Figure 6-3 indicates that before 1990, more black males were being killed by their wives than the reverse; after 1990, the murder rate for black female intimate partners was higher than for black male intimate partners.

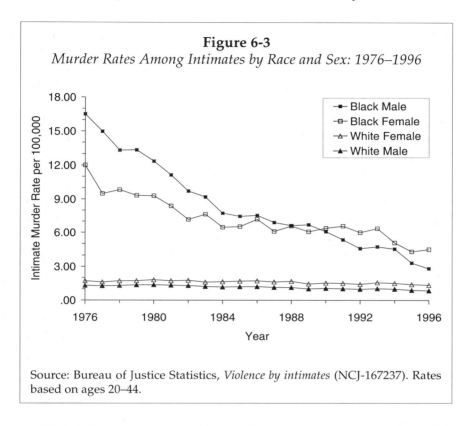

Figure 6-3
Murder Rates Among Intimates by Race and Sex: 1976–1996

Source: Bureau of Justice Statistics, *Violence by intimates* (NCJ-167237). Rates based on ages 20–44.

Trend data on aggravated assaults for intimate partners are difficult to obtain. Although the reliability for NCVS results from 1973 through 1976 is less than for data from the revised survey (see chapter 2), a report covering that period indicates that among violent crimes involving spouses and ex-spouses, 33.9 percent were listed as aggravated assaults (Lentzner & DeBerry, 1980). By comparison, estimates from the 1992 to 1993 redesigned survey indicate that only 1.5 percent of intimate victimizations involved aggravated assaults, clearly a substantial decrease (Bachman & Saltzman, 1995).

Explanations

Research on battered intimate partners has shown a cycle of violence consisting of three stages. The first stage is the *tension-building phase,* during which there is a gradual increase in tension-inducing activities, such as verbal and physical intimidation and physical aggression by the abusing partner. The second stage is the *actual battering incident*, in which the batterer unleashes his aggression and a violent incident occurs. The third stage is one of *loving contrition*, in which the abuser apologizes, shows remorse and numerous kindnesses, and promises that it will never happen again. Of course, because this is a cycle, it is simply repeated with the beginning of the tension-building phase (Walker, 1979).

A single instance of violence toward an intimate partner may, indeed, be a rare and isolated instance in a relationship. Little is known about these occasions, but Browne (1997) cites a number of scholars who suggest that once battering occurs, it often becomes chronic. The first battering incident leaves the victim shaken and vulnerable to expressions of remorse that characterize the third part of the cycle. As the battering is repeated, the battered wife (the most common victim) tries to rationalize what is happening. Beliefs that her husband is under a lot of stress, that she needs to be more understanding, that she is at fault and needs to do a better job as a homemaker, and that she needs to try harder to please her husband are to no avail. She continues to be battered until she either dies of her injuries, moves out and divorces, or kills her tormentor (Browne, 1987).

Other theories include the view that intimate violence is caused by mental abnormalities. Makepeace (1986) finds psychological problems to characterize both male abusers and female victims. Generally, alcohol and substance abuse is a frequent correlate of intimate violence, but the consensus is that neither agent plays a causal role (Browne, 1997; Miller & Wellford, 1997).

Although more research needs to be done, the view that severe physical abuse and neglect in childhood may help to explain intimate violence is supported. Browne et al. state,

> Although later involvement in violence is only one of many potential outcomes of growing up in a violent home, two decades of research on nonlethal assaults by men against female partners documents a sharply increased risk of assaultiveness among men who have experienced or witnessed physical abuse in childhood. (1999, p. 167)

This view receives support from the NSVAW survey. A statistical examination of a large number of causes of intimate partner victimizations revealed a strong link between child maltreatment and subsequent violence. Both women and men who were physically assaulted as children by adult caretakers were more likely to report being victimized by current intimate partners. More research is needed to determine if maltreated children are simply more tolerant of violent behavior and are more likely to get involved with abusive adults. Another possibility is that persons who report child maltreatment are more willing to report other types of victimizations.

For cases of violence that end in homicide, the violent situation is the whole show and the homicidal situation is the final act. Aware that they are going to be beaten yet one more time, battered wives kill because they fear for their lives, because they fear the abuser will harm their children, or simply because, as one woman put it, "I just couldn't take no more beating" (Gillespie, 1989, p. 53).

Short of torture in wartime, it is difficult to find any levels of brutality similar to wife battering. The following case is illustrative:

> Betty and Carl Hundley were married for 10 years. During that time, Carl's abuse of Betty had been constant and severe. He hit her, kicked her, and choked her. He had broken her nose at least five times and had knocked out several of her teeth. He had repeatedly broken her ribs, and he frequently pushed or kicked her down the stairs. She was a diabetic; and a number of times Carl hid her insulin or diluted it with water, causing her to go into diabetic coma. His pattern was to indulge in this sort of violence whenever he was drunk. (Gillespie, 1989, p. 73)

Betty killed Carl and at her trial her sister testified that she had seen Betty beaten so badly that blood poured from her face and stitches were required. In one instance, Betty hid at her sister's home. Carl found her, dragged her from her hiding place by the hair, threw her on the ground, and kicked her until the police arrived.

Six weeks before Carl was killed, Betty was discharged from the hospital from the latest beating. She decided she could take no more, began carrying a gun, and moved into a motel. Carl found her, beat and raped her, and when he threatened to beat her with a beer bottle, she took out the gun and shot him. She was convicted of involuntary manslaughter and sentenced to serve 2 to 5 years in prison (Gillespie, 1989).

The question that frequently arises is, why do women stay in relationships where they are repeatedly and violently attacked? It seems patently apparent to some that there would be no more reason to stay in an intimate relationship of violence than in any other kind of relationship in which a person was harassed or abused.

Several corollaries are consistent with the cycle of violence discussed previously. First, battered women become increasingly socially isolated and lose the "reality check" that contact with friends and family can provide. At the outset of the relationship, the abuser wants her to spend time only with him, which she finds flattering and an indication of her importance to him. As time goes on, however, he gets more and more resentful of any outside contacts with family members, friends, and even eye contact with male strangers. He insists that she not go out shopping or anywhere else without him and to do so is to risk a beating.

Second, the battered woman may be economically dependent on her offender. Without economic skills or a college education, which has been characteristic of women in traditional marriages, what can she do to support herself? This becomes particularly problematic if she has children. Day care is expensive and a minimum wage job is not going to cover the essential living expenses or even make it possible for her to become more marketable through education.

Finally, our earlier discussion of the constraints that battered women face as well as the description of the cycle of violence implies that the most viable theory for why women remain is one of patriarchy. That is, women are viewed as the property of fathers and husbands who may treat them well or badly as they see fit. The view taken here, however, is that the central issue is not patriarchy, but power and control in a relationship—whether a marriage, cohabitation, boy- or girlfriend, or same-sex relationship. Whoever has the greater amount of power and control has the capability to inflict violence on the lesser member without fearing retaliation. The reason patriarchy appears so prominently in discussions of intimate violence is that norms of traditional marriage and their superior capacity to inflict physical injury give males a distinct advantage in relation to power and control. The question that remains unexplored is how intimate partner violence involving males as victims can be explained.

Interventions

Beginning in the 1970s and continuing for the past 30 years, the criminal justice response to domestic violence has proceeded along three parallel tracks: criminal punishment and deterrence of batterers, treatment programs, and restraining orders designed to protect victims (Fagan, 1996). How successful have these changes been?

The most succinct answer is provided by Fagan:

> Thus far, however, research and evaluation on arrest and prosecution, civil or criminal protection orders, batterer treatment, and community interventions have generated weak or inconsistent evidence of deterrent effects on either repeat victimization or repeat offending. For every study that shows promising results, one or more show either no effect or even negative results that increase the risks to victims. (1996, p. 1)

Criminal legal sanctions. The simplest answer to the problem of domestic violence is to arrest the offender. In a Minneapolis experiment, police officers responding to a domestic violence call were randomly assigned three treatments: (1) arresting the suspect; (2) ordering one of the parties out of the residence; or (3) advising the couple. Sherman and Berk (1984) found that subsequent offending was reduced almost 50 percent by arrest.

Replications in five other jurisdictions provided conflicting results. An important factor was the "stake in conformity" hypothesis. Arrest or the threat of arrest was more likely to have a deterrent effect if the offender was employed or married. In short, a criminal justice sanction is effective if it also means the person will lose something he or she values highly, like a job. On the other hand, there are relatively few prosecutions of domestic violence, which may also serve to explain why arrest is not very effective (Fagan, 1996).

Batterer treatment. Treatment programs for batterers vary in their clinical orientation, although most emphasize the need for anger control and attempt to show the batterer the relationship between power and control. Unfortunately, the quality of evaluation research design is such that it is difficult to arrive at any reliable conclusions (Fagan, 1996).

Civil legal sanctions. The use of restraining orders for battered women began in Pennsylvania in 1976. Since that time, every state has provided legislation for protection against domestic violence. The advantages are that protective orders are victim-initiated, rely on a relaxed standard of proof, and offer protection for victims.

Unfortunately, they offer relatively little protection. In one study cited by Fagan (1996), 60 percent of 300 women with protection orders who were interviewed twice in one year suffered abuse at least once. One in five reported threats to kill and severe violence was reported by 29 percent.

The decline in intimate partner homicides. As we have indicated, a wide variety of innovations have been designed to reduce the amount of domestic violence, including homicides. Indeed, as we have seen, domestic homicide rates have declined. The key question is determining what role these legislative and social innovations have played in reducing domestic homicide rates.

A detailed look at the decline in intimate partner homicide was done by Dugan, Nagin, and Rosenfeld (1999). Based on the fact that female intimate partners kill when they are attacked or believe an attack is imminent and on the fact that male violence toward the female is more serious than the reverse, the authors put forth an exposure reduction theory. Exposure reduction theory states that factors that reduce exposure to violent relationships and provide protective alternatives to violence are more closely related to rates at which women kill their partners than rates at which men kill theirs.

The authors found the following:

- The higher the rate of marriage, the higher the rates of male- and female-perpetrated homicide.

- A higher divorce rate lowers the rate at which wives kill husbands, but not the reverse.

- Declining marriage rates and increased divorce rates are associated with increases in the rate of unmarried males killing their partners.

- Results for the effect of educational and economic status differences between partners were mixed.

- The greater availability of hotlines and legal advocacy service is related to a reduction in the rate at which wives kill husbands.

The research on the effectiveness of a number of social changes to protect women in a battering relationship suggests that these changes have a greater effect on whether wives kill husbands than on whether husbands kill wives. One of the most persistent problems in the modern setting is that while battered wives successfully use alternatives to escape violent relationships, laws and policies have been less successful at preventing male intimate partners from pursuing and killing them.

What can be done? Although there is no persuasive evidence to suggest effective responses to the problem of intimate partner violence, the research does offer some useful future avenues. First, the research suggests that legal sanctions are effective when they are reinforced by informal social controls. The "stake in conformity" hypothesis suggests that the deterrent effect of arrests is more likely to work if there is a social cost associated with arrest: loss of job, relationships, and children, and loss of status in the neighborhood. The difficulty with this hypothesis is that offenders may have nothing to lose as a result of arrests. For example, repeat offenders in the Minneapolis experiment as well as in other replications came from neighborhoods characterized by high unemployment, poverty, and divorce rates.

Second, Fagan (1996) suggested that domestic violence cases are not assigned a high priority for prosecution or court action. If prosecutors and courts assign a higher priority to prosecuting other kinds of cases, any deterrent effects will be lost.

Finally, the deterrence logic of criminalization assumes a rational actor—someone who weighs the costs of violence in the form of legal sanctions. In a study of batterers, Dutton (1995) suggested that batterers may have impaired cognition or mental disorders. Clearly, this may be a problem with offenders who pursue their intimate partners after they have left the relationship and who kill them. The behavior may be purposeful, but not rational, which compromises the logic of deterrence.

Violence Toward Other Family Members

The majority of murders do not involve intimate partners or other family members. Using FBI data for the years 1995 through 1997 (for the 32,224 cases on which information was available), 14.5 percent of murders involved intimate partners, 50.1 percent involved other offenders known to victims, and 24.7 percent were stranger murders. Almost 4 percent (3.9 percent) were filicides (the killing of sons and daughters), 1.8 percent were parricides (the killing of parents), 1.4 percent were sororicides or fratricides (the killing of sisters or brothers), and the remainder (3.6 percent) involved "other family" such as stepparents, stepchildren, or in-laws (FBI, 1999).

We discussed intimate partner violence in the preceding section. In this section we discuss the other two most common forms of family violence: parents killing children and children killing parents.

Filicides: Parents Killing Children

Table 6-2 is based on a representative sample of murder cases disposed of in 1988 in 75 of the largest urban counties in the United States. It provides information on patterns for both victims and offenders. Table 6-2 indicates that it is predominantly female parents (54.8 percent) who kill male offspring (55.8 percent). Black parents are prosecuted for killing their children (64.5 percent) more often than white parents (34.5 percent), and black offspring are killed in much higher percentages (65.6 percent) than white children (32.6 percent).

Over half (53.6 percent) of the filicide defendants are under the age of 30. If we include the age 12 to 19 group of victims, almost 90 percent of child victims are 19 years old or younger.

Neonaticides. Neonaticide is the killing of newborns. According to police reports to the FBI for 1995 through 1997, 10.5 percent of parental murder victims are between six days old or younger (FBI, 1999). Although the young mothers are white, poor, and uneducated, there are also those teenage mothers who are terrified at what their parents will think, fear for their physical safety, and are overwhelmed by guilt and shame (Ewing, 1997). Kaiser (1999), writing in the *Chicago Tribune*, reports on an emotionally moving instance of a neonaticide in the small farming community of Poplar Grove, Illinois.

> On February 11, 1996, a newborn baby was found frozen to death in the backyard of one of the townspeople. Police and coroner were called, but despite an extensive investigation, no one was ever charged with the offense. People in this tight-knit commu-

Table 6-2
Sex, Race, and Age Characteristics of Murder Victims and Defendants in 75 Large Urban Counties

		Victims		Defendants	
Characteristic		Parents	Offspring	Parents	Offspring
Sex	Male	57.2	55.8	45.4	81.6
	Female	42.8	44.2	54.8	18.4
Race	White	54.8	32.6	34.5	49.8
	Black	45.2	65.6	64.5	50.2
	Other	0.0	1.8	1.0	0.0
Age	Under 12	0.0	78.5	0.0	0.0
	12–19	0.0	10.9	17.2	38.2
	20–29	0.09	7.7	36.4	30.7
	30–59	56.7	3.0	40.3	29.4
	60 or More	42.4	0.0	6.0	1.7

Source: Dawson, J. M., & Langan, P. A. (1994). *Murder in families* (NCJ-143498), p. 3. Washington, DC: Bureau of Justice Statistics.

nity of 750 were shocked and believed the killing was the work of strangers. Donations paid for the funeral, the town supplied a burial plot, and a monument company contributed a gravestone. 'Baby Doe' was given a name by a group of pastors and said aloud by the townspeople responding as a group at a naming service: 'Angelica Faith Grove.'

Three and a half years later, Kelli Moye, 15 years old at the time of the killing and the daughter of a stable and well-liked family in Poplar Grove, was charged with first-degree murder. Described as 'cheerleader-thin,' she carried the child to term without anyone noticing and gave birth one night as her parents slept downstairs. The boyfriend and father, Michael Mirshak, threatened to reveal Kelli's secret to her parents after they warned him that they would call the police if he continued fighting with her. The parents then questioned the daughter and learned what had happened.

As Ewing (1997) indicates, no one knows how many newborns end up being abandoned by mothers who cannot or will not care for them. He cites figures provided by the American Humane Association, which estimates more than 17,000 children of all ages are abandoned annually by their parents. But the American Humane Association also notes that this is likely an underestimate of a growing problem.

Other child victims. Excluding parental murders during the first year of life, 68.6 percent of parental murders occur to children between the ages of 1 and 5. Only 21.0 percent of parental murders occur after age 5, and most occur before age 18. Even though the number of child murders declines after the age of 5, children frequently remain in a position of abuse and violent victimization. Because they are children, they cannot, like adults, leave deplorable home conditions. In fact, running away subjects the youth to juvenile court intervention.

Juveniles also have far less ability to cope. Many do not know any place of refuge and surviving on their own means doing so with meager financial resources, limited job skills, and incomplete education. Hence, under prolonged conditions of physical, sexual, and psychological abuse, the child may kill the source of his or her pain (Heide, 1992).

Because many child fatalities are not investigated, McClain, Sacks, Froehlke, and Ewigman (1993) integrated police and death certificate data to obtain better estimates. They estimated that the annual number of abuse and neglect fatalities among children under 18 was between 861 and 1814.

As with aggravated assault, there is far more nonlethal child abuse than parental murder. The National Clearinghouse on Child Abuse and Neglect collects extensive data on child abuse and neglect from state child protective services. According to their latest report, just under one million children were victims of substantiated or indicated abuse and neglect in 1997. Fifty-four percent of all victims suffered neglect and 24 percent suffered physical abuse. Two-thirds (67 percent) of all victims were white, and African-American children represented the second largest group (29.5 percent) (U.S. Department of Health and Human Services Administration on Children Youth and Families, 1999).

Parricides: Children Killing Parents

Patterns. Most of what we know about parricides comes from case studies of juvenile homicides referred to mental health professionals for evaluation and treatment. Hence, there is no way of knowing how these offenders differ from other violent juveniles or nonviolent juveniles. Analysis of FBI data from 1977 through 1986 indicates that more than 300 parents and stepparents are killed each year (Heide, 1992). Drawing on data from 75 of the largest urban counties described in Table 6-2, we note that parricide offenders are almost always males (81.6 percent), and defendants are about equally often black and white (49.8 percent versus 50.2 percent). Compared to other groups of children who kill, those who kill their parents are among the youngest; two-thirds of the offenders are under 30 years old (Dawson & Langan, 1994).

The murder of parents by children younger than 12 is very rare, but this does occur and is typically diverted very early in the criminal justice process. There is a general legal consensus that a juvenile under the age of 9 cannot form the notion of criminal intent necessary to make the killing a murder (Heide, 1999). Ewing (1997) gives the example of a 3-year-old boy who watched

> as his intoxicated father beat his mother and threatened her with a pistol. When the man laid the pistol on a table, the boy grabbed it and shot him to death. Later, the boy told authorities, 'I killed him. Now he's dead. If he would have hit my mother, I would have shot him again.' (p. 107)

The view that juvenile killers are on the increase is not supported by the available data. From a low arrested-offender murder rate of 1.6 per 100,000 for juveniles and 7.3 per 100,000 for adults in 1984, both rates increased to a high of 4.9 for juveniles and 8.9 for adults in 1993. Thereafter the rates for both groups declined to 2.5 for juveniles and 5.6 for adults. It is worth noting that juvenile arrest rates in 1997 (2.5) are slightly lower than juvenile offender rates (2.7) in 1978—20 years ago. For the 20-year period, adult offender rates have declined substantially while juvenile rates, except for the peak in 1993, have remained relatively unchanged (Schiraldi, 1999).

As for child abuse, the National Clearinghouse on Child Abuse and Neglect reported on victimization rates from 1990 through

1997. In 1990, the national victimization rate was 13.4 per 1,000 children; it increased to 15.3 by 1993, and by 1997 it had declined to 13.9 per 1,000 children. In short, although child abuse and neglect is still very high (948,000 victims), it has declined steadily since 1993.

Explanations. As with intimate partner violence, the situation involving children that culminates in fatal violence is at the end of a long road of repetitive violence. The most frequent explanation given for violence toward and by children is child abuse. When children are murdered, there is typically a long history of abuse by caregivers, primarily the parents. For small children, the most frequent occasions for abuse are toilet training and colic among infants. Toilet training a toddler requires large amounts of patience and perseverance. Colic occurs among infants who cry without apparent reasons and cause great distress among parents. In either case, parents may lose patience and physically abuse the child.

One of the more frequent expressions of child abuse is **Shaken Baby Syndrome**. This syndrome occurs when the baby's body is vigorously shaken so that the head is repeatedly jerked from back to front, resulting in severe internal bleeding and swelling in the brain, brain stem, spinal cord, or all of these. The outcomes are a variety of neurological damage and, in some cases, death (Ewing, 1997).

There is relatively little known about parents who kill their children. What research is available suggests that child killers come from backgrounds of parental violence, abuse, separation from parents, or the death of a parent.

It has been suggested that cases of neonaticide are the result of dissociative disorders. **Dissociative amnesia** consists of an inability to recall important information, usually of a traumatic or stressful nature. A pregnant teenager who is terrified of what her parents and others will think, fears for her physical safety, and is overwhelmed by guilt and shame may succeed in denying the reality of events until she delivers and is faced with the newborn child. Such a traumatizing event may produce a dissociative state that leads to murder (Kelleher, 1998).

Heide (1992) proposed a three-fold classification of children who kill parents: (1) severely abused children who are pushed beyond their limits; (2) severely mentally ill children; and (3) dangerously antisocial children. Given the role of child abuse in creating parents who kill children, it should come as no surprise that the clinical literature emphasizes the importance of child maltreatment in creating children who kill parents.

Even though most people think of filicide or parricide offenders as mentally ill, mental illness is regarded as playing a less important causal role than child abuse. The research is sparse, but Toupin (1993) classified adolescent homicides into crime-related and conflict-related homicides, and those resulting from mental illness. For 60 homicidal adolescent offenders in Quebec, only five cases, or 8.2 percent, were classified as resulting from psychotic disorders or mental retardation.

There are what Heide (1992) called "dangerously antisocial" offenders. The diagnosis of antisocial personality disorder was attributed to Michelle Ann White, a 14-year-old girl, and her 17-year-old brother, John Jr. The father had obtained custody of the children 10 years before the killing, following his divorce. When John Sr. returned home one evening, he was gunned down by a neighborhood boy while Michelle watched. The two children paid the hit man with three $20 bills from their father's wallet. When the two were arrested, they said the motive for killing their father was that he "had not permitted them to do whatever they wanted" (Heide, 1992, p. 10).

A final characteristic of children who kill distinguishes today's juvenile homicides from those of the past—the unprecedented access to guns. Schiraldi (1999) summarizes the issue:

> Between 1984 and 1994, arrests for gun homicides by juveniles increased an astonishing four-fold, while nongun homicide rates stayed the same. . . . According to one Justice Department study, only 35 percent of America's high school students say that it would be difficult for them to obtain a gun. If America's children had simply become more murder-prone than past generations, one would have expected increases in homicides committed without guns, yet no such increase exists. What is more likely happening is that adolescents today are as together or confused as adolescents have always been, but they have exponentially greater access to handguns. (p. 18)

Interventions. There is little doubt that the problem of child abuse and neglect has been met with legislation encouraging and sometimes requiring reporting by social workers, law enforcement, medical personnel, and educators. Further, treatment and prevention programs and agencies are also available. World Wide Web sites, such as the National Clearinghouse for Child Abuse and Neglect Information (<http://www.calib.com/nccanch/>), provide an abundance of information on how and where to report abuse and neglect as well as publications on various aspects of the problem. Like intimate partner violence, solving the problem of nonlethal violence will contribute to preventing lethal violence.

The law has been active in the more traditional role of providing punishment and deterrence with respect to juvenile homicide offenders, including those who kill parents. In recent decades, however, the public has become outraged at the leniency extended to under-18 homicide murder offenders. As a result, every state has enacted new laws to provide for the prosecution of some juveniles as adults, including the imposition of the death penalty. These laws require that older juveniles who commit the most serious violent crimes (such as homicide, rape, kidnapping, armed robbery, and sodomy) may be prosecuted, convicted, and sentenced to long prison terms and, in some jurisdictions, receive a death sentence.

These laws, variously referred to as transfer, waiver, or certification provisions, can be activated if the court decides that the offender is under 18 and not suitable for treatment as a juvenile. The decision as to whether the offender should be treated as a juvenile is determined by a variety of legal criteria. Joel Eigen (1981) found four factors to be especially predictive of whether a juvenile homicide offender is treated as a juvenile or an adult: (1) the killing takes place during the commission of a felony; (2) the juvenile is 17 years old at the time of the murder; (3) the juvenile is the principal assailant rather than an accessory; and (4) the juvenile has a prior criminal record.

Between 1985 and 1993, nine adults who were juveniles at the time of their crime were executed (Kelleher, 1998). There is little evidence that changes in the law or the imposition of the death penalty account for the decline in juvenile homicides from 1993 through 1997—or have affected the juvenile homicide rate in general. Neither is there evidence that the death penalty is a deterrent and its discriminatory application has been repeatedly demonstrated (Bailey & Peterson, 1998; Bedau, 1982). With respect to changing laws to treat juveniles as adults, remember that harsher punishments have not had a positive effect on adult crime rates. Thus, there is no reason to believe they will be more effective with juveniles (Kelleher, 1998).

Finally, another approach to reduce juvenile homicide has been legislation, and policies to limit access to firearms have been largely unsuccessful. In their study of inner-city youth and guns, Sheley and Wright (1995) point out, first, that simply too many juveniles carry weapons, have access to them, or both, to believe that currently available policies will have any effect. Second, the authors found that self-protection was the most important reason for carrying a weapon. Inner-city dwellers live in a truly dangerous environment; juveniles interact daily with a demographic group characterized by high rates of violence.

Conclusions: Is It Time for Another Look?

The problem of intimate and family violence has been addressed in a typically American fashion: We made laws against it. Although the criminalization of family violence may be an appropriate response, the effectiveness of laws can be questioned. Our conclusion is that arrest in the case of intimate partner violence is of limited value, protection orders are not effective, intimate partner violence does not receive the same kind of attention from the courts as other kinds of crimes, and battering husbands hunt down the wives who have left and kill them.

Other kinds of family violence, though less frequent, are better recorded, but not more effectively treated. Child abuse continues to be a major problem and the consequences of child abuse in adults continue the cycle of violence. Meanwhile, a theme running through all of the preceding is the spotty record of research and evaluation: Not only do we not have adequate knowledge of what works and what does not, we have no knowledge of what works under what kinds of circumstances.

What is needed is not only more research, but a better integration between research and policy. That is, available research on various programs and policies is not organized in a way that informs practices and policies. In addition, the alternatives that have been developed to reduce intimate partner and family violence are often not evaluated in a way that meets minimum methodological standards. Further, continued resources for these programs are made available on the basis of purely political decisions in which evaluations play little or no part.

Finally, intimate partner and family violence occur in what are traditionally and legally viewed as private settings. The prevalence of both types of violence makes it clear that government has a clear and legitimate interest in intervening to protect its citizens. Indeed, the state has a right and obligation to protect its citizens even in private settings. At the same time, privacy and intimacy are central requirements for primary socialization. The challenge is how to reduce intimate partner and family violence without intruding on those important socialization processes that are central to making us humans.

References

Bachman, R., & Saltzman, L. E. (1995). *Violence against women: Estimates from the redesigned survey* (NCJ-154348). Washington, DC: Bureau of Justice Statistics.

Bailey, W. C., & Peterson, R. D. (1998). Capital punishment, homicide, and deterrence: An assessment of the evidence and extension to female homicide. In M. D. Smith & M. Zahn (Eds.), *Homicide studies: A sourcebook of social research* (pp. 257–276). Newbury Park, CA: Sage.

Bedau, H. A. (1982). *The death penalty in America* (3rd ed.). Oxford, UK: Oxford University Press.

Browne, A. (1987). *When battered women kill.* New York: Free Press.

Browne, A. (1997). Violence in marriage: Until death do us part. In A. P. Cardarelli (Ed.), *Violence between intimate partners: Patterns, causes, and effects* (pp. 48–69). Boston: Allyn-Bacon.

Browne, A., Williams, K. R., & Dutton, D. G. (1999). Homicide between intimate partners: A 20-year review. In M. D. Smith & M. A. Zahn (Eds.), *Homicide: A sourcebook of social research* (pp. 149–164). Thousand Oaks, CA: Sage.

Cardarelli, A. P. (1997). Violence and intimacy: An overview. In A. P. Cardarelli (Ed.), *Violence between intimate partners: Patterns, causes, and effects* (pp. 1–9). Boston: Allyn-Bacon.

Caringella-MacDonald, S. (1997). Women victimized by private violence: A long way to justice. In A. P. Cardarelli (Ed.), *Violence between intimate partners: Patterns, causes, and effects* (pp. 144–153). Boston: Allyn-Bacon.

Dawson, J. M., & Langan, P. A. (1994). *Murder in families* (NCJ-143498). Washington, DC: Bureau of Justice Statistics.

Dugan, L., Nagin, D. S., & Rosenfeld, R. (1999). Explaining the decline in intimate partner homicide: The effects of changing domesticity, women's status, and domestic violence resources. *Homicide Studies, 3,* 187–214.

Dutton, D. G. (1995). *The domestic assault of women* (2nd ed.). Boston: Allyn-Bacon.

Eigen, J. (1981). Punishing youth homicide offenders in Philadelphia. *Journal of Criminal Law and Criminology, 72,* 1072.

Ewing, C. P. (1997). *Fatal families: The dynamics of intrafamilial homicide.* Thousand Oaks, CA: Sage.

Fagan, J. (1996, January). The criminalization of domestic violence: Promises and limits. Paper presented at the 1995 Conference on Criminal Justice Research and Evaluation, Washington, DC.

Federal Bureau of Investigation. (1999, May 23). *Supplementary Homicide Reports, 1995–1997.* Available: <http://www.icpsr.umich.edu/cgi/archive.prl>.

Gelles, R. J., & Straus, M. A. (1988). *Intimate violence.* New York: Simon & Schuster.

Gillespie, C. K. (1989). *Justifiable homicide: Battered women, self-defense, and the law.* Columbus: Ohio State University Press.

Greenfeld, L. A. (1998). *Violence by intimates: Analysis of data on crimes by current or former spouses, boyfriends, and girlfriends* (NCJ-167237). Washington, DC: Bureau of Justice Statistics.

Heide, K. M. (1992). *Why kids kill parents: Child abuse and adolescent homicide.* Columbus: Ohio State University Press.

Heide, K. M. (1999). Youth homicide: An integration of psychological, sociological, and biological approaches. In M. D. Smith & M. A. Zahn (Eds.), *Homicide: A sourcebook of social research* (pp. 221–238). Thousand Oaks, CA: Sage.

Kaiser, R. L. (1999, October 24). Mystery gone, not disbelief. *Chicago Tribune,* pp. 1, 12.

Kelleher, M. D. (1998). *When good kids kill.* Westport, CT: Praeger.

Lentzner, H. R., & DeBerry, M. M. (1980). *Intimate victims: A study of violence among friends and relatives* (NCJ-62319). Washington, DC: Bureau of Justice Statistics.

Makepeace, J. (1986). Gender differences in courtship violence victimization. *Family Relations, 35,* 383–388.

———. (1997). Courtship violence as process: A developmental theory. In A. P. Cardarelli (Ed.), *Violence between intimate partners: Patterns, causes, and effects* (pp. 29–47). Boston: Allyn-Bacon.

Martinez-Garcia, A. T. (1988). Culture and wife-battering among Hispanics in New Mexico. In J. F. Kraus, S. B. Sorenson, & P. D. Juarez (Eds.), *Research conference on violence and homicide in Hispanic communities* (pp. 205–214). Los Angeles: UCLA Publication Services.

McClain, P. W., Sacks, J. J., Froehlke, R. G., & Ewigman, B. G. (1993). Estimates of fatal child abuse and neglect, United State, 1979 through 1988. *Pediatrics, 91*, 338–343.

Miller, S. L., & Wellford, C. F. (1997). Patterns and correlates of interpersonal violence. In A. P. Cardarelli (Ed.), *Violence between intimate partners: Patterns, causes, and effects* (pp. 19–26). Boston: Allyn-Bacon.

Renzetti, C. M. (1997). Violence and abuse among same-sex couples. In A. P. Cardarelli (Ed.), *Violence between intimate partners: Patterns, causes, and effects* (pp. 70–89). Boston: Allyn-Bacon.

Riedel, M., & Best, J. (1998). Patterns in intimate partner homicide: California, 1987–1996. *Homicide Studies, 2*, 305–320.

Schiraldi, V. (1999). Making sense of juvenile homicides in America. *America, 181*, 17–19.

Sheley, J. F., & Wright, J. D. (1995). *In the line of fire: Youth, guns, and violence in urban America*. New York: Aldine de Gruyter.

Sherman, L. W., & Berk, R. A. (1984). The specified deterrent effects of arrest for domestic assault. *American Sociological Review, 49*, 261–272.

Sorenson, S. B., Richardson, B. A., & Peterson, J. G. (1993). Race/ethnicity patterns in the homicide of children in Los Angeles, 1980 through 1989. *American Journal of Public Health, 83*(5), 725–727.

Tjaden, P., & Thoennes, N. (2000). *Extent, nature, and consequences of intimate partner violence: Findings from the national violence against women survey* (NCJ 181867). Washington, DC: National Institute of Justice.

Toupin, J. (1993). Adolescent murderers: Validation of a typology and study of their recidivism. In A. V. Wilson (Ed.), *Homicide: The victim/offender connection* (pp. 135–156). Cincinnati, OH: Anderson.

U.S. Department of Health and Human Services Administration on Children Youth and Families. (1999). Child maltreatment 1997: Reports from the states to the national child abuse and neglect data system. Government Printing Office. Available: <http://www.acf.dhhs.gov/programs/cb/stats/ncands97/cm97.htm> [January 10, 2000].

Walker, L. E. (1979). *The battered woman*. New York: Harper & Row.

Wilson, M. I., & Daly, M. (1992). Who kills whom in spouse killings? On the exceptional sex ratio of spousal homicides in the United States. *Criminology, 30*, 189–215.

Zawitz, M. W. (1994). *Violence between intimates: Domestic violence. Selected Findings* (NCJ 149259). Washington, DC: Bureau of Justice Statistics. ✦

Chapter 7

Robbery

Robbery is the theft or attempted theft, in a direct confrontation with the victim, by force or the threat of force. Robbery is one of the most feared crimes in cities, not only because of its relative frequency but also because of its psychological and physical consequences on victims.

Below are three descriptions of actual robbery incidents adapted from a newspaper article (Marder, 1992). What patterns do these incidents suggest about robbery offenses, victims and offenders, settings where robberies occur, and motivations of offenders? How typical do you think these incidents are of most robberies?

In the first incident, two men stopped at an ATM machine after a Saturday evening of dinner and drinks in a fashionable area of the city. Although the hour was late, there was a line. A 17-year-old clutching a .22-caliber handgun approached one man and announced, "This is a stickup." The man hesitated and was shot in the back of the head. Thus ended the life of Richard L. Barbour, Jr., 27, an assistant county prosecutor in New Jersey. Yerodeen Williams, the 17-year-old convicted murderer, later said: "He brung this on himself." Williams said Barbour had failed to follow a basic rule of robbery: When you are approached by a thief, do what he says. "Give it up," Williams said. "If he'd have done that, that man would still be here. If you hesitate, somebody gonna give it to you. Shoot you" (Marder, 1992, p. A01).

In the second incident, Andre Johnson, 16, and two friends were walking through Clark Park in West Philadelphia in October 1988 when they encountered Seung Ki Leung, 25, a University of

Pennsylvania graduate student coming home from a touch football game. Johnson picked up a tree limb and smashed Leung's skull. As the student lay dying, Johnson and his friends went through the student's pockets and took $11.61. He was obliged to kill, Johnson later said from prison, because Leung had looked him directly in the eye. "You walk past somebody, you don't look them right in the eye. . . . You keep walking; you mind your business. If our eyes meet, the dude's looking for trouble" (Marder, 1992, p. A01).

The third incident involved Ruth Wahl, a 22-year-old drugstore cashier in Detroit. Ruth was driving with three friends in her shiny white Suzuki Sidekick, her first car. About midnight, she drove into the parking lot of the Vernor Elementary School and parked. They were just opening a beer when three young men in a brown station wagon drove into the lot and approached. One of the women warned Ruth that nobody comes there, and that they had better go. Ruth drove away with the station wagon in pursuit but lost a race down deserted streets when the wagon finally trapped the Suzuki against a curb. A man with a gun jumped out, shouting, "Gimme your truck, bitch" (Marder, 1992, p. A01). He opened fire, though, killing Ruth Wahl. Unfortunately, such incidents are not rare. Armed robbers are increasingly commandeering cars stopped at traffic lights, restaurant parking lots, automatic-teller machines, pay telephones, and self-serve filling stations (Rand, 1994).

Patterns and Trends

Using official statistics such as the National Crime Victimization Survey (NCVS) and Uniform Crime Reports (UCR) (see chapter 2), we can examine important patterns and trends in robbery over time. As with other types of crimes, the NCVS shows higher rates of robberies than the UCR, even though the NCVS excludes commercial robberies and victims aged less than 12 years. We focus mainly on victimization figures here, because they detect a greater proportion of actual crime that has occurred.

As Figure 7-1 illustrates, robbery rates recorded by the NCVS fluctuated between 1973 and 1999, reaching peaks in 1974, 1981 (the recorded high), and 1994 (Rand, Lynch, & Cantor, 1997). There is some very good news, however: Robbery rates recorded by the

NCVS reached a 27-year low in 1999 (Rennison, 2000). Robbery rates began to decrease sharply after 1994 and have continued to decrease every year since (Figure 7-1). From 1993 to 1999, robbery rates decreased 34 percent (from 6.0/1,000 to 3.6/1,000). The bad news, if any, is that robberies still occur far too frequently. An estimated 810,000 robberies occurred in 1999, accounting for nearly 11 percent of all personal crime victimizations.

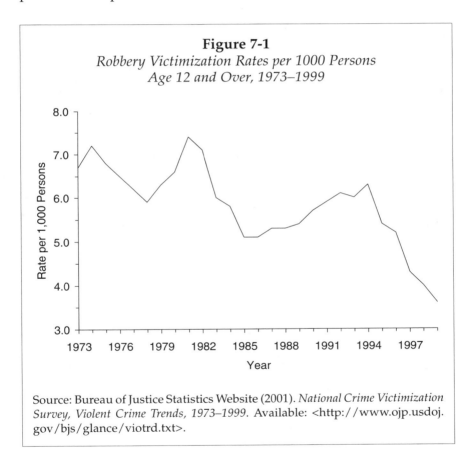

Figure 7-1
Robbery Victimization Rates per 1000 Persons Age 12 and Over, 1973–1999

Source: Bureau of Justice Statistics Website (2001). *National Crime Victimization Survey, Violent Crime Trends, 1973–1999*. Available: <http://www.ojp.usdoj.gov/bjs/glance/viotrd.txt>.

Over a longer period of time (since World War II), however, robberies of banks and convenience stores have increased. The number of robberies of small branch banks has increased tremendously, possibly because these are often located in vulnerable areas, such as small malls in residential areas. Numbers of convenience stores have also increased dramatically, offering potentially attractive targets to offenders. Suitable targets include businesses that are open 24 hours a day, have rapid cash flow, poor visibility from the outside of the store, or poor security features (Cohen & Felson, 1979). We return to this point later in this chapter.

Needless to say, robbery figures are unacceptably high even though recent trends have been encouraging. Next, we attempt to find some general patterns in robbery offenses, offenders, and victims, and perhaps question some popular myths and exaggerations about robbery.

First of all, we examine possible patterns in the offense of robbery. For example, how many robberies result in the **death** of the victim? The answer may surprise you. Estimates suggest that one in 10 homicides is due to a robbery (Cook, 1987). However, police coding of robberies is often difficult because many robbery murders go unsolved and may be classified instead as incidents such as "suspected felony" or "unknown motives." But the likelihood that any one robbery victim will be killed is quite low (about 1.5 out of 1,000). Of course, there are far fewer homicides than robberies, and no slight of hand is involved here. The total number of robberies, rather than homicides, is the appropriate denominator to use in answering this particular question. The appropriate numerator is the number of robbery victims who are killed.

Next, how often does **injury** occur during the course of a robbery? Injuries are common, but serious injuries are rare. About one-third of victims of noncommercial robbery suffer some injury during the robbery, but only 2.6 percent are injured seriously enough to require inpatient care at a hospital (Cook, 1983). Does risk of injury increase with victim resistance? Intuition suggests so, but the evidence is not entirely clear. If we look at completed robberies, 59.8 percent of victims suffering injury reported taking some form of self-protection,[1] while only 45.2 of victims reporting no injury took self-protective measures. If we look at attempted robberies only, victims suffering injury were as likely as those avoiding injury to take self-protective measures—81.3 percent versus 83.6 percent (Bureau of Justice Statistics, 1995).

Wright, Rossi, and Daly's (1983) data further show that offenders' most common self-reported motivations for use of weapons during a crime are, in order of importance, "to intimidate the victim," "to protect myself," and "to get away." Numerous studies have reported high correlations between victim resistance and violence by robbery offenders (Conklin, 1972; Luckenbill, 1981; Block, 1977), but Cook (1986) points out that the actual causal direction of violence is difficult to determine from police records. In other words, do victims "resist" before they are attacked by the robber, thinking it is prudent to do so, or do they "resist" after being attacked, perceiving that the offender is so bent on vicious conduct that the victim has nothing to lose by resisting? In short, it may not be entirely correct to say that resistance is futile, but the weight of the evidence suggests that it is not a good idea.

What, then, do we know about the likelihood of an offender using a **weapon,** or the effect of weapon usage on the **value of the take**? In about one half of all personal robberies, offenders are unarmed, and only about 25 percent of robberies involve a gun (Cook, 1987; Rennison, 2000). For commercial robberies (businesses, such as banks or convenience stores), the likelihood of a gun is much higher (about half). In general, the use of a gun seems to increase the likelihood of robbery success and the amount stolen, but minimizes the chances of the victim being attacked (Cook, 1983). Usually, the "take" is very small. Value of items stolen was less than $50 in 37 percent of cases; value exceeded $250 in only 17 percent of cases (36 percent of cases for commercial robbery).

Where do robberies occur, and why might the **location** be important? Robbery rates are highest in large cities (Bureau of Justice Statistics, 1995). Most robbers reside in poverty areas and strike close to home; those who do travel tend to seek more lucrative targets in commercial areas of the city (Rhodes and Conly, 1991).

Next, we examine **offender and victim demographics** and detect several important patterns. For example, robberies tend to be committed by young (75 percent younger than age 25) males (90 percent); about half of all offenders are black. Juveniles accounted for about 33 percent of all robberies in 1995, according to FBI statistics (Sickmund, Snyder, & Poe-Yamagata, 1997). Victims largely (not exclusively) match the same categories. In other words, blacks were victimized at about three times the rate for whites. Hispanics were twice as likely as non-Hispanics to be victimized. Victimization rates were highest for those aged 16 to 19, but also very high for ages 12 to 15 and 20 to 24 (Ringel, 1997).

The likelihood of robbery victimization corresponds inversely with income: the lower the income, the higher the robbery victimization rate. For example, those earning less than $7,500 (household income) were more than four times as likely to be robbery victims as those earning above $75,000 (Rennison, 2000).

What do we know about the **relationship between robbery victims and offenders**? Unlike other violent crimes, the likelihood that robbery offenders and victims are strangers is much higher. In 1999, for example, 69 percent of victims of rape and sexual assault knew their attackers, in contrast to only 34 percent of robbery victims (Rennison, 2000). The likelihood of a victim reporting a robbery to police (61 percent) was also much greater than for rape or sexual assault (28 percent) (Rennison, 2000). Most robberies involved two or more offenders (58 percent) and a single victim (92 percent) (Ringel, 1997).

Is there a relationship between *drug use* and robbery? Do drug users commit more robberies? The answer isn't clear, although *seriously addicted* drug users commit robberies at a very high rate. The most predatory offenders (high-rate, heroin-addicted offenders) committed 15 times more robberies, 20 times more burglaries, and 10 times more thefts than offenders who did not use drugs (Chaiken, 1986). Studies conducted among heroin users in Baltimore (Ball, Shaffer, & Nurco, 1983) and New York (Johnson et al., 1985) demonstrated that active drug use accelerated the users' crime rate by a factor of four to six and that the crimes committed while people were on drugs were at least as violent, or more so, than those committed by people who did not use drugs. Rand Inmate Surveys (Petersilia, Greenwood, & Lavin, 1977) indicated that among robbers (those who reported committing robbery), drug users had an offense rate twice that of nonusers. Studies of crack users indicate that the robbery rate for this group is as high or higher than heroin-related crime, and their crimes are more violent (Lipton, 1995).

Finally, we want to know if robbers *specialize* in robbery, or if instead, robbery is part of a more general pattern or career of criminal behavior. Evidence suggests that a small number of robbery offenders are indeed very active (Chaiken, 1986), but most commit robbery only opportunistically and occasionally (one or two a year). Robbers are likely to be involved in many other types of crime as well.

Explanations

Now that we have examined some of the most significant patterns and trends associated with robbery, we are better equipped to ask two questions: (1) how can we *explain* such behavior (i.e., what are the causes?), and (2) what can we *do* about it (i.e., what are strategies for intervention and prevention?). Again, we caution that any useful theory must be capable of addressing known patterns and trends. Any theory that is incapable of explaining observable patterns cannot possibly yield useful information. In addition, any useful theory about what causes robbery or motivates offenders should provide useful suggestions for prevention and intervention.

Earlier in this chapter we examined three specific robbery incidents to search for similarities. We return shortly to these young offenders to explore their motivations for committing such terrible crimes. Although their explanations varied, these and many other offenders focused on the negative influence of family, friends, or the brutal environment they had to contend with. Explanations can be broken down into two broad categories: environmental influences (where people live and how they carry out their routine activities) and social psychological explanations (how people perceive themselves and interact with others). As you read the following sections, ask yourself five questions. What are some of the different explanations that offenders offer for committing robbery? To what degree does the evidence suggest individual responsibility on the part of the offender? On the part of the victim? Do external factors, such as the offender's income and environment, help understand robbery? Do different causes or explanations call for different solutions?

Strain Theory and Differential Opportunity Theory

Violence, heavily concentrated in the poorest of neighborhoods, is decimating a generation of young men of color, according to Deborah Prothrow-Stith (1991), Assistant Dean of the Harvard University School of Public Health. She argues that the impact of living in an environment saturated with violence and fear is reshaping the lives of poor children. Disputes that were once resolved by fistfights now end in gun battles, and young men, frequently young black men, willingly use violence for economic gain. Homicides committed by teenagers often occur during robberies or after minor arguments (Marder, 1992).

One convicted offender said that mainstream America has created the formula for violence (Marder, 1992):

> White America is placing drugs into the neighborhood. No black 15-year-old is bringing drugs into the neighborhood. . . . My mind was thinking as a monster. The white community created that. (p. A01)

While the blame-diverting nature of this justification is obvious, some support exists for such views. Prothrow-Stith (1991) argues that white teenagers will never feel the hopelessness or alienation of black teenagers. Such disenfranchisement reduces hope and investment in the future and instead encourages short-term, impulsive (sometimes violent) behavior.

Some offenders said that their behavior was a logical adaptation to an environment in which there are only two readily available means, each illegal, to earn a living (Marder, 1992, p. A01). "The drug dealers are the only ones who can give you a job: lookout person, holder, pusher," one convicted offender said. "You either become a drug dealer or a stickup person." Such statements evoke differential opportunity theory, discussed in chapter 4.

Cloward and Ohlin (1960) argued that individual motivations do not by themselves explain delinquency. Instead, the individual must be in a deviant or conforming environment that allows him or her to learn requisite skills and abilities. Legitimate opportunities may be blocked, but illegitimate ones must be available before the individual can choose one or the other. The deprivation of legitimate means produces a strain toward delinquency, but behavioral adaptations can take many different forms, depending on exactly what specific illegitimate opportunities are available in the environment. If delinquency emerges because of unequal opportunity and the widespread availability of illegitimate opportunities, then the clear policy implications of this theory are that alternatives to delinquent subcultures and illegitimate opportunities must be provided. Cloward and Ohlin's differential opportunity theory heavily influenced social interventions under the Johnson presidency, known as the "War on Poverty" and the

"Great Society" (e.g., education, job training, skill training, community resource centers).

Control Theory

As Hirschi (1969) and others have suggested, weak social bonds to parents, schools, and other institutions of socialization lead to weakened transmission of values and ineffective social and cultural constraints against delinquency. Social bonding, in contrast, is the mechanism by which effective controls and constraints are learned. But most young offenders did not grow up in two-parent families: One parent, grandparents, or foster parents typically raised children. Most do not recount happy family lives (Marder, 1992, p. A01): "Mom's using drugs, Pop's not around, so they bring up their own selves," according to Kerry Marshall, a young offender serving a life sentence for a robbery-murder. He said that even mothers like his, who are hardworking and are not on drugs, are preoccupied. Another offender said he sold drugs and gave some of the proceeds to his mother: "I'd tell her somebody gave it to me. . . . Eventually she knew, but she couldn't do nothing. Mom'd say: 'As long as you don't get caught.' " Andre Johnson, who robbed and killed the student in the incident described earlier in this chapter, never lived with his father and last saw him two years before committing murder:

> 'I barely knew him,' he said. 'I seen him a few times. He's not my father except medically. I give him respect and stuff 'cause he's the dude that brought me into the world. But as far as giving me advice—forget it.' (p. A01)

In such an environment, school is not taken seriously: "I wasn't much interested in learning," one offender said. "School wasn't happening. I'd go to advisory, check in and leave." Nor was the risk of life imprisonment much of a deterrent to committing violent crime: "My brothers used to tell me, don't ever go to jail. . . . But I saw that they went to jail and they were all right. They survived."

Techniques of neutralization. In the first two robbery incidents described in this chapter, the assailants were both young males who expressed justifications for their actions by blaming their victims. Interviews with defendants, lawyers, and family members in 57 cases showed a disturbing pattern: With few exceptions, the teenagers felt little remorse (Marder, 1992). Such expressions are reminiscent of the **techniques of neutralization** described by Sykes and Matza (1957). These are essentially inappropriate extensions of common excuses for rule violations found in the larger culture. According to Sykes and Matza, delinquents are part of the larger culture and subscribe to many of its values, but they episodically "drift" into delinquency by utilizing techniques of neutralization that reduce constraints on their behavior and rationalize deviations from conventional values.

Differential Association Theory

Robberies are increasingly committed by young males, acting in groups of two or more, often in response to peer influence. Among the basic propositions of differential association theory are that criminal behavior is learned in interaction with other persons through a process of communication, primarily within intimate personal groups (Akers, 1997). Learning involves techniques for committing the crime as well as motives, drives, attitudes, and rationalizations.

According to results from the Habitual Offenders Survey (Petersilia et al., 1977), many offenders' careers progressed from auto theft and burglary to an increasing proportion of robberies. Rightly or wrongly, offenders perceived that robberies would require little preparation and few tools, were easy, usually didn't require hurting anyone, and provided unlimited targets. *Juvenile* offenders tended to report expressive needs for committing such crimes (thrills, peer influence). They were less likely to plan their crimes than adults and more likely to use partners. *Adults* tended more often to report motivations of financial need and the desire for high living (drugs, alcohol, women) (for similar findings, see recent research by Jacobs and Wright, 1999). Adults were more likely to plan their offenses and were much less likely to use partners as they got older.

Symbolic Interaction Theory

Symbolic interaction theory focuses on the *meaning* of events as perceived by participants in specific interactions with one another. Those meanings, as we shall soon see, have significant implications for understanding the motives of robbers.

Not all robbers commit their offenses with equal frequency. **Persistent offenders** refers to a small group of criminals who commit an unusually large share of robberies and assaults (Chaiken & Chaiken, 1982). Persistent robbers continue criminal careers despite lengthy periods of incarceration in their youthful years. Violence itself may be part of the attraction of robbery for these offenders (Katz, 1991).

Purely materialistic explanations for robbery are of limited usefulness, according to Katz (1991). Although legitimate opportunities are lacking in the communities where robbery typically occurs and offenders typically live, the rewards of street robbery are minimal (Katz, 1991). In fact, nonviolent forms of criminality, such as burglary, are often more rewarding and present fewer risks. Further, why should robbery be so overwhelmingly (90 percent) a *male* endeavor, if poverty is the primary motivating factor? Instead, Katz suggests, we should focus less on looking for common background factors of persistent robbers and focus more on how persistent robbers, a small and unique group accounting for the largest proportion of robberies, construct and sustain the attractions of robbery, in fact overcoming numerous discouragements, such as the low gain, high risk, and lengthy periods of incarceration accompanied by persistent robbery. Methodologically, this perspective requires less emphasis on statistical data describing biographical and ecological background factors and more emphasis on life histories and narratives told from the perspectives of offenders (Katz, 1988).

Katz argues that persistent robbers recall adolescent years during which they attempt to perfect "badass" identities, demonstrating their willingness to use violence beyond any calculation of legal, material, and physical costs to themselves. Even in younger years, persistent offenders report using violence to silence insults of peers, to avoid being made a fool of, and to dominate a threatening environment. Evidence suggests that violent predators maintain a constant readiness for violence, expecting that others will similarly launch unprovoked attacks (Wright & Rossi, 1994). In robberies, unprovoked violence may also allow the offender to gauge victim compliance, and perhaps fulfill other monetary desires (e.g., kidnapping the victim and escorting him or her to the victim's home or an ATM to increase the take) or nonmonetary desires (e.g., sexual assault, demonstrating to one's peers that one is indeed a "badass"). In spite of such anticipations, "persistent robbers know intimately that the crime is shot through with uncertainties and uncontrollable risk" (Katz, 1991, p. 288). Indeed, it is acting in the face of such wild uncertainty that allows the robber to present himself as a "badass." Persistent robbers, heavily involved in deviant lifestyles, engage frequently in other types of crime, drinking, drug use, gambling, partying, sexual promiscuity, and so on, scoffing at conventional lifestyles and presenting themselves as more brave, more adventurous, more "alive" than others. The pursuit of physical pleasure and awareness, reinforced by constructing and strengthening a "badass" identity, provides strong motivation for persistent robbers.

Similarly, ethnographic research (e.g., interviews) conducted with 86 active armed robbers found that robbery stems most directly from a perceived need for quick cash, but this decision is activated, mediated, and shaped by participation in street culture (Jacobs & Wright, 1999; Wright & Decker, 1997). For example, many offenders had no permanent address, and their lifestyle emphasized a "perpetual search for good times" (p. 155). As Jacobs and Wright (1999) put it,

> The overall picture that emerges from our research is that of offenders caught up in a cycle of expensive, self-indulgent habits (e.g., gambling, drug use, and heavy drinking) that feed on themselves and constantly call for more of the same. (p. 163)

Street culture values the hedonistic pursuit of sensory stimulation, spontaneity, disdain for conventional living, lack of future orientation, and persistent denial of individual responsibility. "Street-corner capitalism" is typified by the need to constantly prove that one is hip, cool, and "in" by conspicuous displays and outlays of cash (Jacobs & Wright, 1999, p. 165). Naturally, such behaviors create the very reinforcing conditions that drive offenders to rob in the first place (i.e., pressing needs for fast cash), but such financial motivations usually become more a matter of maintaining a certain lifestyle and self-image. That is, few persistent offenders said they robbed to support starving children or a family. This sequence of events is diagrammed in Figure 7-2. We have added corresponding references to the various theories discussed in this section.

Figure 7-2
Cycle of Events Leading to Robbery

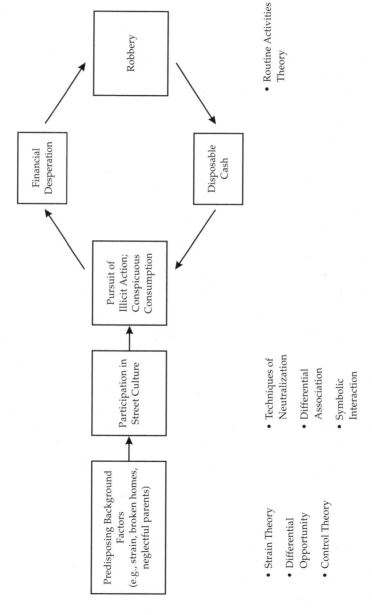

Source: Adapted with permission from Jacobs and Wright (1999, p. 166).

Routine Activities Theory

Why do robberies occur much more often in some places than in others (i.e., the poorest areas of large cities), and why do both offenders and victims tend to be largely young, minority males? The notion of "place" is important to understand and explain these patterns. For our purposes, a "place" typically refers to a specific address, building, or street corner, but it must always be "a fixed physical environment that can be seen completely and simultaneously, at least on its surface, by one's naked eyes" (Sherman, Gartin, & Buerger, 1989, p. 31).

According to routine activities theory, predatory crimes such as robbery are influenced by the convergence in space and time of three necessary elements: (1) motivated offenders, (2) suitable targets, and (3) the absence of capable guardians. All three must be present for a crime to occur. Conversely, crime can be prevented by removing or altering any of these three elements, especially by reducing the attractiveness of targets (e.g., traveling in pairs rather than alone) or improving supervision, security, or natural surveillance opportunities in specific places. In addition, places, like persons, have their own observable routine activities that are subject to both formal and informal regulation (Sherman et al., 1989). Those places that have unusually high rates of robbery or other predatory crime can be called "hot spots," and we are interested in how such place-specific crime rates can be explained.

In a Minneapolis study of hot spots, Sherman and colleagues (1989) found that 4,166 robbery calls between 15 December 1985 and 15 December 1986 were located in only 2.2 percent of all definable "places" in the city. There were 113 places with more than five robberies in one year. Not only was robbery highly concentrated in a relatively small number of places, it was even more concentrated than the offenses of auto theft and rape. But do places "cause" crimes? What makes a spot hot?

Predatory stranger offenses, such as robbery, seem dependent on places where motivated offenders are especially *likely* to come into contact with vulnerable victims and low surveillance (Sherman et al., 1989). Such places seem to share common elements. The five hottest of the hot spots in Minneapolis for robberies, rapes, and auto thefts were the following: (1) an intersection that included bars, a liquor store, and a park, (2) a bus depot, (3) an intersection that included homeless shelters and bars, (4) a downtown mall, and (5) an intersection that included an adult bookstore and several bars. Such places are busy (high number of potential targets), and they provide a clientele that may be engaged in legal (e.g., alcohol consumption) or illegal activities (e.g., prostitution, drug use or sales) that increase their vulnerability and reduce their likelihood of reporting crimes to the police. Police patrols and citizen involvement in crime prevention activities are also less likely in many (but not all) of these hot spots (Sherman et al., 1989).

A research study in Washington, DC (Rhodes & Conly, 1991), investigated how offenders actually select targets for certain offenses and how far they travel (i.e., the "criminal commute"). Like everyone else, offenders obtain environmental cues about people and places from their regular, everyday routine activities (e.g., trips to work, school, shopping, recreation, etc.). Over time, all people construct "cognitive maps" of the urban areas with which they are most familiar. A person's cognitive map depends upon where she goes and what she does. Implications are that offenders will use cognitive maps (based on their own routine activities) to make decisions about where to commit illegal activities. Offenders will commit offenses near their own homes, because these are areas they know best. Further, the more instrumental (goal-oriented) the offense (i.e., robbery), the greater the travel. Social disorganization theory (see chapter 4) has similarly shown us that offenders are clustered in certain areas of the city (i.e., the poorest inner-city neighborhoods with low levels of social cohesion), so it makes sense that crimes such as robbery will also be clustered in certain areas.

In Washington, DC, Rhodes and Conly (1991) looked at three types of crime: robbery, burglary, and rape. They matched up land-use data with offender (i.e., residence) and offense (i.e., crime site) data. They examined characteristics of the immediate environment where offenders lived, the surrounding area, the site of the offense, and the distance traveled. Some places indicated "good" targets to offenders, while others did not.

The distance traveled to commit a crime was greatest for robbery, then burglary, and the least for rape. The majority of all offenses occurred within two miles of the offender's home. When they looked at the site of the offense, the researchers found that victimized areas for robbery and burglary tended to be more transitional[2] and more heavily used for large business and special purposes. Offenders were most likely to move into "transitional" areas to commit robbery and least likely to move into single residential areas and "mixed use" areas. In conclusion, there is distinct movement by robbers into transitional areas and large business areas, but for the most part, offenders commit crimes near their homes (consistent with the ideas of routine activities and cognitive maps).

Interventions

Criminal Justice Approaches

In recent years, criminal justice efforts to reduce robbery have focused mainly on deterrence (i.e., increased law enforcement) and incapacitation (i.e., increased sentences) (Wright & Decker, 1997). For example, strategies have focused on reducing robberies by increasing law enforcement in specific high risk places, such as subways, or by targeting situational correlates of robbery (e.g., mandatory sentences for illegal weapon carrying and use of a weapon during a felony).

During the years 1965 to 1971, New York City dramatically increased the number of uniformed officers patrolling its subway system. Robberies dropped significantly as a result of the increased police presence, but as in many other studies, robberies were simply displaced to different nearby locations (Chaiken, Lawless, & Stevenson, 1974). Studies have failed to consistently demonstrate any clear-cut reduction in crime due to increased police presence alone (e.g., Kelling, Pate, Dieckman, & Brown, 1974).

The Bartley-Fox Gun Law was passed in Massachusetts in 1975. The law provided for a one-year mandatory minimum sentence for anyone convicted of carrying and possessing a firearm in public without a proper license and gun permit. Originally, the bill was intended to punish offenders more harshly and limit the discretion of sentencing judges. However, as eventually adopted, the law did not prohibit prosecutors from reducing a carrying charge to a simple charge of possession, a crime not covered by the minimum sentence. Two years after the law's passage, researchers found decreased gun assaults, gun robberies, and gun homicides (Pierce & Bowers, 1979). After three years, there was still a slight drop in gun robbery rates, but an increase in nongun armed robberies, suggesting that the law's initial deterrent impact may have been only temporary. Process evaluation also suggested that the law had been vigorously enforced initially, but over the next two years increased confusion by police about its applicability and increased discretion by judges had undercut its intent (Beha, 1977; Rossman, Floyd, Pierce, McDevitt, & Bowers, 1979).

Researchers evaluated the impact of mandatory sentences in six cities in three states (Florida, Michigan, and Pennsylvania) where statutes for carrying a firearm while committing a felony were sufficiently similar to permit analysis using a quasi-experimental research design (Loftin & McDowall, 1981). Although the effects of sentence severity (alone) on violent crime rates are often questioned by criminologists, research results in this study indicated that mandatory sentencing provisions clearly reduced the gun homicide rate, but had little to no impact on the nongun homicide rate.

More recently, laws have taken aim at "repeat" offenders (e.g., **three strikes laws**). Some laws have attempted to focus on **career** robbers, but few robbers specialize, making prediction of who will become a **high-rate** offender extremely difficult. It is instructive to look at three strikes laws as an example. Three strikes laws have become extremely popular as a means of putting away repeat offenders (Welsh & Harris, 1999). However, such laws are beset with serious weaknesses, including poorly defined target populations, discrimination against minorities, lack of acceptance and use by prosecutors, and lack of prison space (see chapter 12). Moreover, it is unlikely that criminal justice responses alone are sufficient to produce a substantial decrease in robbery. As Wright and Decker (1997, p. 133) argue, "Threatened criminal penalties for armed robbery already are severe; there is little reason to believe that increasing them will deter the offenders from committing further stickups."

Opportunity Reduction Strategies

Routine activities theory suggests that robbery can be reduced via reducing opportunities to commit robbery. For example, could we reduce robbery by encouraging potential targets to protect themselves: to avoid high crime areas, to not walk alone at night, to not wear expensive jewelry or clothing, and so forth? Could we reduce robbery by increasing surveillance by citizens and businesses in areas at high risk for robbery?

First, evidence suggests that the physical characteristics of stores, buildings, and other places can be manipulated to decrease the risk of robbery. Hunter and Jeffery (1992) reviewed the effects of various measures designed to reduce robbery of convenience stores through a situational strategy called **Crime Prevention Through Environmental Design** (CPTED). Robbery of convenience stores occurred 36,434 times in the United States in 1989 (a 28 percent increase since 1985). Costs included financial losses, physical and mental harm to clerks and clients, loss of business from stores, fear of employees to work in stores, and costs of security and police responses. Positive effects were obtained through the use of CPTED. Four major strategies reduced robbery risk: (1) two or more clerks on duty (employee surveillance), (2) improved cash-handling techniques (i.e., target removal), (3) better access control, and (4) increased natural surveillance. Research methods included physical site assessments, interviews with victims and offenders, and experiments comparing control sites with stores undergoing preventive modifications.

Crow and Bull (cited in Hunter & Jeffery, 1992) examined 349 stores owned by Southland Corporation (i.e., 7-Eleven). A scale of "target attractiveness" was developed based on rankings of different environmental features by former robbers. A field study examined 60 treatment stores and 60 matched control stores. Effective prevention strategies included following limits on available cash and posting of signs to that effect; enhanced visibility and less obstruction of windows; use of security alarms and surveillance cameras; and employee safety training.

Duffala (1976) examined whether *spatial attractiveness* was associated with robbery. He looked at four features: (1) whether a store was located within two blocks of a major street, (2) whether it was located on a street with light amounts of traffic, (3) whether it was located in a residential or vacant land use area or both, and (4) whether it was located in an area with few surrounding commercial activities. No one variable was significant alone, but all four were significant in interaction with one another.

Jeffery, Hunter, and Griswold (cited in Hunter & Jeffery, 1992) assessed 34 convenience stores in Tallahassee, Florida, from January 1981 to July 1985. Thorough security and environmental assessments were conducted at each store, and records of robberies were obtained from police. Risk of robbery was reduced by the following: a cashier located in the center of the store; more than one clerk on duty; clear visibility within the store and from outside the store; stores located near commercial property; stores located near residential property rather than vacant lots; stores near other evening activities; location of gas pumps on the property; and good cash-handling policies.

In Gainsville, Florida, city ordinances were passed in 1986 and 1987 requiring various operational procedures for convenience stores (Clifton & Callahan, cited in Hunter & Jeffery, 1992). In 1986, ordinances required limitation of cash, a security safe, parking lot lighting, removal of visual obstructions, robbery detection cameras, and training of clerks. Robberies, however, continued at an alarming rate. The 1987 ordinances specified that stores had to either close between 8:00 p.m. and 4:00 a.m. or else utilize two clerks on duty. Afterward, a dramatic decline in robberies began, precipitating a decline in convenience store robberies for the state overall. State-recommended security procedures were issued in 1989, and in 1990 the Florida legislature enacted the Convenience Store Security Act. However, the success of prevention still depends mostly on voluntary compliance. Corporations sometimes favor and sometimes oppose specific measures, a "contradiction" resulting from the industry's need to provide protection while holding operating costs to a minimum.

Conclusions

Simple law enforcement or punishment strategies will not have an appreciable impact on reducing robbery. Evidence suggests that robbery is not merely an instrumental (i.e., goal-oriented) crime, as commonly believed, but rather serves offenders' affective (i.e., emotional) needs as well. Robbers often see themselves as "badasses." As such, simple deterrence or incapacitation strategies by themselves are unlikely to work. Broader strategies must focus on reducing risk and opportunity for robbery, both by increasing awareness of routine activities as they relate to risk and by altering physical design of places when such policies can be implemented cost-effectively. Social and cultural correlates of robbery (e.g., growing up in crime-ridden, poverty-stricken neighborhoods with attendant consequences for formative values and behavior) might also be partially addressed by broader social policies including education, job training, and welfare reform. These will be addressed in more detail in the concluding chapter of this book.

Endnotes

1. The NCVS defines *self-protection* in some peculiar ways, including the four most frequent types: "other" measures (24.0 percent), "resisted or captured offender" (18.8 percent), "ran away or hid" (14.7 percent), and "persuaded or appeased offender" (11.9 percent).

2. Consistent with Shaw and McKay's (1942) formulation of social disorganization theory (see chapter 4), "transitional" areas had high rates of instability and population turnover, such as high rates of temporary lodging, construction, and demolition.

References

Akers, R. L. (1997). *Criminological theories* (2nd ed.). Los Angeles: Roxbury Publishing.

Ball, J. C., Shaffer, J. W., & Nurco, D. N. (1983). Day-to-day criminality of heroin addicts in Baltimore: A study in the continuity of offense rates. *Drug and Alcohol Dependence, 12,* 119–142.

Beha, J. A., III. (1977). And nobody can get you out: The impact of a mandatory prison sentence for the illegal carrying of a firearm on the use of firearms and the administration of criminal justice in Boston. *Boston University Law Review, 58,* 106–208.

Block, R. (1977). *Violent crime.* Lexington, MA: Lexington.

Bureau of Justice Statistics. (1995). *Criminal victimization in the United States, 1994* (NCJ-162126). Washington, DC: Department of Justice.

Chaiken, J. M., & Chaiken, M. R. (1982). *Varieties of criminal behavior.* Santa Monica, CA: Rand.

Chaiken, J. M., Lawless, M., & Stevenson, K. A. (1974). *The impact of police activity on crime: Robberies on the New York City subway system* (R-1424-NYC). Santa Monica, CA: Rand.

Chaiken, M. R. (1986). Crime rates and substance abuse among types of offenders. In B. D. Johnson & E. D. Wish (Eds.), *Crime rates among drug-abusing offenders: Final report to the National Institute of Justice.* New York: Narcotic and Drug Research, Inc.

Clifton, W., Jr., & Callahan, P. T. (1987). *Convenience store robberies in Gainesville, Florida: An intervention strategy by the Gainesville Police Department.* Gainesville, FL: Gainesville Police Department.

Cloward, R., & Ohlin, L. (1960). *Delinquency and opportunity.* Glencoe, IL: Free Press.

Cohen, L., & Felson, M. (1979). Social change and crime rate trends: A routine activity approach. *American Sociological Review, 44,* 588–608.

Conklin, J. E. (1972). *Robbery and the criminal justice system.* Philadelphia: Lippincott.

Cook, P. (1980). Reducing injury and death rates in robbery. *Policy Analysis, 6,* 21–45.

———. (1983). *Robbery in the United States: An analysis of recent trends and patterns* (NCJ-91149). Washington, DC: Department of Justice, National Institute of Justice.

———. (1986). The relationship between victim resistance and injury in noncommercial robbery. *Journal of Legal Studies, 15,* 405–416.

———. (1987). Robbery violence. *Journal of Criminal Law and Criminology 78,* 357–376.

Crow, W. J., & Bull, J. L. (1975). *Robbery deterrence: An applied behavioral science demonstration—final report.* La Jolla, CA: Western Behavioral Sciences Institute.

Duffala, D. (1976). Convenience stores, armed robbery, and physical environment features. *American Behavioral Scientist, 20,* 227–246.

Greenwood, P. W., Rydell, C. P., Abrahamse, A. F., Caulkins, J. P., Chiesa, J., Model, K. E., & Klein, S. P. (1994). *Three strikes and you're out: Estimated benefits and costs of California's new mandatory-sentencing law.* Santa Monica, CA: Rand.

Hirschi, T. (1969). *Causes of delinquency.* Berkeley: University of California Press.

Hunter, R. D., & Jeffery, C. R. (1992). Preventing convenience store robbery through environmental design. In R. V. Clarke (Ed.), *Situational crime prevention: Successful case studies.* Albany, NY: Harrow & Heston.

Jacobs, B., & Wright, R. T. (1999). Stick-up, street culture, and offender motivation. *Criminology, 37,* 149–173.

Jeffery, C. R., Hunter, R. D., & Griswold, J. (1987). Crime prevention and computer analysis of convenience store robberies in Tallahassee, Florida. *Security Systems,* August, 1987, and *Florida Police Journal,* Spring, 1987.

Johnson, B. D., Goldstein, P. J., Preble, E., Schmeidler, J., Lipton, D. S., Spunt, B., & Miller, T. (1985). *Taking care of business: The economics of crime by heroin abusers.* Lexington, MA: Lexington Books.

Katz, J. (1988). *Seductions of crime.* New York: Basic Books.

——. (1991). The motivation of the persistent robber. In M. Tonry (Ed.), *Crime and justice: A review of research* (Vol. 14, pp. 277–306). Chicago: University of Chicago Press.

Kelling, G. L., Pate, T., Dieckman, D., & Brown, C. E. (1974). *The Kansas City preventive patrol experiment: A summary report.* Washington, DC: Police Foundation.

Lipton, D. S. (1995). *The effectiveness of treatment for drug abusers under criminal justice supervision* (NCJ 157642). Washington, DC: Department of Justice, Office of Justice Programs, National Institute of Justice.

Loftin, C., & McDowall, D. (1981). One with a gun gets you two: Mandatory sentencing and firearms violence in Detroit. *Annals of the American Academy of Political and Social Science, 150,* 455.

Luckenbill, D. (1981). Generating compliance: The case of robbery. *Urban Life, 10,* 25–46.

Marder, D. (1992, December 6). A new generation of killers, feeling no blame and no shame. *Philadelphia Inquirer,* A01.

McDonald, D. C., & Carlson, K. E. (1993). *Sentencing in the courts: Does race matter? The transition to sentencing guidelines, 1986–90.* Washington, DC: Department of Justice, Bureau of Justice Statistics.

Petersilia, J., Greenwood, P., & Lavin, M. (1977). *Criminal careers of habitual felons.* Santa Monica, CA: Rand.

Pierce, G. L., & Bowers, W. J. (1979). *The impact of the Bartley-Fox gun law on crime in Massachusetts.* Unpublished manuscript. Boston: Northeastern University, Center for Applied Social Research.

Prothrow-Stith, D. (1991). *Deadly consequences.* New York: Harper Collins.

Rand, M. R. (1994). *Carjacking* (NCJ-147002). Crime Data Brief, National Crime Victimization Survey. Washington, DC: Department of Justice, Office of Justice Programs, Bureau of Justice Statistics.

Rand, M. R., Lynch, J. P., & Cantor, D. (1997). *Criminal victimization, 1973–95* (NCJ-163069). Washington, DC: Department of Justice, Office of Justice Programs.

Reiss, A. J., Jr., & Roth, J. A. (Eds.). (1993). *Understanding and preventing violence 1.* Washington, DC: National Academy Press.

Rennison, C. M. (2000). *Criminal victimization 1999. Changes 1998–99 with trends 1993–99* (NCJ-182734). Washington, DC: Department of Justice, Office of Justice Programs.

Rhodes, W. M., & Conly, C. (1991). *Crime and mobility: An empirical study.* In P. J. Brantingham & P. L. Brantingham (Eds.), *Environmental criminology* (pp. 167–188). Prospect Heights, IL: Waveland.

Ringel, C. (1997). *Criminal victimization 1996. Changes 1995–96 with trends 1993–96* (NCJ-165812). Washington, DC: Department of Justice, Office of Justice Programs.

Rossman, D., Floyd, P., Pierce, G. L., McDevitt, J. L., & Bowers, W. (1979). *The impact of the mandatory gun law in Massachusetts.* Boston: Boston University School of Law, Center for Criminal Justice.

Shaw, C. R., & McKay, H. D. (1942). *Juvenile delinquency and urban areas.* Chicago: University of Chicago Press.

Sherman, L., Gartin, P., & Buerger, M. (1989). Hot spots of predatory crime: Routine activities and the criminology of place. *Criminology, 27,* 27–55.

Sickmund, M., Snyder, H. N., & Poe-Yamagata, E. (1997). *Juvenile offenders and victims: 1997 update on violence* (NCJ-165703). Washington, DC: U.S. Department of Justice, Office of Justice Programs, Office of Juvenile Justice and Delinquency Prevention.

Sykes, G., & Matza, D. (1957). Techniques of neutralization: A theory of delinquency. *American Journal of Sociology, 22,* 664–670.

Tonry, M. (1987). *Sentencing reform impacts.* Washington, DC: Department of Justice, National Institute of Justice.

Welsh, W. N., & Harris, P. W. (1999). *Criminal justice policy and planning.* Cincinnati, OH: Anderson.

Wright, J. D., & Rossi, P. H. (1994). *Armed and considered dangerous.* New York: Aldine de Gruyter.

Wright, J. D., Rossi, P. H., & Daly, K. (1983). *Under the gun: Weapons, crime, and violence in America.* Hawthorne, NY: Aldine de Gruyter.

Wright, R. T., & Decker, S. H. (1997). *Armed robbers in action.* Boston: Northeastern University Press. ✦

Chapter 8

Rapes and Sexual Assaults

Rapes and sexual assaults take many different forms. Victims are young as well as old, male as well as female, and from various racial backgrounds and income levels. Definitions of rape and sexual assault have changed substantially over time in response to criticism and advocacy by women's groups. Rape at one time was commonly (but mistakenly) assumed to be caused by sexual desire alone. This assumption caused various misconceptions about the offender, the offense, and the victim, and it failed to distinguish between different *types* of rape and sexual assault. In the first section of this chapter, we examine important definitions, patterns, and trends in rape and sexual assault. We then turn to causal theories and interventions informed by current knowledge. We begin with a look at a few examples that illustrate the diversity of sexual assault incidents, offenders, and victims.

- A "Code R" (sexual assault victim) comes into a hospital emergency room for help. A young teenager was abducted by a stranger, tied up, and held for many hours. The ER is busy, so she has to wait many hours for a physical exam (required for legal purposes); and until she has the exam, she is not allowed to eat or drink. A family member asks if the girl's story will be on the news ("Community Voices," 1997).

- A woman comes into the busy rape crisis office of a downtown unit for help in coping with her assault of a few months ago. Her biggest concern is how to tell her husband. The couple is from a country where sexual assault is shameful and can permanently scar a family name. Not only does the woman fear retaliation by the rapist, a family friend, but she dreads her husband's response ("Community Voices," 1997).

- It is a typical day in Family Court. A number of child sexual abuse cases are heard. Similarities in these cases become apparent—the accused is a parent, stepparent, mom's boyfriend, or cousin. The incident happened in the living room, near the bed, at the video store, or at grandma's or grandpa's house. The child is asked to describe, in court terms, what happened—which part of the perpetrator touched him and how ("Community Voices," 1997).

- According to police reports, two 15-year-old girls went to an apartment complex to visit a friend. When the two did not come home that night, their parents called the police. Police entered an apartment inhabited by two young men known to be acquainted with the missing girls. Police found the two teenagers, a suspect, and the drug rohypnol ("roofies," the so-called date-rape drug). Rohypnol, an illegal sedative, is about 10 times the strength of valium and has no taste or odor when dissolved in drinks. The girls said they were drinking soda and then couldn't remember anything until about 5:00 a.m. the following morning. Police believe the girls were given the drug and then raped (KRON-TV, 1996).

Definitions, Patterns, and Trends

Three major statistical series measure rape: the National Crime Victimization Survey (NCVS), the FBI's Uniform Crime Reports (UCR), and the National Incident-Based Reporting System (NIBRS).[1] We briefly examine how each defines rape and sexual assault before looking at some important patterns and trends. Please refer to chapter 2 for detailed discussions of these measures.

The NCVS currently provides the most detailed data on rape and sexual assaults. **Rape** is defined as forced sexual intercourse in which the victim may be either male or female and the offender may be of the same sex or a different sex from the victim. In contrast, **sexual assault** refers to a wide range of victimizations, separate from rape or attempted rape. These crimes include attacks that involve unwanted sexual contact between victim and offender (e.g., grabbing, touching, fondling). Both measures count attempts as well as completed crimes. Victims interviewed by the NCVS must be at least 12 years old; victims less than age 12 are excluded from all estimates.[2]

The UCR, based upon police reports, defines **forcible rape** as "the carnal knowledge of a female forcibly and against her will." The UCR definition includes attempts as well as completed rapes. In contrast to the NCVS, the UCR excludes statutory offenses, in which either no force is used or the victim is under the age of consent. Forcible rape is a Part I offense. In contrast, other **sex offenses** have traditionally been categorized by the UCR as Part II offenses. Sex offenses include sodomy, statutory rape, and offenses against chastity, decency, and morals.

As noted in chapter 2, the NIBRS was designed to improve the definition, accuracy, and measurement of crime reported by police authorities. The NIBRS, in contrast to the UCR, provides more precise definitions of rape and other sexual offenses. For example, **forcible rape** is the carnal knowledge of a person forcibly or against that person's will or both; or not forcibly or against the person's will, at a time during which the victim is incapable of giving consent because of his or her youth or because of his or her temporary or permanent mental or physical incapacity. This offense includes both male and female victims and threats and attempts. **Statutory rape** is the carnal knowledge of a person without force or the threat of force when that person is below the statutory age of consent. The ability of the victim to give consent is a determination by the law enforcement agency. **Forcible sodomy** is oral or anal sexual intercourse with another person, forcibly or against that person's will or both; or not forcibly or against that person's will where the victim is incapable of giving consent because of his or her youth or because of his or her temporary or permanent mental or physical incapacity. **Sexual assault with an object** is a crime in which the offender uses an instrument or object to unlawfully penetrate the genital or anal opening of the body of another person, forcibly or against that person's will, or both. **Forcible fondling** is the touching of the private body parts of another person for the purpose of sexual gratification, forcibly or against that person's will or both. Forcible fondling also includes indecent liberties and child molesting. **Incest** is nonforcible sexual intercourse between persons who are related to each other within the degrees wherein marriage is prohibited by law.

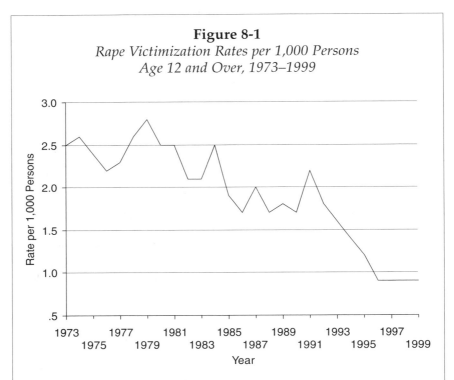

Figure 8-1
Rape Victimization Rates per 1,000 Persons Age 12 and Over, 1973–1999

Source: Bureau of Justice Statistics Website (2001). *National Crime Victimization Survey violent crime trends, 1973–99.* Available at <http://www.ojp.usdoj.gov/bjs/glance/rape.htm>.

Note: Includes both attempted and completed rapes measured by the National Crime Victimization Survey (NCVS). Because of changes made to the NCVS, data prior to 1992 were statistically adjusted to make them comparable to data collected under the redesigned methodology. The adjustment methods are described in Ran, Lynch, and Cantor (1997). Estimates for 1993 to 1999 are based on collection year while earlier estimates are based on data year.

Although we focus mainly on rape in this chapter, it is clear that rape and sexual assault cover a wide variety of behaviors. We emphasize that definitions are critical in the social construction of a crime (see chapter 1): They influence statistical estimates of a crime, perceptions of causes, and official responses to it. The question of consent has been especially controversial in defining rape, and we will examine in this chapter how that issue has been addressed by criminal justice legislation and policy.

Rape victimization rates have fluctuated over time, but have gradually decreased since 1979. Rape victimization rates from 1996 to 1999 reflected the lowest levels recorded since the inception of the NCVS in 1973 (Figure 8-1). Decreases have been noted almost every year since 1991, although rape rates showed no change from 1996 to 1999.[3]

If we look at arrest rates provided by the UCR over time, similar (but not identical) patterns emerge (Figure 8-2). The conclusion that rape and other sex offenses have been declining gradually since 1991 is basically the same. However, arrests for rape (unadjusted for the size of the population) increased fairly steadily between 1980 and 1990, then decreased gradually after 1991. Neverthelss, as we saw in chapter 2, arrests may reflect a number of forces besides actual crimes (e.g., reporting by victims and witnesses, accuracy of police record systems, and reporting of crime data to the FBI by local and state law enforcement agencies).

The highest rate of forcible rape recorded by law enforcement agencies was in 1992 (Figure 8-2), when police agencies recorded 109,060 forcible rapes nationwide. In 1995, the number of forcible rapes per capita among women of all ages reported to law enforcement agencies was the lowest since 1985, and the per capita number of arrests for rape and other sex offenses was the lowest recorded by law enforcement authorities since 1983 (Greenfeld, 1997).

Characteristics of Victims, Offenders, and Offenses

Victims. According to NCVS estimates, 201,000 people aged 12 or older were victims of attempted (30 percent) or completed (70 percent) rapes in 1999, and 182,000 others experienced sexual assaults other than rape (Rennison, 2000). Police statistics indicate that slightly less than a third of victims (32 percent) reported the rape or sexual assault to a law enforcement agency (Greenfeld, 1997). The most common reason given by victims for reporting the crime to the police was to prevent further crimes by the offender against them. The most common reason cited by the victim for not reporting the crime to the police was that it was considered a personal matter. Victims were also more likely to report the crime if they were injured and if the offender was armed.

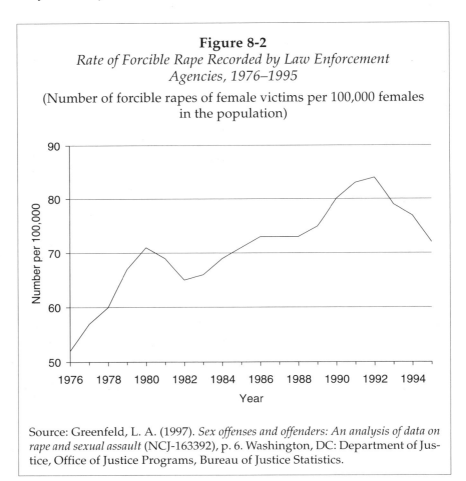

Figure 8-2
Rate of Forcible Rape Recorded by Law Enforcement Agencies, 1976–1995

(Number of forcible rapes of female victims per 100,000 females in the population)

Source: Greenfeld, L. A. (1997). *Sex offenses and offenders: An analysis of data on rape and sexual assault* (NCJ-163392), p. 6. Washington, DC: Department of Justice, Office of Justice Programs, Bureau of Justice Statistics.

The vast majority of violent sex offending involved male offenders assaulting female victims. Overall, nearly 99 percent of the offenders described by victims in single-victim incidents were male, and an estimated 91 percent of the victims of rape and sexual assault were female (Greenfeld, 1997). Like other types of violent crime, rape and sexual assault victims were disproportionately low-income, urban residents of the same race as their attackers.

In a high percentage of rapes and sexual assaults, the victims are children. According to the NCVS, teenagers aged 16 to 19 reported the highest per capita rates of victimization in 1999 (Rennison, 2000). Data drawn from police-recorded incidents of rape in three states revealed that 44 percent of rape victims were under the age of 18 (Greenfeld, 1997). Two-thirds of convicted rape and sexual assault offenders serving time in state prisons reported that they had victims under the age of 18, and 58 percent said their victims were age 12 or younger.

About 40 percent of rape victims suffered some kind of injury, although only 5 percent suffered a major injury, such as severe lacerations, fractures, internal injuries, or unconsciousness (Greenfeld, 1997). Injuries were most common among victims age 30 or older and victims of rapists armed with a knife. Nearly six in 10 rapes involving a knife resulted in victim injury. About one in 11 rape and sexual assault victims reported that they suffered some economic loss as a consequence of the crime. The average economic loss was about $200, and nearly 7 percent of victims reported losing time from work (Greenfeld, 1997).

Although **date rape** has received much media attention recently, it is the norm rather than the exception that sex offenders and victims know one another. Victims of rape and sexual assault report that in nearly three out of four incidents, the offender was not a stranger (Greenfeld, 1997). Victim and offender are likely to have had a prior relationship as family members, intimates, or acquaintances (especially the latter). Based on police-recorded incident data, in 90 percent of the rapes of children younger than 12, the child knew the offender; two-thirds of the victims aged 18 to 29 had some prior relationship with the rapist.

The most comprehensive study of date rape so far was conducted by Mary Koss (1988), who sampled 6,000 students at 32 colleges across the United States. A majority of women (53 percent) reported having experienced some kind of unwanted sexual contact. Fifteen percent had been victims of completed rapes and 12 percent had been victims of attempted rapes. Fully 83 percent of the victims of completed rapes knew their attacker, and 57 percent of the victimizations occurred while on dates. However, only 10 percent of the victims reported the assault to police or rape crisis centers.

Offenders. Nearly 99 in 100 rapists are male, six in 10 are white, and the average offender is in his early 30s (Greenfeld, 1997). About 42 percent of offenders are 30 or older at the time of the offense, 32 percent are aged 21 to 29, about one-quarter (26 percent) are under 21. The racial distribution of arrestees for rape is similar to the racial distribution for all violent UCR arrests—56 percent of arrestees for rape in 1995 were white, 42 percent were black, and 2 percent were of other races. Whites accounted for a large proportion of arrests (75 percent) for sex offenses other than rape (Greenfeld, 1997).

Offenders typically have a single victim with whom they have had some prior relationship. The vast majority of rapes and sexual assaults (91 percent) involve a single offender, usually a family member (13 percent), intimate (6 percent), or acquaintance (35 percent) of the victim (Greenfeld, 1997). Only about 30 percent of rapists and less than 15 percent of sexual assaulters reported that their victim had been a stranger to them.

Rapists rarely murder their victims, contrary to media stereotypes and popular fiction.[4] Between 1976 and 1994, an estimated 405,089 murders occurred in the United States. Of these, the circumstances surrounding the murder were known in 317,925, or 78.5 percent. Among the cases with known circumstances, only an estimated 4,807, or 1.5 percent, were classified as involving rape or another sex offense (Greenfeld, 1997).

Offenses. Rape occurs much more frequently in large cities, although rates in smaller cities and rural counties have been slowly increasing (Greenfeld, 1997). Most of the rapes reported to police are completed rapes. In 1995, 87 percent of recorded rapes were completed crimes; the remainder were classified as attempts. About 8 percent of rapes reported to law enforcement agencies were later determined to be *unfounded* (i.e., police investigation resulted in the decision that no crime had occurred). Only half of all reported rapes are ever cleared by an arrest.

As one might expect from routine activities theory (see chapter 4), rape occurs more frequently at certain times and places where motivated offenders and suitable targets converge. In summer months, for example, more rapes occur when people are outdoors and moving around. The highest volume of rape reported to police in 1995 (9.9 percent of the annual total) was recorded in August, and the lowest (6.8 percent) was recorded in December (Greenfeld, 1997). Rape is also more likely to occur during the times when most people are off work. About two-thirds of rapes and sexual assaults occur during the 12 hours from 6 p.m. to 6 a.m.

Rape does not always occur in isolated, out of the way places. Nearly six out of 10 rape and sexual assault incidents in one study were reported by victims to have occurred in their own home or at the home of a friend, relative, or neighbor. More than half of rape and sexual assault incidents were reported by victims to have occurred within one mile of their home or at their home (Greenfeld, 1997).

Weapons are not used in the typical rape. Although physical force or threats or both are always used by rapists (by definition), only about one of every 16 rape and sexual assault victims reported that a firearm was present during the commission of the offense. Most victims (84 percent) reported that no weapon was used by the offender (Greenfeld, 1997). Similar (but not identical) results were found by surveys of convicted offenders in state prisons (Greenfeld, 1997). Offenders convicted of rape or sexual assault were substantially less likely than other violent offenders to have used a weapon during the commission of the crime. Seventeen percent of rapists and 6 percent of sexual assaulters reported using a weapon during their crime. While 30 percent of all violent offenders reported having used a firearm, only about 5 percent of rapists and 2 percent of sexual assaulters used a firearm during the crime. Rapists were about as likely as all violent offenders to report having used a knife while committing the crime (10 percent of rapists versus 11 percent of all violent offenders).

Explanations

Over the years, many people have assumed that rape is motivated *mainly* by sexual desire. If this explanation is incorrect, as now seems to be the case, then many types of interventions intended to reduce sexual desire (e.g., chemical castration, censorship of pornography) remain unlikely to affect the incidence of rape. Identifying the relevant range of causes of this behavior is an essential precursor to doing something about it.

Psychoanalytic Theories

No one theory has been able to explain the majority of offenders or offenses. However, a number of background characteristics significantly increase the *likelihood* of a person becoming a rapist. These *risk factors* include experiencing sexual trauma as a child or being victimized sexually. Although only one-third of sexual assault offenders reported that they had ever been physically or sexually abused while growing up, these offenders were substantially more likely than any other category of offenders to report such abuse (Greenfeld, 1997). Alcohol and drug use are also common among rape offenders, symptomatic of attempts to cope with high levels of anxiety and distress. Psychoanalytic theorists emphasize that although substance abuse may lower inhibitions against committing acts of violence, it is not necessarily the major causative factor.

Psychoanalytic interpretations of rape examine unresolved needs and conflicts in the offender's past: "His unfulfilled needs for acceptance, affection, and intimacy result in depression . . ." (Groth, 1990, p. 77). Many rapists have episodic careers in which particular incidents often seem related to negative life events and feelings of helplessness (Groth, 1990). A majority of adult rapists reported committing their first offense by the age of 16, although most incidents go undetected or are not treated as serious crimes (Groth, 1990).

Insecurity about masculine identity is not uncommon. Often, failures in multiple areas of life make the rapist experience doubts about his manhood. He may compensate by attempting to aggressively display his masculinity. Poor social relationships, poor social skills, and high anxiety in dealing with other people are often found. As a result, the rapist fails to develop successful interpersonal relationships. He is often detached or self-centered in interactions with others. Convicted rapists often report chronic unhappiness due to a sense of inadequacy and a feeling of isolation from others.

Clinical studies illustrate that rape serves nonsexual needs of offenders, not just sexual desires. In particular, strong needs of control and hostility have been observed (Groth & Binbaum, 1979). Rape may symbolize an offender's attempt to regain control, to punish someone, or do both of these for his perceived mistreatment (i.e., a victim identifies with the role of aggressor in order to overcome a sense of powerlessness and helplessness). In fact, many rapists report difficulty in maintaining an erection during the offense. According to psychologists (Groth, 1990; Groth & Binbaum, 1979), there are at least three distinct types of rape. Although any one rape may contain elements of all three types, one tends to predominate, and offenders tend to fit better into one of these three categories than the others.

In an **anger rape,** the assault is characterized by physical brutality, far more than is necessary to overpower the victim. Sex is used to express pent-up feelings of anger; the offender seeks to harm and degrade his victim. These rapists report feeling angry or depressed before the rape, and not particularly aroused sexually. During the rape, they often have difficulty achieving or maintaining an erection. The sexual assault in this case is typically unplanned and impulsive.

In the **power rape,** the offender seeks to dominate his victim sexually, not necessarily hurt her. Sex is a means of compensating for feelings of inadequacy. Such offenders often attempt to humiliate their victims by forcing them to engage in various acts. Like the anger rapist, the power rapist does not find the offense very satisfying sexually. Typically these rapes are planned, although opportunistic.

The **sadistic rape** is the most rare and the most violent form of sexual assault. Here, aggression itself is eroticized; sex and aggression are fused in the mind of the offender. The offender becomes aroused or excited only through violence. The attack often involves torture or mutilation. Thankfully, such types are relatively rare.

Feminist Theories

Although psychologists and psychiatrists focus on individual offender characteristics, we also need to consider sociocultural aspects (e.g., norms and values regarding sexuality and attitudes toward women). Rape is seen by feminists as a violent assault that inflicts emotional as well as physical trauma upon victims. The causes of rape, according to feminists, lie deep within a society and culture dominated by male attitudes, values, and beliefs. Male-dominated culture, in many ways, objectifies relationships with women, eschews female value and belief systems, and limits female rights and opportunities. Feminists argue that, historically, rape has been inappropriately defined, investigated, prosecuted, and punished by male-dominated legislative and justice systems. Rape law reform thus became a major research and policy agenda for feminists.

Susan Brownmiller, one of the best known early feminist theorists, focused her analysis on the historical power advantage that men have enjoyed over women, resulting in the unequal status and unfair treatment of women in our society. A broader feminist critique has important implications for explaining rape:

> Man's discovery that his genitalia could serve as a weapon to generate fear must rank as one of the most important discoveries of prehistorical time, along with the use of fire and the first crude stone axe. From prehistoric times to the present I believe rape has played a critical function. It is nothing more or less than a conscious process of intimidation by which *all* men keep *all* women in a state of fear. (Brownmiller, 1975, pp. 14–15)

Traditional socialization patterns, according to feminist theory, have encouraged men to associate masculinity with power, dominance, strength, virility, and superiority and femininity with submissiveness, passivity, and weakness. Various cultural expectations, including those embodied in male-dominated legislative and justice systems, historically tended to view women as little more than male property.

Research has been largely supportive of the sociocultural view of rape described by feminists. Sanday (1981) conducted a cross-cultural study of 156 tribal societies existing between 1750 B.C. and 1960. At the extremes of her sample, she found that rape was rare or absent in 47 percent of the societies studied, but a frequent and accepted practice against women in 18 percent of the societies. In the most rape-prone societies, female authority and power were low, and masculinity was frequently expressed by interpersonal violence and toughness.

Scully and Marolla (1985) conducted interviews with 114 convicted rapists in a Virginia prison. Rewards or justifications for rape perceived by offenders included a means of exacting revenge or punishment, achieving a "bonus" while committing another crime (such as burglary or robbery), obtaining sexual access to women who would otherwise be unavailable, exercising sexual power and control, and participating in an "adventure." Supporting a sociocultural interpretation, the authors warned that rape could not be seen as merely the act of a few sick men. Rather, "rape can be viewed as the end part in a continuum of sexually aggressive behaviors that reward men and victimize women" (Scully & Marolla, 1985, p. 262).

Malamuth (1981, 1984) conducted studies to assess male views associated with sexual aggression. He asked different male samples (mostly college students) to determine the likelihood that they would commit a rape if they could be assured of not being caught and punished. Responses to various questions were given on five-point scales ranging from very likely (5) to not likely at all (1). On average, about 35 percent of respondents across samples indicated some likelihood of raping (LR) by scoring a 2 or higher. High LR was associated with callous attitudes toward rape and belief in various rape myths (e.g., that women really enjoy rape in spite of their protests), providing support for sociocultural theories of rape.

Although supportive of sociocultural theories of rape, these research studies have not yet adequately answered the question of why most men do not rape or commit other sexual offenses in a society and culture that is, to some degree, accepting of rape myths and aggressive male sexual behavior (Chappell, 1989). The samples used in many studies are unrepresentative of the male population and may in fact target those with more aggressive sexual attitudes and behaviors. Sociocultural views also do not fully explain sexual violence directed against children or adult males. More interdisciplinary perspectives are needed that incorporate individual as well as sociocultural views. Although certain cultures may be "rape prone" to varying degrees, the individual offender must still have a motivation to sexually aggress, must overcome internal and external inhibitors against sexual aggression, and must formulate a strategy to overcome victim resistance (Finkelhor, 1984).

Feminist theories, informed and modified by research findings over time, have retained their influence (Chappell, 1989). Early feminist theories that emphasized rape as a direct extension of biology and characterized rape as a strictly nonsexual, violent crime are now regarded as dubious (Russell, 1984). However, the early emphasis on rape as a purely nonsexual, violent crime served important social functions of raising awareness, changing public attitudes about rape, and reforming laws based on rape myths (Scully & Marola, 1985). Because many people (including male justice officials and male jurors) mistakenly assumed that rape was the result of a single motive, sexual desire, the victim was often assumed to somehow have been provocative or irresponsible, thus contributing to her victimization.

Cognitive Distortions and Rape Myths

Another set of causal theories, consistent with feminist interpretations but focused more on individual factors, addresses thinking errors and distortions that are supportive of rape. Attitudes and behaviors supportive of rape can be learned and reinforced through social interactions with others, and beliefs may be further reinforced through socialization (e.g., in the family, school, etc.), membership in various groups, and witnessing media portrayals of coercive male-female relationships (Russell, 1984).

Can men learn to be rapists? Ellis (1989) suggests that four learning processes are facilitated by media portrayals. First, men may imitate witnessed acts of coerciveness or violence toward women. Second, men may increasingly associate sex and violence by viewing material that exhibits sex and violence in the same context. Third, rape myths are perpetuated and reinforced by the media. Fourth, heavy viewers of television may become desensitized to sexual aggression and more tolerant of the pain, fear, and humiliation associated with such acts.

The mythology of rape allows an individual both to engage in illegal sexual behavior and to rationalize and justify it after it occurs (Weis & Borges, 1975). Rape myths can serve to provide men with an ideology that justifies acts of violence toward women (Brownmiller, 1975; Burt, 1983; Scully & Marolla, 1984). These rationalizations or justifications for deviant behavior are similar to what Sykes and Matza (1957) have referred to as "techniques of neutralization" (see also chapter 4).

One popular rape myth is the belief that "no means yes": that is, the belief that women make initial protests, but they never really mean it (Koss & Harvey, 1993). Another myth is that women are swept off their feet by sexually forceful men. In reality, women fantasize more frequently about sexual encounters during which they choose their partner as well as the specific acts involved (Koss & Harvey, 1991). Another myth is that "nice girls don't get raped"; in other words, the offender may believe that the victim teased or sexually provoked him, or both. Another myth states that "it is impossible to rape an unwilling woman." This myth perpetuates stereotypes that a woman must have consented unless serious and obvious physical injuries resulted. Evidence for the existence of such myths has been found in samples of convicted rapists (Burt, 1980, 1983; Scully & Marolla, 1985) and noncriminal adult and juvenile males (Burt, 1983; Koss, Gidycz, & Wisiniewski, 1987; Meuhlenhard & Hollabaugh, 1988).

Although feminist theories argue that rape myths must be addressed through large-scale cultural and social change including changes in sex role socialization, cognitive-behavioral and social learning theories focus upon altering individual, learned patterns of thinking and behavior that increase the likelihood of rape. It is the level of analysis (individual versus sociocultural) that distinguishes these theories (Gilmartin, 1994).

Interventions

Rape Law Reform

As seen in chapter 1, criminal law is a "social construction." In other words, both definitions of illegal behaviors and corresponding penalties result from social processes. Many critics have perceived serious problems with legal definitions of rape and how rape cases are processed in court. Rape law reform has proceeded vigorously since the 1970s, initially spurred by the advocacy of women's groups, but joined increasingly by researchers and academics. By 1980, almost every state in the United States had passed some form of rape law reform legislation (Bienen, 1980). Debate and legislative reform continue, however.

Traditional definitions of rape that relied upon proof of vaginal penetration, for example, were criticized as inaccurate, incomplete, and unfair to victims. Sexual assault takes many different forms, and serious harm to victims (both female and male, and both children and adults) can occur with or without penetration, often referred to in criminal codes as "carnal knowledge." Rape and different sexual offenses are increasingly defined in gender-neutral terms that attempt to describe the specific behavior involved.

Michigan was one of the earliest states to undergo extensive rape law reform, serving as a model for many other states. In 1975, Michigan legislation abandoned the term *rape* in favor of *criminal sexual conduct*. Four degrees of criminal sexual conduct were established, based upon the seriousness of the offense, the amount of coercion used, the infliction of personal injury, and the age and incapacitation of the victim (Marsh, Geist, & Caplan, 1982). Thus, it was hoped, sexual offenses could be classified using relevant, important legal criteria, displacing a host of outdated, confusing labels that failed to distinguish the actual behavior involved (e.g., "assault with intent to commit rape," "indecent liberties," "carnal knowledge of a female ward by a guardian," and "debauchery of youth").

Defining certain sexual behaviors as a series of violent, coercive behaviors is often controversial, however, because it is not always entirely clear how much force was used or was necessary for the offender to gain compliance (Chappell, 1989). In other words, some assaults display elements involving the exploitation of power relationships more clearly than any element of physical force.

California, in contrast to Michigan and other states that attempted to base rape law reform upon behavioral criteria, adopted a multifaceted approach that included four major elements: (1) sentence enhancements for the use of weapons or violence, (2) a **rape shield law** to constrain the use of prior sexual history by defense attorneys attempting to establish victim consent, (3) establishing gender-neutral language in defining rape, and (4) removing the spousal exception to cases of rape (Polk, 1985).

To determine whether rape law reform in California led to changes in processing or punishment, Polk (1985) examined California data for the years 1977 to 1982. In general, effects were small and were limited more toward the tail end (e.g., sentencing, incarceration) of the criminal justice system. Police were no more likely to make an arrest following rape law reforms, although prosecutors were somewhat more likely to file rape cases as felonies. But the felony conviction rate for rape did not increase. Even though incarceration rates increased for rape during the period of the studies, they increased at similar rates for other serious felonies as well, reflective of a larger national trend toward tougher penalties.

Similar results were found in Michigan (Caringella-MacDonald, 1985). Sexual assault cases were more likely than nonsexual assault cases to be authorized for prosecution, but offense severity rather than rape law reforms may have confounded these results (i.e., differences in case characteristics were not controlled for in analyses). Among the cases authorized for prosecution, a higher proportion of the sexual assault cases also involved victim credibility problems (e.g., implausible or inconsistent statements). At subsequent stages of criminal justice processing, there were no significant differences in the rate of case convictions or plea bargains for the two types of assaults. Where plea bargains did occur, however, sentences for sexual assaults were reduced to a lesser extent than for other assaults.

Studies of the rape shield law in Indiana (LaFree, 1989) showed similar disappointing results. Based on 38 trials during 3 years following passage of the law, LaFree examined detailed data including victim, defendant, juror, trial, and courtroom characteristics. In each case, he examined the influence of several types of "nontraditional" victim behavior including alcohol or drug use (in general, and at the time of the incident), extramarital sexual activity, having illegitimate children, and having a reputation as a partier. The rape shield law appeared to be almost totally ineffective. It was invoked in only one-third of the cases examined, and in almost every one of these cases, evidence had already been presented in court (in the presence of jurors) that the victim had allegedly engaged in one or more forms of nontraditional behavior. Further, cases that used a defense based upon victim consent were less likely than other cases to result in a guilty verdict. Last, but not least, victim behavior was important only in those cases where defenses attempted to prove either that the victim gave consent or that no sex occurred. In such cases, though, interviews revealed that jurors were less likely to perceive the defendant was guilty when the victim engaged in premarital sex, used alcohol or drugs regularly, knew the assailant, or was black. These are hardly the effects intended by passage of rape reform laws.

Rape shield laws have since been passed in more than 45 states, and the requirement of corroboration of the victim's testimony has been eliminated in all states. However, rape law reforms have proved to be quite limited in reducing the role of victim character-istics or increasing conviction rates in sexual assault cases. Victim credibility remains a central issue in the processing of sexual as-sault cases (Kruttschnitt, 1994).

Incarceration

How many rapists are in prison? About 234,000 offenders con-victed of rape or sexual assault in 1994 were under correctional su-pervision—either local jail, state prison, federal prison, probation, or parole (Greenfeld, 1997). About 60 percent of these offenders were under conditional supervision in the community (e.g., proba-tion or parole). Sex offenders account for just under 5 percent of the total population under correctional supervision on a given day.

Since 1980, the average annual growth in the number of prison-ers has been about 7.6 percent (Greenfeld, 1997). The number of prisoners sentenced for violent sexual assault other than rape has increased by an annual average of nearly 15 percent, faster than any other category of violent crime and faster than all other crime categories except drug trafficking.

While the average sentence of convicted rapists has remained stable at about 10 years, the average time served has increased from about 3½ years to about 5 years (Greenfeld, 1997). For those released after serving time for sexual assault, the sentence has been a stable 6½ years, and the average time served has grown from about 6 months to just under 3 years.

How often do rapists recidivate once released from prison? In two 3-year BJS followup studies of samples of felons placed on probation and of felons released from prison, rapists had a lower rate of rearrest for a new crime (52 percent) than other violent of-fenders (60 percent). Of former rapists released from prison and followed for 3 years, 52 percent were rearrested for any crime, 28 percent were rearrested for a new violent crime, and 8 percent were rearrested for a new rape. While recidivism generally speak-ing is high, therefore, it cannot be stated that recidivism for *rape* is especially high (Greenfeld, 1997).

Victim Resistance

Does resisting one's attacker decrease or increase the likeli-hood of rape? Bart and O'Brien (1985) attempted to answer this question by conducting a nonrandom survey of 94 volunteers so-licited through newspaper ads. Their sample was not entirely rep-resentative of rape victims nationally: Volunteers for the study were more likely to be young, unmarried, and working or attend-ing school. Offenders in these incidents were also more likely to be a stranger than is usually the case. Even though the study did not obtain representative samples of rape victims or offenders, it pro-vided valuable insights about the effects of victim resistance, and its main findings have since been fairly well supported (Greenfeld, 1997).

Researchers interviewed victims, asking questions about de-mographic factors and situational and background variables asso-ciated with the rape. Six possible defense strategies were described: (1) flee or try to flee; (2) scream or yell; (3) beg or plead; (4) "cognitive verbal" techniques (try to reason with offender or con him, or make him see her as a person); (5) take advantage of en-vironmental intervention or opportunity; and (6) respond with physical force.

Study results showed that those who avoided rape used a greater number of strategies than those who did not. **Avoiders** ($N =$ 51) were more likely to flee or try to flee, yell or scream, use physi-cal force, and take advantage of environmental opportunity (e.g., a bystander or car passing nearby). **Raped** women ($N = 43$) were more likely to beg or plead. Avoiders and raped women were equally likely to use cognitive strategies (i.e., appealing to the of-fender's sense of decency or humanity).

Avoiders were more likely to experience a gut reaction of rage. **Raped women** were more likely to think about avoiding death or mutilation (fear). Even for raped women, those who used physical strategies were less depressed than raped women who did not. They were less likely to take the blame for the rape (e.g., attribute it to some personality defect of their own). *There was no evidence that physical resistance significantly increased the use of force by the rapist.*

Similar results have been found in victimization surveys (Greenfeld, 1997). About seven out of 10 victims (72 percent) of rape and sexual assault reported that they took some form of self-protective action during the crime. The most common form of self-defense was to resist by struggling and yelling. Among vic-tims who took a self-protective action, just over half felt that their actions had helped the situation. About one in five victims felt that their actions either had made the situation worse or simultaneously had helped and worsened the situation.

Victim Counseling and Assistance

As a result of advocacy by women's groups and increased public awareness of the difficulties faced by rape victims, many victim counseling and assistance programs have been developed since the 1970s. Most of these programs are run by nonprofit groups that rely partially or wholly upon grants, charitable contributions, or funding by local, state, or federal government agencies. One example is provided by Women Organized Against Rape (WOAR), based in Philadelphia (Urban Archives, 1999).

WOAR is a social service and social change organization established as a nonprofit corporation in May 1973 with three major goals: (1) to eliminate rape in our society, (2) to provide needed support and referral to victims of rape, and (3) to empower women to gain control over their lives. Since its inception, WOAR has adopted a feminist interpretation of rape and its effects on victims:

> Rape, the threat of rape, and the fear of rape are forms of physical and mental violence that have been used continuously throughout recorded history to control women and substantially limit their roles in society. . . . Rape is the ultimate denial of rights to women. . . . In short, the socialization of women is a continual exercise in restriction by fear which makes it a struggle for women to fulfill their potential as human beings. WOAR unites women who wish to work actively to eliminate rape and thus help create a healthy and enlightened environment for women. (Urban Archives, 1999)

WOAR provides services in three main areas: direct service to victims, community education and training, and advocacy.

Direct service to victims. Rape victims and their families need specialized support and counseling to deal with medical, legal, and personal aftermath of rape. WOAR provides information and support to allow victims to understand the professional and institutional services and processes confronting them and to make informed choices about their options. Services include crisis counseling and support 24 hours a day through a telephone hotline; crisis counseling and support through hospital emergency room accompaniment; accompaniment and advocacy for survivors at court; and individual and group counseling for survivors and their families.

WOAR staff and experienced volunteers provide counseling and support for victims and survivors receiving medical treatment in the emergency rooms at Episcopal Hospital in North Philadelphia and Thomas Jefferson University Hospital in Center City Philadelphia. Because court proceedings can be confusing and upsetting for sexual assault victims and survivors, and especially so for child and adolescent survivors and their families, WOAR staff and experienced volunteers provide accompaniment, information, and support for survivors at preliminary hearings, trials, and sentencings. WOAR provides individual and group counseling services for women and girls and men and boys who have experienced sexual victimization. WOAR's confidential counseling services are provided free of charge. Support groups are generally conducted for 10 sessions and are led by experienced WOAR counselors. They also offer counseling for the parents and other family members of victims.

One counselor described an individual counseling session with a female client in her mid-30s ("Community Voices," 1997). She had been seeing this client for a number of months to help her deal with being sexually abused throughout her childhood and teenage years by an adult male (a family acquaintance). They began with some breathing and relaxation exercises to calm the client. She was able to talk about some images—smells, touches, sounds—that still trigger uncomfortable flashbacks (e.g., seeing a man and a child together, the feel of facial hair, the smell of alcohol on a man's breath). She said her body felt completely numb as she talked about these memories. The counselor remarked how much courage it takes to will oneself to discuss the details of old wounds.

Another counselor described a meeting with a teenage rape victim scheduled to go to court the next day for her preliminary hearing. The girl was so nervous and anxious that the counselor was worried that she might not be able to testify. The victim was terrified of the perpetrator, and the thought of having to see him in court and explain what he did to her made her feel very scared. The counselor set up a pretend courtroom in the office so that the victim could practice some relaxation techniques to help reduce her anxiety ("Community Voices," 1997).

Community education and training. WOAR brings educational programs about sexual assault and personal safety to children and adults in classrooms, community centers, and workplaces throughout Philadelphia. They distribute brochures and other informational materials on rape and child sexual abuse; materials are available in English and in Spanish. WOAR also provides specific training and information to medical, legal, and counseling personnel who serve rape victims, to improve the timeliness, sensitivity, and substance of these services (Urban Archives, 1999). WOAR has sponsored numerous conferences and workshops including the series Nursing and Management of Sexual Assault Victims, A Training Workshop for Medical Professionals.

Advocacy. WOAR has organized public demonstrations focused on raising public awareness of specific issues (e.g., judicial handling of sexual assault issues, child sexual assault issues, rapes on public transportation, violence against women, etc.). WOAR has also worked to reform the way victims are treated in the legal system (Urban Archives, 1999). The Criminal Justice Model, developed by WOAR in 1977, contributed to the formation of the Rape Prosecution Unit in the office of the Philadelphia District Attorney in January 1978, and eventually to the formation of the Sex Crimes Unit of the Philadelphia Police Department in 1981. WOAR has testified at the Pennsylvania State Legislature, contributing to landmark rape reform rulings, such as the Pennsylvania Rape Shield Law in 1976, making prior sexual history inadmissible; the Confidential Communications Law in 1982, which established confidentiality between rape crisis counselors and victims; and the Marital Rape Law in 1985, which enabled spousal rape victims to benefit from improved stipulations for treatment by medical and legal systems afforded any other rape victim. WOAR helped develop the Pennsylvania Coalition Against Rape (PCAR), a statewide coalition of rape-crisis centers, and was one of the founding members of Women's Way, Philadelphia's fundraising agency for services to women, in 1976.

Sex Offender Treatment Programs

According to inmate surveys conducted by the Bureau of Justice Statistics, about 14 percent of imprisoned sex offenders reported that their sentence included a special court condition that they receive psychological or specialized sex offender treatment (Greenfeld, 1997). Overall, about 4 percent of the sentences of confined violent offenders had a similar requirement.

No unanimous expert opinion exists about the effectiveness of sex offender treatment. Very different approaches are often used in different states, and different emphases on treatment versus punishment have characterized responses to sex offenders over time. The impact of treatment on sexual offenders remains largely unknown due to a shortage of convincing empirical data, inadequate sample sizes and research designs, and inadequate followup periods of offenders released back into society (Furby, Weinrott, & Blackshaw, 1989). Newer programs that use a combination of cognitive and behavioral approaches have shown promise, though, and a consensus is developing that successful treatment models must address deviant sexual interests, social skills deficits, and cognitive distortions about sexual offending (Marques & Nelson, 1992). Two examples illustrate the potential of sex offender treatment programs for reducing recidivism: (1) the Vermont Treatment Program for Sexual Aggressors and (2) California's Sex Offender Treatment and Evaluation Project (SOTEP).

The Vermont Treatment Program for Sexual Aggressors was created by a special appropriation from the state legislature in 1982 (Pithers, Martin, & Cumming, 1989). The program includes three residential (prison) and 20 outpatient (community) treatment sites. The program is multimodal, including individual and group psychotherapy, substance abuse counseling, vocational training, behavioral interventions, and psychohormonal therapies. Offenders learn cognitive and behavioral skills to reduce the likelihood of reoffending. One critical requirement for eligibility is that offenders accept responsibility for their crime. An extensive battery of psychological and physiological assessment procedures are used to identify and target specific cognitive and behavioral patterns for change.

Treatment generally begins with victim empathy groups, to encourage the offender to acknowledge the harm done to his victim and recognize the victim as a thinking, feeling person. Treatment then moves on to training in specific sets of skills, including social skills, sexual knowledge, emotional management skills, and decision-making processes. Treatment then focuses on helping clients to recognize the events, emotions, fantasies, and thoughts that typically accompany a relapse to sexual aggression. Offenders learn specific skills and strategies for coping with these triggers and lowering the risk of reoffending.

Group therapy focuses on issues of personal victimization (e.g., sexual and/or physical abuse in one's own past), cognitive distortions (e.g., rape myths), behavioral therapies, problem-solving skills, and transition from prison to community life. Individual therapy is also offered on a selective basis.

To qualify for outpatient (i.e., community) treatment, offenders must demonstrate consistent progress in cognitive and behavioral change. Clients must be able to describe the situations that personally increase their individual risk of reoffending. For each of these situations, clients must be able to verbalize or role-play coping responses that reduce the chance of sexual aggression. They must be able to anticipate new high-risk situations and develop effective coping responses. Clients need to demonstrate that they can perceive, report, and modify an appropriate range of emotions, expressing these emotions verbally and appropriately, rather than sexually. Clients must show an understanding and respect that each person has the right to define his or her own sexual role. Finally, they must demonstrate (through physiological measures) a decrease of sexual arousal to deviant sexual stimuli and increased arousal to appropriate stimuli (e.g., consensual sexual behavior between adults).

If progress continues in outpatient treatment, the client eventually may qualify for work release, where he is closely monitored and supervised in the community, and subsequently, parole. Although strict control groups were not used to evaluate treatment programs, the study's authors report slightly lower rates of relapse compared to less intensive forms of treatment (Pithers et al., 1989).

California's Sex Offender Treatment and Evaluation Project (SOTEP) also uses a relapse prevention model that emphasizes teaching specific cognitive and behavioral skills to reduce the likelihood of recidivism (Marques & Nelson, 1992). The relapse prevention perspective emphasizes two major steps: (1) identify the steps that increase the risk of relapse, and (2) develop, plan, and practice coping responses to the unique factors that increase personal risk of reoffending. Multiple risk elements must be identified and addressed for any individual offender. These risk factors may be environmental (e.g., access to potential victims in particular places or at particular times, interpersonal stressors) or intrapersonal (e.g., deviant sexual arousal patterns, negative emotional states, drug or alcohol intoxication, and cognitive distortions and misinterpretations).

This program was created in 1985, four years after the state legislature required that all convicted rapists and child molesters be incarcerated by the Department of Corrections, rather than face commitment to state hospitals for treatment. According to law, however, offenders can be transferred to a state Department of Health facility during the last two years of their prison terms. The SOTEP treatment project is housed in a 46-bed unit at Atascadero State Hospital.

An evaluation of the SOTEP program was described by Marques and Nelson (1992). In the selection phase, project staff screened and recruited inmates who met eligibility criteria. Eligibility was restricted to male inmates convicted of one or more offenses of rape or child molestation and inmates who were between 18 and 30 months of their release from prison, had no more than two felony convictions, admitted their offense, had IQs greater than 80, were between 18 and 60 years of age, spoke English, lacked serious medical or mental illness, and did not present serious management problems in prison. Qualified inmates who volunteered were then matched on the characteristics of type of offense, age, and criminal history, and randomly assigned to either the Treatment Group or the Volunteer Control Group. A third group, the Nonvolunteer Control Group, consisted of qualified inmates who did not volunteer.

Only 20 percent of eligible offenders actually volunteered for the program (low volunteer rates for sex offender treatment programs typically weaken the generalizability of results to other sex offenders). Volunteers were somewhat more likely than the total population of incarcerated sex offenders to be child molesters rather than rapists, and were slightly younger and less violent. The Treatment Group examined in the study consisted of 107 offenders: 49 heterosexual child molesters, 23 homosexual child molesters, 9 bisexual child molesters, and 26 rapists.

Several in-treatment clinical improvements were observed over a minimum 1-year period (Marques & Nelson, 1992): decreases in the use of justifications and cognitive distortions associated with sexual aggression, fewer symptoms of depression and social introversion, and reductions in deviant patterns of sexual arousal.

By the end of the study, 66 Treatment graduates (minimum of 1 year of treatment completed), 66 Volunteer Controls, and 56 Nonvolunteer Controls had been released from prison. The mean time since release for the three groups varied between 18 and 22 months. The Nonvolunteer Control Group had a sex offense reincarceration rate (4 percent) twice that of the Treatment Group (2 percent), while the Volunteer Control Group had a sex offense reincarceration rate (6 percent) three times that of the Treatment Group. Although study samples are small and the followup periods brief (typical problems with research in this area), the outcome results are strengthened by the quality of the experimental research design. Comprehensive treatment of sex offenders can significantly lower rates of reoffending and reincarceration, but stronger evaluation research is still needed to determine the range and magnitude of treatment effects over time.

Conclusions

Definitions of rape and sexual assault have changed substantially over time, largely in response to advocacy by women's groups. Measurement of these offenses has also improved, although many crimes still go unreported. Rape victims are disproportionately young, while offenders are typically white males in their early 30s. Victims and offenders frequently knew one another prior to the offense. Rape and sexual assaults have decreased gradually over the past eighteen years, although rates are still high. Many different causes have been suggested, but major theories focus either upon the individual rapist (e.g., psychodynamic and cognitive theories) or the sociocultural forces that maintain or justify coercive male sexual behavior (e.g., feminist theories). Responses to rape and sexual assault have often been contradictory and ambiguous. Changes in legal responses to rape since the 1970s have been most dramatic, although it is not clear that victims have greatly benefited from rape law reforms. Victim assistance and counseling programs are now widespread, but often lack stable resources to meet the needs of their clients. Sex offender treatment programs in recent years show promise, but offenders must be willing to admit responsibility for their offense and demonstrate consistent cognitive and behavioral change prior to release. Even though better outcome studies are still needed to adequately determine the effectiveness of treatment programs, punishment alone seems to provide inadequate protection against sex offenders.

Endnotes

1. Other sexual assault definitions and statistics can be found in U.S. statistical series such as the National Pretrial Reporting Program (NPRP) and the National Judicial Reporting Program (NJRP); see Greenfeld (1997, pp. 31–32).

2. Recently, the Bureau of Justice Statistics (BJS), with assistance from the Committee on Law and Justice of the American Statistical Association, tried to improve the measurement of rape, sexual assault, and domestic violence in the National Crime Victimization Survey (NCVS) (see chapter 2). New questions and procedures were added in 1992 and 1993, which broadened the scope of sexual incidents covered to include sexual assaults and other unwanted sexual contacts (Greenfeld, 1997).

3. Note that post-1992 data were statistically adjusted to reflect changes in the redesigned victimization survey (see Ran, Lynch, & Cantor, 1997). Observed decreases in rape should thus be interpreted cautiously.

4. See *Red Dragon*, *Silence of the Lambs*, or *Hannibal* by Thomas Harris for lurid (but popular) examples of this genre.

References

Bart, P. B., & O'Brien, P. H. (1985). *Stopping rape: Successful survival strategies.* New York: Pergamon.

Bienen, L. (1980). National developments in rape reform legislation. *Women's Rights Law Reporter, 6,* 171–213.

Brownmiller, S. (1975). *Against our will: Men, women, and rape.* New York: Simon & Schuster.

Burt, M. (1980). Cultural myths and support for rape. *Journal of Personality and Social Psychology, 38,* 217–230.

———. (1983). Justifying personal violence: A comparison of rapists and the general public. *Victimology: An International Journal, 8,* 131–150.

Caringella-MacDonald, S. (1985). The comparability in sexual and nonsexual assault case treatment: Did statute change meet the objective? *Crime and Delinquency, 31,* 206–222.

Chappell, D. (1989). Sexual criminal violence. In N. A. Weiner & M. E. Wolfgang (Eds.), *Pathways to criminal violence* (pp. 68–108). Newbury Park, CA: Sage.

Community Voices: Working With WOAR. (1997, March 16). *Philadelphia Inquirer,* p. E5.

Ellis, L. (1989). *Theories of rape: Inquiries into the causes of sexual aggression.* New York: Hemisphere.

Finkelhor, D. (1984). *Child sexual abuse: New theory and research.* New York: Free Press.

Furby, L., Weinrott, M., & Blackshaw, L. (1989). Sex offender recidivism: A review. *Psychological Bulletin, 105,* 3–30.

Gilmartin, P. (1994). *Rape, incest, and child sexual abuse.* New York: Garland.

Greenfeld, L. A. (1997). *Sex offenses and offenders: An analysis of data on rape and sexual assault* (NCJ-163392). Washington, DC: Department of Justice, Office of Justice Programs.

Groth, A. N. (1990). Rape: Behavioral aspects. In N. A. Weiner, M. A. Zahn, & R. J. Sagi (Eds.), *Violence: Patterns, causes, public policy* (pp. 73–79). San Diego, CA: Harcourt, Brace, Jovanovich.

Groth, A. N., & Binbaum, H. J. (1979). *Men who rape: The psychology of the offender.* New York: Plenum.

Koss, M. P. (1988). *Hidden rape: Sexual aggression and victimization of students in higher education.* In A. W. Burgess (Ed.), *Rape and sexual assault* (Vol. 2, pp. 3–25). New York: Garland.

Koss, M., Gidycz, C., & Wisiniewski, N. (1987). The scope of rape: Incidence and prevalence of sexual aggression and victimization in a sample of higher education students. *Journal of Consulting and Clinical Psychology, 55,* 162–170.

Koss, M. P., & Harvey, M. H. (1993). *The rape victim: Clinical and community interventions.* Newbury Park, CA: Sage.

KRON-TV. (1996). Date-rape drug. Aired: June 19, 1996. KRON-TV, Prince William, VA. Available: <http://www.kron.com/nc4/use/stories/daterape.htm>.

Kruttschnitt, C. (1994). *Gender and interpersonal violence.* In A. J. Reiss, Jr. & J. Roth (Eds.), *Understanding and preventing violence: Social influences* (Vol. 3). Washington, DC: National Academy Press.

LaFree, G. (1989). *Rape and criminal justice: The social construction of sexual assault.* Belmont, CA: Wadsworth.

Malamuth, N. (1981). Rape proclivity among males. *Journal of Social Issues, 37,* 138–157.

———. (1984). *Aggression against women: Cultural and individual causes.* In N. M. Malamuth & E. Donnerstein (Eds.), *Pornography and sexual aggression* (pp. 19–52). New York: Academic.

Marques, J. K., & Nelson, C. (1992). The relapse prevention model: Can it work with sex offenders? In R. D. Peters, R. J. McMahon, & V. L. Quinsey (Eds.), *Aggression and violence throughout the lifespan* (pp. 222–243). Newbury Park, CA: Sage.

Marsh, J. C., Geist, A., & Caplan, N. (1982). *Rape and limits of law reform.* Boston: Auburn House.

Muehlenhard, C. L., & Hollabaugh, L. C. (1988). Do women sometimes say no when they mean yes? The prevalence and correlates of women's token resistance to sex. *Journal of Personality and Social Psychology, 54,* 872–879.

Pithers, W. D., Martin, G. R., & Cumming, G. F. (1989). Vermont treatment program for sexual aggressors. In D. R. Laws (Ed.), *Relapse prevention with sex offenders* (pp. 292–310). New York: Guilford.

Polk, K. (1985). Rape reform and criminal justice processing. *Crime and Delinquency, 31,* 191–205.

Ran, M. R., Lynch, J. P., & Cantor, D. (1997). *Criminal victimization, 1973–95* (NCJ-163069). Washington, DC: Department of Justice, Office of Justice Programs.

Rennison, C. M. (2000). *Criminal victimization 1999. Changes 1998–99 with trends 1993–99* (NCJ-182734). Washington, DC: Department of Justice, Office of Justice Programs.

Russell, D. E. (1984). *Sexual exploitation, rape, child sexual abuse, and workplace harassment.* Beverly Hills, CA: Sage.

Sanday, P. R. (1981). The sociocultural context of rape: A cross-cultural study. *Journal of Social Issues, 37,* 5–27.

Scully, D., & Marolla, J. (1984). Convicted rapists' vocabulary of motive: Excuses and justifications. *Social Problems, 31,* 530–544.

———. (1985). Riding the bull at Gilley's: Convicted rapists describe the rewards of rape. *Social Problems, 32,* 251–263.

Sykes, G., & Matza, D. (1957). Techniques of neutralization: A theory of delinquency. *American Journal of Sociology, 22,* 664–670.

Urban Archives, Temple University Libraries. (1999). Women organized against rape (WOAR). *Records, 1972–.* Available: <http://www.library.temple.edu/urbana/woar-tp.htm>.

Weis, K., & Borges, S. (1975). Victimology and rape: The case of the legitimate victim. In L. G. Schultz (Ed.), *Rape victimology* (pp. 91–141). Springfield, IL: Charles C. Thomas. ✦

Chapter 9

Collective and Political Violence

We turn in this chapter to a very different type of violence: behavior that is directed by specific groups of people at other specific groups of people, usually with a specific goal or purpose. The term *collective* violence suggests that violence can be largely a group-level phenomenon, and we need to examine the processes that may trigger, promote, or tolerate collective violence in certain situations (Gurr, 1989b).

In particular, we examine social structural influences of violence, including the use of *power* in conflicts between different groups. Collective violence can be a double-edged sword: Violence has often been used by the powerful to preserve existing power relations, but violence has also been used by groups who feel oppressed to challenge a class-based social system and initiate social change. In this sense, your terrorist may be my freedom fighter, or vice versa.

Brown (1989) has examined numerous historical examples in which collective violence has been used for various causes, some seemingly justified, others less so (see chapter 3). He reminds us that violence is the instrument not only of the criminal, but also of the honorable. Violence has often been used as a means to end the perceived oppression of one group by another, but it has also been used as a means of preserving it. For example, the Revolutionary War represented colonists' resistance to British oppression; the American Civil War represented a deep split over ending slavery and its economic consequences. Rebellious groups, as Rubenstein (1989) noted, often conceive of themselves as cultural entities struggling for some form of self-determination. The Southern elite prior to and throughout the Civil War provide an extreme example of that honorable objective.

Violence has also been used by specific groups to resist social change or to enforce behavioral compliance by others. Three examples illustrate this point. First, the post-Civil War reconstruction period in the United States was accompanied by widespread resistance to the newly granted rights of former slaves. During the first decade after the Civil War, nearly 80 riots by whites occurred in the South against freed slaves and the new federal government. The Ku Klux Klan gained support in the "Old South" and lynch mobs became common. In fact, over 2,000 blacks were killed in this manner between 1882 and 1903 (Brown, 1989). Second, Indian Wars in the United States throughout the eighteenth and nineteenth centuries were marked by settlers' ruthless attempts to seize land and squash resistance. Third, in the late 1800s, lynching was widely used in the so-called Wild West at the same time as it was growing in the South; but in the West, it took place in response to conditions of lawlessness (e.g., protecting one's property, family). Many a suspected horse thief, rapist, or murderer was lynched without a trial.

In the latter 1800s and early 1900s, violence was also used by agents of government or big business to preserve the existing social order (e.g., to end legal as well as illegal strikes). For instance, the Industrial Revolution was propelling society from an agrarian economy to a factory and manufacturing economy; there was mass migration to the cities in a search for work. Many people were displaced from farms in the country; many more had emigrated from other countries to escape oppression and seek opportunity in the idealized democracy of the "New World." Such massive social change resulted in turbulence that led to rising unemployment and masses of povertized people who were concentrated in slums. Various outbreaks of mob violence during this period included labor violence, as workers tried to form unions to reform wretched conditions. Organized crews of strikebreakers were sent in to quell the disturbances, using swift and brutal force. As a result, hundreds of violent clashes between workers and employers occurred between 1870 and 1930.[1]

Three major lessons have emerged over the years (Gurr, 1989a). First, political violence, when it occurs, is often a predictable consequence of certain kinds of social conditions and conflicts. Theorists rarely think of group violence today as pathological, or a breakdown of normal social relationships involving criminals and misfits. Rather, group violence is seen as a consequence of real or at least perceived grievances over underlying social, economic, and political issues.

Second, violence generated by social movements has patterned consequences that are often recognized and used by parties to the conflict. Groups in conflict with rivals or authorities have choices about how to press their claims. Whether violence occurs or not depends upon the choices made by both groups. However, the resort to violence is the result of a complex combination and interaction of fear, belief, and calculation, as well as underlying social conditions. Scholars disagree about which of these (or other) factors are most important.

Third, outbreaks of collective violence in American history seem to be connected with larger cycles of political change. Although risky, violence is often effective in winning concessions or compliance or both, especially when it grows out of a sustained social movement. In this sense, there is always something vaguely democratic about collective violence, even when we disagree with the claims of the aggrieved group. Most groups, whether farmers, strikers, or campus activists, are seeking some form of autonomy or benefits for their group. They typically pursue reforms on behalf of their group and are rarely revolutionaries intent on overthrowing the state (Gurr, 1989a).

Obviously, the extreme example of group conflict (on a continuum of scale) involves open war between tribes, opposing political factions, or entire nations. It is far beyond the intended scope of this text to offer an examination of international conflicts, wars, or genocide, even were there sufficient space to do so. Other disciplines (e.g., history, political science), courses, and books (e.g., Dyer, 1985; Wright, 1965) offer detailed, focused analyses of those topics. Indeed, even narrowing our focus to all types of collective violence in the United States would extend beyond the boundaries of a single chapter.[2] In this chapter, instead, we apply the tripartite framework (chapter 1) to analyze two specific, pressing types of group violence in the United States—urban riots and domestic terrorism. Although both are related to social structural and cultural conditions, and both imply goals of structural and political change, their causes and histories in the United States are somewhat distinct.

Urban Riots

Patterns

On Saturday, May 2, 1992, the Los Angeles riot became the deadliest in recent U.S. history, surpassing by one casualty the 43 killed in the Detroit riots of 1967 (Woestendiek, 1992). The violence had begun 3 days earlier, shortly after a jury found four white police officers not guilty in the videotaped beating of black motorist Rodney King. The so-called flashpoint was the intersection of Florence and Normandie in South Central Los Angeles, a low-income, predominantly black area that had never totally rebounded from the Watts riots of 1965.

A total of 4,500 federal troops had been ordered to Los Angeles by President Bush to assist the 6,000 National Guardsmen who had already spent long hours on patrol. The combined force of soldiers, federal agents, and police from the state, city, and neighboring communities numbered more than 20,000. Authorities patrolled the streets Sunday as people cleaned their neighborhoods, coped with disrupted services, and mourned their losses amid the devastation left by 3 days of rioting. Mayor Tom Bradley extended the dusk-to-dawn curfew except for roving police cars, rumbling armored military vehicles, and National Guard troops standing sentry at street corners and storefronts. Despite sporadic reports of fires, looting, gunshots, and violence, the streets were relatively calm by Sunday, May 3. Fires, once reported at a rate of 50 an hour, had dropped almost to normal levels. Courts began processing the first 700 of more than 6,300 people arrested since the rioting had begun.

Damage from the riots—which injured 2,000 people, destroyed 3,800 buildings, and left 10,000 other structures burned, vandalized, or looted—was estimated at $550 million by Mayor Bradley. Work crews, under escort by California Highway Patrol officers, entered the ravaged South Central area to begin restoring service to the 24,000 homes that were left without power, water, or phone service. Long lines of people formed outside post offices, gas stations, and grocery stores. With many grocery stores destroyed, and many merchants afraid to open, necessities were hard to come by. Mail delivery, like public transportation and trash pickup, was suspended indefinitely. President Bush declared the riot-torn neighborhoods of Los Angeles a disaster area, making them eligible for federal financial help.

The carnage in 1992 Los Angeles was all too familiar to many. During the 1960s, more than 500 race riots broke out in American cities, wreaking an enormous toll in damages, injuries, and lives. At least 167 U.S. cities experienced civil disorders (e.g., riots, violent protests) during the summer of 1967. Although few full-blown riots were recorded in the United States during the 1970s and 1980s, several outbreaks preceded the L.A. riots of 1992.

One of the most serious incidents occurred in the Hispanic neighborhood of Mount Pleasant in Washington, D.C., in May 1991 (Hernandez, 1991). The trigger for the riot was a rumor that a policewoman had shot and killed a handcuffed Latino man during an arrest for public drunkenness. Two days of rioting ensued, where vehicles were burned and businesses looted on Mount Pleasant Street. Police in riot gear eventually fired tear gas to disperse the crowds. Subsequent facts revealed the rumor to be inaccurate. The officer had managed to get handcuffs on only one hand when the suspect broke free, the suspect threatened the officer with a knife and ignored three warnings to halt, and the suspect survived a single gunshot wound to the chest. However, long-seated feelings of mistrust and hostility have typically characterized relations between poor, inner-city minorities and police (Toch, 1992).

In addition to the rumored police brutality in D.C., residents blamed the 1991 rioting there upon a city political structure that had long ignored and disrespected Hispanic citizens. Grievances included rough evictions, callous city officials, exploitative employers, and uncaring teachers. The devastating Los Angeles riots came a year later. In both cases, experts drew striking parallels to the riots of the 1960s:

> The same substandard, overcrowded housing; dreary, poorly paid jobs (or no work at all) and poor schools; the same resentment on the part of the neighbors; the same voicelessness; the

same complaints of police brutality; and the same feeling that nobody cared. (Raspberry, 1991, p. A22)

Explanations

Social structural explanations. Relative deprivation is usually
the wellspring of collective action (Gurr, 1989a). People are not
likely to risk organized conflict unless they are seriously discontented about conditions perceived as unjust: "The perception that
other groups or circumstances prevent people from realizing their
value expectations is a necessary condition for political protest
and rebellion" (Gurr, 1989a, p. 14). Thus, the sources, distribution,
and intensity of discontent in response to perceived injustice influence the mobilization, growth, and shape of group action.

The causes of riots by minority groups nationwide in the 1960s
and in 1992 Los Angeles are strikingly similar (Associated Press,
1992). The Commission on Civil Disorders (known as the Kerner
Commission after its chairperson) was appointed by President
Johnson in 1967 specifically to look at the causes of urban riots. The
major cause was identified as institutional racism: Black rioters felt
that material and political resources available to others were being
denied to them by a white society ruled by the ideology and practices of institutionalized racism. Three major recommendations
followed: (1) Mechanisms for expression of legitimate grievances
and participation in policy formation needed to be created; (2) improvements in the criminal justice system were needed to remove
discrimination and protect the safety of all citizens in all neighborhoods; and (3) there was a need to create a national identity aimed
at removing racial and ethnic barriers (Ball-Rokeach & Short,
1985).

A second commission, the National Commission on the Causes
and Prevention of Violence, was appointed by President Johnson
in 1968 to study individual and collective violence in America. Its
creation was precipitated by such events as assassinations (e.g., M.
L. King, Jr., R. Kennedy), campus violence surrounding Vietnam
War protests, and widespread urban riots the year before. The
commission rejected Johnson's idea that an organized group of
conspirators was responsible for the violence. According to the
commission, the cause of collective violence was a political system
that had failed in two ways: (1) It blocked *legitimate* expression of

grievances, and (2) it prevented policymakers from recognizing and effectively responding to legitimate grievances. Some of the more tangible grievances expressed by rioters included deprivation in housing, employment, and educational opportunities. The common theme of the two 1960s commissions was that the root causes of urban violence lay deep in the social fabric (Ball-Rokeach & Short, 1985).

Curiously, urban riots virtually ceased after the peak year of 1967 (150 civil disorders reported) until the 1990s. Why? Social, political, and economic conditions improved only marginally for the poorest minorities, institutional racism was not cured, and the Kerner Commission recommendations remained largely unfulfilled. Wilson (1987) argued that the majority of blacks had experienced a regression in economic and social conditions since the 1960s. At least four other possible reasons for the hiatus in urban violence must be explored (Ball-Rokeach & Short, 1985).

First, the expansion of social control may have helped repress violence (Ball-Rokeach & Short, 1985). For example, the 1970s witnessed massive increases in police expenditures, especially in large cities. A second explanation has to do with declining expectations: Cuts in federal programs, the failure of other social programs, and the diminished promise of civil rights advancements following the slaying of Martin Luther King may have produced lowered expectations for reform. Third, unique social-historical conditions may also have played a role. The climate in the 1960s was one of reform and hope (e.g., the civil rights movement). Events in history sometimes converge at certain times to produce peaks in demands for change. Riots and protests of the 1960s were partially, at least, a reflection of uniquely organized social movements as well as long-term underlying social conditions (Ball-Rokeach & Short, 1985). Last, but not least, changes in economic structure help explain declines in collective violence. Wilson's (1987) concept of the "urban underclass" reflects a concentration in physical and emotional space of the worst social and economic conditions to be found: unstable families, dependence on social agencies, high crime rates, and a large, unemployable population. According to Wilson, the underclass can become inactive because of economic dependency and psychological despair. As we have now witnessed, the seeds of anger and despair that helped fuel the 1992 L.A. riots nevertheless lie dormant; they have not disappeared. Allegations of police brutality often spark riots, although social and historical conditions shape responses (McCartney, 1992).

Organizational explanations. The City of Los Angeles and the LAPD were, at best, poorly prepared to address the 1992 riots when they first broke out. Useem (1997) argued that a public safety agency (e.g., the LAPD) must balance competing needs to be democratically accountable and maintain administrative capacity. Accountability refers to the objective of controlling state responses to ensure that decisions and practices are consistent with democratic values. Unfortunately, attempts to be accountable may reduce the state's capacity to respond effectively to emergency conditions. For example, the state's capacity to respond to riots involves at least three major elements: (1) strategy, (2) command, and (3) preparation. Although hindsight is easier than foresight, LAPD officials performed poorly in 1992 (Useem, 1997). Based upon interviews conducted with city officials and LAPD officers, Useem illustrated how specific choices and actions by LAPD and city officials help explain responses to riots.

Strategy is an important component of police response. That is, some crowds may be calmed through a strategy of diplomacy rather than a massive show of force. But the success or failure of either strategy is not easily predictable. For example, police use of force can antagonize potential rioters and undermine diplomatic efforts. However, if a diplomatic strategy proves ineffective, it will take time and skill to reconfigure a strategy that includes forceful social control. Early on in the 1992 riots, the LAPD remained committed to a strategy of diplomacy that ignored flagrant, serious law violations (e.g., assaults and vandalism near Florence and Normandie). Officers were specifically instructed to adopt a strategy of "soft patrol" (e.g., to dress in regular patrol uniforms rather than riot gear, to display a cordial demeanor to residents by waving and engaging in casual conversation, and to avoid making arrests). Not until 6:00 p.m., when rioting was already gaining momentum, were officers reconfigured into a riot-ready force (Useem, 1997).

The LAPD was hesitant to respond quickly and forcefully when riots first broke out because of widespread and long-standing public perceptions of unpunished, unrestrained police brutality toward minorities (indeed, that was the very topic of the criminal trial that triggered the rioting). In particular, officials feared that an overly forceful response early on would inflame rioting rather than quell it.

Command is a second critical component of organizational response to riots. A crisis situation creates dilemmas of organization: Who will exercise authority over and coordinate the response of social control agents? A major disturbance heightens the need to be clear about unity of command (e.g., unified versus fragmented), level of command (e.g., centralized versus decentralized authority), and location of command (e.g., at the site of the disturbance versus away from it). In 1992, questionable decisions about command were made in each case, Useem (1997) argued.

Trade-offs accompany decisions about where to set up command operations. Location near the incident may permit the decision-maker to see the situation more clearly and rapidly, more readily take advantage of temporary opportunities as they occur, and communicate more directly with responding officers, perhaps resulting in a more cohesive response. However, it takes time to establish and staff a command post in the field (as opposed to downtown offices), and immediately available resources at the scene may be inadequate. In the L.A. riots, the lieutenant in charge questionably opted for a field command post. Numerous problems included severe congestion (i.e., inadequate room for emergency equipment and personnel to operate) and poor communication (e.g., telephone lines were too few and overcrowded, forcing time-consuming face-to-face transmission of critical information and commands). This resulted in critical delays in information processing and resource deployment. Numerous officers who had rushed to the command post reported during postriot interviews that they had waited around for as long as 3 hours to get their assignments, contributing to declining morale and contempt toward those in command. A second command post at a different location (i.e., the bus depot) was established by the captain of the Metropolitan Division. Interviews revealed that there was no coordination whatsoever between the two posts.

Preparation for a possible riot, a third dimension of organizational response, was surprisingly weak in Los Angeles. In spite of LAPD claims that the force had been well-briefed about a possibly negative trial verdict and that authorities had issued directives that officers were to be fully trained and prepared for a riot, postriot interviews indicated that many officers, including the field post commander, had received no training and no briefing of any sort. Some analysts (Useem, 1997) cited dissension between the mayor and the police chief as a source of confusion: No communication occurred at critical junctures where joint action could have made a difference (e.g., recognizing that the diplomacy strategy favored by city officials was failing badly). The impending retirement of Chief Gates, for example, may have contributed to power struggles and interpersonal conflict among high-ranking LAPD officials, further reducing the likelihood of a coordinated and prepared response to a potential emergency. During the initial rioting, Chief Gates himself left the station early during the disturbance to attend a fund raiser; moreover, two-thirds of the city's 18 area captains were at a conference 60 miles away. In spite of a directive by the assistant chief that a tactical alert was to be declared the moment the King verdicts were read, no tactical alert was announced until 6:55 p.m., 4 hours afterward. A tactical alert would have allowed commanders to keep hundreds of officers beyond their regular shifts, including specifically the South Bureau officers who had been specially trained to staff a field command post.

Useem's (1997) analysis reminds us that agents of social control make important decisions that may reduce or inflame riot conditions. Such organizational explanations provide an important counterpoint to the social structural approaches discussed earlier. Underlying social conditions and frustration may be stronger and more intractable preconditions for a riot, but more proximal causes (triggers) must be identified and examined as well.

Social psychological explanations. Social psychological theories also help explain (partially) the triggering factors associated with mob identity and behavior. **Deindividuation** refers to a process whereby the internal restraints (e.g., internalized rules and norms) that normally keep people from behaving aggressively may be reduced or removed by a person's anonymity within a group. In a mob, people act without fear of consequences because they feel they cannot be identified. Individuals are not easily recognizable, and they may perceive that the likelihood of individuals being held accountable for their behavior is low. As a result, perceived responsibility for behavior, such as rioting, is dispersed throughout the crowd: **diffusion of responsibility**. The intersection of anonymity and diminished responsibility contributes to the escalation of group violence (Scherer, Abeles, & Fischer, 1975), perhaps heightened by various factors including emotional arousal, an emphasis on the present (rather than the future), sensory overload, physical action, reliance upon noncognitive interactions and feedback, novel or unstructured situations, and altered states of consciousness (e.g., lack of sleep) (Zimbardo, 1969).

Similar conditions may contribute to urban riots, although empirical evidence is incomplete. An analysis of press quotations documenting rioters' remarks during the 1965 Watts riots in Los Angeles provides some support for Zimbardo's arguments (Toch, 1992, pp. 192–209). Perceived grievances were clearly present in rioters' motivations (e.g., police brutality, retaliation against white exploitation, and unemployment). Feelings expressed by rioters included a sense of hopelessness, anonymity, and lack of identity.

Collective grievances may have interacted powerfully with social psychological processes to shape the course of events in the emergent riot. As Toch (1992, p. 198) argued, "The influence of other rioters is an obviously important factor in riot motivation, especially among people who become involved as the disturbance expands." Toch further suggests, "The availability of like-minded companions and the example set by riot-initiators often facilitate the translation of despair into destruction and explosion." The targets of riots are symbolic: "The target of collective violence thus symbolically represents persons and agencies who have remained unresponsive to human aspirations" (Toch, 1992, p. 199).

Interventions

According to Gurr (1979), history and contemporary evidence in the United States has taught us that popular opinion tends to sanction violence in favor of the status quo (e.g., maintaining social order). However, prolonged use of violence or force by any group to advance its interests may impede and even prevent reform, because it will elicit strong (defensive) counterviolence. Long-term solutions must address the underlying causes that give rise to grievances.

Historically, American officials have used at least three major responses to political violence: acquiescence, control, and remedial strategies (Gurr, 1979). **Acquiescence** means to stand by and do nothing. This is rarely possible or acceptable in modern times, although government officials often stood by and did nothing in the past (e.g., vigilante violence in the Wild West; black lynchings in the South).

Control refers to the official use of force to restore order. The most common response by the state has been to *suppress* outbreaks of violence, not to ignore them. The greater the perceived threat to the nation's political and economic institutions, the greater the response. There are two specific forms of control. *Preemptive control* refers to the proactive use of strategic tactics (e.g., informers, surveillance) or force before violence breaks out. Frequently, as witnessed by FBI strategies regarding the Black Panthers during the 1960s, such strategies include harassment and arrest of activists, plus saturation policing during marches or protests. *Reactive control*, in contrast, refers to strong reactions *after* violence breaks out (e.g., sending in federal troops, the National Guard, and all available police officers to restore order).

Remedial strategies consist of at least three types. First, a *paternalistic strategy* suggests attacking the immediate symptoms only (e.g., increasing public assistance to address the problem of unemployment). *Accomodation* refers to increasing opportunities within the existing system for the aggrieved group (e.g., creating jobs, offering improved education or job training, or both). Such a strategy may lead to slow but significant change. The rarest type, *radical reform*, requires a direct adjustment in the structure of political and economic power by improving the status of certain groups. Groups would acquire some of the means necessary to resolve grievances themselves (e.g., control over local funding and local political power). For example, in the award-winning PBS documentary series *Eyes on the Prize* (in a segment called "Two Societies, Separate and Unequal"), black community leaders shout to a seemingly deaf white majority, ". . . black people want control over black communities!" Thus, optimal strategies must be a mix of control and remedial strategies (Gurr, 1979). Reforms cannot be introduced if order is totally lacking; order cannot be restored for long if no reforms are made.

Remedial responses to the L.A. riots were slow, controversial, and in the long run, quite limited. An emergency aid bill was finally approved on June 18, 1992, after weeks of stalemate in Congress. Following threat of veto by then-President George Bush, the bill was cut in half from the original $2 billion sought by Democrats (Welch, 1992). The revised bill included $495 million to replenish federal accounts providing business loans and emergency grants to rebuild Los Angeles neighborhoods torn by rioting. An additional $81 million was to be provided to other Small Business Administration loan programs. The bill also included $500 million for a summer jobs program for disadvantaged teenagers. Funds were projected to help create 360,000 summer jobs. Although the stated intention was to help inner-city youth, only about $100 million was targeted to the nation's 75 biggest cities, with the remainder distributed to states under existing Labor Department formulas.

When the bill was finally passed, House Majority Leader Richard A. Gephardt (D., Mo.) stated: "This bill is not nearly as much as I wanted it to be. . . . But at least it's something to begin to resolve the problem, to get young people off the streets" (Welch, 1992, p. A03). Cut out of the original bill was money for summer Head Start, disadvantaged schools, and other social and law-enforcement programs for inner cities that had been added by the Senate. The revised bill also reduced the money for summer jobs from $675 million to $500 million, the maximum amount Bush had said he was willing to accept. Opponents complained that the money allocated was still excessive and contended that the money intended to create jobs could not be well spent in so short a time. Both Democrats and Republicans claimed that the bill was only the first round of legislation to address urban problems. Longer-term initiatives, such as federally funded Urban Enterprise Zones, were planned to jump-start stagnant economies in America's large cities. However, subsequent legislation restricting welfare eligibility has hurt America's poorest minorities.

The Welfare Reform Act of 1998 reduced substantially the ability of individual states to provide welfare benefits to needy citizens (Goodman, 1998). States had to scramble to develop programs to get welfare recipients working in exchange for benefits. In Pennsylvania, 38,000 adults were targeted to lose their welfare benefits by March 3, 1999, unless they were working at least 20 hours a week. Even with new welfare-to-work programs, such as Philadelphia Works, few current heads of households on welfare were working 7 months later (Yant, 1999). Program organizers reported disappointing enrollment, job placement, and retention rates despite a vigorous economy. Of 15,000 Philadelphia welfare recipients targeted for the program, only 7,995 enrolled. Of the 3,800 placed in jobs, half of those quit or were fired (Yant, 1999).

Welfare recipients in work programs struggled with numerous obstacles, including the logistics and expenses of child care and transportation, family stress, mental health problems, substance abuse, and bureaucratic requirements (e.g., required meetings during the day with caseworkers, teachers, and court officials) (Yant, 1999). Even for those who were actually put to work, little financial security was achieved. A 50-family study of welfare reform conducted by Philadelphia Citizens for Children and Youth offered three major conclusions: (1) Although 60 percent of the parents said they were working, 85 percent had incomes below the poverty line; (2) the average wage was $6.32 an hour, or $8,000 a year for a family of three, well below the poverty line of $13,884; and (3) only 40 percent received any health-care benefits from their jobs; only 12.5 percent received any child-care assistance (Yant, 1999, p. A18). We have yet to discover what long-term effects welfare reform may have on families or on children whose parents can no longer provide for them.

Given the emphasis on jobs and loans in the post-Los Angeles emergency aid bill, legislative responses seem to illustrate quite well the accomodation strategy described by Gurr. In the absence of radical reform (i.e., changes in the distribution of power to aggrieved groups) and in light of the recently enacted welfare reform laws (i.e., paternalism), time will tell if scaled-down accommodation strategies are sufficient to avert further riots. There is little reason to be optimistic, given what we have learned (and failed to learn) from riots in the 1960s and 1990s.

Terrorism

On Friday, February 26, 1993, a huge explosion occurred in the underground garage of the Vista Hotel at the World Trade Center complex in New York City. The bomb, consisting of 1,200 pounds of explosives, caused $500 million in damage, killed six, and injured more than 1,000 people. According to the FBI agent who arrested Ramzi Ahmed Yousef, the convicted architect of the bombing, Yousef proudly admitted to being a terrorist. He stated that his only regrets were that the casualties and destruction had not been greater, and that if he had had more money he could have built a bigger, more effective bomb. (Kushner, 1998)

On Wednesday, April 19, 1995, a yellow rental van exploded in front of the Alfred P. Murrah Federal Building in Oklahoma City, killing 168 people and injuring 850 others. Timothy McVeigh was pulled over on Interstate Highway 35 about 75 minutes later for driving without a current registration tag, and was arrested for carrying a concealed weapon. A search of the car uncovered anti-government propaganda and other evidence that eventually implicated McVeigh and accomplices as the Oklahoma bombers. The FBI affidavit filed in federal court stated that McVeigh was extremely agitated about the federal government's assault on the Branch Davidian compound near Waco, Texas, exactly two years earlier (Hamm, 1997). McVeigh was sentenced to death and eventually executed on June 11, 2001.

Definition and Patterns

According to Kushner:

Terrorism is the use of force (or violence) committed by individuals or groups against governments or civilian populations to create fear in order to bring about political (or social) change. (1998, p. 10)

However, terrorism is a diverse, multifaceted concept that can potentially include many different behaviors and groups (Combs, 1997; Kushner, 1998). Definitions of terrorism commonly include some combination of the following elements (Schmid, 1983):

- Violent methods are intended to inspire fear and anxiety among a particular group.

- Those carrying out violent acts may include individuals, groups, or state officials.

- The immediate victims of violence are often not the main targets of the immediate act.

- Immediate victims may be chosen randomly or selectively (representative or symbolic targets).

- Violent acts may be motivated by idiosyncratic, criminal, or political reasons.

- Violence is often intended as a strategy for making demands, gaining attention, or spreading propaganda.

The U.S. Code and the FBI define **terrorism** as "the unlawful use of force or violence against persons or property to intimidate or coerce a government, the civilian population, or any segment thereof, in furtherance of political or social objectives" (FBI, 1998). For purposes of counting, a **terrorist incident** is defined as the following:

> A violent act or an act dangerous to human life in violation of the criminal laws of the United States, or of any state, to intimidate or coerce a government, the civilian population, or any segment thereof. Terrorism is either domestic or international, depending on the origin, base, and objectives of the terrorist organization. (FBI, 1998, p. ii)

According to the FBI, **domestic terrorism**

> is the unlawful use, or threatened use, of force or violence by a group or individual based and operating entirely within the United States or Puerto Rico without foreign direction and whose acts are directed at elements of the U.S. government or its population, in the furtherance of political or social goals. (FBI, 1998, p. ii)

And **international terrorism**

> is the unlawful use of force or violence committed by a group or an individual, who has some connection to a foreign power or whose activities transcend national boundaries, against persons or property to intimidate or coerce a government, the civilian population or any segment thereof, in furtherance of political or social objectives. (FBI, 1998, p. ii)

We will focus our brief inquiry in this chapter on domestic terrorism, using the growing right-wing militia movement in the United States as a primary example. Even though international terrorism is fully deserving of separate, in-depth analysis, we lack space to do justice to the topic here. For both domestic and international terrorism, there is a burgeoning literature (e.g., Combs, 1997; General Accounting Office [GAO], 1997; Hamm, 1997; Mullins, 1997; Weinberg & Davis, 1989), suggesting that the continued development of appropriate theories and responses to terrorism will be a priority in coming years.

Although the number of terrorist incidents both worldwide and in the United States has declined in recent years, the level of violence and lethality has increased. The State Department reported that the number of international terrorist incidents (i.e., acts involving citizens or the territory of more than one country) fell from a peak of 665 in 1987 to 296 in 1996, a 25-year low (GAO, 1997). Seventy-three of the international incidents in 1996 (25 percent) were against U.S. citizens and facilities overseas. Casualties, however, were high: 311 persons killed (including 24 Americans) and 2,652 wounded (including 250 Americans).[3]

Similarly (see Figure 9-1), FBI counts of incidents of domestic terrorism declined from a high of 51 in 1982 to just one incident in 1995 (i.e., the Oklahoma City bombing). However, the Oklahoma attack in 1995 was the deadliest in history on U.S. soil, killing 168 and wounding 500 more. Conventional explosives continue to be the weapon of choice for both domestic and international terrorists, although concern is growing about the potential misuse of

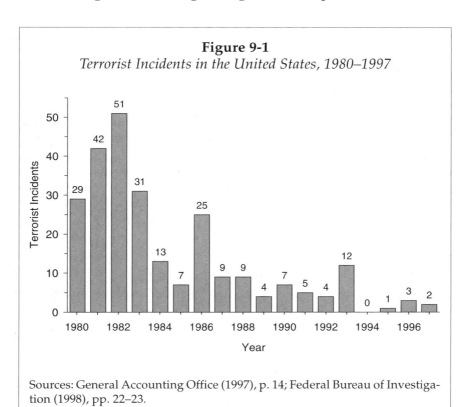

Figure 9-1
Terrorist Incidents in the United States, 1980–1997

Sources: General Accounting Office (1997), p. 14; Federal Bureau of Investigation (1998), pp. 22–23.

chemical or biological weapons (GAO, 1997). The FBI (1999) describes four types of groups that present domestic terrorism threats: (1) right-wing extremist groups, (2) other antigovernment groups, (3) Puerto Rican extremist groups, and (4) special interest extremists.

Right-wing extremist groups include militias and white-separatist groups. Right-wing extremist groups encourage massing weapons, ammunition, and supplies in preparation for a confrontation with federal law enforcement (FBI, 1999). The stated goal of the militia movement is to defend and protect the United States Constitution from those who want to take away the rights of Americans. Militia activity varies from states with almost no militia activity (e.g., Hawaii, Connecticut) to states with thousands of active militia members (e.g., Michigan, Texas). Current membership in such groups, estimated by the American Defense League and the Southern Poverty Law Center, is about 35,000, but inclusion of friends, sympathizers, and allies would add thousands more (Kushner, 1998).

The American militia movement has grown over the last decade. Specific issues include conflicts over guns, state laws, mistrust of federal law enforcement, taxes, and the threat of foreign takeover. The right to bear arms is an issue that rallies most militia members. For example, the national system of instant background checks for all gun buyers mandated by the 1993 Brady Act angered many militia groups. Militias resent state laws forbidding them to gather together to fire weapons. Sixteen states have laws that prohibit all militia groups and 17 states have laws that prohibit all paramilitary training. Mistrust of federal law enforcement is frequently cited in militia literature. FBI and Bureau of Alcohol, Tobacco, and Firearms (ATF) actions, such as Ruby Ridge and Waco, are frequently cited as examples of federal abuses of power. Militia members also believe that tax dollars are wasted by a huge, uncaring, and inefficient bureaucracy in Washington, D.C. Since the Internal Revenue Service collects federal taxes, it is especially hated. Further, the United Nations is perceived as an organization bent on taking over the world and destroying American democracy to establish the "New World Order." This conspiracy theory holds that the United Nations will one day lead a military coup against the nations of the world to form a one-world government. United Nations troops, consisting of foreign armies, will commence a military takeover of America. The United Nations will mainly use foreign troops on American soil because foreigners will have fewer reservations about killing American citizens. Captured U.S. military bases will be used to help conquer the rest of the world (FBI, 1999).

Many right-wing groups adhere to the Christian Identity belief system, which holds that the world is on the verge of a final apocalyptic struggle between God/Christ and Satan (i.e., The Battle of Armageddon), in which Aryans (i.e., European Caucasians) must fight Satan's heirs: Jews, nonwhites, and their establishment allies (i.e., the federal government). The Christian Identity belief system (also known as Kingdom Identity) provides a religious base for racism and anti-Semitism as well as an ideological rationale for violence against minorities and their white allies. Christian Identity teaches that the white race is the chosen race of God, whites are the "true Israelites," and Jews are the children of Satan. Adherents believe that Jews have gained control of the U.S. federal government and are attempting to enslave the white population by enacting laws subjugating white people, such as affirmative action, prochoice, and antigun statutes.

To prepare for Armageddon, many Identity adherents engage in survivalist and paramilitary training, storing foodstuffs and supplies, and caching weapons and ammunition. More extreme adherents may take actions including armed robbery to finance the upcoming battle, destroying government property and infrastructure, and targeting Jews and nonwhites.

Due to widespread propaganda efforts and Christian Identity's broad racist, anti-Semitic, and antigovernment appeal, a number of churches and diverse organizations throughout the United States have embraced these doctrines. Identity beliefs are increasingly found in the rhetoric of all types of right-wing extremist groups including militias, survivalist communes, the Ku Klux Klan, skinheads, tax protesters, Freemen, Populists, gun enthusiasts, militant antiabortionists, secessionists, millenialists, neo-Nazis, white supremacists, and Common Law Courts (FBI, 1999; Hamm, 1997; Kushner, 1998).

Other antigovernment groups include the Freemen, Sovereign Citizens, and Common Law Courts. The Freemen and Sovereign Citizens believe they have the right to renounce their citizenship, after which they do not have to comply with federal laws or rules (FBI, 1999). Some, like the Freemen, believe they have the right to issue their own money, called "certified comptroller warrants." Some groups have formed their own system of laws to replace the existing court system. These Common Law Courts have no basis in federal jurisprudence, but participants claim legitimacy based on the laws of the Old Testament, English common law, the Magna Carta, and commercial law (FBI, 1999).

The **Posse Comitatus** movement, founded by Henry Lamont Beach in Portland in 1969, became the foundation for many of the current antigovernment groups (Kushner, 1998). The term is Latin, meaning "power to the county." Dating back to medieval England, the sheriff could enlist local residents to help enforce the laws and pursue accused criminals. A form of common law belief called "quiet title" provides justification for refusal to pay taxes, obtain driver's licenses, or submit to other forms of state and federal regulation. This procedure supposedly frees a person from state or federal regulation by emphasizing localized custom and authority (Kushner, 1998). For example, the Nullification Doctrine, a concept dating back to 1798, argues that states (or so-called sovereign citizens and militias) have the right to void repugnant federal laws within their jurisdiction. Posse membership grew throughout the 1970s and 1980s, especially in the Midwest, as many family-owned farms failed. Posse leaders offered phony loan schemes, bigoted conspiracy theories, and armed confrontation as solutions to economic problems. More than 100 county sheriffs in Kansas received letters demanding the arrest of judges for ordering seizures of private property. Posse members since 1980 have been arrested, charged, and convicted of offenses including counterfeiting, illegal arms dealing, manufacturing explosives, conspiracy to commit murder of judges and government officials, and murder (Kushner, 1998).

The growing antigovernment movement has been well documented since at least 1994 (Kushner, 1998). The Anti-Defamation League (ADL) released a fact-finding report in 1994 entitled "Armed and Dangerous: Militias Take Aim at the Federal Government." The Southern Poverty Law Center (SPLC), known for advocacy against hate crimes and civil rights violations, announced in 1994 that it was forming a Militia Task Force to monitor developments in the antigovernment movement (Kushner, 1998). On November 1, 1994, Morris Dees of the SPLC sent a letter to U.S.

Attorney General Janet Reno warning of the potential for violence by heavily armed extremist groups. A total of 441 armed militias in 50 states were known as of 1996 (SPLC, 1996).

Puerto Rican extremist groups have occasionally targeted U.S. interests in an effort to gain Puerto Rican independence (FBI, 1999). July 25, 1998, marked the 100-year anniversary of the United States invasion of Puerto Rico during the Spanish-American War. On December 13, 1998, Puerto Ricans voted in a nonbinding referendum concerning Puerto Rico's political status. Despite a lack of popular support (independence garnered only 2.5 percent of the vote), militant independence activists continue to pursue their goals. Several convicted Puerto Rican terrorists remain incarcerated within the federal prison system, and pro-independence activists continue to lobby for their release.

Special-interest extremist groups may advocate violence with the goal of effecting change in one specific policy area. The most recognizable single-issue extremists are those involved in the violent antiabortion and environmental protection movements. The FBI continues to investigate various bombings of abortion clinics and incidents of violence targeting abortion providers across the country (FBI, 1999). The January 1998 bombing of an abortion clinic in Birmingham, Alabama, and the assassination of Dr. Barnett Slepian in Buffalo, New York, serve as reminders of the threat posed by antiabortion extremists.

Terrorists frequently time events and attacks to coincide with dates of symbolic significance (Hamm, 1997; Kushner, 1998). April 20 is the anniversary of Adolph Hitler's birth and has served to mark various right-wing ceremonies and events. April 19, however, is the most important symbolic date for right-wing militia groups: Ruby Ridge, Waco, and the Oklahoma bombings all occurred on April 19. Many antigovernment groups note the April 19 anniversary of the Battle of Lexington in 1775, applauding the efforts of those opposed to the tyranny of the federal government.

Ruby Ridge. The Ruby Ridge incident began on April 19, 1992, creating a fervor for antigovernment propagandists. In a 10-day shoot-out and standoff with federal agents, white separatist Randy Weaver and his family held federal agents at bay following an aborted attempt to arrest Weaver for failure to appear on a federal firearms charge (manufacturing and selling two sawed-off shotguns). After mailing notice of Weaver's scheduled court date

(March 20, 1991), the U.S. Attorney's office received an envelope addressed to the "Servant of the Queen of Babylon." The letter stated that "the stink of lawless government" had reached Yahweh (God) and that "Whether we live or whether we die, we will not bow to your evil commandments" (Hamm, 1997, p. 19). A quote followed from the writings of Robert Mathews:

> A long forgotten wind is starting to blow. Do you hear the approaching thunder? It is that of the awakened Saxon. War is upon the land. The tyrant's blood will flow. (Hamm, 1997, p. 19)

The letter, signed by Mrs. Vicki Weaver, transformed a $300 gun violation into what federal authorities perceived to be a neo-Nazi conspiracy to incite revolution (Hamm, 1997).

After learning of the issue of a failure-to-appear warrant on February 20, 1991, Weaver retreated with his family to his Ruby Ridge cabin where he became increasingly militant and prepared for possible siege. Over a year later, on March 27, 1992, a plan code-named "Northern Exposure" was designed by the U.S. Marshal's office to bring in Weaver (Hamm, 1997). The three-phase plan included (1) attempts to negotiate a settlement through Weaver's friends, (2) intelligence gathering and surveillance, and (3) based on intelligence efforts, figuring out a way to secure Weaver's arrest. A fantastic array of media, federal agents, and equipment (e.g., night goggles, microwave transmitters, and armored assault vehicles) followed.

In preparation for a possible future assault on the cabin, six U.S. Marshals scouting the area around Weaver's cabin came upon a large, yellow Labrador baying wildly and killed it. Weaver's son Sammy, 14, yelled and opened fire on the agents. He was shot and killed as he tried to run up the hill. His companion, Kevin Harris, 23, shot and killed U.S. Marshal William Degan while trying to retreat to the cabin. Larry Potts, head of the FBI Criminal Division, then dispatched the elite Hostage Rescue Team, which included snipers and FBI advisors. As agents circled Ruby Ridge, armored personnel carriers moved up the hill, helicopters hovered overhead, and trucks rumbled into the meadow, the Weavers prepared for Armageddon (Hamm, 1997).

In the ensuing shoot-out, Weaver's wife Vicki was shot dead as she held her 11-month-old baby in her arms. Weaver and Kevin Harris were wounded but survived. During the 11-day standoff,

300 federal agents camped in the meadow as growing crowds of antigovernment protesters became increasingly incensed. Weaver was eventually convinced to surrender by Vietnam veteran Colonel James "Bo" Gritz, Populist Party candidate and a well-known adherent of Christian Identity.

Weaver and Harris were acquitted on murder charges regarding Degan's death. Weaver was convicted of failing to appear in court on the previous weapons charges and served a 16-month sentence. Upon his release, he filed a $170 million lawsuit against the government alleging the wrongful deaths of Vicki and Sam Weaver. A settlement was reached in which each of Weaver's three daughters received $1 million. Weaver himself received a $100,000 settlement on the condition that he bring no further charges against the federal government (Hamm, 1997, p. 242).

Waco. At Waco, Texas, agents of the Bureau of Alcohol, Tobacco, and Firearms launched the biggest raid in their history to seize what they believed was an illegal cache of weapons at the Branch Davidian compound. Four ATF agents and six Davidians were killed in a shoot-out. A tense, 51-day standoff followed, until April 19, when federal agents launched a renewed assault that was followed by a fire that burned the compound to the ground. Eighty followers, including 21 children, were dead. Controversy ensued about whether federal agents started the fire with incendiary tear gas grenades, or whether Davidians set the fire themselves. Attorney General Janet Reno appointed a special prosecutor in 1999 to investigate the circumstances surrounding the fire and what role, if any, the federal government had played. The inquiry eventually substantiated the charges that federal agents had used incendiary devices at Waco and had attempted to cover up their use. In a stunning development on February 6, 2001, former U.S. Prosecutor Bill Johnston plead guilty in federal court in St. Louis to obstruction of justice for withholding information about the FBI's use of pyrotechnic gas canisters before the lethal 1993 fire. The discovery that such materials were indeed used triggered probes, including one by former Senator John Danforth, who called for the indictment. According to reports, prosecutors will recommend three years of probation for Johnston ("News in Brief," 2001). Such events can serve only to further solidify and fuel the fears of antigovernment groups, who for years to come will rally around Waco as the exemplar of government misbehavior and conspiracy.

Explanations

Strain theory. Adherence to right-wing belief systems constitutes a particular type of adaptation to "anomie" or normlessness in American society (see chapter 4). In the United States, widely held cultural goals include monetary success and achievement. Success is thought of as possible for all who work hard, regardless of ascribed characteristics such as socioeconomic status (Merton, 1957). However, not everyone has equal access to culturally sanctioned (legitimate) means for achieving success. Years of quality education and training are often required for the best jobs, and not everyone is extended equal opportunities to these means. Thus, social structure creates a strain between goals and means. The gap between means and goals creates pressure toward nonconformity (deviant behavior), with the greatest pressure on those facing the greatest disjuncture. Individuals experiencing strain may adapt in different ways.

In the **rebellion** adaptation, cultural goals and means are rejected, but new ones are substituted. Rebels attempt to alter society and create a new world where a new set of goals and means is adopted. As Scherer and colleagues (1975) suggested, "This course of action may also lead to violence to the degree that it develops into a revolutionary social movement" (p. 193). Little consensus exists about psychological theories of terrorism (e.g., Crenshaw, 1990; Kaplan, 1978; Ross, 1996; Weinberg & Davis, 1989), but evidence is mounting that some of the major right-wing extremists in the United States to date have been impressive "losers and loners" (Hamm, 1997). Examples illustrate the strain experienced by individuals and how rebellion becomes a viable adaptation. Forceful rejection of cultural goals and means can be found as well as substitution of a well-developed alternative set of goals and means.

Randy Weaver, when asked by a gun dealer (an ATF informant) in 1989 how he was surviving, stated: "Just that. Surviving" (Hamm, 1997, p. 18). Weaver said that times were tough and he was moving his family back to their mountain cabin. He added: "It's all goin' down the tubes." At the prompting of the gun dealer, Weaver's short foray into illegal firearms sales began. When two ATF agents approached Weaver with an offer to drop pending federal weapons charges in return for providing information about right-wing gunrunners, Weaver responded bluntly, "You can go to

hell" (Hamm, 1997, p. 19). In fact, this incident served to fuel
Weaver's growing militancy. At the base of the Ruby Ridge property, Weaver built a wooden cross inscribed with the Biblical quote:
"Every Knee Shall Bow to Yashua Messiah" (Hamm, 1997, p. 18).
Weaver and his son shaved their heads. Weaver's children patrolled the area armed with guns, displaying swastikas, and shouting at neighbors, "Niggers! Go back home!" (Hamm, 1997, p. 20).
In preparation for the coming Armageddon, Weaver stocked the
cabin with six rifles, six revolvers, and several thousand rounds of
ammunition. Like many Identity followers, Weaver's family referred to the U.S. government as the Zionist Occupation Government (ZOG).

Roger Moore was a member of the right-wing Patriots and a
gun collector who knew Timothy McVeigh well through the gun
show circuit. Of McVeigh, Moore said: "I made the mistake of be-
friending him. . . . He was always saying he had no money, no place
to go" (Hamm, 1997, p. 166). "He was always spouting this far-out
stuff. He was to the right of Attila the Hun" (Hamm, 1997, pp.
166–167). Later, when McVeigh moved to Kingman, Arizona, Mike
Fortier recounted, "I thought he was still in the army when he
showed up at my door. . . . When you saw him, it was like he [had]
never left" (Hamm, 1997, p. 167). Likewise, convicted Oklahoma
coconspirator Terry Nichols had accumulated his own impressive
record of failure, unemployment, grinding poverty, and misery
long before the Oklahoma incident (Hamm, 1997, pp. 162–163).

Christian Identity beliefs and politics can provide ample motivations and justifications for violence:

> For the religious terrorist, violence is first and foremost a sacra-
> mental act or divine duty executed in response to some theologi-
> cal demand or imperative. Terrorism thus assumes a
> transcendental dimension, and its perpetrators are consequently
> undeterred by political, moral, or practical constraints. Whereas
> secular terrorists, even if they have the capacity to do so, rarely
> attempt indiscriminate killing on a massive scale—because such
> tactics are inconsistent with their political aims and therefore are
> regarded as counter-productive, if not immoral—religious ter-
> rorists often seek to eliminate broadly defined categories of ene-
> mies and accordingly regard such large-scale violence not only as
> morally justified but as a necessary expedient to attain their
> goals. (Hoffman, 1998, p. 14)

A profound sense of alienation (anomie) intersects with right-wing religious beliefs to set the stage for violence:

> Whereas secular terrorists regard violence as a way to instigate the correction of a flaw in a system that is basically good, religious terrorists see themselves not as components of a system worth preserving at all but as 'outsiders' seeking fundamental changes in the existing order. This sense of alienation further enables the religious terrorist to contemplate far more destructive and deadly types of terrorist operations than secular terrorists—and reinforces the tendency to embrace a far more open-ended category of 'enemies' for attack. (Hoffman, 1998, p. 15)

Christian Identity beliefs remain the most significant bond between today's antigovernment movement followers (FBI, 1999; Hamm, 1997; Kushner, 1998). Immersion into right-wing Christian Identity groups and beliefs, however, may be well advanced by the time that terrorists experience or evidence any obvious "strain," and it is difficult to determine to what degree anomie has preceded, accompanied, or followed immersion into right-wing attitudes and behavior. Certainly, further theory-driven research, including biographical and life history accounts, is needed.

Hamm (1997, p. 176) uses the Levi-Strauss concept of **homology** as a further explanatory device for violent terrorism: There is a dynamic interaction of music, beliefs, and lifestyle that is not linear or predictable, but chaotic and dynamic. Immersion into a particular lifestyle interacts concomitantly with beliefs and individual personality to shape one's thoughts, intentions, and behaviors. Hamm's examples include McVeigh, a frequent user of crystal methamphetamine, whose growing alienation, anger, and excitement interacted with his immersion into right-wing culture and literature, including the infamous Turner Diaries, his adopted manifesto. Extremist beliefs and an alienated, angry personality fed off of and fueled each other over a long period of time.

Cultural deviance. Turk (1990) argued that conflicts between dominant and subordinate groups may be resolved not only by consensual methods, but also by deception and force. Violence is a resource that may be used frequently or infrequently, effectively or ineffectively. In this view, terrorism and terror are associated with the breakdown of traditional authority structures and with efforts to create new ones. Awareness and resentment of political coercion and social inequality do not usually lead to terrorism, Turk stated, although lower-class socialization is more likely to reflect experiences of material and cultural deprivation and defeat, while higher-class socialization reflects experiences of privilege and success. Lower-class individuals are more likely to be resentful without actively resisting, however. Most subordinate persons do not readily move from resentment to resistance or violence. Within lower-class ranks, however, the imagery of terrorism is most likely to attract the young and the politically inexperienced, who have not internalized the accommodations of dominance and deference that characterize well-established authority structures.

Interventions

The first and most immediate challenge to government, military, police, and security services, according to Hoffman (1998), is simply to identify the many diverse and amorphous right-wing extremist groups and more accurately assess their intentions, capabilities, and capacity for violence. A second challenge is to identify reasons why some hitherto peaceful groups suddenly embark on campaigns of terrorism. Due to the diversity of terrorist groups and ideologies, no one magic bullet is likely to be found. Through a broad range of strategies, however, the goals of prevention and intervention should be to ameliorate the underlying causes of terrorism and not just its violent manifestations (Hoffman, 1998).

The federal response to domestic terrorism. The U.S. government has adopted a three-pronged strategy to combat terrorism focused on efforts to (1) prevent and deter terrorism, (2) respond to terrorist threats and incidents, and (3) manage the consequences of a terrorist act (GAO, 1997). Under sponsorship of the National Security Council (NSC), an Interagency Intelligence Committee on Terrorism composed of more than 40 federal agencies, bureaus, and offices has been formed to coordinate policy, plan interagency activities, share intelligence and other information, and coordinate responses to crises. In its Strategic Plan for 1998–2003, the FBI identified as its highest priority foreign intelligence, terrorist, and criminal activities that directly threaten the national or economic security of the United States.

In a statement to the U.S. Senate Committee on Appropriations, FBI Director Louis J. Freeh stressed development of Rapid Deployment Teams capable of responding to multiple terrorist incidents. With funding provided by the Omnibus Consolidated Appropriations and Emergency Supplemental Act of 1999, the FBI announced plans to establish rapid deployment teams in New York City, Washington, D.C., Miami, and Los Angeles.

The FBI counterterrorism effort focuses heavily on intelligence collection, analysis, and dissemination (FBI, 1999). The FBI Counterterrorism Center, established in 1995, encompasses the operations of the FBI's International Terrorism Operations Section and Domestic Terrorism Operations Section.[4] A planned National Domestic Preparedness Office would become a partner with the Counterterrorism Center to ensure that domestic preparedness programs and activities can benefit from the most up-to-date threat information.

Current interagency capacity for terrorism prevention and intervention remains more an ideal than a reality (National Institute of Justice, 1999). The Anti-Terrorism and Effective Death Penalty Act of 1996 required the National Institute of Justice (NIJ) to determine what technologies are needed by state and local law enforcement agencies to combat terrorism. To fulfill this task, NIJ sponsored a survey of state and local law enforcement officials and representatives of other groups that could be involved in preventing and managing terrorist attacks.

The NIJ project was carried out in two phases: Phase I involved an inventory of the technology needs of state and local law enforcement, sent to respondents in all 50 states and the District of Columbia, while Phase II involved analyses of respondents' needs to determine whether existing or developing technology is adequate or whether new technologies are required. Researchers conducted interviews and formed focus groups involving state and local law enforcement officers and other officials (e.g., emergency management officials), who coordinate agency responses to terrorist incidents. A total of 108 interviews and group sessions were held; 195 individuals representing 138 agencies from 50 states and the District of Columbia took part.

By far, the most commonly expressed needs were for ready access to current intelligence and communications regarding terrorism, especially command, control, and communications

("C3")—the ability to communicate information and data and to direct and coordinate the activities of individuals and organizations (particularly first responders) to achieve a common goal. The cost of improving communications security so that plans are not compromised was considered a major shortfall. Other technology needs mentioned were identifying, disarming, and disabling explosives; defending against weapons of mass destruction; apprehending and disarming terrorists; crowd and riot control; and surveillance. The need for more and better training for state and local law enforcement officers in how to combat terrorism was also discussed.

Preventive approaches to domestic terrorism. Improved negotiation and nonconfrontational approaches should receive as much attention as more intrusive technological and military options. Here, the goal is to prevent conflicts from becoming violent. Hoffman (1998), for example, points to the nonviolent resolution of the 81-day standoff between the Freemen, a Montana militia organization, and the FBI in April 1996, an incident that stands in marked contrast to earlier fiascoes in Waco, Texas, and Ruby Ridge:

> By skillfully employing the tactics of negotiation and the non-confrontational approaches developed during previous encounters with antigovernment and white supremacist groups, the authorities defused a potentially explosive situation, obtained the surrender of 16 heavily armed Freemen who had barricaded themselves at the isolated ranch they had dubbed 'Justus Township,' and avoided the bloodshed that had accompanied previous incidents. (p. 16)

As Hoffman (1998) suggests, we must also consider how the more alienating aspects of American society and culture (anomie) support violent, extremist views, and find ways to reduce that sense of alienation among so many people:

> Above all, the profound sense of alienation and isolation of these cults and religious movements needs to be vigorously counteracted. A bridge needs to be found between mainstream society and the extremists so that they do not feel threatened and forced to withdraw into heavily armed, seething compounds or to engage in preemptive acts of violence directed against what they regard as a menacing, predatory society. (p. 15)

Here, the challenge is to develop educational programs that confront and refute right-wing rhetoric before it takes hold. Some progress can be seen: A number of community and nonprofit groups are attempting to counter the spread of right-wing conspiracy theories used to acquire new recruits (see, for example, educational curricula discussed in the next chapter on hate crimes). Through presentations that communicate important lessons in accessible and relevant language, people may gain a more critical perspective from which they can challenge the assertions of right-wing belief systems.

Conclusions

Historically, responses to collective violence have included acquiescence, control, and remedial strategies. Although reactive responses to urban riots and domestic terrorism may be necessary in the short term to restore order, long-term solutions must more proactively address the underlying causes that give rise to grievances. Unless we can learn to better identify and address the root causes that lead people to commit such acts, it seems that urban riots will remain a profound possibility and domestic terrorism a viable option for some of the most alienated, angry members of our society.

Endnotes

1. Although Hollywood movies rarely portray historical events with great accuracy, one could gain a fairly realistic sense of the nature of labor violence in early twentieth-century American cities by watching the movies *F.I.S.T.* (with Sylvester Stallone) and *On the Waterfront* (with Marlon Brando). These films also illustrate how group conflict can lead to criminal violence. Organized crime during this period grew as immigrant groups, first the Irish and then the Italians, found many legitimate opportunities in the "New World" closed to immigrants. Organized crime often infiltrated worker unions (e.g., dockworkers in New York) as a means of controlling important economic and job opportunities.

2. We refer interested readers to the timeless volume edited by Ted Gurr (1989b).

3. Ninety deaths and 1,400 injuries in 1996 resulted from a single truck bombing in Sri Lanka.

4. Federal agencies assigning personnel to the Center include the Bureau of Alcohol, Tobacco, and Firearms, the Central Intelligence Agency, the Defense Intelligence Agency, the Department of Commerce, the Department of Defense, the Department of Energy, the Department of Transportation, the Environmental Protection Agency, the Federal Aviation Administration, the Federal Emergency Management Agency, the Immigration and Naturalization Service, the Internal Revenue Service, the National Security Agency, the United States Customs Service, the United States Marshals Service, and the United States Secret Service.

References

Associated Press. (1992, October 3). Group lists the causes of L.A. riots. *Philadelphia Inquirer*, p. A02.

Ball-Rokeach, S. J., & Short, J. F., Jr. (1985). Collective violence: The redress of grievance and public policy. In L. A. Curtis (Ed.), *American violence and public policy*. New Haven, CT: Yale University Press.

Brown, R. M. (1989). Historical patterns of violence. In T. R. Gurr (Ed.), *Violence in America: Vol. 2. Protest, rebellion, reform* (pp. 23–61). Newbury Park, CA: Sage.

Combs, C. C. (1997). *Terrorism in the twenty-first century*. Upper Saddle River, NJ: Prentice-Hall.

Crenshaw, M. (1990). The logic of terrorism: Terrorist behavior as a product of strategic choice. In W. Reich (Ed.), *Origins of Terrorism* (pp. 7–24). Cambridge, UK: Cambridge University Press.

Dyer, G. (1985). *War*. New York: Dorsey.

Federal Bureau of Investigation (FBI). (1998). *Terrorism in the United States, 1997*. Washington, DC: U.S. Department of Justice, Federal Bureau of Investigation, Counterterrorism Threat Assessment and Warning Unit, National Security Division.

———. (1999). The threat to the United States posed by terrorists. Statement for the Record of Louis J. Freeh, Director, Federal Bureau of Investigation, Before the United States Senate Committee on Appropriations, Subcommittee for the Departments of Commerce, Justice, and State, the Judiciary, and Related Agencies, Feb. 4, 1999. Available: <gov/pressrm/congress/freehct2.htm>.

General Accounting Office (GAO). (1997). *Combating terrorism: Federal agencies' efforts to implement national policy and strategy*. Washington, DC: U.S. General Accounting Office, National Security and International Affairs Division (GAO/NSIAD-97-254).

Goodman, H. (1998, April 19). Rendell hopes 'Philadelphia Works' works for poor, but even if it does, he warns, much more needs to be done. *Philadelphia Inquirer*, p. D1.

Gurr, T. R. (1979). *Alternatives to violence in a democratic society.* In H. D. Graham & T. R. Gurr (Eds.), *Violence in America: Historical and comparative perspectives.* Newbury Park, CA: Sage.

———. (1989a). The history of protest, rebellion, and reform in America: An overview. In T. R. Gurr (Ed.), *Violence in America, Vol. 2: Protest, rebellion, reform* (pp. 101–130). Newbury Park, CA: Sage.

———. (Ed.). (1989b). *Violence in America: Vol. 2. Protest, rebellion, reform,* (pp. 240–265). Newbury Park, CA: Sage.

Hamm, M. S. (1997). *Apocalypse in Oklahoma: Waco and Ruby Ridge revenged.* Boston: Northeastern University Press.

Hernandez, R. E. (1991, May 11). How Hispanics got attention in D.C. *Philadelphia Inquirer*, p. A07.

Hoffman, B. (1998). Revival of religious terrorism begs for broader U.S. policy. *Rand Review, 22*(2), 12–17.

Kaplan, A. (1978). The psychodynamics of terrorism. *Terrorism: An International Journal, 1,* 237–254.

Kushner, H. W. (1998). *Future of terrorism: Violence in the new millennium.* Thousand Oaks, CA: Sage.

McCartney, S. (1992, May 3). Black leaders say warnings went unheeded for years. *Philadelphia Inquirer*, p. A05.

Merton, R. K. (1957). *Social theory and social structure.* New York: Free Press.

Mullins, W. C. (1997). *Sourcebook on domestic and international terrorism: An analysis of issues, organizations, tactics, and responses* (2nd ed.). Springfield, IL: Charles C. Thomas.

National Institute of Justice. (1999). *Inventory of state and local law enforcement technology needs to combat terrorism. Research in Brief* (NCJ 173384). Washington, DC: Department of Justice, Office of Justice Programs, National Institute of Justice.

"News in Brief." (2001, Feb. 7). *Philadelphia Inquirer*, p. A02.

Raspberry, W. (1991, May 10). Problems of harassed and poverty-ridden Hispanics come to the fore in D.C. riots. *Philadelphia Inquirer*, p. A22.

Ross, J. I. (1996). A model of the psychological causes of oppositional political terrorism. *Journal of Peace Psychology, 2,* 129–141.

Rubenstein, R. E. (1989). Rebellion in America: The fire next time? In T. R. Gurr (Ed.), *Violence in America: Vol. 2. Protest, rebellion, reform* (pp. 307–328). Newbury Park, CA: Sage.

Scherer, K. R., Abeles, R. P., & Fischer, C. S. (1975). *Human aggression and conflict.* Englewood Cliffs, NJ: Prentice-Hall.

Schmid, A. P. (1983). *Political terrorism: A research guide to concepts, theories, data bases and literature.* New Brunswick, NJ: Transaction Books.

Southern Poverty Law Center (SPLC). (1996). *False patriots: The threat of antigovernment extremists.* Montgomery, AL: Southern Poverty Law Center.

Toch, H. (1992). *Violent men* (Rev. ed.). Washington, DC: American Psychological Association.

Turk, A. (1990). *Social dynamics of terrorism.* In N. A. Weiner, M. A. Zahn, & R. J. Sagi (Eds.), *Violence: Patterns, causes, public policy* (pp. 212–218). Orlando, FL: Harcourt Brace Jovanovich.

Useem, B. (1997). The state and collective disorders: The Los Angeles riot/protest of April, 1992. *Social Forces, 76,* 357–377.

Weinberg, L., & Davis, P. B. (1989). *Introduction to political terrorism.* New York: McGraw-Hill.

Welch, W. M. (1992, June 19). Congress approves urban aid bill. Scaled-back measure sent to Bush. *Philadelphia Inquirer,* p. A03.

Wilson, W. J. (1987). *The truly disadvantaged.* Chicago: University of Chicago Press.

Woestendiek, J. (1992, May 3). L.A. begins to pick up pieces. Troops patrolling streets; Toll at 44. *Philadelphia Inquirer,* p. A01.

Wright, Q. (1965) *A study of war.* Chicago: University of Chicago Press.

Yant, M. (1999, October 19). Welfare results fall short of hopes. *Philadelphia Inquirer,* pp. A1, A18.

Zimbardo, P. G. (1969). The human choice: Individuation, reason, and order vs. deindividuation, impulse, and chaos. In W. J. Arnold (Ed.), *Nebraska symposium on motivation* (pp. 237-307). Lincoln, NE: University of Nebraska Press. ✦

Chapter 10

Hate Crimes

It was just after midnight on a cold Sunday morning, February 23, 1997. Two black 17-year-olds, Raheem Williams and his cousin Warren, were walking home from the 24-hour Pathmark store on Grays Ferry Avenue in Philadelphia. Raheem was carrying a grocery bag. They remember a sole white man in a black leather jacket and blue jeans, standing on the corner. The man was bathed in light from the front door of St. Gabriel's Social Hall, where a "beef and beer" party was winding down inside. "Got anything in that bag for me?" Raheem said the man had asked. "You're drunk," Raheem had said. "Why don't you go home and sleep it off?" Raheem had to walk past the man to reach his house, and they bumped into each other. Words were exchanged, then shoves and blows. The fight soon involved dozens of whites from inside the hall as well as Raheem's cousin and his mother, Annette Williams, who was punched and kicked on the porch of her home as she tried to intervene. Mrs. Williams was briefly hospitalized; her son and nephew were treated and released. Some whites claimed the mob attacked the Williamses in retaliation for an attack on a white man by blacks hours earlier; authorities never confirmed the earlier attack.

The attack on the Williams family was followed by the March 14, 1997, slaying of white teen Christopher Brinkman by an alleged black robber (Dawsey, Giordano, Fish, & Rhor, 1997, p. A01). Brinkman was shot as robbers held up Squire Drugs, where he was a clerk. Two black men were arrested and charged with the crime. Christopher Brinkman's funeral was held at St. Gabriel's, the center of community life for white, Irish-Catholic residents in Grays

Ferry (Dawsey et al., 1997, p. A01). Over the next 6 weeks, racial tension threatened to boil over into a riot, with Minister Louis Farrakhan's Nation of Islam calling for a 5,000-man march through Grays Ferry and local white residents dismayed to see themselves labeled nationally as violent racists (Bowden, 1997, p. A01). In the attack on the Williams family, six white men were eventually convicted on a variety of charges, including ethnic intimidation, riot, and making terroristic threats. The stiffest sentence was from 9 to 23 months in jail.

Such tragedies illustrate how racial tensions can escalate to violence. But what is a **hate crime** exactly? A whole new category of crime was created with passage of the Hate Crime Statistics Act (HCSA) of 1990. The 1990 HCSA required the collection of nationwide hate crime data for the first time. The goals of the HCSA were to gather information on the frequency, location, extent, and patterns of hate crime, increase law enforcement awareness of the problem and responses to it, raise public awareness of the problem, and send a message that the government is concerned about hate crime. The HCSA requires the Department of Justice (through the FBI) to collect and report data on hate crimes involving the **predicate offenses** of murder, non-negligent manslaughter, forcible rape, aggravated assault, simple assault, intimidation, arson, and vandalism. A predicate offense means two things: (1) A criminal offense has occurred, and (2) that offense was motivated wholly or in part by prejudice (Jacobs & Potter, 1997).[1]

HCSA defines a *hate crime* as "a criminal offense committed against a person or property, which is motivated, in whole or in part, by the offender's bias against a race, religion, ethnic/national origin group, or sexual orientation group." **Bias**, according to FBI guidelines, is "a performed negative opinion or attitude toward a group of persons based on their race, religion, ethnicity/national origin, or sexual orientation" (Jacobs & Potter, 1997, p. 8).

The term *hate crime* is somewhat misleading, because it refers to criminal behavior motivated by prejudice. The label distinguishes criminal behavior motivated by prejudice from criminal behavior motivated by lust, jealousy, greed, and so forth (Jacobs & Potter, 1997, p. 2). Prejudice can be against a wide variety of groups, although only 18 states include gender or sexual orientation in their definitions of hate crimes. However, prejudice is a complex concept, not easy to define in either legal or behavioral terms.

For criminal conduct to be a hate crime, then, it must be motivated by prejudice. The criminal conduct must be *causally related to the prejudice.* But how strong must that relationship be? If the hate crime must be wholly motivated by prejudice, there would be an extremely small number of such crimes. What gets counted in hate crime statistics, therefore, is very much dependent on the definition. It is often difficult to tell whether a given act was a hate crime or a senseless act of violence. Determining this would require one to actually know the motivation of the offender. For example, the infamous Central Park Jogger incident in New York was originally thought to be a hate crime (i.e., a white woman victimized by black and Hispanic attackers), but it was later established that these youths were on a "reign of terror," harassing or attacking anyone in their path. One woman took the brunt of their fury, unfortunately converging in the wrong place at the wrong time with the wrong people (Levin & McDevitt, 1993).

Patterns and Trends

Trends

Many journalists, politicians, and academics have described a "hate crime epidemic" in recent years, but no reliable empirical data exist to support this conclusion (Jacobs & Potter, 1997). Until 1990, the only data were those provided by advocacy groups such as the Anti-Defamation League, the Southern Poverty Law Center, and the Gay and Lesbian Anti-Violence Project. Several problems exist with these data: Each agency pays attention to only limited segments of the population, all lobby for increased attention to the problem, and all compete for scarce government or private funds to support their causes. Further, these agencies use diverse sources of data, including newspaper reports, victim reports to the agency, police data, and so on.

Even though a problem certainly can be identified, there are two main reasons to be skeptical about the existence of an "epidemic": (1) Criminologists are familiar with the considerable difficulties of trying to accurately measure crime, and (2) there have been numerous, vicious bias-motivated attacks against various groups throughout history (e.g., Native Americans, blacks, ethnic and religious groups, women, and homosexuals). We next examine hate crimes measured by the FBI since 1990 (see Table 10-1).

Table 10-1

Hate Crimes Reported to the FBI by Law Enforcement, 1991–97

Year	Number of Hate Crimes Reported	Number of States Reporting	Number of Law Enforcement Agencies Reporting
1991	4,755	32	2,771
1992	7,466	41 + D.C.	6,181
1993	7,587	46 + D.C.	6,551
1994	5,852	43 + D.C.	7,200
1995	7,947	45 + D.C.	9,500
1996	8,759	49 + D.C.	11,000
1997	8,049	49 + D.C.	11,211
1998	7,755	46 + D.C.	10,730
1999	7,876	48 + D.C.	12,122

Source: Federal Bureau of Investigation. "Crime in the United States, Uniform Crime Reports" (*Annual Reports 1991–1999*). Washington, DC: U.S. Department of Justice.

In spite of passage of the 1990 HCSA, which made collection and reporting of hate crimes to the FBI by local law enforcement agencies mandatory, only 11 states submitted any 1990 hate crimes data to the FBI at all, making any reliable conclusions impossible. Part of the problem, the FBI said, was that each state responded to its own unique needs and statutory requirements, and thus collected data quite differently. For 1991 hate crimes, 32 states reported data. However, within those 32 states, only 2,771 of 12,805 law enforcement agencies nationwide reported any data. Of these, 73 percent reported no hate incidents at all. The problem is apparent: Police agencies do not necessarily have the motivation, time, or personnel to collect and code additional data for the federal government. The FBI's first report in 1991 found 4,755 hate crimes nationwide, but because over 14 million total crimes were reported that year, this seems a small number indeed.

The second FBI report covered 1992 hate crimes. Forty-one states plus the District of Columbia reported 7,466 hate crimes. The 1993 report revealed that 46 states plus the District of Columbia reported 7,587 hate crimes to the FBI. In 1994, there was a drop in reported crimes. Trends were up again in 1995 and 1996, then down slightly from 1997 to 1999. Although reported hate crime incidents *appear* to have increased between 1991 and 1999, observable increases are likely due to an increase in the number of agencies and states reporting rather than a true increase.

Passage of a new law requiring the collection and reporting of hate crime statistics is not sufficient to ensure reliable or meaningful data, although the FBI has expended considerable effort to train law enforcement agents in definitions and procedures. The FBI has published two manuals: *Hate Crime Data Collection Guidelines* (FBI, 1990) and *Training Guide for Hate Crime Data Collection* (FBI, 1991). The *Training Guide* instructs police to answer 19 questions about an offense to determine whether to count it as a hate crime or not (Jacobs & Potter, 1997, pp. 15–17). Guidelines are often ambiguous, though. For example, they do not specify how much weight should be given to each of the 19 questions or how many questions need to be answered affirmatively for an incident to qualify as a hate crime. Consider the following examples.

First, FBI guidelines ask whether the victim is a member of a "target" racial, religious, ethnic or national origin, or sexual-orientation group. But are all ethnic and religious groups target groups? Are whites in target groups (Jacobs & Potter, 1997, p. 16)? Second, guidelines ask whether offenders are of a different group than the victim. But what if one or more offenders is from the same group as the victim? Third, guidelines ask whether the incident would have taken place if the victim and offender were of the same group. This judgment seems to rely entirely upon subjective perceptions of the police officer rather than objective evidence. Other guidelines ask the police officer to consider whether the neighborhood where the attack occurred has any previous history of such altercations, whether the victim(s) are outnumbered significantly in a specific area, and whether there is any history of negative sentiment against a specific group. Again, such judgments may require historical and sociological analysis, and even affirmative answers beg the question about offender motivation. There remains considerable subjectivity, therefore, as to what gets defined, investigated, or eventually counted as a hate crime.

Offenses, Offenders, and Victims

Levin and McDevitt (1993), after examining police data in Boston in the early 1990s, suggested several distinguishing features of hate crimes. First, such crimes were excessively brutal.[2] In Boston, about half of reported hate crimes were acts of violence; 30 percent required treatment at hospitals. In contrast, comparisons to national reports (UCR) showed that only about 7 percent of all offenses reported to police were assaults (Levin & McDevitt, 1993). Second, hate crimes were often perpetrated at random, on total strangers. In 85 percent of Boston hate crimes, victims did not know their attackers. But if we compare this to National Crime Victimization Survey (NCVS) figures, fewer than half of violent crimes on average are committed by strangers. Third, a majority of hate crimes in Boston (64 percent) were committed by multiple offenders (often juveniles). If we compare to the NCVS, only 25 percent of violent crimes on average involve multiple offenders. Thus, a group may encourage or support violence against other groups; a group may also offer a sense of anonymity and diffusion of blame.

Levin and McDevitt (1993) also identified three types of hate crimes. In the first type, **thrill-seeking** hate crimes, the individual acts with a group to achieve acceptance. The second type, **reactive** hate crimes, involve incidents in which the individual acts to protect himself or his group from perceived threats from outsiders. In the third type, **mission** hate crimes, an individual or a group targets members of a particular group, which is seen as a cause of personal or societal problems. The relative frequency of each of these types is unknown.

On the basis of national (FBI) hate crime data,[3] Jacobs and Potter (1997) reported that the majority of crimes are not committed by organized hate groups, but by teenagers, primarily white males often acting in a group. Of apprehended offenders, 51 percent were white and 35 percent were black. Researchers estimate that a large percentage of hate crime offenders go unapprehended, at least 42 percent (the arrest rate is especially low for vandalism). Nationally, incidents are typically low-level criminal conduct. According to Jacobs and Potter, hate crimes involved intimidation (29.5 percent), destruction/damage/vandalism (25.7 percent), and simple assault (16.5 percent). But patterns vary from one city and state to another, perhaps because of differences in crime, definitions, or counting. For example, Boston police reported that the most common hate crime was assault and battery with a dangerous weapon (Levin & McDevitt, 1993), but Boston police may undercount or ignore less serious hate crimes (Jacobs & Potter, 1997, p. 20). Nationally, there were only 15 bias-motivated murders and 13 bias-motivated rapes reported in 1993.

Martin (1996) conducted a more detailed examination of hate crime incidents, victims, and offenders which compared two jurisdictions: New York City and Baltimore County, Maryland (excluding the city of Baltimore, but including its surrounding suburban area). The study design included examination of police incident reports of hate crimes in both districts during the same time period, but researchers also examined nonbias crimes of the same penal code classification (e.g., assaults were classified as either "bias-related" or "nonbias-related"). Case-based data were supplemented by interviews with police and telephone interviews of small samples of victims. The data include 2,000 New York City and 700 Baltimore County cases, divided equally between bias and nonbias crimes.

Martin (1996, p. 465) found that most of the bias crimes involved either assaults (32 percent) or harassment (37 percent). Overall, New York City showed a larger proportion of total crimes against persons compared to Baltimore (77 percent versus 59 percent). In New York City, 57 percent of bias crimes were racially motivated (Martin, 1996, p. 464) compared to 77 percent for Baltimore. Of the racially motivated crimes in New York City, antiblack crimes were more likely to involve harassment (46 percent) than physical assault (34 percent), while the reverse was true for antiwhite crimes (harassment, 26 percent versus assault, 57 percent). In New York City, a higher rate of ethnic (e.g., anti-Hispanic) and religious crimes (anti-Semitic) were reported than in Baltimore. Anti-Semitic crimes were more likely to involve vandalism or criminal mischief.

Martin (1996) examined differences between bias and nonbias crimes. Because of differences in location, nonbias crimes were more likely than bias crimes to occur in and around *private* residences. Bias crimes were more likely to occur in *public* places, such as the street, church, or school grounds. Consistent with previous studies, bias crimes were much more likely than nonbias crimes to involve multiple offenders. Offenders were mostly male (80 to 90 percent), and high proportions of these crimes were committed by juveniles. In New York City and Baltimore, 42 and 41 percent, respectively, of offenders were under age 18 (compared to 24 and 22 percent for nonbias offenders).

According to Martin (1996), bias crime victims were more likely than nonbias crime victims to be male, juvenile, and black. Moreover, the offender was more likely a stranger to the victim (89 percent of bias incidents in New York City and 75 percent of incidents in Baltimore). Victims of bias assaults were somewhat less likely to be injured than victims of nonbias assaults. However, victims of bias crimes reacted more strongly than victims of similar, nonhate crimes. In New York City, 40 percent of bias crime victims said they still felt great effects on their lives 2 to 3 months after the incident; only 14 percent of nonbias crime victims reported such long-term effects.

Explanations

Group Conflict Theories

A rich tradition of research in social psychology has examined causal explanations of prejudice, although much more focused research on theories of hate crimes is needed. We know that the more strongly individuals identify with certain groups they belong to ("in-groups"), the more they experience competition and conflict with other groups ("out-groups"). Such in-group versus out-group conflict, even in childhood and temporary groups, is well documented.

The work of Sherif and his colleagues (Sherif & Sherif, 1953; Sherif, Harvey, White, Hood, & Sherif, 1961) illustrated that group membership serves strong individual needs for affiliation and acceptance, and intergroup conflict strongly facilitates group cohesiveness and identity. In the famous "Robber's Cave" experiments, temporary groups of adolescent campers quickly formed strong in-group attachments and strong dislike of out-group members under conditions of relatively mild competition.

In general, experiments have shown that intergroup competition for scarce resources increases the level of cohesiveness within groups. Members are more likely to report that group membership is important to them under heightened competition with another group. Intergroup competition also increases the rejection of the other group's members, as shown by group members' tendencies to emphasize between-group differences and minimize between-group similarities (Cooper & Fazio, 1979; Coser, 1956). Intergroup conflict facilitates distortions of the other group's intentions and behaviors. The other group is frequently stereotyped, dehumanized, or seen as immoral or malevolent, while one's own group is idealized as moral, powerful, and completely justified in its views and actions toward others (e.g., Linville & Jones, 1980).

Tajfel (1981) argued that all that is necessary for group conflict to occur is individuals' perception that they are members of one group and that others are members of a different group, a naturally occurring process he called **social categorization**. Studies have consistently demonstrated systematic in-group preferences and out-group biases even when the out-group was one with whom in-group members never met, never interacted, and about whom they knew very little (Tajfel, 1981).

Strain Theory

As noted in chapter 4, strain results when individuals experience a gap between culturally emphasized goals (e.g., success, wealth, material possessions) and the legitimate means available to achieve those goals (e.g., access to high quality education, participation in social networks). Strain is most acutely experienced by lower-income groups, for whom the gap is the largest (Merton, 1957). Although diverse adaptations to strain are possible, violence against perceived competitors might be predicted under the adaptation of *innovation* (i.e., acceptance of cultural goals, but rejection of legitimate means to achieve them).

Intergroup conflict between different ethnic groups may be heightened by the perceived competition for scarce economic resources. Some experts argue that as America's racial and ethnic makeup diversifies, racial tensions are being heightened: "The rapid increase of a minority population in an area almost invariably leads to conflict," according to Howard J. Ehrlich of the National Institute Against Prejudice and Violence (Welch, 1991, p. A04). "A good deal of what is going on is genuine culture conflict, which then calls out the sort of underlying prejudice and racism that exists in society as a whole." Danny Welch, who monitors hate crimes for the Southern Poverty Law Center in Montgomery, Alabama, stated that:

> We're seeing more and more of it. Ten years ago you saw classic black-and-white issues . . . nowadays . . . people are struggling for the same jobs—blacks, whites, Asians, Hispanics. It can create problems. (Welch, 1991, p. A04)

Indeed, the 1990 Census documented a changing racial mix in American society, with large growth in Hispanic and Asian-American populations and a relative decline in the majority white population. Much of the increase has resulted from immigration, resulting in a doubling of the Asian-American population to 3 percent and a more than 50 percent increase in Hispanics, who now make up 9 percent of the population. Blacks make up about 12 percent of the nation's population, but if current trends continue, Hispanics will surpass blacks as the largest minority group within 20 years.

These demographic shifts may translate into increased racism and resentment of minorities. According to Lynn Duvall, a researcher and writer with the Southern Poverty Law Center's Klanwatch project:

> As diversity grows, hate crime statistics rise, and dealing with tensions caused by competition for jobs and housing, exacerbated by language barriers and cultural misunderstandings, becomes increasingly complicated. (Welch, 1991, p. A04)

Attacks on Asian Americans may reflect resentment of the economic success of Asia and the attention given to achievements by Asian Americans. Tensions between blacks and Asian-American businesspersons, such as Korean grocery store operators in black neighborhoods, have been seen in New York, Los Angeles, Philadelphia, and elsewhere.

Such trends are also characteristic of Grays Ferry in Philadelphia, the example that began this section (Dawsey et al., 1997). The neighborhood's physical landscape is dominated by St. Gabriel's Roman Catholic Church, built in 1909 to accommodate the neighborhood's growing number of Irish Catholics. Over the decades, however, the white population began to give way to an increasing influx of African Americans. In 1970, according to U.S. Census Bureau figures, blacks accounted for 27 percent of the neighborhood; whites, 73 percent. By 1990, whites made up 62 percent of the community; blacks, 36 percent. The census tracts immediately surrounding Grays Ferry are 76 percent black. The declining numbers of whites in the area make many feel insecure. But racial tensions between blacks and Irish-Catholic Americans in the neighborhood go back a long way. In 1832 and 1834, riots took place in the areas south of South Street and east of Grays Ferry. In 1842, the violence moved west and broke out in Grays Ferry and in the neighborhoods to the north. Blacks and Irish lived in the same dilapidated housing in the same alleys and courtyards of South Philadelphia, but had never blended into a community. The violence persisted throughout the 1800s as each group competed for the same menial jobs and as the Irish tried to maintain a tenuous hold on political power. Even today, it seems, the two groups ignore their similarities:

> . . . to stroll the streets here, to talk to residents, is to learn that Grays Ferry is a neighborhood of contradictions. Where love and loathing exist in tandem. Where neighbors tolerate poverty but not each other. Where groups of have-nots duel over nothing more than a ratty playground. (Dawsey et al., 1991, p. A01)

Social Learning Theory

Social learning theories also offer relevant hypotheses about offender motivations and behavior. One's attitudes, values, and beliefs about individuals who belong to specific groups do not surface in a vacuum; they are learned through interaction with others. According to differential association theory (Sutherland, 1947), criminal behavior is learned through interaction with other persons through direct communication. One may learn techniques for committing a crime, but also specific motives, drives, rationalizations, and attitudes associated with the act. One learns definitions of certain behaviors as favorable or unfavorable, and one becomes "free" to commit delinquent or criminal acts when definitions favorable to committing the crime exceed definitions unfavorable to committing the crime (see also Sykes & Matza, 1957). Differential associations vary in terms of frequency, duration, priority, and intensity. Differential learning of attitudes and behaviors occurs most strongly within primary groups, such as peers and family. Learning of attitudes and behaviors conducive to criminality is subject to all of the mechanisms that are involved in other learning. As a result, values and behaviors that are rewarded are likely to increase in frequency, while those that are not tend to diminish.

It is likely that mistrust, stereotypes, and animosity toward other ethnic groups are learned and reinforced through one's interactions with intimate acquaintances and family members, and those associations provide both justifications and rewards for committing acts of violence or harassment against out-group members. Juvenile perpetrators of hate crimes, for example, often voice justifications that they believe they are protecting their neighborhood from the threat of invaders, and the majority of their acts are committed in the company of one or more peers or family members (Levin & McDevitt, 1993).

A recent British study cites similar factors relating individual, group, and community prejudice (Sibbitt, 1997). Case studies were conducted in two London boroughs. Researchers interviewed a wide variety of people in the two areas, including staff in government agencies (police, housing departments, schools, the Youth Service, and the Probation service) as well as victims, perpetrators, and residents of local communities. Perpetrators of racial harassment and violence frequently acted together as friends or even families. Views held by perpetrators toward ethnic minorities tended to be shared by the wider communities to which they belong. For perpetrators and community residents expressing racist views, racism served to divert attention from underlying problems and a sense of powerlessness in their lives. In this sense, ethnic minorities may serve as *scapegoats* for some segments of the population, especially in times of economic hardship (Allport, 1954).

Interventions

Police Bias Investigation Units and Conflict Prevention Units

Many cities have formed police **bias units** to investigate possible bias crimes. Despite media focus on a few well-publicized incidents, little is known about the more frequent, less visible offenses typically identified as hate crimes, and we know little about the structure, processes, or effectiveness of bias-crime units found in police agencies (Martin, 1996). Careful examination of police responses was conducted by Martin in New York City and Baltimore County, Maryland, in 1988. Both police departments, in spite of differing practices and procedures, were recognized as leaders in formulating responses to hate crimes.

In New York City, a Bias Incident Investigating Unit (BIIU) was created in December 1980. The Unit consisted of 18 investigators citywide. The procedure for investigating bias crimes is as follows: Initially, if the first officer on the scene suspects bias, he or she notifies a shift sergeant, who contacts the precinct commander. Both officials respond, as well as a BIIU officer. Then, BIIU decides whether the crime was likely motivated by bias or not. At this point, BIIU becomes responsible for the case, and a special review is needed to reclassify the case as not a hate crime. Thus, the first officer on the scene has enormous influence in determining whether an incident is labeled as a bias crime or not. In New York, bias need only be responsible in part for the offense. Factors considered in the determination of bias include display of offensive symbols, date and time of occurrence, and statements by the suspect at time of attack (e.g., racial epithets). The duties of BIIU officers include working closely with precinct detectives, paying special attention to victims (e.g., reassure, link with neighbors, and refer to organizations and agencies who can help), and monitoring progress of cases through the criminal justice system. In 1987 and 1988, 1,200 cases were reviewed, including 150 that were later determined unfounded.

In Baltimore County, Maryland, the population of 655,000 is 85 percent white. The department initiated a special approach to bias crimes in 1981 following several reported KKK incidents. Unlike New York City, there is no special bias investigation unit. Responsibility for investigating bias cases rests with individual beat officers, precinct supervisors, and Community Service Officers (CSOs). If organized hate groups are involved, precinct officers may request assistance from the department's Community Relations Division (CRD) or from its Intelligence Division. This approach has grown with the department's emphasis on community-oriented policing in general. Between 1981 and 1986, one detective was assigned to bias crime investigations. In 1986, verification criteria were modified, investigative responsibility shifted to precinct personnel, and oversight and record keeping shifted to CRD. CRD monitors cases and maintains close ties with community groups and with each precinct's CSO. Cases are handled according to department procedures and then reviewed at monthly meetings attended by officers from CRD, a representative from the state Human Relations Commission, the county executive's minority affairs specialist, and at least one precinct CSO. All cases are reviewed and classified as either verified, unverified (i.e., not enough evidence to determine), or unfounded (i.e., clearly not a bias incident). Criteria for classification, as in New York City, are based on FBI guidelines. Between 1982 and 1988, 690 bias incidents were reported in Baltimore County—581 involved a criminal offense; 407 incidents and 346 criminal offenses were later verified.

Clearance rates (i.e., percentage of cases in which an arrest was made) for bias crimes were typically higher than for similar, nonbias crimes. In Baltimore, the clearance rate was 20 percent for bias crimes and 14 percent for nonbias crimes. In New York City, the clearance rate was 24 percent for bias crimes and 9 percent for nonbias crimes. Results seem to reflect more intensive police investigations of bias crimes (Martin, 1996). In both jurisdictions, witnesses were less likely for bias than for nonbias crimes (13 versus 21 percent). However, in New York City, police conducted a follow-up interview with the victim in 95 percent of bias versus only 14 percent of nonbias cases. In Baltimore, officers were only slightly more likely to conduct follow-up interviews in bias versus nonbias cases. Police activities that occurred more frequently for bias crimes in both sites included canvassing for witnesses, taking photos of the crime scene, and showing photos of suspects to crime victims.

These are two very different policing strategies operating in the two areas. Neither is cheap, and both require substantial police resources and training. Further, the two jurisdictions differ considerably, and an appropriate intervention strategy needs to take into consideration relevant community characteristics, such as demographic makeup, needs, priorities, histories, and so on. The community-oriented approach is probably more difficult in New York City, where the population is more diverse, more transient, and less middle class than in Baltimore County. Martin (1996) argued, however, that a visible police response has great symbolic importance, and police agencies have a responsibility to set a *moral tone* in their departments and in their communities.

Hate Crime Legislation

Forty-seven states have now enacted some kind of hate crime legislation (exceptions are Nebraska, Utah, and Wyoming). According to Levin and McDevitt (1993), common types of state legislation include institutional vandalism in 36 of the 47 states (e.g., vandalism against churches, synagogues, and schools); bias-motivated violence and intimidation (29 of the 47 states); and interference with religious worship (18 of the 47 states), such as crimes that disrupt religious services or desecrate religious symbols.

Although legislation varies a great deal from one state to another, Jacobs and Potter (1997) describe three major types of hate crime laws (recall that individual states have the constitutional authority to develop their own criminal laws). Each has different functions, and each provides important options for law enforcement and courts.

The first type, **substantive laws**, are largely based on the Anti-Defamation League's (ADL) Model Hate Crime Law (1992), which establishes a separate *intimidation* offense. State laws vary a great deal in designating which offenses are predicate crimes.[4] Most hate crime laws do not use the word *motivation*. Instead, they refer to a person who commits an offense *because of* or *by reason of*. Nevertheless, state courts have generally interpreted hate crime statutes to require proof of a prejudiced motive (Jacobs & Potter, 1997). The second type, **sentence enhancements**, are statutes that either upgrade an existing offense or increase the maximum penalty for offenses motivated by prejudice. In Pennsylvania, for example, an offender is charged with a crime one degree higher than the predicate offense (thus allowing stronger penalties). State laws vary greatly in regard to the magnitude of the enhancement for bias motivation. In federal law, the 1994 Crime Bill mandated a revision of the U.S. sentencing guidelines to allow enhancements for hate crimes of three offense levels (sentencing guidelines depend on offense level and previous record) above the base level for the underlying offense (Jacobs & Potter, 1997). The third type, **reporting statutes,** are laws that specify requirements for hate crime data collection and reporting. The exemplar is the Hate Crimes Statistics Act (HCSA) of 1990, which required the collection of nationwide hate crime data for the first time.

The prosecution of hate crimes, unfortunately, remains relatively rare, although defendants charged with criminal acts (e.g., assault) have been and continue to be prosecuted under other criminal laws. The prosecutor faces a considerable burden in trying to prove that the person was motivated by hate. A Catch-22 exists: A hate crime is very difficult to prosecute successfully, but failure to pursue criminal charges could result in anger and retaliation in the victim's community. At the same time, prosecution may anger those in the alleged offender's group or community. Either way, the prosecutor risks the possible escalation of community tensions, and selecting an impartial jury is often extremely difficult (Jacobs & Potter, 1997).

For laws to be effective, police must arrest, prosecutors must charge, juries must convict, and judges must sentence. For various reasons, hate crimes (like all crimes) undergo much case attrition: Cases are filtered out of the criminal justice system as they are processed (Levin & McDevitt, 1993). In Boston, of 452 cases reported to police, only 60 resulted in arrest, 38 were charged (in the other 22 cases there was insufficient evidence or diversion), 30 were convicted, and 5 were incarcerated. Numerous difficulties explain such attrition. For example, hate crime statutes are fairly new laws, and prosecutors may be hesitant to pursue charges vigorously. There are relatively few arrests, and most offenders are strangers to the victim. The evidence is often insufficient to sustain conviction (e.g., offender motivations of bias are difficult to prove), and judges may not be sure how to proceed with punishment (e.g., specialized sentencing enhancements further complicate existing state sentencing guidelines).

Some cases are prosecuted under the Federal Civil Rights Act (e.g., fair housing laws, fair hiring practices, etc.), although a much larger number of prosecutions occur today at the state level (Levin & McDevitt, 1993). There are four main types of federal legislation: (1) **civil rights protections against conspiracies** (e.g., neighbors conspiring to keep out certain ethnic groups); (2) **forcible interference with civil rights** (e.g., preventing someone from eating in a public restaurant, enrolling in school); (3) **deprivations of civil rights under cover of law** (i.e., actions committed by public officials, especially police, who intentionally deprive an individual of his or her constitutional rights),[5] and (4) **willful interference with civil rights under the Fair Housing Act** (i.e., interference with an individual's rights to buy, rent, or live in a home; includes incidents of firebombing and harassment).

Like state laws, however, federal statutes are only rarely enforced. Between 1987 and 1989, the U.S. Department of Justice prosecuted only 31 cases of racial violence (Levin & McDevitt, 1993). Although it is not entirely clear why prosecutions are so rare, at least two main explanations have been offered. First, a markedly reduced emphasis on civil rights during the Reagan/Bush era was reflected by conservative nominees to the U.S. Supreme Court and a lack of federal funding for enforcement of civil rights legislation. Second, the remedies available under federal law are extremely limited. They only protect citizens who are threatened or attacked while exercising a federally protected right (e.g., buying a home). This would exclude a majority of victims.

Civil Remedies

On a November evening, 1988, in Portland, Oregon, Mulugeta Seraw, an Ethiopian graduate student, was being dropped off by two friends. Three skinheads from a group called East Side White Pride spotted them. The skinheads blocked the Ethiopians' path and ordered them to move. When the Ethiopians did not respond immediately, one of the skinheads took a baseball bat and smashed their car windows. Another skinhead turned the baseball bat on Seraw, crushing his skull with repeated blows. Seraw was dead on the scene before the ambulance arrived. (Dees & Bowden, 2001)

On a July evening in 1998, at Hayden Lake, Idaho, Victoria Keenan and her teenage son, Jason, were driving past the 22-acre Aryan Nations compound when their car backfired, a sound that Aryan Nation security guards apparently mistook for a gunshot.

A truckload of guards gave chase, firing shots until the Keenans' car went into a ditch. Jesse Warfield, then chief of security, pulled Keenan by the hair and threatened to kill her. The other guards beat her son. (Dees & Bowden, 2001)

What do these two incidents have in common? First, both provide grievous examples of violent hate crimes. Second, both resulted in major civil lawsuits by Morris Dees and the Southern Poverty Law Center that intentionally bankrupted two of the most notorious white supremacist organizations in the United States. The Southern Poverty Law Center (SPLC), founded in 1971, is a nonprofit organization that combats hate, intolerance, and discrimination through education and litigation. Its programs include Teaching Tolerance (see following) and the Intelligence Project, which collects and disseminates detailed information about the location, operations, and activities of major hate groups operating in the United States. The organization and its director, attorney Morris Dees, are probably best known for winning several major lawsuits against organized hate groups (Dees & Bowden, 2001).

In the Seraw case, Dees and the SPLC won $12.5 million in damages against the defendants, Tom Metzger and his son, John, leaders of the White Aryan Resistance (WAR) movement. Dees successfully proved that the Metzgers, by their actions in sending skinheads to Portland to propagate the racist and violent mission of WAR, and by inciting youth to commit acts of violence against minorities and foreigners, were legally liable for Seraw's death even though the Metzgers were 1,500 miles away when the crime occurred. The Seraw case established a strong precedent for future litigation based on legal principles of "vicarious liability." That is, hate groups can be held legally liable for spawning violence even when they do not directly participate in the actual crimes. The U.S. Supreme Court refused to hear Metzger's appeal, and the judgment stood.

In the other verdict, an Idaho jury on September 7, 2000, returned a $6.3 million civil judgment against the Aryan Nations, its founder Richard Butler, and former security guards. Butler, an 82-year-old rural Idaho pastor who has often been called the elder statesman of American hate, was held liable for the actions of his security force. Dees established that the Aryan Nations guards were poorly trained, guards were hired without any background checks, and the organization attempted to cover up a lack of proper procedures after the lawsuit was filed. Further, Dees convincingly demonstrated that the Aryan Nations had a long history of promoting violent racism. Through an extensive publishing network and a prison outreach program, Aryan Nations had for years promoted the supremacy of the white race and the notion of a separate white homeland. Its annual summer conferences in Idaho were well known as the largest and most visible meetings for white supremacists in the United States. In a final insult to Butler, the entire 20-acre Aryan Nations compound was seized and awarded to plaintiffs. Dees said that the property may be used to build a center for tolerance. In sum, the Butler case provided Dees and the SPLC with a golden opportunity to pursue crippling damages against one of the most well-organized hate groups in the United States. Civil lawsuits thus provide important strategic weapons to reduce hate-related violence.

Teaching Tolerance

If values and attitudes conducive to committing hate crimes can be learned, as suggested by social learning theories, then it is possible that they can be unlearned. In-group biases and stereotypes can potentially be reduced through regulated contact between persons from each group, especially if the contact is between persons of equal status, the contact is in-depth and not superficial, the social climate for contact is friendly, the behavior during such contact challenges previously formed stereotypes, and the contact occurs within an environment favoring cooperation rather than competition. Such principles have been used effectively to reduce conflict between various adversarial groups, such as members of different ethnicities and nationalities (e.g., Amir, 1969; Foley, 1976). Various curricula have also been designed to dispel stereotypes and increase tolerance between different groups.

The SPLC (1999) offers free or low-cost resources to educators at all levels. The SPLC began the *Teaching Tolerance* project in 1991 as an extension of the center's various legal and educational efforts. *Teaching Tolerance* curriculum resources include two video-and-text teaching kits, *America's Civil Rights Movement* and

The Shadow of Hate, which chronicle the history of hatred and intolerance in America and the struggle to overcome prejudice. A third kit, *Starting Small*, is a teacher-training package for early childhood educators. Other resources include a set of eight-color "One World" posters, accompanied by a 12-page teacher's guide and grants of up to $2,000 for K-12 teachers. The program also offers a 1-year research fellowship for educators with strong writing skills and an interest in equity issues. A magazine titled *Teaching Tolerance* is distributed free twice a year to a half-million educators throughout the United States and 70 other countries. It features contributions of writing and artwork that address classroom themes of tolerance, respect, and community building.

Other strategies have combined school curricula with broad-based school-community partnerships to reduce hate crime. In Massachusetts, the Student Civil Rights Project attempts to reduce hate through several initiatives (Mahoney, 1999). First, a summer internship program brought together a diverse group of college and high school students from across the state to explore, identify, review, and recommend curricula and resources that school communities could implement to prevent hatred and prejudice in schools. Students had to confront their own feelings and attitudes toward different groups, as well as their own experiences with victimization and discrimination. Interns received training in civil rights laws and history from legal experts and civil rights organizations.

A centerpiece of the internship program was creation of a youth-focused web site (<www.stopthehate.org>), an on-line educational-reporting mechanism designed to provide students, teachers, and administrative professionals with tools and resources to combat and reduce bias within schools. The site provides information on victim assistance, diversity awareness training, and peer mediation as strategies to reduce bias-related incidents. An on-line history section features information on the Holocaust and the Civil Rights Movement. An on-line bulletin board is featured. Further, an on-line reporting form is available: Students can report incidents of hate-motivated harassment or violence directly through the Internet. On-line reports are received by a student civil rights director who may then establish contact with school officials or law enforcement, or both. The student site is linked to the Governor's Task Force on Hate Crimes webpage.

The project has developed a resource manual called the *Educator's Resource Manual,* containing a comprehensive overview of hate crime laws and prevention steps for schools and communities as a well as the *Hate Crimes Resource Manual for Law Enforcement and Victim Assistance Professionals.* The project has also focused upon raising student awareness about hate crimes through distribution of pamphlets and posters as well as its website. The project provides extensive community outreach, mainly through designing and offering collaborative training symposia for schools, educators, and law enforcement. In collaboration with a local UPN television station, the group also works on strengthening media resources to raise awareness about issues and resources to prevent hate crimes. A 1-hour special, entitled *The Teen Files: The Truth About Hate*, was created and produced, and a diversity awareness curriculum was designed to complement the television special and integrate with web-based resources.

The project has requested through the governor's office that all Massachusetts high schools designate a civil rights coordinator who will serve as a contact for the student civil rights director in the event of a hate-related incident; the coordinator will also act as a liaison between the school and local law enforcement. A training session is being planned for all school-based civil rights coordinators. The project is expanding its efforts throughout the state, including creation of pilot civil rights teams in 10 to 15 high schools. Although such efforts are laudable, we hope that necessary resources will be allocated to properly evaluate the degree to which programs achieve their objectives over time (e.g., reductions in hate-related attitudes and behaviors).

Conclusions

Creating a new crime category may serve important symbolic and political functions. Hate crime laws attempt to rectify past wrongs by translating civil rights into the criminal law (Jacobs & Potter, 1997). However, passing new laws does not necessarily improve crime control. Definition and measurement of hate crimes remains problematic, gathering data from police agencies has been difficult, and enforcement and prosecution of hate crime laws have been minimal. Efforts aimed at providing better training for criminal justice personnel may help in the future. Civil lawsuits have provided an important supplemental weapon against hate crime, as witnessed by major lawsuits won by the Southern Poverty Law Center. At the very least, the ability of laws to change human behavior is limited. We still need to address the individual and social causes that underlie hate and prejudice. It is unlikely that legal strategies alone will suffice. Well-designed educational and social learning strategies aimed at promoting and assessing an increase in tolerance must be part of a multifaceted strategy to reduce hate crime.

Endnotes

1. As an analogy, consider the predicate in a written sentence. The predicate (some specific action) depends on (requires) the subject (some specific actor, place, or object). The predicate cannot exist alone (in a proper sentence) without the existence of a subject. In predicate *crimes*, similarly, the bias statute depends upon an already existing criminal statute.

2. Subsequent analyses of national-level data suggest that Boston was somewhat unique in its high level of reported hate-crime violence. See Martin (1996) and Jacobs and Potter (1997) for further discussion.

3. FBI data do not provide very much data on offenders. See Martin (1996) and Jacobs and Potter (1997) for further discussion.

4. *Ibid.*, Note 1.

5. The federal civil rights convictions of police officers in the Rodney King case in Los Angeles certainly provide the best known example, although successful prosecutions under these provisions are extremely rare; in fact, charges are rarely even initiated.

References

Allport, G. (1954). *The nature of prejudice*. Cambridge, MA: Addison-Wesley.

Amir, Y. (1969). Contact hypothesis in ethnic relations. *Psychological Bulletin, 71*, 319–342.

Anti-Defamation League. (1992). *Hate crimes statutes: A 1991 status report*. New York: Anti-Defamation League.

Bowden, M. (1997, April 13). How a Grays Ferry street fight became a racial crisis. The strife in the neighborhood had been brewing. Some unlikely alliances had to form to prevent it from boiling over. *Philadelphia Inquirer*, p. A01.

Cooper, J., & Fazio, F. H. (1979). The formation and persistence of attitudes that support intergroup conflict. In W. G. Austin & S. Worchel (Eds.), *The social psychology of intergroup relations*. Pacific Grove, CA: Brooks/Cole.

Coser, L. A. (1956). *The functions of social conflict*. Glencoe, IL: Free Press.

Dawsey, D., Giordano, R., Fish, L., & Rhor, M. (1997, March 23). Grays Ferry: Decades of racial divide. Recent crimes have heightened tension. Residents feel forgotten. *Philadelphia Inquirer*, p. A01.

Dees, M., & Bowden, E. (2001). *Taking hate groups to court*. Montgomery, AL: Southern Poverty Law Center. Available: <http://www.splcenter.org/legalaction/la-3.html>.

Federal Bureau of Investigation. (1990). *Hate crime data collection guidelines*. Washington, DC: Government Printing Office.

———. (1991). *Training guide for hate crime data collection*. Washington, DC: Government Printing Office.

———. (*Annual Reports*, 1991–1999). *Crime in the United States* (Uniform Crime Reports). Washington, DC: Department of Justice.

Foley, L. A. (1976). Personality and situational influences on changes in prejudice. *Journal of Personality and Social Psychology, 34*, 846–856.

Hate Crime Statistics Act. (1992). 28 U.S.C. § 534 (Supp. IV).

Jacobs, J. B., & Potter, K. A. (1997). Hate crimes: A critical perspective. In M. Tonry (Ed.), *Crime and justice, a review of research* (Vol. 22, pp. 1–50). Chicago: University of Chicago Press.

Levin, J., & McDevitt, J. (1993). *Hate crimes: The rising tide of bigotry and bloodshed*. New York: Plenum.

Linville, P. W., & Jones, E. E. (1980). Polarized appraisals of out-group members. *Journal of Personality and Social Psychology, 38*, 689–703.

Mahoney, J. (1999, August). Stop the hate: Massachusetts task force creates student civil rights project to combat problem. *Corrections Today*, pp. 82–86.

Martin, S. (1996). Investigating hate crimes: Case characteristics and law enforcement responses. *Justice Quarterly, 13*, 455–480.

Merton, R. K. (1957). *Social theory and social structure*. Glencoe, IL: Free Press.

Sherif, M., Harvey, O. J., White, B. J., Hood, W. R., & Sherif, C. W. (1961). *Intergroup conflict and cooperation: The Robber's Cave experiment*. Norman, OK: Institute of Group Relations.

Sherif, M., & Sherif, C. W. (1953). *Groups in harmony and tension*. New York: Harper & Row.

Sibbitt, R. (1997). *Perpetrators of racial harassment and racial violence.* London, England: Great Britain Home Office Research and Statistics Directorate.

Southern Poverty Law Center. (1999). *Teaching tolerance.* Available: <http://www.splcenter.org/teachingtolerance/tt-mainbtm.html>.

Sutherland, E. H. (1947). *Principles of Criminology* (4th ed.). Philadelphia: Lippincott.

Sykes, G., & Matza, D. (1957). Techniques of neutralization: A theory of delinquency. *American Journal of Sociology, 22,* 664–670.

Tajfel, H. (1981). *Human groups and social categories: Studies in psychology.* New York: Cambridge University Press.

Welch, W. M., of Associated Press. (1991, September 10). New racial diversity fuels hate-crime wave. *Philadelphia Inquirer,* p. A04. ✦

Chapter 11

The Role of Firearms in Violence

On April 20, 1999, two teenage gunmen stormed Columbine High School in suburban Littleton, Colorado, killing 12 fellow students and a teacher before committing suicide. Few events in recent history have so shocked the public consciousness. Colorado Governor Bill Owens was sitting in his office, ready to sign legislation to expand the right to carry concealed firearms, when gunshots rang out at Columbine High (Paulson, 2000). Instead, the Republican governor refused to sign the measure and asked lawmakers to take all gun legislation off the table pending further review. They complied.

According to Governor Owens, the Columbine murders forced officials to examine current gun laws for potential loopholes and reforms. Owens admitted that he was previously unaware of straw purchases or the ease of acquiring a weapon at gun shows (Paulson, 2000). A straw purchase refers to the practice of a "clean" buyer (e.g., no criminal record) buying a gun for someone who legally cannot do so. Owens was also surprised to discover that many guns are sold by unlicensed gun dealers at gun shows, where no background checks are conducted. In fact, the two Columbine assassins had purchased one of their weapons at a gun show.

Nine months after the Columbine murders, Governor Owens voiced support for gun-control measures (e.g., banning straw purchases, requiring safe storage of firearms, raising the age for buying a handgun from 18 to 21, adding juvenile records to background checks, and requiring criminal background checks at gun shows). The Columbine incident has given gun-control bills a similar boost in other states. Even gun-control advocates were surprised when California legislators passed bills limiting handgun sales to one a month and strengthening the assault-weapons ban. In Pennsylvania, a bill requiring gun buyers to purchase trigger locks finally passed after failing in a previous session (Paulson, 2000).

Situational Correlates of Violence

The Columbine incident provides a tragic example regardless of one's political beliefs. It illustrates the need to examine *situational* correlates of violence: What role do firearms play? What role does alcohol and drug use play? What role do specific settings (e.g., hot spots) play?

Although our major focus to this point has been on specific *types* of violence, we turn now to an examination of specific *settings and objects* frequently associated with violent behavior. Social scientists have long recognized that human behavior results from complex interactions between persons and their environments (e.g., Monahan & Klassen, 1982; Brantingham & Brantingham, 1991; Parsons, 1951). This idea is frequently summarized by the equation $B = f(P, E)$, in which *Behavior* (B) is a *function* (f) of both *Person* (P) and *Environment* (E). Similarly, according to criminologists, criminal acts depend upon both offender motivation and opportunity, and each shapes the other over time (Brantingham & Brantingham, 1991). Any violent act is always the result of an interaction between two or more individuals *and* characteristics of the specific situations they find themselves in, never solely one or the other.

Even though definitions vary, a good general definition of a *situation* is offered by Pervin:

> . . . an organism's engagement with an array of objects and actions which covers a time span. A situation is defined by who is involved including the possibility that the individual is alone, where the action is taking place, and the nature of the action or activities occurring. (1978, pp. 79–80)

This definition acknowledges that behavior in any given place and time is influenced simultaneously not only by characteristics of the individuals involved (i.e., their individual personalities and learning experiences), but also by the availability of specific objects (e.g., weapons), characteristics of the physical environment (e.g., design characteristics of a particular bar, street corner, school, or public park), and the social setting (e.g., the presence of others, role expectations, the use of alcohol and drugs). The study of situations and settings where violence frequently occurs has begun to yield some consistent findings and conclusions. In this chapter, we examine the role of firearms in violence. In the next chapter, we focus upon the role of alcohol and other drugs.

Patterns and Trends

Crimes Involving Firearms

Guns are involved in a large number of violent crimes. Results from the National Crime Victimization Survey (NCVS) reveal that 670,500 victims of serious violent crimes (rape and sexual assault, robbery, and aggravated assault) faced an offender with a firearm in 1998 (U.S. Department of Justice, 2000a). Victimizations involving a firearm represented 23 percent of the 2.9 million violent crimes of rape and sexual assault, robbery, and aggravated assault.

These numbers are certainly cause for concern, although recent declines in felony gun use have been encouraging. As the data in Figure 11-1 indicate, the number of crimes committed with firearms declined dramatically from 1993 to 1998, falling to levels last experienced in the mid-1980s (U.S. Department of Justice, 2000b).

The use of firearms is more frequent for certain types of crime than others. Uniform Crime Reports (UCR) data show that more than two-thirds (68 percent) of the 18,209 murders occurring in 1997 were committed with firearms. In 1998, about 65 percent of all murders, 32 percent of all robberies, and 19 percent of all aggravated assaults reported to the police were committed with a firearm (U.S. Department of Justice, 2000b).

Injuries

To what degree does the presence of a gun during a crime increase or decrease the likelihood of the victim being attacked, or the victim being injured? Fortunately, victims of crimes involving the use of a firearm are only rarely shot. Of the victims of nonfatal violent crime who faced an assailant armed with a firearm, only 3 percent suffered gunshot wounds in 1997. An estimated 57,500 nonfatal gunshot wounds from assaults were treated in hospital emergency departments from June 1992 through May 1993 (U.S. Department of Justice, 2000a). The answer also depends upon the type of crime under consideration.

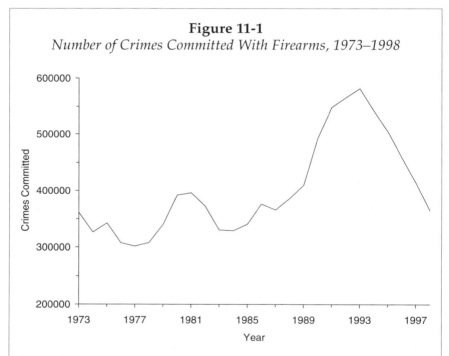

Figure 11-1

Number of Crimes Committed With Firearms, 1973–1998

Source: Bureau of Justice Statistics Website (2001). *Crime facts at a glance: Crimes committed with firearms, 1973–98.* Available at <http://www.ojp.usdoj.gov/bjs/glance/guncrime.htm>.

Death is a rare outcome of violent crime. Cook (1991) found that 5.7 nonfatal gunshot injuries occur for every homicide, but the risk of death is highly elevated for young people (ages 15–34), particularly black males. Among teenagers aged 15 to 19, the gun homicide rate was 83.4/100,000 for black males, compared with 7.5 for white males of the same age.

Further, although death is a rare outcome relative to the total number of violent crimes committed with firearms, a significant percentage of firearm-related deaths are homicides. According to data from the National Center for Health Statistics, in 1996 about 41 percent of the deaths that resulted from firearms injuries were homicides, 53 percent were suicides, 3 percent were unintentional, and 2 percent were of undetermined intent (U.S. Department of Justice, 2000b).

Some researchers have argued that the use of a gun during a crime, such as robbery, enables the perpetrator to achieve his or her goals without firing the weapon, and thus attack and physical harm may actually be prevented (Kleck, 1991). National Crime Survey data for the time period 1973 to 1982 show that escalation from threat to attack was less likely when the offender was armed with a gun (probability = .14) than when he or she was unarmed (.30), armed with a knife (.25), or armed with another weapon (.45) (Reiss & Roth, 1993).

It is equally likely, however, that possession of a gun may encourage the perpetrator to challenge potential victims whom they might otherwise have avoided (Cook, 1981). Fully 55 percent of commercial robberies involve guns; only 13 percent of personal robberies involve guns. Guns may also be fired impulsively (e.g., conflicts between intimates and acquaintances). For example, between 1976 and 1987, twice as many women were shot and killed by their partners as by strangers (Reiss & Roth, 1993).

In incidents where a gun is actually fired, significant injuries are likely. For example, Zimring (1968) reported fatality rates of 12.2 percent for gun attacks and only 2.4 percent for knife attacks, the second most lethal weapon. Even though robbers who carry a gun are more likely to complete their robberies without experiencing victim resistance and without injuring their victims (Cook, 1991), gun injuries are clearly more dangerous. In cases where the victim received medical attention, gun victims were more likely (84 percent) than knife victims (74 percent) to be hospitalized. Overall, though, the probability of being hospitalized following victimization by a gun-using offender was only 6 percent, the same as when the offender was unarmed.

Characteristics of Offenders

Weapons arrest rates per 100,000 population are highest for teens, males, and blacks (U.S. Department of Justice, 2000a). Juveniles have been involved in an increasing proportion of weapons arrests in recent years, creating enormous concern about a future crime wave by violent juvenile "superpredators." While many researchers (Cook & Laub, 1998; Harris, Welsh, & Butler, 2000) have expressed skepticism about these predictions, there is certainly cause for concern.

Reliable long-term statistics on juvenile gun use are scarce, but official statistics since 1980 provide a chilling picture (Snyder, 1998). Juvenile arrests for weapon law violations doubled between 1987 and 1993. Gun homicides by juveniles in the United States tripled between 1983 and 1997, while homicides involving other weapons declined. From 1983 through 1995, the proportion of homicides in which a juvenile used a gun increased from 55 percent to 80 percent (Greenbaum, 1997). In fact, *the overall increase in juvenile homicide witnessed in the mid-1980s was entirely firearm-related* (Snyder, Sickmund, & Poe-Yamagata, 1996). Correspondingly, recent *decreases* in juvenile homicides since 1993 are entirely attributable to decreases in murders committed with firearms (Snyder, 1998).

Juveniles report having easy access to guns. In a survey of 758 male students in inner-city high schools and 835 male serious offenders incarcerated in six different detention facilities (Sheley & Wright, 1993), it was found that 83 percent of inmates and 22 percent of students possessed guns. These firearms tended to be high-quality, powerful revolvers. Most detainees and students stated it was easy to acquire a gun; only 35 percent said it would be difficult. Fifty-three percent of students said they would "borrow" a gun if they needed one (from family members or friends); 37 percent of students and 54 percent of detainees said they would get one off the street. Though involvement in drug sales was more common among those reporting that they carried a gun, the main reason given for carrying a gun was self-protection.

Firearm Acquisition and Use

An important question concerns a person's motivation for using a gun: What situations increase the likelihood of one person using a firearm against another? According to the National Research Council (Reiss & Roth, 1993, p. 262), "establishing the motive for an instance of gun use is a formidable, time-consuming, judgmental task, often with an uncertain outcome." Available evidence, however, provides some interesting results.

In a survey of 1,874 incarcerated felons interviewed during 1982 by Wright and Rossi (1985), 184 reported firing a gun while committing an offense. Of these, the most commonly reported motivations for using a gun included "to protect myself" (48 percent), "to scare the victim" (45 percent), and to "kill the victim" (36 percent) (note: categories are not mutually exclusive). Fully 76 percent of the felons who used a gun during an offense claimed that they had no prior intent to fire the gun, suggesting that the presence of a gun alone greatly increases the chances of using it. The 1991 Survey of State Prison Inmates (Beck et al., 1993), based upon interviews with a representative national sample of 14,000 inmates, found similar results. The most frequently reported reasons for using a gun were to scare the victim (54 percent), for protection (30 percent), to kill the victim (14 percent), and to get away (12 percent). The conclusion to be drawn is that many criminals who use guns do so for instrumental reasons (i.e., to expedite commission of the offense or escape or both).

Inmates were also questioned about the sources (i.e., from whom) and means (i.e., what type of transaction) of gun acquisitions (Wright & Rossi, 1985). The most frequent source was family or friends (44 percent), followed by illegal gun markets (26 percent), retail outlets (21 percent), and other (9 percent). The most common means or type of transaction was a cash purchase (43 percent), followed by theft (32 percent), a loan (9 percent), a gift (8 percent), or trade (7 percent). The 1991 Survey of State Prison Inmates (Beck et al., 1993) found similar results: Among those inmates who possessed a handgun, 31 percent acquired it through family or friends; 28 percent acquired it through an illegal market, drug dealer, or a fence; 9 percent acquired it through theft. About one-quarter of offenders (27 percent) acquired guns through retail outlets. The most criminally active offenders were especially likely to obtain guns from nonretail sources (Wright & Rossi, 1985), suggesting serious limitations (but not futility) of prevention strategies aimed at regulating retail sales (see following). It should be noted, however, that even legitimately purchased guns can end up being used in violent crimes. In one study, Cook (1981) found that of each new cohort of handguns sold, about one third are involved in a crime at least once in their lifetimes.

Motivations by citizens to use a gun, not surprisingly, are different. Self-defense is often reported as a primary motive for gun ownership, although the actual frequency of self-defense incidents is a point of considerable disagreement among researchers. For example, Kleck (1991) estimates incidents of self-defense gun use at between 700,000 and 1 million times per year, about 10 times higher than estimates obtained by Cook (1991). To interpret such findings, however, numerous questions must be asked about the reliability of different data sources (e.g., self-report surveys versus arrest statistics), problems associated with definitions and measurement of self-defense, and how researchers adjust data to address possible alternative explanations of results.

Overall, results from the National Crime Victimization Survey indicate that crime victims very rarely defend themselves with firearms: 1.2 percent of robberies, 1.4 percent of assaults, and 3.1 percent of residential burglaries (Reiss & Roth, 1993, p. 266). However, victims reporting self-defense appear to experience slightly lower injury rates. For example, of intended robbery victims who defended themselves with a gun, the self-reported injury rate was 17 percent compared to 25 percent for those who made no self-defense attempt.

Explanations

Symbolic Interaction Theory

A landmark study by Luckenbill (1977) illustrated how disputes become violent through a series of interpersonal exchanges. The concept of a *situated transaction* refers to a series of interactions between people in a specific setting, time, and social context. The presence of a weapon during such a dispute greatly increases the likelihood of its use. Luckenbill examined 71 homicide cases drawn from one county over a ten-year period. Data included police, probation, psychiatric, and witness reports; offender interviews; victim statements; and grand jury and court testimony. Luckenbill illustrated that criminal homicide frequently resulted from some conflict between offender and victim that escalated over time, resulting in attempts by one or both parties to "save face" at the other's expense.

Six stages were used to summarize the typical progression of events. At stage 1, the victim makes an initial move toward the offender: a statement or insult. At stage 2, the offender interprets the victim's previous move as offensive. At stage 3, the offender retaliates physically or verbally to restore face. At stage 4, the victim responds to the offender's challenge, essentially forming a "working agreement" for violence. At stage 5, physical combat ensues, ending in the death of the victim. Although weapons can be brought into play at any stage in a violent interaction, their use is especially likely at stage 5. In 36 percent of the cases examined by Luckenbill, offenders had carried weapons into the setting. In 64 percent of the cases, the offender either left to get a weapon or used an existing prop as a weapon (e.g., a knife, baseball bat, beer bottle, or glass). Stage 6 refers to the termination of the transaction, at which point the offender either remains at the scene or flees.

Luckenbill's research showed that murder is often the result of an intense two-way interchange between offenders, victims, and bystanders in particular settings. The availability and presence of guns in situated transactions greatly increases the likelihood of their use. The 1991 Survey of Prison Inmates (Beck et al., 1993) confirmed that 90 percent of offenders who carried a weapon into a particular setting to commit a crime actually used it. More than half of the inmates who committed murder (64 percent), robbery (51 percent), and assault (57 percent) regularly carried a weapon.

Routine Activities and Illegal Markets

Is gun crime more concentrated in some places than others? Evidence suggests that focusing on the specific places and activities where gun crime is the most frequent may provide promising explanations and strategies for the prevention of gun violence.

Routine activities (see chapter 4) refer to recurrent and prevalent activities that provide for basic population and individual needs, including work, provision for food, shelter, recreation, socializing, learning, and raising a family (Cohen & Felson, 1979). According to the theory, offenders commit offenses near places where they spend most of their time, and major pathways in between. Further, individuals are victimized near places where they spend most of their time, and major pathways in between. Routine activity patterns influence crime rates by affecting the convergence in space and time of three elements required for direct personal victimization to occur: (1) motivated offenders, (2) suitable targets, and (3) the absence of capable guardians.

Cohen and Felson used national data to describe population routine activities and crime rates, but others have argued that a smaller, more appropriate unit of analysis is *places*, "fixed physical environments that can be seen completely and simultaneously, at least on surface, by one's naked eyes" (Sherman, Gartin, & Buerger, 1989, p. 31).

Places, like people, have their own routine activities that partially explain different frequencies and types of crime. While the population in certain places may be transient (people come and go), the *activities* that occur there are often patterned in regular (routine) ways. Examples of routine activities in specific places include typical types of social and economic interactions, the relative wealth or poverty of participants, approved and disapproved activities, and typical moral values. Places, like people, then have their own distinct "characters."

Sherman and colleagues (1989) found that specific crimes in Minneapolis between 1985 and 1986 were heavily concentrated in specific places. Over half of all calls to police were to only 3.3 percent of all places, and the top 5 percent of all locations generated an average of 24 calls each (i.e., nearly one every two weeks). When researchers focused on specific crimes, hot spots became even more concentrated: 4,166 robberies were reported in only 2.2 percent of places; 3,908 auto thefts were reported in only 2.7 percent of places; and 1,729 sex crimes were reported in only 1.2 percent of places. The hottest spots for robberies, rapes, and auto thefts included an intersection located near bars, a liquor store, a park, a bus depot, an intersection with homeless shelters and bars, a downtown mall, and another intersection near an adult bookstore and bars.

Do places *cause* crimes, however, or merely *host* them? According to Sherman and colleagues, some places actually facilitate crime, especially predatory crime. In particular, robberies (e.g., near 24-hour cash businesses), sex crimes (e.g., in public parks), and stranger violence (e.g., low opportunities for surveillance) were found to be very place specific.

Some illegal market offenses, such as prostitution and drug sales, may create their own routine activities (Sherman et al., 1989). Such activities in and around these specific hot spots tend to overwhelm legitimate activities in the area and increase the likelihood of convergence of motivated offenders, competitors for illegal market sales, and perhaps potential victims (e.g., drug buyers) who, fearing danger, routinely carry firearms in these areas (Decker, Pennell, & Caldwell, 1997).

Using data obtained from over 7,000 arrestees in 11 major urban areas involved in the Drug Use Forecasting (DUF) program, Decker and colleagues (1997) found strong evidence relating involvement in illegal markets to gun carrying, use, and victimization. They found that a higher percentage of arrestees than in the general population have ever owned a firearm; they acquire firearms easily, and a substantial number have used them to commit crime. The groups reporting the easiest access to firearms were those most likely to be involved in illegal markets: drug sellers and gang members.

Research findings suggest the existence of a small but violent subculture in which the possession and use of guns is common and tolerated. Gang membership, drug selling, gun carrying, and gun use were all highly related. Among the entire sample of arrestees, gang members (50 percent) and drug sellers (42 percent) were much more likely than other arrestees (23 percent) to use a gun to commit a crime. Both were more likely to be victimized by other gun users as well: 50 percent of juvenile males and more than 75 percent of gang members reported being shot at. Similar to other studies (Beck et al., 1993; Sheley & Wright, 1993), reasons most commonly cited by arrestees (two thirds) for carrying a gun were protection or self-defense.

Repeat gun criminals are particularly attracted to gun-carrying hot spots because of illegal market activities, and these high-risk offenders are much more likely to use guns in these high-risk places (Sherman & Rogan, 1995). Gun crimes, unsurprisingly, are highly concentrated in specific areas (Sherman, Shaw, & Rogan, 1995). The good news, if any, is that place-specific opportunities for intervention may also be afforded by such places (see following).

Cultural Theories and Firearm Availability

To what degree is the easy availability of firearms partially or largely responsible for high rates of violence in American society? Does the United States experience higher rates of violent crime (especially homicide) than other countries because of its permissive laws regarding gun ownership and sales? What evidence can we bring to bear upon such important questions?

No precise gun count exists, but the Bureau of Alcohol, Tobacco, and Firearms (ATF) estimated in 1990 that there were 200 million guns in the United States (Reiss & Roth, 1993). The proportion of households owning any gun has remained stable at about 50 percent for three decades. The biggest increase in gun ownership occurred between 1959 and 1978, when the portion of citizens owning handguns increased from 13 percent to 25 percent. Rates of gun ownership are generally highest in rural areas and small towns, higher for whites than blacks, highest in the South, and higher for high-income households (Reiss & Roth, 1993). Simple "subcultural" interpretations suggesting that some groups are more predisposed toward owning and using guns than others are not easy to support; there is considerable diversity in the membership of gun owners.

A review of various studies using cross-national, interjurisdictional, and longitudinal analyses to examine the relationship between gun availability and violence found no relationship between gun availability and the number of nonfatal gun crimes (Cook, 1991). For crimes that ended in death, greater gun availability was associated with somewhat higher rates of felony murder, but this factor did not account for a large proportion of total violence.

A comparison of Seattle and Vancouver (two cities that are similar in demography, geography, and socioeconomic status, but located in different countries) showed that gun ownership had no effect on the prevalence of robbery rates, but Seattle had an overall homicide rate 60 percent higher and a firearm homicide rate that was 400 percent higher (Sloane et al., 1988). More permissive gun laws in Seattle were implicated by the researchers as the major explanation for these dramatic differences.

Although some researchers have claimed that increased handgun availability among the population actually provides a deterrent to would-be criminals (Kleck, 1991; Lott, 1998), easy availability may also mean that guns can be used more often in violent crimes, and perpetrators in high-availability jurisdictions may even increase their firepower because of fear that potential victims may be armed (Reiss & Roth, 1993). Research suggesting that gun availability deters would-be criminals typically suffers from inadequate controls for important cross-jurisdictional variations in poverty rates, gang and drug activity, and local and state governmental gun laws and anticrime programs (Ludwig, 1999).

Available evidence, although not entirely conclusive, suggests that gun availability alone cannot explain high rates of violent crime in the United States. As Reiss and Roth (1993) caution, *the direction of causality* in such studies is not always clear. For example, in household surveys, some respondents who report owning guns may be arming themselves in response to higher crime rates in their community, producing a spurious correlation between gun ownership and violence rates. Differences may also reflect regional differences in culture and attitudes, which are difficult to measure and control for in cross-jurisdictional studies. Research is further complicated by the lack of a national data system to track unique identifiers of firearms and by their frequent movement, through burglary, unregulated sales, and simple carrying from one situation to another (Reiss & Roth, 1993). The best evidence comes from controlled evaluations of changes in laws that reduce firearms availability (see following).

Interventions

Disrupting Illegal Gun Markets

As already noted, some evidence indicates that gun availability is related to gun homicide rates. However, some researchers (e.g., Sherman et al., 1995) argue that it is not simply the total number of guns in circulation that increases gun violence, but the carrying of guns in high-risk places at high-risk times. If this is true, then greater enforcement of existing laws against carrying concealed weapons might reduce gun crime.

This was the question posed by the **Kansas City Gun Experiment**, an evaluation of a police patrol project to reduce gun violence. If police could get more guns off the street, would there be fewer gun crimes? The experiment developed out of a federal grant awarded to the Kansas City (Missouri) Police Department (KCPD) under the Bureau of Justice Assistance (BJA) "Weed and Seed" program in 1991. The intervention was based on the theory that additional, proactive police patrols to detect gun violations would increase gun seizures, which, in turn, would reduce gun crime either by deterring potential offenders or by incapacitating greater numbers of gun-using criminals.

The target beat was an 80-by-10-block area with a 1991 homicide rate of 177 per 100,000 persons, about 20 times the national average. The population was almost entirely nonwhite; the area had very low property values and consisted predominantly of single-family detached homes. A comparison beat with very similar population demographics and similar crime rates (e.g., total firearm-related crimes, shots fired per incident, drive-by shootings, and homicides) was chosen.

For 29 weeks, from July 7, 1992, to January 27, 1993, the Kansas City Police Department focused extra patrol attention on gun crime "hot spots" in the target area. The actual techniques the officers used to find guns included stop-and-search frisks based upon reasonable suspicion, searches incident to an arrest on other charges (i.e., the basis for a legitimate arrest had already been established), and safety frisks associated with car stops for traffic violations. Officer overtime was paid for by the federal grant. No special efforts were made to limit police activities in the comparison beat, but neither were special funds available for extra patrol time in that area. The hot spot locations were identified by a computer analysis of all known gun crimes.

The extra patrol was provided in rotation by officers from Central Patrol in a pair of two-officer cars working on overtime under the federal Weed and Seed program. Four officers thus worked 6 hours of overtime each night from 7 p.m. to 1 a.m., 7 days a week, for a total of 176 nights, with two officers working an additional 24 nights, for a total of 200 nights, 4,512 officer-hours, and 2,256 patrol car-hours. They focused exclusively on gun detection through proactive patrol and did not respond to calls for service.

Because the extra patrol hours were federally funded, separate bookkeeping was required to document the time. In addition, an evaluator accompanied the officers on 300 hours of hot spots patrol and coded every shift activity narrative for patrol time and enforcement in and out of the area. Property room data on guns seized, computerized crime reports, calls for service data, and arrest records were analyzed for both areas under the study.

The primary data analyses compared all 29 weeks of the Phase 1 patrol program (July 7, 1992, through January 25, 1993, when the Phase 1 funding for the special patrols expired) to the 29 weeks preceding Phase 1. Other analyses added all of 1991 and 1993. The 1993 data included 6 months with no overtime patrols and Phase 2 overtime patrols for 6 months in the second half of 1993. Analyses thus covered six 6-month periods, two of which had the program and four of which did not.

The officers generated a lot of activity. Both in and out of the target beat, the directed patrols issued 1,090 traffic citations, conducted 948 car checks and 532 pedestrian checks, and made 170 state or federal arrests and 446 city arrests, for an average of one police intervention for every 40 minutes per patrol car.

The results of the evaluation indicated that directed police patrols in gun crime hot spots reduced gun crimes by increasing the seizures of illegally carried guns. Gun *seizures* by police in the target area increased significantly from 46 before the intervention to 76 afterward (an increase of 65 percent), while *gun crimes* declined significantly from 169 to 86 (a decrease of 49 percent). Traffic stops were the most productive method of finding guns, with an average of one gun found in every 28 traffic stops. The numbers of guns found during car checks tripled. During the same time period, neither gun crimes nor guns seized changed significantly in the comparison beat several miles away. If anything, the number of guns seized in the comparison beat dropped slightly from 85 to 72, and the number of gun crimes increased very slightly from 184 to 192. Further, drive-by shootings dropped from 7 to 1 in the target area, doubled from 6 to 12 in the comparison area, and showed no displacement to adjoining beats. Homicides decreased significantly in the target area, but not in the comparison area.

Data analyses ruled out several alternative hypotheses. First, only gun crimes were affected by the directed patrols, with no changes in the number of calls for service or in the total number of violent or nonviolent crimes reported. Second, there was no measurable displacement of gun crimes to patrol beats surrounding the target area, as gun crimes remained stable in the seven contiguous beats. Before and after surveys of citizens showed that respondents in the target area became less fearful of crime and more positive about their neighborhood than respondents in the comparison area.

Although the before-after study of the target beat and the comparison beat could not eliminate all possible competing explanations for the results, the inverse correlation between gun seizures and gun crime suggests that proactive policing of gun crimes in high-risk places is a promising strategy deserving of further research. Reiss and Roth (1993) similarly suggest that gun violence may be best reduced through tactics that police already apply in illegal drug markets, including buy-bust operations, high-priority investigation and prosecution of unregulated gun dealers, use of minors as informants against illegal dealers, phony fencing operations for illegal guns, high-priority investigation and prosecution of felonies in which guns are stolen, and high mandatory minimum sentences for those who steal or illegally sell guns (p. 280).

The Boston Violence Prevention Project

This project has claimed remarkable success in reducing juvenile homicides (Goldman, 1997). Along with other efforts launched concurrently, the National Institute of Justice supported a problem-solving project to devise, implement, and evaluate strategic interventions to reduce youth homicide (Kennedy, 1997). The working group included representatives from Harvard University, the Boston Police Department, the U.S. Department of Alcohol, Tobacco, and Firearms (ATF), the U.S. Attorney's Office, the Suffolk County District Attorney's Office, the Massachusetts Department of Probation, and city-employed gang outreach and mediation specialists, known as street workers.

The approach focused first on analyzing the supply and demand for guns, and then on trying innovative methods to disrupt illegal firearm markets and deter youth violence. Researchers found that both victims and offenders typically had histories of gang membership and high rates of offending. For example, 75 percent of offenders and victims had been arraigned for some offense, and 55 percent had been on probation. Twenty-five percent of the offenders were on probation at the time they committed murder. Further, youth homicides were concentrated in neighborhoods that hosted an estimated 61 gangs involving about 1,300 juveniles.

Intervention strategies focused on both supply and demand. A stern message was delivered to gang members, warning that continued violence would lead to a comprehensive and intensive system of responses, including severe personal restrictions for those on probation and parole (e.g., bed checks, room searches, and enforcement of warrants), intensive police presence in neighborhoods (e.g., federal agents), search and seizure of unregistered cars, vigorous arrest and prosecution for disorder offenses such as drinking in public, and strict enforcement of curfew laws by probation and police officers. Kennedy points to one vivid example where a gang member with a 15-year history of violent felonies was arrested for carrying a single bullet. When his prior convictions were taken into account, he was indicted as an armed career criminal and sentenced to nearly 20 years in prison. Kennedy (1997) stated: "Stunned gang members soon turned over their handguns, and the neighborhood became quiet" (p. 2).

Officials explicitly acknowledged that youth violence is much more than just a law enforcement problem. City, state, and federal representatives helped establish and support a large network of community-based job, recreation, and prevention programs for juveniles. Between July 1995, when the program began, and January 1997, the city of Boston reported zero juvenile homicides. For 1996, the homicide rate for those under 24 dropped 70 percent; arrests for assault with a gun by a juvenile dropped 81 percent from 1993 (Goldman, 1997).

Gun Control Legislation

Four broad strategies of gun legislation are possible (Reiss & Roth, 1993, pp. 270–281): (1) alter gun uses or storage (e.g., carrying), (2) change gun allocation across different user categories (i.e., who can purchase a gun), (3) reduce lethality of guns (e.g., through technology such as user identification mechanisms and trigger locks), and (4) reduce the number of guns (i.e., availability). We briefly examine each, focusing on interventions in which evaluation has been conducted.

Altering gun uses or storage refers broadly to regulations and policies affecting the legal carrying, storage, and use of a firearm.

For example, the Bartley-Fox Laws in Massachusetts in 1974 expanded gun licensing procedures and mandated a 1-year sentence for unlicensed carrying of a firearm. The law was most effective in the short term due to vigorous law enforcement. Results suggest that the law decreased gun use in assaults and robberies and decreased gun homicides during a 2-year evaluation period (Pierce & Bowers, 1981). Evaluations of sentencing enhancements for the use of a gun during a felony in six jurisdictions showed a decrease in gun homicides, but no change in nongun homicides, and no consistent effect on gun robberies or assaults (McDowall, Loftin, & Wiersema, 1992).

A good example of *changing gun allocation* is provided by the Federal Gun Control Act of 1968, which prohibited gun dealers from selling to "dangerous" categories of persons including juveniles, convicted felons, drug users, and former mental patients. The law also restricts gun imports and retail sales to federally licensed dealers. No significant effect on firearms injuries or deaths was found in an evaluation study (Zimring, 1975), although weak enforcement of the laws may be at least partially responsible for weak effects. In Washington, DC, increased enforcement of federal law in 1970 resulted in a six-month decrease in gun homicides, but no change in nongun homicides (Reiss & Roth, 1993).

More recently, the federal Brady Act, in effect since February 1994, mandated background investigations and prohibited retail sales of guns to persons in high-risk categories (identical to the categories specified by the Federal Gun Control Act of 1968). The interim provisions of the Brady Act specified that licensed firearm dealers request a presale check on all potential handgun purchasers from the chief law enforcement officer (CLEO) in the jurisdiction where the prospective buyer resides. The CLEO must make a reasonable effort to determine whether the purchaser is legally prohibited from possessing a handgun. Unless earlier approval is obtained, the dealer must wait five days before transferring the weapon to the buyer.

This interim system remained in effect until November 30, 1998, when an instant background check became mandatory for purchasers of all firearms. Under the "permanent provisions" of the Brady Act, presale inquiries are now made through the National Instant Criminal Background Check System (NICS) operated by the FBI. The background check determines, based on available records, if an individual is prohibited under the Federal Gun Control Act or state law from receiving or possessing firearms. As of November 30, 1998, the procedures related to the waiting period of the interim system were eliminated.

An estimated 312,000 felons, fugitives, and other prohibited persons were prevented from buying handguns during the Brady Act's interim period from March 1, 1994, through November 29, 1998 (Manson, Gilliard, & Lauver, 1999). The statutorily prescribed rejections amounted to about 2.4 percent of 12,740,000 Brady presale background checks during that period. From January 1, 1998, through November 29, 1999, there were about 70,000 rejections among the 2,384,000 inquiries or applications. About 63 percent of the rejections were for a prior felony conviction or a current felony indictment. Domestic violence misdemeanor convictions accounted for 10 percent of the rejections, and domestic violence protection orders prompted 3 percent of the rejections.

No systematic evaluations of the Brady Act have yet been conducted, and no significant reductions in violence attributable to its influence have yet been found. Given the small percentage of refusals relative to applicants, the cost-effectiveness of this measure also requires further analysis (Welsh & Harris, 1999, chap. 5).

The third strategy, *reducing lethality of guns,* includes measures that designate certain firearms dangerous because of concealability, firepower, or other risk. It also includes measures that restrict access to certain types of weapons or ammunition by law, or that make weapons less dangerous by requiring specific types of safety technology (e.g., trigger locks). Little evaluation evidence of these strategies exists at this time.

A fourth strategy attempts to *reduce the number of guns available* in a specific jurisdiction. For example, the 1977 District of Columbia Firearms Control Act prohibited ownership of handguns by virtually anyone except police officers, security guards, and previous gun owners. During periods of vigorous enforcement in the three years following implementation, the law reduced rates of gun robbery, assault, and homicide (Jones, 1981; Loftin, McDowall, Wiersema, & Cottey, 1991). However, increases in gun homicides were noted in 1988 when crack markets exploded (Cook, 1991).

Conclusions

Because of evidence that felons most frequently obtain their firearms through unregulated sales, the benefits of further federal regulation of guns may be small. This doesn't mean that such strategies should be abandoned. Quite the contrary, they provide an essential foundation and companion to the other strategies reviewed in this section (e.g., disruption of illegal markets, interagency and community prevention efforts).

Although a diverse array of legislation has been attempted in recent years, much more rigorous, controlled evaluations of different interventions are needed (Cook, 1991; Reiss & Roth, 1993, chap. 6). We still know little about the effectiveness of different types of gun legislation, and only a few studies adequately control for alternative explanations of results.

References

Beck, A., Gilliard, D., Greenfeld, L., Harlow, C., Hester, T., Jankowski, L., Snell, T., Stephan, J., & Morton, D. (1993). *Survey of state prison inmates, 1991* (NCJ-136949). Washington, DC: U.S. Department of Justice, Office of Justice Programs, Bureau of Justice Statistics.

Brantingham, P. J., & Brantingham, P. L. (Eds.). (1991). *Environmental criminology.* Prospect Heights, IL: Waveland.

Cohen, L., & Felson, M. (1979). Social change and crime rate trends: A routine activity approach. *American Sociological Review, 44,* 588–608.

Cook, P. J. (1981). Guns and crime: The perils of long division. *Journal of Policy Analysis and Management, 1,* 120–125.

———. (1991). The technology of personal violence. In M. Tonry (Ed.), *Crime and justice: A review of research* (Vol. 14, pp. 1–72). Chicago: University of Chicago Press.

Cook, P. J., & Laub, J. H. (1998). The unprecedented epidemic in youth violence. In M. Tonry & M. H. Moore, (Eds.), *Youth violence. Crime and justice: A review of research* (Vol. 24, pp. 27–64). Chicago: University of Chicago Press.

Decker, S. H., Pennell, S., & Caldwell, A. (1997). *Illegal firearms: Access and use by arrestees* (NCJ-163496). Washington, DC: U.S. Department of Justice, Office of Justice programs, National Institute of Justice.

Goldman, H. (1997, January 26). Death takes a holiday among Boston teens. *Philadelphia Inquirer,* p. 1.

Greenbaum, S. (1997). Kids and guns: From playgrounds to battlegrounds. *Juvenile justice, Journal of the Office of Juvenile Justice and Delinquency Prevention,* Volume III, Number 2 (NCJ-165925). Washington, DC: U.S. Department of Justice, Office of Justice Programs, Office of Juvenile Justice and Delinquency Prevention.

Harris, P. W., Welsh, W. N., & Butler, F. (2000). A century of juvenile justice. In G. LaFree, R. Bursik Jr., J. Short, & R. Taylor (Eds.), *Criminal justice 2000: Vol. 1. The changing nature of crime* (pp. 359–425). Washington, DC: U.S. Department of Justice, National Institute of Justice.

Jones, E. D., III. (1981). The District of Columbia's firearms control regulations act of 1975: The toughest handgun control law in the United States—Or is it? *Annals of the American Academy of Political and Social Science, 455,* 138–149.

Kennedy, D. M. (1997). *Juvenile gun violence and gun markets in Boston.* Research Preview. Washington, DC: U.S. Department of Justice, Office of Justice programs, National Institute of Justice.

Kleck, G. (1991). *Point blank: Guns and violence in America.* New York: Aldine de Gruyter.

Loftin, C., McDowall, D., Wiersema, B., & Cottey, T. (1991). Effects of restrictive licensing of handguns on homicide and suicide in the District of Columbia. *New England Journal of Medicine, 325,* 1615–1620.

Lott, J. R., Jr. (1998). *More guns, less crime: Understanding crime and gun control laws.* Chicago: University of Chicago Press.

Luckenbill, D. (1977). Criminal homicide as a situated transaction. *Social Problems, 25,* 176–186.

Ludwig, J. (1999). Review: *More guns, less crime: Understanding crime and gun control laws. Contemporary Sociology, 28,* 466–467.

Manson, D. A., Gilliard, D. K., & Lauver, G. (1999). *Presale handgun checks, the Brady interim period, 1994–1998* (NCJ-175034). U.S. Department of Justice, Bureau of Justice Statistics.

McDowall, D., Loftin, C., & Wiersema, B. (1992). A comparative study of the preventive effects of mandatory sentencing laws for gun crimes. *Journal of Criminal Law and Criminology, 83,* 378–394.

Monahan, J., & Klassen, D. (1982). Situational approaches to understanding and predicting individual violent behavior. In M. E. Wolfgang & N. A. Weiner (Eds.), *Criminal Violence* (pp. 292–319). Beverly Hills, CA: Sage.

Parsons, T. (1951). *The social system.* New York: Free Press.

Paulson, S. K. (2000, January 11). Colorado Governor changes stance on guns. *The Philadelphia Inquirer,* p. A01.

Pervin, L. A. (1978). Definitions, measurements, and classifications of stimuli, situations, and environments. *Human Ecology, 6,* 71–105.

Pierce, G. L., & Bowers, W. J. (1981). The Bartley-Fox gun law's short-term impact on crime in Boston. *Annals of the American Academy of Political and Social Science, 455,* 120–132.

Reiss, A. J., Jr., & Roth, J. A. (Eds.). (1993). *Understanding and preventing violence* (Vol. 1). Panel on the Understanding and Control of Violent Behavior, National Research Council. Washington, DC: National Academy Press.

Sheley, J. F., & Wright, J. D. (1993). *Gun acquisition and possession in selected juvenile samples* (NCJ-145326). Washington, DC: U.S. Department of Justice, Office of Justice Programs, National Institute of Justice.

Sherman, L. W., Gartin, P., & Buerger, M. (1989). Hot spots of predatory crime: Routine activities and the criminology of place. *Criminology, 27,* 27–55.

Sherman, L. W. & Rogan, D. (1995). Effects of gun seizures on gun violence: Hot spots, patrol in Kansas City. *Justice Quarterly, 12,* 673–693.

Sherman, L. W., Shaw, J. W., & Rogan, D. P. (1995). *The Kansas City gun experiment* (NCJ-150855). Washington, DC: U.S. Department of Justice, Office of Justice Programs, National Institute of Justice.

Sloane, J., Kellermann, A., Rey, D., Ferris, J., Koespell, T., Rivara, F., Rice, C., Gray, L., & LoGerfo, J. (1988). Handgun regulations, crimes, assaults, and homicide. *New England Journal of Medicine, 319,* 1256–1262.

Snyder, H. N. (1998). *Juvenile arrests 1997* (NCJ-173938). Washington, DC: U.S. Department of Justice, Office of Justice Programs, Office of Juvenile Justice and Delinquency Prevention.

Snyder, H. N., Sickmund, M., & Poe-Yamagata, E. (1996). *Juvenile offenders and victims: 1996 update on violence* (NCJ-159107). Washington, DC: U.S. Department of Justice, Office of Justice Programs, Office of Juvenile Justice and Delinquency Prevention.

U.S. Department of Justice, Bureau of Justice Statistics. (2000a). *Firearms and crime statistics.* Available: <http://www.ojp.usdoj.gov/bjs/guns.htm>.

————. (2000b). *Since 1993, the number of crimes committed with firearms has declined, falling to levels last experienced in the mid-1980s.* Available: <http://www.ojp.usdoj.gov/bjs/glance/guncrime.htm>.

Welsh, W. N., & Harris, P. W. (1999). *Criminal justice policy and planning.* Cincinnati, OH: Anderson.

Wright, J. D., & Rossi, P. H. (1985). *The armed criminal in America: A survey of incarcerated felons.* National Institute of Justice Research Report (July).

Zimring, F. E. (1968). Is gun control likely to reduce violent killings? *The University of Chicago Law Review, 35,* 721–737.

———. (1975). Firearms and federal law: The Gun Control Act of 1968. *Journal of Legal Studies, 4,* 133–198. ✦

Chapter 12

The Role of Drugs and Alcohol in Violence

Evidence linking drug and alcohol use to violence is striking. For example, prior alcohol use by the victim, perpetrator, or both is consistently found in more than half of all violent events (Reiss & Roth, 1993). Such prevalence rates alone are insufficient, however, to demonstrate that alcohol or drug use causes violence.

For example, problem drinkers are more likely to have previous histories of violence. But how do we make sense of this? Are violent people more likely to drink, or are heavy drinkers more likely to be violent? The two questions are quite different. One requires examination of violent offenders; the other requires examination of problem drinkers. Although these two populations overlap, they are far from identical.

In this chapter, we explore links between alcohol or drug use and violence. As in previous chapters, we examine major patterns, explanations, and interventions. However, to productively explore this broad, complex, and growing field of knowledge, we begin with a more general description of relationships between drug use and *behavior*, then narrow our focus to *criminal* behavior, and then zero in on *violent* behavior. To limit our focus strictly to violent behavior could lead us to miss important patterns, explanations, and interventions. We believe a wiser course is to bring in broader perspectives relevant to violence, though not strictly limited to violent behavior. As such, relevant material from psychology, sociology, public health, and criminal justice informs our inquiry, although violence reduction remains our central goal. In short, broad, interdisciplinary problems of violence require broad, interdisciplinary solutions (Reiss & Roth, 1993).

Patterns

Offenders who have a severe drug problem are responsible for a high proportion of crime (Ball, Shaffer, & Nurco, 1983; Chaiken, 1989; Inciardi, 1979). We know from Drug Use Forecasting (DUF) data that many arrestees, about two-thirds, test positive for drug use of at least one illegal drug, although we cannot automatically claim any "causal" relationship between drug use and crime. The proportion of all arrestees who test positive for substance abuse has never fallen below 60 percent and has been as high as 85 percent (Wish & O'Neil, 1989; National Institute of Justice, 1994).

The successor to DUF, the Arrestee Drug Abuse Monitoring (ADAM) program, now tracks drug use among booked arrestees in 35 large urban areas. In 1998, the ADAM program conducted interviews and drug tests with more than 30,000 recent arrestees in 35 metropolitan areas (National Institute of Justice, 1999). A total of 20,716 adult males, 6,700 adult females, 3,134 juvenile males, and 434 juvenile females participated in the program during 1998. In 15 sites, about two-thirds of the adult arrestees and more than half of the juvenile male arrestees tested positive for at least one drug. Among adult males, marijuana was the drug most frequently detected in 22 of the 35 sites; cocaine was the drug most likely to be detected in 11 sites. Among females, cocaine was the drug most frequently detected in 28 of 32 sites; methamphetamine was the most frequently detected drug in three of the sites. Among juveniles, marijuana was by far and away the most frequently detected drug in sites collecting juvenile data.

The National Center on Addiction and Substance Abuse (CASA; 1998) reported that 60 percent to 80 percent of all prison inmates (federal, state, and county) have been involved with drug use or drug-related crimes in some fashion. Of $38 billion in correctional expenditures in 1996, more than $30 billion was spent incarcerating individuals with a history of drug or alcohol abuse, or both. For chronic users, activities and behaviors surrounding drug acquisition and use pervade their lifestyle (Johnson et al., 1985; Walters, 1992). Many of these drug-abusing offenders are repeatedly incarcerated, but untreated, with the result of a high rate of re-lapse into drug use and crime after release. Moreover, drug-using felons are a primary source of failure on parole (Wexler, Lipton, & Johnson, 1988).

We know that there is a higher frequency of offending for the most frequent drug users. However, there is a lower rate of drug use among arrestees for violent offenses than arrestees for other types of offenses. This evidence argues against the claim that the use of psychoactive drugs directly causes violent behavior (Reiss & Roth, 1993).

Although the risk of drug-related homicide varies dramati-cally by city and place, about 10 percent of homicides are estimated to be drug-related. Research has demonstrated no direct link be-tween prevalence of cocaine use and homicide rates in five major cities (Reiss & Roth, 1993, p. 188).

Unfortunately, research has not always properly distinguished between three major types of drug-related violence: (1) **pharmaco-logical**, (2) **economic**, and (3) **systemic** (Goldstein, 1989). The na-ture and frequency of each is different, and the implications for explanation and prevention are also quite different. Remember, there is no automatic connection between drugs and violence. In-stead, we must ask: *Under what conditions and in what settings are which individuals more likely to display violent behavior?*

Pharmacological effects refer to the physiological effects of a drug on the body. In some cases, biological effects may help trigger violent behavior, although many interactions involve other fac-tors. For alcohol, no simple dose-response relationship is evident, but low, acute doses are more likely to facilitate aggression, while high doses are more likely to lead to lethargy. For marijuana and opiates, higher doses generally lead to decreased aggression, al-though opiate withdrawal may lead to increased aggression. For amphetamines, cocaine, LSD, and PCP, increased aggression oc-curs only inconsistently and occasionally. For example, small doses of amphetamines increase activity levels and competitive-ness, not necessarily violent behavior. Increased activity and com-petitiveness, however, may create or escalate conflicts with other persons. Thus, interactions with psychological and sociological factors are once again important. Similarly, no direct link between cocaine use and violence has been found.

Economically compulsive violence refers to crimes committed to obtain drugs or money for purchasing drugs. Except during withdrawal, heroin users tend to avoid violent crimes if nonviolent alternatives (e.g., burglary, theft) are available. A classic study by Johnson et al. (1985) examined 201 active street opiate users in Harlem. Each subject provided at least 33 consecutive days of data in a storefront ethnographic field station. During the study period, 72 percent committed no robberies; 23 percent committed occasional but irregular robberies; 5 percent were classified as "high-rate" robbers (i.e., committed 45 percent of all reported robberies). The high-rate robbers were more likely to be heroin users. Because the vast majority of heroin users are not robbers, a very small percentage of them therefore commit a good deal of robbery. Economically compulsive violence has been less clearly demonstrated among adult users of other illegal drugs.

Systemic violence refers to violence associated with the illegal sale and distribution of drugs. Such disputes include violence associated with gangs or illegal drug organizations (e.g., disputes with rival organizations over territory; enforcement of organizational rules; battles with police; punishment of enemies; protection of drugs or sellers). It includes transaction-related violence (i.e., robberies of drugs or money from the seller or buyer during a drug transaction); assaults to collect debts; and disputes over the quality or quantity of drugs exchanged between buyer and seller. It may also include violence involving third parties: bystanders, or participants in related illegal markets (e.g., firearms, hired enforcement, prostitution). One could view the crack problem in the late 1980s and early 1990s as a large industry with a very large supporting or "service" economy (everything that goes with drug use and selling).

How often does each type of drug-related violence occur? Goldstein, Brownstein, Ryan, and Bellucci (1989) classified police records of 414 homicides in New York in 1988. They classified 53 percent of the deaths as drug-related. Of these, 39 percent were systemic; 2 percent were economic; 8 percent were pharmacological; and 4 percent had multiple drug-related causes. Judgments about which incidents are drug-related, however, are far from straightforward and objective, especially when multiple causal factors exist in each event. Officers and researchers both classified more events as systemic than any other category, but officers used the economic category far more often than did the researchers. Researchers classified as economic only crimes in which it was clear that the motive was to finance drug use.

Such research likely understates the role of economics (Reiss & Roth, 1993). For example, the drug motivation for robbery and burglary is often concealed and unknown to police. Second, many crimes classified as systemic may contain economic motives such as robbery of drugs from a dealer. Third, crimes in which the drug motive was more indirect are likely undercounted (e.g., the original motive for the crime may have been to get money for groceries or some other purpose). The low rate of economic violence reported by Goldstein may also be related to alternative access to other sources of income among users of cocaine and synthetic drugs. For example, dealing cocaine offers attractive alternatives to robbery or burglary as a means of getting drugs directly, or getting money to buy drugs. In addition, wholesalers usually distribute crack to street dealers on a consignment basis, and the negotiation often allows for some personal use by the retailer. For many others, part-time drug dealing is a supplement to legal income.

Explanations

Although links between substance abuse (especially alcohol) and violence are well-known, these relationships are not easily interpreted as *causal* mechanisms. In other words, many but not all violent offenders have substance abuse problems. These offenders are likely to be young males. But only small proportions of young males commit acts of serious violence (e.g., robbery, rape, assault, murder). Neither do most substance abusers commit acts of serious violence. For some, however, substance abuse is part of a much broader lifestyle that increases the risk of violent offending or victimization. The challenge is to separate the causal effects of social structural, cultural, and lifestyle factors from individual causes (e.g., psychological and biological). In general, the violence-producing effects of drugs are strongest among heavy, chronic users (which are a small proportion of all users).

Miczek and colleagues (1993) provide the most thorough review to date of animal and human studies examining the effects of drugs on violent behavior. Especially useful are 13 tables (spanning 101 pages) that summarize the results of numerous studies examining the effects of drugs (e.g., alcohol, opiates, amphetamines, cocaine, cannabis, and hallucinogenics) on both animals and humans.

As Miczek et al. (1993) point out, data from animal studies provide the primary means to investigate experimentally the causes of aggressive behavior, whereas studies in humans most often attempt to infer causative relationships mainly by correlating the incidence of violent behavior with past alcohol intake or abuse of other drugs. There are limitations in our ability to study these effects with human subjects. Experimental studies offer the best means of controlling for extraneous variables (i.e., threats to internal validity), but have low external validity (i.e., generalizability). Field (i.e., nonexperimental) studies with humans offer the least control over extraneous variables, but have high generalizability. Ethical constraints prevent us from manipulating dosages of different drugs to human subjects at high levels where effects on violent behavior are most likely.

A common methodological problem is that past and current conditions (individual and social) influence human behavior, in addition to the type of drug and dosage. For example, psychopathology (e.g., psychosis, depression, antisocial personality) often predates and accompanies substance abuse in human research. It is difficult to separate such effects. In spite of these limitations, some consistent effects of specific types of drugs have been found.

Alcohol is the drug most consistently linked with aggressive behavior (Miczek et al., 1993). However, individuals vary considerably in their responses to alcohol (even at high doses), and group-level studies rely mainly upon correlational evidence. Alcohol has acute (immediate) and chronic (long-term) biological effects on brain functions, including memory. Alcohol intoxication leads to impaired cognitive skills and interpersonal communication, which in turn increases the risk of violence. It is also difficult to sort out the effects of heavy drinking from the settings in which it occurs. For example, a person who regularly frequents certain bars and drinking parties may be exposed to many opportunities for conflict.

Parker (1998) argues that there is a remarkable correspondence over a 62-year period (1934–1995) between alcohol consumption and homicide rates. In fact, even holding poverty, income, and the proportion of males aged 15 to 24 constant, homicide rates for both whites and nonwhites were significantly related to alcohol consumption over this 62-year period. Parker suggests two mechanisms that contribute to this relationship. First, depending upon the situation, setting, and the people involved, alcohol use can lead to **selective disinhibition**, whereby social norms that normally limit violence are temporarily suspended or neutralized. Secondly, at the community or neighborhood level, locations with large concentrations of alcohol outlets are often **hot spots** of crime (see chapters 4, 7, and 11), attracting many visitors who engage in a wide variety of illegal activities. The concentration of alcohol outlets may facilitate an atmosphere of "time out" or "anything goes." Combined with the fact that alcohol use and crime rates are already higher in neighborhoods with high concentrations of alcohol outlets, the connection between high alcohol use and high homicide rates is plausible.

No data suggest a direct pharmacological link between *opiates* such as heroin and aggression (Parker, 1998, p. 393). Where violence occurs, it is more likely to be associated with withdrawal among addicted users or attempts to obtain more of the drug, or both.

Some strong evidence links *amphetamine* abuse to violence in humans, but mainly for heavy, chronic abusers and intravenous users. Chronic amphetamine abuse appears to increase the likelihood of irritability, psychosis, and communication impairments that increase the risk of violence.

Cocaine is linked to violent behavior primarily through its role in illegal drug markets (sale and distribution). Biological effects on violent behavior are less clear. Violent behavior occurs occasionally (but not consistently among different individuals or different groups), but it seems secondary to the paranoia and psychosis that can be triggered by heavy, chronic cocaine use.

Most reviews conclude that *cannabis* (e.g., marijuana, hashish) either has no discernible effects on aggression or actually decreases aggression. There is still some concern about the role of these drugs in violence associated with illegal drug markets, but their use is much more widespread than other drugs, their availability and cost is lower, and profit margins are generally much smaller.

Similarly, use of *hallucinogenics* is only rarely associated with violent behavior. Low, acute doses generally stimulate defensive and timid reactions in animals. Hallucinogenics are infrequently associated with human violence, although some evidence suggests that preexisting psychopathology may stimulate hypersensitive or aggressive responses to environmental stimuli.

The effects of *PCP* are not entirely clear. In animal studies, exposure to PCP leads to very unpredictable results. In human studies, there is no consistent association between PCP intake and violent behavior, contrary to popular stereotypes. In humans, PCP abuse is usually part of a pattern of heavy, polydrug use, making causal inferences difficult. Violence is infrequent, but when it occurs, it is usually associated with the secondary effects of heavy, acute, or chronic exposure (e.g., psychosis) and with preexisting aggressive personality and social background characteristics.

Others, noting that men are much more likely to behave violently than women when intoxicated, have suggested that biological differences associated with gender are at work. However, the same evidence also implicates the interactive causal roles of psychological, social structural, and cultural factors (Reiss & Roth, 1993).

Evidence from biological studies suggests that higher alcohol doses reduce concentrations of the male hormone testosterone. Animal studies show that acute, low alcohol doses increased aggressive behavior in individuals who already had high blood testosterone levels. There is little experimental evidence on endocrinological effects for humans, but available evidence is consistent with animal studies in that alcohol intoxication is more likely to lead to aggression in low doses than high doses (Reiss & Roth, 1993). Psychological factors also play a role in mediating the alcohol-gender relationship (Reiss & Roth, 1993).

Gender is of fundamental importance in understanding the relationship between alcohol use and violent behavior. For example, male drinking patterns are much more likely to include binge drinking and aggressive behavior associated with male peer interactions. Individual histories of aggressive behavior are also a critical determinant of whether drug or alcohol use leads to violent behavior or not. Men, once again, are much more likely than women to have had aggressive experiences in their development. Emotions also play a role. Male users are more likely to select specific drugs to dampen or intensify certain emotions such as anger. Such drinking patterns are often related to one's individual developmental experiences or family pathology, or both.

Social processes (e.g., social structure and culture) also mediate relationships between alcohol use, gender, and violence. These relationships are neither uniform nor unanimous across different cultures. There are different cultural norms and customs regarding use of alcohol and behavior while intoxicated, different states that MacAndrew and Edgerton (1969) have referred to as **drunken comportment.** The Yuruna Indians in the South American rain forest consistently become withdrawn when drunk, acting as though no one else existed. In a rural Japanese fishing village, drunkenness regularly leads to camaraderie, laughter, jokes, songs, and dances. In a small northern Colombian village, residents remain somber, controlled, and morose, regardless of the degree of intoxication they achieve.

There are also different stresses in different cultures that influence the likelihood of violent behavior under conditions of drunkenness (Fagan, 1990). For example, among the Naskapi Indians of northern Canada, the least successful men (iron miners) were the most aggressive drinkers. Or, in contrast to Guatemalan immigrants to the United States, male Dominican immigrants tended to bring their entire families with them. They also enjoyed greater economic opportunities (perhaps because of more established kinship and cultural networks in the United States) and drank at home more often than in bars. On the other hand, drinking resulted in greater aggression for Guatemalan men, who were more likely to live alone, experience greater economic hardship, and drink at bars rather than at home.

Different cultures or groups may have very different social expectations about the effects of alcohol in different settings (Miczek et al., 1993). For example, one ethnographic study found that a group of youths was quiet and deferential when drinking among their elders in a neighborhood bar, but much more aggressive in other surroundings after they left their company. Repeated observations suggested that the youths occasionally sought out different settings where expression of aggressive behavior was more acceptable. One's company and one's social setting thus influence one's behavior strongly, even when alcohol or drugs are being used.

In sum, three major factors interact to explain how drugs affect behavior: **set**, **setting**, and **pharmacological** effects (Goode, 1993). *Set* refers to the psychic, mental, or emotional state of the person taking the drug. Set includes the person's expectations, intelligence, personality, imagination, and mood. *Setting* refers to the social and physical environment in which drug use takes place. Setting includes whom one uses drugs with and where, such as one's immediate surroundings (e.g., at home, in a car, at a bar, at a party) as well as the larger social and cultural backdrop. Third, as discussed earlier, *pharmacological* effects refer to the physiological effects of drugs (e.g., neurobehavioral changes). Again, we emphasize that these three influences on behavior interact with one another and are not always easy to separate.

Interventions

Although the War on Drugs may seem a tired cliché to many, it remains a flashpoint for public fear and the massive mobilization of political and law enforcement resources. The "war" began in 1980 under President Reagan and continued under his successor, President Bush. In fact, drug abuse was perceived as a problem so severe and so threatening that its eradication became, to many, a matter of primary national security and importance (Gates, 1998). However, the drug problem, like other social problems, is socially constructed; it is only partly based in reality (see chapter 1). In other words, certain social and political dynamics produce social policy and legislation (i.e., the "War on Drugs") as well as consequences (e.g., high incarceration rates). Many critics argue that the "casualties" in this war have been too high.

What is meant by the *War on Drugs*? It includes a diverse array of reactions to drug and alcohol abuse: tougher laws aimed at punishing drug users and sellers (e.g., mandatory minimum sentences of up to life imprisonment for trafficking in cocaine), drug interdiction efforts at U.S. borders and overseas (including the use of armed forces and diplomatic initiatives in countries such as Colombia and Mexico), targeted police strikes in neighborhoods where illegal drug markets flourish, mandatory drug-testing policies for probationers and parolees as well as employees of government and private corporations, efforts to address presumed social correlates of drug abuse (e.g., chronic poverty, unemployment), drug awareness education in schools, and drug treatment (e.g., in communities and in prison). The major emphases, though, have clearly been punishment and interdiction.

Although American presidents are fond of declaring war on targeted problems, war implies aggression against an enemy (Heath, 1998). The enemy in the war on drugs has tended to be the stereotypical drug user and dealer: blacks or Hispanics, the poor, and those unwilling to work. Such stereotypes are contradicted by national surveys showing that middle-class, white, employed adults constitute the majority of occasional drug users. Drug use is not novel, nor is it limited to the United States. However, whether or not drug use is perceived as a problem in any specific place or time depends largely upon the tolerance of the dominant culture. In America, drug use is commonly associated with the criminal element and ethnic minorities, with the consequences that minorities have been incarcerated in record numbers for drug offenses (Heath, 1998). Drug laws have contributed to institutionalized racial discrimination by mandating tougher sentences for crack cocaine than for powdered cocaine offenses (Jensen & Gerber, 1998).

The war on drugs has led to various unintended consequences, such as overcrowded courts and prisons, increased crime (i.e., economically motivated crime), official corruption (e.g., law enforcement and political officials), eroded civil rights and race relations, and new public health crises (Chepesiuk, 1999; Eldredge, 1998). In spite of massive efforts by U.S. government officials, only an estimated 10 to 25 percent of illegal drugs are stopped at the border. In fact, the purity of cocaine, heroin, and marijuana have increased due in part to law enforcement efforts that have led smugglers to decrease the bulk of their product. Still, the number of deaths due to drug trafficking far exceeds those due to drug use. Street prices of illegal drugs have actually declined since the 1980s, reflecting market forces where a growing supply surpasses the huge demand (Eldredge, 1998).

Some argue that the federal drug budget, $17 billion in 1999, should be equalized between supply and demand strategies so that adequate resources are available for drug treatment and prevention, including providing young people with good schools, decent housing, recreational programs, and meaningful job prospects (Massing, 2000). Others argue that, without a continuing, multifaceted war on drugs, public health and safety will suffer dearly, and hard-fought gains realized in recent years will be quickly lost (Gates, 1998). Regardless of one's opinions, it is clear that valid information about the problem and its causes is sorely needed, as are sound evaluations of the multitude of programs and policies generated by the War on Drugs. We turn now to a closer examination of several major intervention strategies.

Weed and Seed

Weed and Seed is a federally funded strategy intended to mobilize and coordinate antidrug resources in targeted high-crime communities. Started in 1991, the strategy targets drug trafficking, gang activity, and violence for intervention, enforcement, community policing activities, human services programs, and neighborhood improvement initiatives. Four key components are included in this strategy (Dunworth & Mills, 1999). First, *weeding* refers to concentrated and enhanced law enforcement efforts to identify, arrest, and prosecute violent offenders, drug traffickers, and other criminals operating in the target areas. Second, *seeding* refers to human services, such as after-school, weekend, and summer youth activities; adult literacy classes; parental counseling; and neighborhood revitalization efforts to prevent and deter further crime. Third, *enhanced coordination* refers to coordinated analysis of local problems and developing strategies to address them. The federal oversight responsibility for each participating site rests with the U.S. Attorney's Office for the corresponding district. Fourth, *community policing* refers to proactive police-community engagement and problem solving in which police officers are assigned to specified geographic locations. This effort is seen as the bridge between weeding and seeding. By gaining the trust and support of the community, police engage residents and businesses as problem-solving partners in the law enforcement effort (e.g., neighborhood watches, citizen marches and rallies, and graffiti removal). Weed and Seed has grown since 1991 to include 200 sites nationwide. A national evaluation of eight case-study cities examined various aspects of program implementation as well as measurable effects on crime and public safety (Dunworth, Mills, Cordner, & Greene, 1999). Although each site had its own distinctive crime problems, they all shared high rates of violent crime related to drug trafficking and drug use. The evaluation included a review of funding applications and other significant program documents; individual interviews with key program administrators, senior law enforcement staff, managers of seeding activities, service providers, and community leaders; analysis of automated, incident-level records of crimes and arrests; group interviews with participants in seeding programs; and two surveys of residents in target areas conducted in 1995 and 1997.

Developing an appropriate seeding strategy was among the greatest challenges for Weed and Seed (Dunworth et al., 1999). Seeding efforts (e.g., youth prevention and recreation programs, family support services, community economic development) required participation and commitment from many diverse organizations with different goals, whereas weeding, operating mainly within the established structures of law enforcement and criminal justice, had a relatively clear mission. For seeding, more time was needed for planning, relationship-building, and gaining consensus and commitment from the wide range of participants involved.

Within the target areas of each site, evaluators compared Part 1 crime (see chapter 2) trends for the year prior to implementation of Weed and Seed and the second year after the program began (Dunworth et al., 1999). Five target areas had double-digit percentage decreases: Stowe Village in Hartford, 46 percent; Crawford-Roberts in Pittsburgh, 24 percent; North Manatee, 18 percent; the Shreveport target area, 11 percent; and the Central District in Seattle, 10 percent. One target area (West Las Vegas) had a single-digit decrease (6 percent), and three target areas experienced increases in Part 1 crime (South Manatee, 2 percent; Meadows Village in Las Vegas, 9 percent; and Salt Lake City, 14 percent).

Like so many other evaluations that attempt to compare crime rates across different communities and time periods, researchers could not state definitively the extent to which different factors contributed to the observed changes in crime (Dunworth et al., 1999). However, a number of factors appear related to observed crime changes. First of all, overall crime rates in the surrounding (nontarget) areas of the target sites mirrored increases or decreases in the target areas, suggesting that Weed and Seed had little influence on crime rates. Hartford and Pittsburgh, which experienced the largest Part 1 crime decreases in nontarget areas, are the same two sites whose target areas achieved the largest Part 1 crime decreases. Salt Lake City, the site with the largest Part 1 crime increase in its smaller target area, also exhibited the largest Part 1 crime increase overall.

Changes in drug arrest rates appeared to be associated with changes in the overall Part 1 crime rate. Among the six target areas for which arrest data were available, the four areas reporting decreases in Part 1 crime from the year prior to Weed and Seed through the second year of implementation (Hartford, Pittsburgh, North Manatee, and Shreveport) all experienced initial high rates of drug arrests, suggesting an initial period of intense weeding activities followed by declining drug arrest rates. Assuming the level of law enforcement has remained somewhat constant, this trend may reflect some success in reducing drug activity (Dunworth et al., 1999).

To gain the perspective of community residents whom the seeding programs were intended to benefit, participant interviews and community surveys were also conducted. According to the residents interviewed, the seeding programs provided services that otherwise would not have been available in the target areas. Most of those interviewed indicated that participation in the seeding programs was a positive experience that helped them feel more secure emotionally, physically, or both. Benefits perceived by participants included providing additional structure and discipline in the lives of target area youths, and opportunities and assistance for adults to work toward personal and professional growth. Community surveys, however, suggested inconsistent impacts. Residents in two areas (Manatee and Pittsburgh) perceived substantial improvements in severity of crime and police effectiveness in controlling crime. Residents in Akron and Seattle perceived some improvement in drug-related crime; Hartford residents perceived some reduction in violent and gang-related crime. Residents in three areas (Las Vegas, Salt Lake City, and Shreveport) perceived little improvement in general public safety or the severity of specific types of crime.

In conclusion, the effectiveness of weeding and seeding activities varied across the eight sites (Dunworth & Mills, 1999). The evaluation found that pre-existing community features may enhance or weaken Weed and Seed efforts. Important factors included the strength of the existing social and institutional infrastructure (e.g., an established network of community-based organizations and community leaders), the severity of crime problems, geographical advantages favoring economic development, and transiency of the community population. Finding the appropriate mix and sequence of weeding and seeding activities are important factors in gaining community support for the program.

Drug Courts

The drug court movement began in the mid-1980s. Although the number of drug-related court cases had been growing rapidly, traditional law enforcement and criminal justice policies were not having significant impacts on reducing drug supply and demand. In the summer of 1989, an administrative order from the chief judge of Florida's 11th judicial circuit established the first drug court (Goldkamp, 1994).

The drug court approach departs from tradition by systematically offering drug treatment to drug-abusing offenders entering the court system. Previously, the court would occasionally refer selected offenders to outside treatment agencies as a condition of probation. In the drug court model, the judge has the authority to hold the defendant or offender personally and publicly accountable for treatment progress. In exchange for successfully completing treatment, the drug court may dismiss the original charge, reduce or set aside the sentence, or offer a lesser penalty or any combination of these options. Their innovation lies in the premise that effective and flexible programs of court-supervised drug treatment can reduce demand for illicit substances and hence reduce substance abusers' involvement in crime and reinvolvement in the court system.

In the Miami Drug Court, the judge works with the prosecutor, defender, and drug treatment specialists as a team to select the appropriate treatment approach, monitor progress in the courtroom, and help overcome problems (e.g., housing and employment) that may hinder treatment progress. The Miami Drug Court model incorporated nontraditional roles for court actors and a specially adapted program of outpatient treatment for substance abuse (Goldkamp & Weiland, 1993). The program was designed initially to accept defendants charged with third-degree felony drug possession offenses and with no prior convictions. Presumably, these persons were not serious risks to public safety and were at the beginning of their criminal involvement. By the time of the study, however, the Drug Court was accepting persons with initial charges of selected second-degree drug felonies as well as some defendants with prior convictions.

The Miami Drug Court referred defendants to an outpatient treatment program with sites in four locations in Dade County. Treatment consisted of a four-phase program that required about one year to complete. Phase 1 centered on detoxification (e.g., a goal of seven consecutive negative urine tests). Phase 2 focused on counseling (two to three visits per week, with urine testing at each visit). In Phase 3, educational and vocational assessment and training were provided. Phase 4 was graduation; Phase 5 (informal suspension) was invoked only if the defendant accumulated three consecutive, unauthorized failures to keep required clinic appointments.

The supervisory role of the judge is unique (Goldkamp & Weiland, 1993). In frequent encounters in court, the judge hears reports of the defendant's progress, discusses treatment progress with the defendant, and offers encouragement where appropriate. The judge's facilitation of treatment includes assistance in resolving criminal-justice issues and in social service problems such as housing and employment. Support may yield to sanctioning if the defendant shows a poor record of performance or is rearrested. Occasionally, a 2-week period of incarceration ("motivational jail") is used or a case is transferred to be tried in a typical felony court.

When researchers compared Miami Drug Court defendants over an 18-month period with similar defendants not in the program, they found the Drug Court defendants had fewer cases dropped; lower incarceration rates; less frequent rearrests; longer times to rearrest; and higher rates of failure to appear, due largely to the relatively frequent appearances required of Drug Court defendants. The treatment sample was a cohort of defendants ($n = 326$) admitted to Drug Court in August and September of 1990. The comparison samples consisted of other types of felony defendants processed at the same time: (1) eligible defendants who did not enter Drug Court ($n = 89$); (2) felony defendants who were ineligible for Drug Court ($n = 199$); and (3) nondrug felony defendants ($n = 185$).

The number of drug court programs and the availability of funding have increased substantially in recent years. Subsequent evaluations, however, have not been entirely conclusive. In the largest study to date, the U.S. General Accounting Office (1997) conducted a review of 134 government-funded drug courts and 20 evaluation studies as of December 1996. The programs were extremely diverse in their approaches, characteristics, and completion and retention rates. The available studies did not support firm conclusions about the overall impact of drug court programs.

In another review of 30 evaluations pertaining to 24 drug courts throughout the United States, Belenko (1998) found that drug courts provided closer, more comprehensive supervision and much more frequent drug testing and monitoring during the program than other forms of community supervision. More important, drug use and criminal behavior were substantially reduced while offenders participated in the program. Drug courts generated cost savings, at least in the short term, from reduced prison use, reduced criminality, and lowered criminal justice system costs. In addition, drug courts were quite successful in bridging the gap between the court and the treatment-public health systems and spurring greater cooperation among the various agencies and personnel within the criminal justice system.

Prison-Based Drug Treatment

Nearly 1.8 million inmates were incarcerated in U.S. jails and prisons in 1998, a rate of 461 per 100,000 adults (up from 292 in 1990). Drug offenses were a leading cause of those increases (Beck & Mumola, 1999). About two out of three inmates admit drug histories, but less than 15 percent receive any systematic treatment while in prison (Mumola, 1999). Many drug-abusing offenders are repeatedly incarcerated, but untreated, with the result that a high proportion relapse into drug use and crime after release. The time that drug-involved offenders are incarcerated presents a unique opportunity to provide them with treatment. More than 70 percent of active street addicts have never been in treatment nor intend to enter treatment for their addiction (Lipton, Morales, & Goldsmith, 1989; Peyton, 1994). The need for expanding drug abuse treatment was recognized in the Violent Crime Control Act of 1994, which for the first time provided substantial drug treatment resources for federal and state jurisdictions.

Although there is yet little consensus about what types of treatment work best for what types of offenders in what settings, several studies suggest that in-custody treatment, especially intensive Therapeutic Community (TC) programming, can be effective in reducing relapse and recidivism among seriously drug-involved offenders (Lipton, Falkin, & Wexler, 1992; Lipton, 1995; Simpson, Wexler, & Inciardi, 1999).

TC is an intensive, long-term (12–18 months), highly structured, residential treatment modality for hard-core drug users. In particular, TC emphasizes the necessity of the inmate taking responsibility for his or her behavior before, during, and after treatment, and inmates play an important role in structuring group norms and sanctions.

Inmates typically move through three phases of treatment in a 12-month program. The first phase consists of orientation, diagnosis, and an assimilation process. In the second phase, lasting 5 to 6 months, inmates are expected to take on increased responsibility and involvement in the program. Those who have been in the program longer are expected to share their insights by teaching new members and assisting in the day-to-day operation of the TC. Encounter groups and counseling sessions focus on self-discipline, self-worth, self-awareness, respect for authority, and acceptance of guidance for problem areas. Seminars take on a more intellectual approach. Debate is encouraged as a means of self-expression. During the third phase—preparation for community reentry—which lasts 1 to 3 months, inmates strengthen planning and decision-making skills and design their individual exit plans.

Effectiveness is related specifically to the length of time an individual remains in treatment (Lipton, 1995). Evaluations of New York's Stay'n Out program (Wexler, Falkin, & Lipton, 1990; Wexler, Lipton, Falkin, & Rosenbaum, 1992), Oregon's Cornerstone Program (Field, 1984, 1989, 1992), Delaware's Key-Crest programs (Inciardi, 1995; Inciardi, Martin, Buzin, Hooper, & Harrison, 1997), California's Amity Prison TC program (Wexler, 1995), the Texas In-Prison TC (Knight, Simpson, Chatham, & Camacho, 1997), and the Federal Bureau of Prisons (1998) Triad program illustrate the potential of prison-based therapeutic communities.

The most recent and state-of-the-art research on prison-based TC was reported in a special issue of the *Prison Journal* (e.g., Knight et al., 1999; Martin et al., 1999; Wexter, Melnick, Lowe, & Peters, 1999). Evaluations of prison-based treatment are described in three states (California, Delaware, and Texas) that have mounted major treatment initiatives in correctional settings. The three studies all used a common time interval (3 years) for tracking follow-up outcomes including performance indicators extracted from official criminal justice records in each state.

The overall consistency of findings from these three independent evaluations strengthens the case for treatment effectiveness in correctional settings. Each found that graduates of prison TC have lower rates of rearrest, drug relapse, and return to custody than comparison samples, especially when prison TC is combined with structured aftercare following release from prison. In Delaware, for example (Martin, Butzin, Saum, & Inciardi, 1999), 3-year followups showed that rearrest rates were lowest for those who graduated prison TC and successfully completed an aftercare program (31 percent). Those who completed TC but no aftercare still did significantly better (45 percent) than those who dropped out (72 percent) or those who received no treatment (71 percent). In California (Wexler et al., 1999), those who successfully completed prison TC plus aftercare showed a rearrest rate of 27 percent in 3-year followup studies, compared to 75 percent for a no-treatment comparison group. In Texas (Knight, Simpson, & Hiller, 1999), those who completed TC plus aftercare had a 3-year rearrest rate of only 25 percent, compared to 42 percent of a no-treatment comparison group. A comprehensive review of almost 30 years of research (Pearson & Lipton, 1999) further supports the positive impact of intensive therapeutic community programs.

Griffith, Hiller, Knight, and Simpson (1999) examined costs for prison-based treatment in Texas. Adding prison-based treatment and aftercare raised the base costs for prison incarceration and 3 years of parole supervision (approximately $18,000) by about 25 percent, an increase that was shown to be highly cost-effective for inmates with serious drug-related problems and who completed treatment.

Even though evaluation results are promising, many studies of prison TC have been vulnerable to criticisms of inadequate research design, unknown or compromised program implementation, inadequate measures of treatment process and outcome, or all of these (Austin, 1998; Fletcher & Tims, 1992). Furthermore, self-selection is the main guide inmates use to navigate through treatment options, which complicates the clarity of scientific interpretations (Simpson et al., 1999). Thus, we need to know more about risk factors that represent barriers to treatment participation and completion (Hiller, Knight, & Simpson, 1999) as well as ways to engage inmates in the treatment process more effectively (Blankenship, Dansereau, & Simpson, 1999). Human subjects guidelines restrict the use of research designs that withhold services, such as drug treatment, from people who need them (which would provide control groups in a classic experimental design).

Questions remain about what kinds of inmates benefit most from such programs, how treatment needs are assessed, how need assessments influence program placement decisions and treatment planning, and how treatment process (e.g., program content, staffing, and inmate processing) influences outcomes (Inciardi, Martin, Lockwood, Hooper, & Wald, 1992).

Drug Abuse Resistance Education

The school-based Drug Abuse Resistance Education Program (D.A.R.E.) is one of the most widespread programs in the United States. It is well known for its use of trained, uniformed police officers in the classroom and its combination of local control and centralized coordination. The original D.A.R.E. program was created in 1983 by the Los Angeles Police Department and the Los Angeles Unified School District as a substance abuse prevention program for grades K-12. D.A.R.E. uses a core curriculum consisting of 17 hour-long weekly lessons taught to fifth- and sixth-graders. Since it was founded, D.A.R.E. has expanded to encompass programs for middle and high school students, conflict resolution, gang prevention, parent education, and after-school recreation and learning. D.A.R.E. targets multiple drugs, including alcohol and tobacco. The curriculum has been revised over the years to become more interactive.

A study conducted by the Research Triangle Institute (Ringwalt et al., 1994) found that the program enjoyed widespread public and official support, and that its appeal cut across racial, ethnic, and socioeconomic lines. More than half (52 percent) of the school districts nationwide adopted the program in one or more of their schools. Researchers used meta-analysis, a method involving synthesis of findings from different studies, to examine the short-term effectiveness of D.A.R.E.'s core curriculum. They also compared the effectiveness of D.A.R.E. to other school-based substance abuse prevention programs. Substance abuse was defined as use of marijuana, alcohol, or tobacco by school-age children. D.A.R.E. programs appeared best at increasing students' knowledge about substance abuse and enhancing their social skills (Ringwalt et al., 1994). Effects on students' attitudes toward drugs, attitudes toward the police, and self-esteem were more modest. Short-term effects on reducing substance abuse by fifth- and sixth-graders were very small indeed. Only the findings for tobacco use were statistically significant.

Other large-scale reviews of drug-abuse prevention programs have found similar effects (Botvin, 1990; Botvin, Baker, Dusenbury, Botvin, & Diaz, 1995; Dryfoos, 1990; Durlak, 1995; Hansen, 1992; Hawkins, Arthur, & Catalano, 1995; Tobler, 1986, 1992). Relatively ineffective approaches include those based primarily on information dissemination (e.g., different drugs and their effects), fear arousal (e.g., emphasize the risks associated with drug use), moral appeal (e.g., teach students about the evils of drug use), or affective education (e.g., focus on building self-esteem, responsible decision-making, and interpersonal growth) (Botvin, 1990). More effective approaches included some kind of resistance-skills training, that is, teach students about social influences of substance use and specific skills for effectively resisting these pressures, alone or in combination with broader-based life-skills training, such as assertiveness skills.

Conclusions

As indicated by Reiss and Roth,

The link among alcohol, other psychoactive drugs, and violence turns out to be not an example of straightforward causation, but rather a network of interacting processes and feedback loops. (1993, p. 183)

Biological effects of drugs on behavior differ considerably according to the specific type of drug and dosage, and biological effects interact with diverse psychological and sociological processes to influence behavior. Because causal influences connecting drug abuse to violence are so diverse, so must be the potential solutions. In this chapter, we focused on four important types of prevention and intervention: Weed and Seed, Drug Courts, Prison-Based Drug Treatment, and Drug Abuse Resistance Education (DARE) for adolescents. Comprehensive strategies are needed that target both juveniles and adults, both demand and supply, and both individuals and public policy. Strategies that emphasize punishment and interdiction alone have not yielded productive results in the past, nor should they be expected to do so in the future.

References

Austin, J. (1998). The Limits of prison drug treatment. *Corrections Management Quarterly, 2*, 66–74.

Ball, J. C., Shaffer, J. W., & Nurco, D. N. (1983). Day-to-day criminality of heroin addicts in Baltimore: A study in the continuity of offense rates. *Drug and Alcohol Dependence, 12*, 119–142.

Beck, A. J., & Mumola, C. J. (1999, August). *Prisoners in 1998* (Bureau of Justice Statistics Bulletin). Washington, DC: U.S. Department of Justice, Office of Justice Programs.

Belenko, S. (1998). Research on drug courts: A critical review. *National Drug Court Institute Review, 1*, 1–42.

Blankenship, J., Dansereau, D., & Simpson, D. (1999). Cognitive enhancements of readiness for corrections-based treatment for drug abuse. *The Prison Journal, 79*, 431–445.

Botvin, G. J. (1990). Substance abuse prevention: Theory, practice, and effectiveness. In M. Tonry & J. Wilson (Eds.), *Drugs and crime* (pp. 461–519). *Crime and Justice, A Review of Research.* (Vol. 13). Chicago: The University of Chicago Press.

Botvin, G., Baker, E., Dusenbury, L., Botvin, E., & Diaz, T. (1995). Long-term follow-up results of a randomized drug abuse prevention trial in a white middle-class population. *Journal of the American Medical Association, 273*, 1106–1112.

Chaiken, M. R. (1989). In-prison programs for drug-involved offenders. *Research in Brief.* Washington, DC: National Institute of Justice.

Chepesiuk, R. (1999). *Hard target: The United States war against international drug trafficking, 1982–1997.* Jefferson, NC: McFarland.

Dryfoos, J. G. (1990). *Adolescents at risk: Prevalence and prevention.* New York: Oxford University Press.

Dunworth, T., & Mills, G. (1999). *National evaluation of Weed and Seed* (NCJ-175685). Washington, DC: U.S. Department of Justice, National Institute of Justice.

Dunworth, T., Mills, G., Cordner, G., & Greene, J. (1999). *National evaluation of Weed and Seed: Cross-site analysis* (NCJ-176358). Washington, DC: Department of Justice, National Institute of Justice.

Durlak, J. A. (1995). *School-based prevention programs for children and adolescents.* Thousand Oaks, CA: Sage.

Eldredge, D. C. (1998). *Ending the war on drugs: A solution for America.* Bridgehampton, NY: Bridge Works Publishing.

Fagan, J. (1990). Intoxication and aggression. In M. Tonry & J. Wilson (Eds.), *Crime and justice: A review of research, Drugs and crime* (Vol. 13, pp. 241–320). Chicago: University of Chicago Press.

Federal Bureau of Prisons. (1998). *TRIAD Drug treatment evaluation.* Six-month report: executive summary. Washington, DC: Department of Justice, Federal Bureau of Prisons.

Field, G. (1984). The cornerstone program: A client outcome study. *Federal Probation, 48,* 50–55.

Field, G. (1989). A study of the effects of intensive treatment on reducing the criminal recidivism of addicted offenders. *Federal Probation, 53*(10), 51–56.

Field, G. (1992). Oregon prison drug treatment programs. In C. Leukefeld & F. Tims (Eds.), *Drug abuse treatment in prisons and jails* (pp. 246–260). NIDA Monograph No. 118. HHS. Rockville, MD: Government Printing Office.

Fletcher, B. W., & Tims, F. M. (1992). Methodological issues: Drug abuse treatment in prisons and jails. In C. G. Leukefeld & F. M. Tims (Eds.), *Drug abuse treatment in prisons and jails* (pp. 142–159). Washington, DC: Government Printing Office.

Gates, D. F. (1998). Some among us would seek to surrender. In J. A. Schaler (Ed.), *Drugs: Should we legalize, decriminalize, or deregulate?* (pp. 80–82). Amherst, NY: Prometheus Books.

Goldkamp, J. (1994). *Justice and treatment innovation: The drug court movement* (NCJ-149260). Washington, DC: Department of Justice, National Institute of Justice.

Goldkamp, J. S., & Weiland, D. (1993). *Assessing the impact of Dade County's felony drug court.* Final report. Philadelphia: Crime and Justice Research Institute.

Goldstein, P. J. (1989). Drugs and violent crime. In N. A. Weiner & M. E. Wolfgang (Eds.), *Pathways to criminal violence* (pp. 16–48). Newbury Park, CA: Sage.

Goldstein, P. J., Brownstein, H. H., Ryan, P. J., & Bellucci, P. A. (1989). Crack and homicide in New York City, 1988: A conceptually based event analysis. *Contemporary Drug Problems, 16,* 651–687.

Goode, Erich. (1993). *Drugs in American society* (4th ed.). New York: McGraw-Hill.

Griffith, J., Hiller, M., Knight, K., & Simpson, D. (1999). A cost-effectiveness analysis of in-prison therapeutic community treatment and risk classification. *The Prison Journal, 79,* 352–368.

Hansen, W. B. (1992). School-based substance abuse prevention: A review of the state of the art of curriculum: 1980–1990. *Health Education Research, 7,* 403–430.

Hawkins, J. D., Arthur, M. W., & Catalano, R. F. (1995). Preventing substance abuse. In M. Tonry & D. Farrington (Eds.), *Building a safer society: Strategic approaches to crime prevention* (pp. 343–427). *Crime and justice: A review of research* (Vol. 19). Chicago: University of Chicago Press.

Heath, D. B. (1998). War on drugs as a metaphor in American Culture. In J. A. Schaler (Ed.), *Drugs: Should we legalize, decriminalize or deregulate?* (pp. 135–154). Amherst, NY: Prometheus Books.

Hiller, M., Knight, K., & Simpson, D. (1999). Risk factors that predict dropout from corrections-based treatment for drug abuse. *The Prison Journal, 79,* 411–430.

Inciardi, J. (1979). Heroin and street crime. *Crime and Delinquency, 25,* 333–346.

———. (1995). The therapeutic community: An effective model for corrections-based drug abuse treatment. In K. C. Haas & G. P. Alpert (Eds.), *The dilemmas of punishment* (pp. 406–417). Prospect Heights, IL: Waveland Press.

Inciardi, J., Martin, S., Butzin, C., Hooper, R., & Harrison, L. (1997). An effective model of prison-based treatment for drug-involved offenders. *Journal of Drug Issues, 27,* 261–278.

Inciardi, J. A., Martin, S. S., Lockwood, D., Hooper, R. M., & Wald, B. M. (1992). Obstacles to the implementation and evaluation of drug treatment programs in correctional settings: Reviewing the Delaware KEY experience. In C. G. Leukefeld & F. M. Tims (Eds.), *Drug abuse treatment in prisons and jails* (pp. 176–191). Washington, DC: Government Printing Office.

Jensen, E. L., & Gerber, J. (1998). *The new war on drugs: Symbolic politics and criminal justice policy.* Cincinnati, OH: Anderson.

Johnson, B., Goldstein, P. J., Preble, E., Schmeidler, J., Lipton, D. S., Spunt, B., & Miller, T. (1985). *Taking care of business: The economics of crime by heroin abusers.* Lexington, MA: Lexington Books.

Knight, K., Hiller, M., & Simpson, D. (1999). Evaluating corrections-based treatment for the drug-abusing criminal offender. *Journal of Psychoactive Drugs, 31*(3), 299–304.

Knight, K., Simpson, D., Chatham, L., & Camacho, L. (1977). An assessment of prison-based drug treatment: Texas' in-prison therapeutic community program. *Journal of Offender Rehabilitation, 24,* 75–100.

Knight, K., Simpson, D., & Hiller, M. (1999). Three-year reincarceration outcomes in-prison therapeutic community treatment in Texas. *The Prison Journal, 79,* 321–333.

Lipton, D. S. (1995). *The effectiveness of treatment for drug abusers under criminal justice supervision* (NCJ 157642). Washington, DC: U.S. Department of Justice, Office of Justice Programs, National Institute of Justice.

Lipton, D. S., Falkin, G. P., & Wexler, H. K. (1992). Correctional drug abuse treatment in the United States: An overview. In C. G. Leukefeld & F. M. Tims (Eds.), *Drug Abuse Treatment in Prisons and Jails,* 8–30. NIDA Monograph No. 118. HHS. Rockville, MD: Government Printing Office.

Lipton, D. S., Morales, E., & Goldsmith, D. S. (1989). *Pathways into treatment: A study of the drug treatment entry process.* Final Report of NIDA Project 1 R01 DA-03929-01. New York: Narcotic and Drug Research, Inc.

MacAndrew, C., & Edgerton, R. B. (1969). *Drunken Comportment.* Chicago: Aldine.

Martin, S., Butzin, C., Saum, C., & Inciardi, J. (1999). Three-year outcomes of therapeutic community treatment for drug-involved offenders in Delaware: From prison to work release to aftercare. *The Prison Journal, 79,* 294–320.

Massing, M. (2000). *The fix.* Berkeley: University of California Press.

Miczek, K., DeBold, J. F., Haney, M., Tidey, J., Vivian, J., & Weerts, E. M. (1993). Alcohol, drugs of abuse, aggression, and violence. In A. J. Reiss, Jr. & J. A. Roth (Eds.), *Understanding and preventing violence: Vol. 3. Social Influences* (pp. 377–570). Panel on the Understanding and Control of Violent Behavior, National Research Council. Washington, DC: National Academy Press.

Mumola, C. J. (1999, January). *Substance abuse and treatment, state and federal prisoners, 1997* (Bureau of Justice Statistics Special Report). Washington, DC: U.S. Department of Justice, Office of Justice Programs.

National Center on Addiction and Substance Abuse (CASA). (1998). *Behind bars: Substance abuse and America's prison population.* New York: Columbia University.

National Institute of Justice. (1994). *Drug use forecasting 1993.* Annual report on adult arrestees: Drugs and crime in America's cities. Research in Brief. Washington, DC: U.S. Department of Justice.

———. (1999, April). *1998 annual report on drug use among adult and juvenile arrestees* (NCJ 175657). Washington, DC: Department of Justice.

National Institute on Drug Abuse. (1981). *Drug abuse treatment in prisons.* Treatment Research Report Series. Washington, DC: National Institute on Drug Abuse, Government Printing Office.

Parker, R. N. (1998). Alcohol and homicide in the United States, 1934–1995, or one reason why U.S. rates of violence may be going down. *National Institute of Justice Journal, 237,* 14–15.

Pearson, F., & Lipton, D. (1999). A meta-analytic review of the effectiveness of corrections-based treatments for drug abuse. *The Prison Journal, 79,* 384–410.

Peyton, E. A. (1994, March 11). *A coordinated approach to managing the drug involved offender.* The Second Report of the Treatment Access Committee, Delaware Sentencing Accountability Commission.

Reiss, A. J., Jr., & Roth, J. A. (Eds.). (1993). *Understanding and preventing violence* (Vol. 1). Panel on the Understanding and Control of Violent Behavior, National Research Council. Washington, DC: National Academy Press.

Ringwalt, C. L., Greene, J. M., Ennett, S. T., Iachan, R., Clayton, R. R., & Leukefeld, C. G. (1994). *Past and future directions of the D.A.R.E. program: An evaluation review.* Draft Final Report, September 1994. Washington, DC: U.S. Department of Justice, Office of Justice Programs, National Institute of Justice.

Simpson, D., Wexler, H., & Inciardi, J. (1999). Introduction. *The Prison Journal, 79,* 291–293.

Tobler, N. S. (1986). Meta-analysis of 143 adolescent drug prevention programs: Quantitative outcome results of program participants compared to a control or comparison group. *The Journal of Drug Issues, 16,* 537–367.

———. (1992). Drug prevention programs can work: Research findings. *Journal of Addictive Diseases, 11*(3), 1–28.

U.S. General Accounting Office. (1997). *Drug courts: Overview of growth, characteristics, and results* (NCJ-169764). Washington, DC: U.S. General Accounting Office.

Walters, G. (1992). Drug-seeking behavior: Disease or lifestyle. *Professional Psychology: Research and Practice, 23*(2), 139–145.

Wexler, H. K. (1995). *Amity/prison TC: One-year outcome results.* Unpublished report to NDRI.

Wexler, H. K., Falkin, G. P., & Lipton, D. S. (1990). Outcome evaluation of a prison therapeutic community for substance abuse treatment. *Criminal Justice and Behavior, 17*(1), 71–92.

Wexler, H. K., Lipton, D., Falkin, G. P., & Rosenbaum, A. B. (1992). Outcome evaluation of a prison therapeutic community for substance abuse treatment. In C. G. Leukefeld & F. M. Tims (Eds.), *Drug abuse treatment in prisons and jails* (pp. 156–175). Washington, DC: Government Printing Office.

Wexler, H. K., Lipton, D. S., & Johnson, B. D. (1988). *A criminal justice system strategy for treating cocaine-heroin abusing offenders in custody.* Issues and Practices Paper in Criminal Justice (U.S. GPO. No. 1988-202-045:8-0082). Washington, DC: National Institute of Justice, March.

Wexler, H., Melnick, G., Lowe, L., & Peters, J. (1999). Three-year reincarceration outcomes for Amity in-prison therapeutic community and aftercare in California. *The Prison Journal, 79,* 321–333.

Wish, E. D., & O'Neil, J. A. (1989, September). *Drug use forecasting (DUF).* Research Update, January to March, 1989. Washington, DC: U.S. Department of Justice, National Institute of Justice. ✦

Chapter 13

Prevention and Intervention Strategies

In previous chapters we explored different types of violence (e.g., homicide, rape, robbery, hate crimes) using the *tripartite approach* (i.e., major patterns, explanations, and interventions). We have thus already had much to say about how to reduce each type of violence. Why, then, a separate chapter on prevention and intervention? This concluding chapter summarizes several important but more *general* approaches to prevention and intervention that don't fit neatly into any one specific subtopic.

We draw upon both criminal justice and public health perspectives (see chapter 1) to argue for a more balanced approach to prevention and intervention. The main challenges are threefold: (1) We need to more carefully consider the appropriate balance of punishment and prevention required to reduce different types of criminal violence; (2) we need to develop better programs and policies based upon valid information and knowledge; and (3) we need to better evaluate which strategies are effective and which are not.

Traditionally, the public health approach has been more inclusive, and this is the perspective that largely guides our discussion of prevention. Informed by a broad range of interdisciplinary theory and research, this multimodal approach has much to add to the criminal justice approach which traditionally emphasizes the roles of law enforcement, the courts, and corrections. More and more, we are witnessing the development of creative, multimodal approaches to violence prevention and intervention.

Criminal Justice Approaches

Criminal justice approaches aimed at reducing violence have traditionally emphasized deterrence, rehabilitation, or incapacitation goals (see chapter 1), although distinctions between programs and policies based on these goals are less pronounced than they once were. Here, we briefly summarize some of the major evidence for the effectiveness of each. We then discuss two controversial examples of punishment (i.e., three strikes laws and the death penalty) and examine major limitations.

Deterrence

Theories of deterrence predict that reduced crime will result as the certainty, swiftness, and severity of sanctions are increased. Indeed, some studies have found a reduction in crime rates (some more than others) related to the increased likelihood of apprehension, conviction, or imprisonment (Greenwood, 1982). A National Academy of Sciences panel that conducted the most thorough review of deterrence research to date found that, overall, the evidence did not strongly support the existence of deterrent effects (Blumstein, Cohen, & Nagin, 1978). Where effects were found, however, they seemed to be stronger when the probability of arrest and incarceration was increased (i.e., *certainty*). The effect of increasing length of sentences (on crime rates) was minimal. Evidence suggests that *certainty is much more important than severity.*

A number of studies have examined whether an increased police presence in certain areas reduces violent crime. For example, a study of crime in the New York subways between 1965 and 1971 showed that robberies dropped significantly after the number of uniformed officers patrolling the subway system was increased (Chaiken, Lawless, & Stevenson, 1974). However, crimes were displaced to nearby locations. In the well-known Kansas City Preventive Patrol Experiment (Kelling, Pate, Dieckman, & Brown, 1974), researchers varied the amount of preventive patrol (i.e., officers in patrol cars cruising neighborhoods) in different districts. Areas were matched for similarity in crime rates, population demographics, income, and calls for service. In some areas, patrols were doubled or quadrupled (proactive patrol). In others, nothing was changed (control group). In another, preventive patrol was eliminated entirely (reactive policing). After one year, there were no significant differences in crime rates or citizens' perceptions of safety. Studies have failed to consistently demonstrate any clear-cut reduction in crime due to increased police presence alone.

Although the evidence is mixed, testing deterrence theory is in reality quite difficult and complex (Nagin, 1998). First of all, much of the research has been based on aggregate, official statistics (e.g., UCR) that contain known limitations (see chapter 2). Second, interpreting crime rates is an extremely complex task. Many studies are unable to eliminate other factors that could account for observed deterrent effects (e.g., biases in measures, regional variations in criminal statutes and procedures, differences in data collection and reporting, and other influencing factors). Third, it is difficult to determine how many *potential* offenders are deterred by any specific strategy. Doing so would require large samples of survey or interview respondents, including honest citizens as well as offenders. Some researchers attempt to assess offenders' calculation of benefits versus costs associated with specific offenses, although only occasionally in response to any specific intervention strategy (Clarke & Cornish, 1985), and only occasionally with positive benefits (Clarke, 1992). In sum, deterrent effects of sanctions on crime rates are not impossible to achieve, but the weight of the evidence to date has been somewhat mixed and stronger research methods are needed (Nagin, 1998).

Rehabilitation

Numerous, diverse attempts at reforming offenders have been attempted over the years, including psychotherapy, behavior modification, vocational training, alcohol and drug treatment, and violent offender and sex offender programs. A National Academy of Sciences panel (Sechrest, White, & Brown, 1979) concluded that we know very little about what works and what does not. A major problem is that evaluation methodologies have often been inadequate. At least three other situations limit conclusions about rehabilitation: (1) There are few programs available to prisoners (e.g., many want drug treatment but can't get it); (2) many inmates refuse to participate; and (3) sometimes inmates are not allowed to participate for security reasons. More recently, researchers (e.g., Andrews et al., 1990; Gendreau, 1996) have argued that the "nothing works" rhetoric about rehabilitation is highly misleading. They argue that the best studies show that some types of treatment indeed work for some types of offenders, at least some of the time. However, we still need to know much more about how different factors influence treatment outcomes for different offenders.

Incapacitation

Incapacitation refers to the argument that offenders cannot commit further crimes while in prison. Generally what is recommended is increasing sentence length to keep convicted offenders in prison longer, particularly "career criminals." However, serious problems are associated with this type of *selective incapacitation* (Blumstein, Cohen, Roth, & Visher, 1986). Most important, we cannot predict with any accuracy whatsoever *who* is likely to become a career criminal until *after* he or she has already amassed a lengthy criminal career. It would be highly unethical and illegal to simply lock somebody up forever because we think they might become a serious criminal. There is, in other words, a huge false positive problem: A large percentage of those who are predicted to re-offend (based upon various models) indeed do not. *General incapacitation*, in contrast, argues that if we simply locked up all offenders for longer periods of time, we would significantly reduce crime. However, such indiscriminate increases in punishment would strain criminal justice resources (e.g., overcrowded jails and prisons) even further than they are already (Welsh, 1995), and projected expenses would far exceed available resources unless gigantic tax increases were imposed (Welsh & Harris, 1999).

The Death Penalty

Capital punishment was used widely in the United States until 1968, when it was suspended by the U.S. Supreme Court. In *Furman v. Georgia* (1972), the Court ruled that the death penalty, at least as administered, constituted cruel and unusual punishment because it was administered in an arbitrary and discriminatory manner. The death penalties of 39 states and the District of Columbia were rendered invalid.

The death penalty was banned in the United States until a followup decision by the Supreme Court was issued in *Gregg v. Georgia* (1976). Revising its earlier decision, the Court ruled against mandatory death penalty laws, but allowed "aggravating and mitigating circumstances" for which the death penalty could be permitted (e.g., a murder committed in the course of a felony). Because of the seriousness and finality of the punishment, capital cases must be conducted according to higher standards of due process and more careful procedures than other cases.

Instead of deciding the defendant's guilt and imposing the death sentence in the same court proceeding, most states created "bifurcated" (two-step) proceedings with a separate trial and punishment phase. In the punishment phase, the court must consider specific aggravating factors set forth in state law (e.g., excessive cruelty, murder of a police officer, commission of a murder during a felony) as well as specific mitigating factors (e.g., offender's youthfulness, diminished intent, lack of a previous criminal record). These factors must be weighed together before a judge or jury imposes the death penalty in any case. Executions resumed in 1977, as most states revised their legislation to meet the requirements set forth by *Gregg v. Georgia*. As of 1998, 38 states had capital punishment statutes (Snell, 1999).

The *Gregg* decision stood until 1987, when Georgia's death penalty was challenged once again on constitutional grounds, this time on the basis of racial discrimination. In *McCleskey v. Kemp* (1987), the defendant's attorneys claimed that Georgia's law discriminated on the basis of race. Research by David Baldus and his colleagues (Baldus, Woodworth, & Pulaski, 1994) examined over 2,000 Georgia murder cases and found that defendants charged with killing whites received the death penalty 11 times more often than those charged with killing blacks. Even after controlling for 230 factors, such as viciousness of the crime and the quality of the evidence in each case, the death sentence was still four times more likely to be imposed when the victim was white. Even though a majority (60 percent) of homicide victims in Georgia were black, six out of seven offenders put to death between 1977 and 1987 were black men convicted of killing white men (Baldus et al., 1994). The Supreme Court rejected McCleskey's claim by a 5 to 4 vote. To show that the death penalty in Georgia was being administered in an unconstitutional manner, the Court ruled, McCleskey would have had to prove that decision makers discriminated in his own individual case, not just in a "generalized statistical study." McCleskey was executed in 1991.

Although about 200 to 300 new offenders have been added to death row every year since 1977, the number of executions per year since 1977 has never exceeded 74 (in 1997) (Snell, 1999). The major reason is the lengthy and expensive appeals process required since the Supreme Court ruling in *Gregg v. Georgia*. Between 1977 and 1998, 500 death row prisoners were executed (Snell, 1999). The average amount of time lapsed between sentencing and execution was 113 months (i.e., nearly 9½ years). Death sentences must be reviewed by both state and federal courts until the appeals process has been exhausted. From 1973 to 1998, a total of 6,431 persons were sentenced to death, but only 500 (7.8 percent) were executed. Fully 2,124 (33 percent) had their sentence or conviction overturned as a result of appellate court decisions; 180 (2.8 percent) died while awaiting execution; 146 (2.3 percent) had their sentence commuted (Snell, 1999).

During 1998, 68 persons in 18 states were executed. Lethal injection was by far the most popular method (88 percent), followed by electrocution (10 percent). From 1977 to 1998, Texas was the runaway leader in executions with 164 (33 percent of all executions in the United States during this period), followed by Virginia with 59 (12 percent), Florida with 43 (9 percent), Missouri with 32 (6 percent), Louisiana with 24 (5 percent), and Georgia with 23 (5 percent). Thus, only six states (five of them in the South) accounted for 70 percent of all executions in the United States since 1977. Overall, southern states performed 407 (81 percent) of all executions in the United States between 1977 and 1998 (Snell, 1999).

Death sentences and executions are disproportionately likely for African Americans, given their representation in the general population (about 12 percent of the U.S. population). Of the 5,709 persons who entered prison under sentence of death since 1977 (i.e., post-*Gregg* decision), 2,830 (50 percent) were white; 2,347 (41 percent) were black; 449 (8 percent) were Hispanic; and 83 (1 percent) were classified as "other." From 1977 to 1998, 281 (56 percent) of the 500 prisoners executed were white; 178 (36 percent) were black; 34 (7 percent) were Hispanic; and seven (1 percent) were classified as "other."

Among inmates under sentence of death on December 31, 1998 (for whom criminal histories were available), 65 percent had a prior felony conviction and 9 percent had a previous homicide conviction (Snell, 1999). There was little difference by race: 63 percent of whites and 69 percent of blacks under sentence of death had prior felony convictions; 8 percent of whites and 9 percent of blacks under sentence of death had a prior homicide conviction.

Diverse arguments are commonly made for and against the death penalty (for further reading, see Baldus et al., 1994; Bohm, 1989; Bohm, 1999; Zimring & Hawkins, 1986). At least four major arguments are commonly made in favor of the death penalty: (1) public support, (2) deterrence, (3) retribution, and (4) cost-effectiveness.

First, public opinion strongly favors the death penalty, some argue, and thus democratic values should prevail. Between 1953 and 1999, the Gallup poll asked the question, "Are you in favor of the death penalty for a person convicted of murder?" Support has been as low as 42 percent in 1966 and as high as 80 percent in 1994, but hasn't dropped below 70 percent since 1985. In 1999, 71 percent favored the death penalty for persons convicted of murder (Maguire & Pastore, 1999b).

A second major argument addresses deterrence: Does the death penalty deter criminals from committing violent acts? Research conducted by Ehrlich (1975) is often cited as support for deterrent effects due to the death penalty. However, that study has been severely criticized for its weak methodology, and most experts have questioned its conclusions (Blumstein et al., 1978; Conrad & van den Haag, 1983; Vandaele, 1978). The research evidence in favor of deterrent effects is not convincing (Blumstein et al., 1978). The great majority of murderers, for example, commit their crimes impulsively and irrationally, without much reasoning or anticipation of consequences (see chapters 4 and 9). Indeed, it would be folly to suggest that laws determine human behavior completely or even to a great extent (Packer, 1968). What about all the other diverse causes of human (and violent) behavior? Why should individual free will (or pathology) predominate among all the diverse causes of homicide suggested by social science research (Zahn, 1990)?

Some advocates (e.g., Conrad & van den Haag, 1983) argue that the death penalty achieves justice by paying back killers for the seriousness of their crimes. Retribution becomes a moral justification for the death penalty. According to this position, the death penalty helps define the most serious of all crimes (and punishments), showing society's disapproval. The death penalty alone, advocates argue, provides sufficient retribution and reparation for surviving family members of homicide victims. Advocates also point to incapacitation as a justification; the death penalty prevents offenders from doing further harm. However, the portion of released homicide offenders who recommit murder is quite low (Zahn, 1990). Of those on death row at the end of 1998, only 9 percent had a previous homicide conviction (Snell, 1999). However, moral justifications really can't be answered by any empirical evidence, but rather by faith: Retribution is punishment for its own sake.

Advocates may also argue that the death penalty is more cost-effective than holding prisoners for the rest of their lives. This position is weak (Bohm, 1989, 1999; Conrad & van den Haag, 1983). The mandatory appeals process in many cases ends up being more expensive than the cost of incarcerating a prisoner for life, and there is no justifiable reason in a democratic society to place a priority on cost-effectiveness where human lives are concerned. Besides, evidence suggests that it is actually more expensive to carry out a death sentence under current laws than it is to keep someone in prison for life (Bohm, 1999; Zimring & Hawkins, 1986).

Opponents of the death penalty often point to at least three arguments: (1) improper use of state power, (2) racial discrimination, and (3) the possibility of errors. First, opponents argue, it is wrong for the government to intentionally kill citizens. How can the state advocate murder while at the same time prohibiting murder? Further, in countries (e.g., apartheid-era South Africa) and regions of the United States (e.g., southern states) where the death penalty has been most widely used, its use has departed most conspicuously from standards of equity and humanity (Bohm, 1999; Bowers, 1974). It is hard to ignore historical lessons where the death penalty has been justified and applied under the auspices of religion (e.g., the Christian crusades) and the coercive use of power by the state (e.g., Stalinist Russia) to enforce compliance (Bowers, 1974; Foucault, 1977).

Second, there is substantial evidence that the death penalty discriminates against minorities (Bohm, 1999; Bowers, 1974). Minorities are more likely to be arrested, charged, and convicted of capital crimes, even holding constant legal variables, such as previous criminal record; and they are at least four times more likely to be executed (Baldus et al., 1994). Statistics show clearly that blacks receive death penalty sentences far more frequently than would be expected on the basis of their criminal history alone (Snell, 1999).

Third, opponents argue, the death penalty is irreversible, but a surprising number of people convicted of capital crimes were later found to be innocent (Bohm, 1999). Recall also that a significant percentage (33 percent) of those sentenced to death later had their convictions or sentences overturned (Snell, 1999).

Regardless of one's views, one cannot ignore the constitutional requirements outlined by the Supreme Court. Nor can one ignore the moral arguments that fuel public support for the death penalty. On the other hand, both sides could benefit from careful examination of existing research and further valid research on critical arguments associated with the death penalty (Bohm, 1999).

Three Strikes Laws

Three strikes laws have become extremely popular as a means of putting away repeat offenders (Welsh & Harris, 1999). However, such laws are beset with a number of weaknesses, including poorly defined target populations, discrimination against minorities, lack of acceptance by prosecutors, and lack of prison space (Shichor & Sechrest, 1996). Further, although these laws attempt to focus on career criminals, few offenders specialize, and prediction of who will become a high-rate offender is extremely difficult, as we saw earlier in this chapter.

Democratic values, such as equity, are compromised by these laws. A California study found that blacks were sent to prison under the three strikes law 13 times more often than whites (Greenwood et al., 1994). Forty-three percent of the third-strike inmates in California were African American, although they made up only 7 percent of the state's population and 20 percent of its felony arrests. In analyses of the Federal sentencing guidelines, researchers found that African Americans received longer sentences than whites, not because of differential treatment by judges but because they constituted the large majority of those convicted of trafficking in crack cocaine, a crime Congress had singled out for especially harsh mandatory penalties (McDonald & Carlson, 1993).

Target populations for three strikes laws seem particularly poorly defined. In California, about 1,300 offenders have been imprisoned on third-strike felonies and more than 14,000 have been incarcerated for second-strike felonies. California's law calls for a doubling of the prison sentence for a second felony and for a sentence of 25 years to life for a third conviction. The California law was written to cover 500 felonies, including many nonviolent offenses. Some of the felonies include petty theft, attempted assault, and burglary. Thus, about 85 percent of all those sentenced under the three strikes laws were involved in nonviolent crimes. For instance, 192 marijuana possessors have been sentenced for second and third strikes, compared with 40 murderers, 25 rapists, and 24 kidnappers.

State prosecutors have avoided the three strikes laws because they see little need for them with existing sentencing laws (Welsh & Harris, 1999). Another reason is that some laws have been narrowly written, making them difficult to apply. Plea bargaining and charge bargaining have become common methods for circumventing three strikes laws.

The criminal courts rely on a high rate of guilty pleas to speed case processing and avoid logjams. Officials offer inducements to defendants to obtain guilty pleas. Three strikes laws disrupt established plea-bargaining patterns by preventing a prosecutor from offering a short prison term (less than the minimum) in exchange for a guilty plea. However, prosecutors usually can shift strategies and bargain on charges rather than on sentences. The findings of research on the impact of mandatory sentencing laws are instructive (Tonry, 1987). Officials make earlier and more selective arrest, charging, and diversion decisions; they also tend to bargain less and to bring more cases to trial. Indeed, 25 percent of three strikes cases go to trial compared with 4 percent overall for felonies.

The California law created a need to build 15 new prisons, costing $4.5 billion (Greenwood et al., 1994). California's prison population was expected to grow by 70 percent following passage of the law, resulting in a 256 percent capacity rate, meaning that without new prisons, three inmates would be housed in space for one.

Last, but not least, evidence suggests that felons are neither widely aware of the provisions of new three strikes laws nor deterred by them. Even worse, violent behavior could be unintentionally increased, inciting some felons to murder witnesses or resist arrest by police officers to avoid getting caught.

Get-tough policies, such as three strikes, provide a dramatic response to a serious problem, but it is unlikely that such intervention is sufficient by itself to produce a substantial decrease in violent crime. Given the complexity of human behavior and the interaction of multiple causes of violence (e.g., biological, psychological, and sociological), it must be emphasized that the criminal justice system is limited in its ability to prevent violent crime.

The Limits of Punishment

The criminal justice system is intended, at least in part, to prevent crime. But how much impact do responses by police, courts, and corrections have on violent crime? Many researchers have concluded after careful reviews of the evidence that the criminal justice system is, at best, quite limited in its ability to reduce violent behavior (Blumstein et al., 1978; Greenwood, 1982; Packer, 1968; Reiss & Roth, 1993). Punishment is a necessary but not sufficient condition to prevent violent crime, argued Packer:

> The criminal sanction is indispensable; we could not, now or in the foreseeable future, get along without it. Yet we resort to it in far too indiscriminate a way, thereby weakening some of the important bases upon which its efficacy rests and threatening social values that far transcend the prevention of crime. (1968, p. 364)

What are some of these limits, then, and what values are threatened?

First of all, criminal justice system processing is imperfect and inefficient. If the criminal justice system is to have any success in preventing violence, it must first be able to identify and apprehend violent offenders. However, clearance rates (the percentage of reported crimes in which police make an arrest) are not very high. The clearance rate for murder, the highest of any offense, was only 66 percent in 1997 (Maguire & Pastore, 1999a). Clearance rates are even lower for certain offenses, such as aggravated assault (59 percent), forcible rape (51 percent), and robbery (26 percent). Most cases, if solved at all, are solved either by an on-scene arrest or a witness identifying the offender. If these factors do not occur, arrest is unlikely (Greenwood, 1982).

Second, even if an arrest is made, cases are filtered out at each stage of court processing (primarily because of the quality of evidence) (Cole & Smith, 1998). For example, considerable portions of those who are arrested are not prosecuted. Even if prosecutions are initiated, many cases will be dismissed after closer review. Even if charges are not dismissed, offenders are not always convicted, and many plead guilty to lesser charges. Indeed, only about half of all arrests for violent crime result in a conviction. Of those, less than half are sentenced to state prison (Greenwood, 1982). Given such serious limitations, under what circumstances can we reasonably expect the criminal justice system to prevent crime, and what else is needed?

Violent offenders should not escape punishment. However, the vast majority will be released from prison at some point, better or worse equipped to become productive members of society. To what degree can prison reduce the likelihood of recidivism? Do *some* prison programs (e.g., drug treatment, education, vocational training) work at least for *some* offenders under at least *some* circumstances? And even more important, are there any effective strategies to prevent acts of criminal violence in the first place, before violators come to the attention of the criminal justice system? As Packer argues, the use of punishment must be qualified to some degree by other social purposes, including the enhancement of freedom and the doing of justice.

Does the criminal justice system discriminate against minorities? We find it troubling that advocates of harsher punishments often ignore evidence that minorities receive the harshest punishments. Overrepresentation of minorities in the criminal justice system, from arrest to disposition to incarceration, remains one of the most troubling problems in the adult and juvenile justice systems of the United States (Welsh, Harris, & Jenkins, 1996). Minorities come into contact with the criminal justice system at much higher rates than whites (Hagan & Peterson, 1995). For example, African Americans make up one-third of all arrests and half of all incarcerations, although they compose only 12 percent of the general population. African American, Latino, Asian American, and Native American youth are incarcerated in detention facilities and public training schools at rates three to four times those of whites (National Prison Project, 1990). Although incarceration rates vary across counties and states, minority youth make up more than half of all juveniles incarcerated nationwide (Feyerherm, 1995).

At least two major explanations have been offered: (1) Minorities commit more crimes and (2) the criminal justice system is racist. There is likely some truth to both, although it is extremely difficult to measure either with precision or to determine their exact balance. First, official statistics are themselves flawed (see chapter 2). Second, racial disparities in conviction and incarceration rates are reduced (but not eliminated) when certain variables, such as the offender's current and prior offense severity, are taken into consideration (Walker, Spohn, & DeLeone, 1996). Ample evidence points to discrimination, although its exact prevalence is unclear. Much evidence suggests that high rates of minority youth incarceration are attributable at least partly to case processing disparities, and not merely to higher crime rates by minority youth (Pope & Feyerherm, 1992). In spite of increasing public and scholarly concern about relationships between race, crime, and punishment,[1]

> program initiatives/policy designed to reduce minority overrepresentation and ensure fairness in juvenile justice processing either do not exist or at least not in any significant numbers. (Pope & Feyerherm, 1992, p. 46)

As Carl Pope suggests,

> Policy initiatives must not only address problems in the case processing of juvenile offenders, as noted earlier, but also preexisting social conditions. Only by such a two-pronged attack can we have any chance of reducing crime among our youths and the disproportionate overrepresentation of minorities within the juvenile justice system. (1995, pp. 215–216)

Public Health Approaches to Punishment and Prevention

With some modifications to include a greater role for individual offender characteristics, the public health risk-based approach to prevention has gained considerable attention from criminal justice researchers and policy makers. Two striking examples are provided by the National Research Council's *multilevel risk approach*

(Reiss & Roth, 1993) and the Office of Juvenile Justice and Delinquency Prevention's (OJJDP) *Comprehensive Strategy for Serious, Violent, and Chronic Juvenile Offenders* (Howell, 1995).

The Multilevel Risk Approach

Despite abundant social science evidence over the years that violent crime is related to time, place, culture, and social structure, criminological researchers and policymakers over the past century have heavily emphasized individual offenders' motivations (Harris, Welsh, & Butler, 2000). Calls for multilevel, interdisciplinary approaches (e.g., examining the relative explanatory power of individual, institutional, social structural, and cultural factors associated with violence) have become more frequent in recent years, partially as a result of the greater sophistication of information and computing systems, and partially as a result of the influence of the public health perspective.

The National Academy of Sciences *Panel on the Understanding and Causes of Violent Behavior,* composed of an international panel of experts from a variety of disciplines, was established in 1989 to review existing knowledge and make recommendations to control violence (Reiss & Roth, 1993). One of their main conclusions was that we have many promising directions for intervention and prevention to pursue from research findings, but better measures and more controlled research (especially evaluations of promising efforts) are needed to identify causes and opportunities for prevention. Using the risk approach to classify different predictors, they proposed a matrix consisting of two main dimensions: (1) *temporal proximity* (closeness in time) of a predictor to the violent event, and (2) the *level of analysis* at which that predictor is observed.

Levels of analysis refer to different units of observation and analysis, including *macrosocial, microsocial, psychosocial,* and *biological* (e.g., *neurobehavioral*). Macrosocial factors are characteristics of large social units such as communities, cities, states, and countries. Macrosocial risk factors for violence include both social structural (e.g., poverty, unemployment) and cultural (e.g., group and subgroup values about the acceptability of violence in specific circumstances, exposure to media violence, etc.) variables. Microsocial factors are characteristics of encounters among people (e.g., family and group dynamics, situational factors such as availability of weapons, organizational and institutional processes). Psychosocial factors include individual characteristics (e.g., personality, learned rewards) or temporary states (e.g., influence of alcohol, stress) that influence interactions with others. Biological or neurobehavioral factors, primarily in the brain, include chemical, electrical, and hormonal influences on behavior.

The multilevel approach carries important implications for the study and prevention of violence. Consistent with the risk-based approach of the public health perspective, the panel suggested that the effective prevention and intervention of violence will depend upon breaking one or more specific links in the chain of events preceding a violent incident. Instigating multiple options for intervening, and increased interagency collaboration is called for:

> Violence problem-solving will require long-term collaboration and new organizational arrangements among local law enforcement, criminal justice, schools and public health, emergency medicine, and social service agencies, all working with program evaluators and other researchers. (Reiss & Roth, 1993, p. 10)

OJJDP's Comprehensive Strategy for Serious, Violent, and Chronic Juvenile Offenders

Delinquency theory, research, and policy have also been influenced by the public health perspective. The National Juvenile Justice Action Plan, part of the OJJDP Comprehensive Strategy for Serious, Violent, and Chronic Juvenile Offenders (Howell, 1995), encourages helping youths throughout their development while responding to juvenile crime in a way that ensures public safety. Although public attitudes, legislation, and justice system responses toward juvenile crime in the United States have toughened in recent years (Torbet et al., 1996), the National Juvenile Justice Action Plan calls for a more balanced approach between punishment and prevention.

The *Comprehensive Plan* was based upon an influential risk-based approach known as the Social Development Strategy (Catalano & Hawkins, 1996; Hawkins & Catalano, 1992; Howell, 1995). According to this strategy, known risk factors for delinquency and substance abuse can be reduced by enhancing known "protective" factors. Healthy beliefs and clear standards for behavior in the family, school, and community (i.e., protective factors) directly promote healthy behavior in children. By encouraging bonding with people and institutions (e.g., families, peer groups, schools, and communities) that promote healthy beliefs and clear standards, the model suggests, youths will be encouraged to adopt similar beliefs and standards. Individual characteristics (e.g., prosocial orientation, intelligence, resilient temperament), however, are important because they affect a child's ability to perceive opportunities, develop skills, and obtain recognition.

The OJJDP Comprehensive Plan is based on decades of research, statistics, and evaluations in the fields of criminal and juvenile justice, public health, and youth development (Bilchik, 1998). Research has consistently documented certain risk factors for violent juvenile offending (Greenwood, 1992; Hawkins, Arthur, & Catalano, 1995; Howell, 1995; Loeber & Farrington, 1998; Reiss & Roth, 1993; Roth, 1994). At the individual level, risk factors include pregnancy and delivery complications; hyperactivity; concentration problems; restlessness; risk-taking behavior; early aggressiveness; early involvement in other forms of antisocial behavior; and beliefs and attitudes favorable to deviant or antisocial behavior. Family factors that increase risk include delinquent siblings; criminal behavior of parents; harsh discipline; physical abuse or neglect; poor family management practices; low levels of parent-child involvement; high levels of family conflict; parental attitudes favorable to violence; and separation of the child from family. School factors associated with higher risk include academic failure; low commitment to education; truancy; early dropout; frequent changes of schools; association with delinquent peers; and gang membership. Community or neighborhood factors include high population density; high residential mobility; high poverty rate; availability of weapons and drugs; and a high rate of adult involvement in crime. We summarize here five key objectives of the Comprehensive Plan and briefly review corresponding prevention and intervention strategies.

Objective #1. The first objective of the plan is to provide immediate intervention and appropriate sanctions and treatment for delinquents. Through various federal grants, states have been provided with funds to strengthen their juvenile justice systems. States, in turn, funnel funds to specific cities and counties to develop and implement programs to prevent and control delinquency. A wide variety of strategies has been implemented including *graduated sanctions*. Sanctions refer to a system of responses to delinquency that combine individual accountability with intensive treatment and rehabilitation services. These sanctions are graduated to the degree that they fit the offense and the juvenile's previous history of delinquency. This requires consideration and balancing of various criteria, such as the seriousness of the delinquent act, the potential risk for re-offending, the risk to public safety, and the offender's rehabilitation needs. The most intensive treatments are reserved for juveniles who most need them (e.g., intensive, residential drug and alcohol treatment), while the most intensive punishments (e.g., secure detention, rather than camps, ranches, or farms) are reserved for those who earn them. Comprehensive, valid risk and needs assessments are required to determine the appropriate punishment or treatment response for any juvenile.

Safe Futures provides a programmatic response to the first objective. Under the Safe Futures Project, OJJDP is providing approximately $1.4 million a year for 5 years to each of six communities: Boston, Seattle, St. Louis, Contra Costa County and Imperial County (both in California), and the Fort Belknap Indian Community in Montana. Safe Futures assists communities in developing collaborative efforts to reduce youth violence and seeks to improve the service delivery system by creating a continuum of care for youths and their families. Both primary and secondary prevention strategies are used. Collaborative efforts include the participation of local human service and juvenile justice systems; health and mental health services; child welfare and education; and police, probation, courts, and corrections agencies. In Boston, for example, a coalition of community and government agencies is attempting to establish a total support network to address the multiple needs of juvenile offenders and their families. Extensive participation includes neighborhood residents and youth, community-based service providers, schools, churches, housing authorities, probation, police, and corrections. A key aspect of this program is its emphasis on increasing local administrative control and decision-making through neighborhood governance boards established in each of the three target areas (Kracke & Special Emphasis Division Staff, 1996).

Objective #2. The second objective of the plan is to prosecute serious, violent, and chronic juvenile offenders in criminal court. The primary focus is on offenders who have committed serious crimes, have a lengthy history of delinquency, have failed to respond to treatment, or all of these. In public health parlance, tertiary prevention is emphasized by Objective #2. In particular, almost every state has adopted or strengthened waiver and transfer mechanisms that allow juveniles, under specific conditions, to be tried as adults in criminal court. Such legislation varies dramatically from one state to another, however, and reliable information on the impact of such strategies is still lacking. OJJDP is currently funding several studies to determine the outcome and impact of waiver and transfer provisions on juvenile offenders. Related policies include changing state laws to make juvenile records more accessible to school, human services, and justice personnel. In many states, no longer does a juvenile's record become sealed when he or she reaches adulthood; previous juvenile offenses can now be used in criminal proceedings. Confidentiality of juvenile records, once a cornerstone of the *parens patriae* philosophy, has also been weakened, ostensibly to improve sharing of information among human service personnel, and to improve coordination of different treatment services delivered by different agencies.

Objective #3. The third objective of the plan attempts to reduce youth involvement with guns, drugs, and gangs. As argued earlier (see chapter 11), the availability of firearms in the United States is at least partly related to high rates of violent crime. *Partnerships to Reduce Juvenile Gun Violence,* a recent effort funded by OJJDP, attempts to enhance and coordinate prevention, intervention, and suppression activities by strengthening linkages among community groups, schools, law enforcement, and the juvenile justice system. For example, if law enforcement agents become more acquainted with community residents, they will, it is hoped, learn more about problems in neighborhoods and be more successful in enlisting support for community crime prevention efforts. Three critical factors are addressed: (1) juvenile access to guns, (2) the reasons young people carry guns, and (3) the reasons they choose to use guns to resolve conflicts. Similarly, in the Boston Violence Prevention Project (Kennedy, 1997), city, state, and federal representatives helped establish and support a large network of community-based job, recreation, and prevention programs for juveniles. Such efforts, illustrative of secondary and tertiary prevention techniques, coincided with police and probation crackdowns on high-risk offenders.

Other strategies focus specifically on reducing gang violence. Research supported through OJJDP's *National Youth Gang Suppression and Intervention Program,* based on the work of Irving Spergel in Chicago, suggests that effective strategies to reduce gang violence must focus upon individuals, institutions, and communities (Burch & Chemers, 1997). Coordinated strategies that appear to be associated with the sustained reduction of gang problems include community mobilization (e.g., citizens, youth, community groups, and agencies); social and economic opportunities, such as special school, training, and job programs; social intervention (especially youth outreach and work with street gangs); gang suppression (i.e., formal and informal social control procedures administered by justice agencies and community groups); and organizational change and development (i.e., appropriate organization and integration of strategies and potential reallocation of resources among involved agencies). Based upon these findings, OJJDP is currently implementing and testing its Comprehensive Response to America's Youth Gang Initiative in five jurisdictions (Mesa and Tucson, Arizona; Riverside, California; Bloomington, Illinois; and San Antonio, Texas). In the first year, each site began the process of community mobilization, identifying the nature and extent of the gang problem, and exploring ways to address these problems. In the second year, sites began implementing appropriate strategies to reduce gang violence. Evaluation is currently underway, as are training and technical assistance to the agencies and groups involved in this collaborative effort. OJJDP has also established the National Youth Gang Center to promote effective and innovative strategies, collect and analyze statistical data on gangs, analyze gang legislation, and review research literature. Boys' and Girls' Clubs of America's Gang Prevention Through Targeted Outreach, a program funded by this initiative, has served over 6,000 youths at risk for gang involvement. Through a referral network that includes courts, police, schools, social services, and other agencies, as well as direct outreach, at-risk youths are recruited into local Club programs in a nonstigmatizing way (i.e., they are not segregated into separate programs from other youths). Once they join, youths are provided with case-managed recreation and education activities focused on personal development to enhance communication skills, problem solving, and decision making. Unlike other strategies funded under Objective #3, primary prevention is emphasized by these programs.

Objective #4. The fourth objective is to provide opportunities for children and youth. Prevention activities focused on enhancing prosocial skills and increasing opportunities for youth have, when well-planned and well-implemented, proven effective in reducing delinquency (e.g., Howell, 1995). Such programs, emphasizing primary prevention techniques, include mentoring, after-school activities, conflict resolution training, remedial education, and vocational education. Boys' and Girls' Clubs, described above, have provided after-school activities that increased school attendance, improved academic performance, and reduced juvenile crime (Ingersoll, 1997). Welsh, Jenkins, and Harris (1999) found that participation in five community-based after-school programs run by nonprofit groups reduced rearrest rates for juveniles in one community (Harrisburg, PA) but not another (Philadelphia). Program implementation and organizational stability were important factors influencing program impact.

Mentoring programs, such as the Juvenile Mentoring Programs (JUMP) funded by OJJDP, have also enjoyed some success in reducing delinquency. Advocates of mentoring argue that such programs address at-risk children's critical needs for positive adult contact, support, monitoring, and child advocacy. Such needs are particularly high in povertized communities where delinquency rates are highest. Mentors and youths make a significant commitment of time and energy to develop relationships devoted to personal, academic, or career development, and social, athletic, or artistic growth. In the Big Brothers/Big Sisters program (BB/BS), the youth and the volunteer mentor meet for about 4 hours, two to four times per month, for at least 1 year. Developmentally appropriate activities may include taking walks; attending a play, movie, school activity, or sporting event; playing catch; visiting the library; grocery shopping; watching television; and sharing thoughts and ideas about life. Professional staff and national operating standards provide uniformity in recruitment, screening, matching, and supervision of volunteers and youths. Opportunities and support are provided for volunteers, as well as youths and their parents. A national evaluation of the Big Brothers/Big

Sisters of America mentoring program found that youths involved in the program were 46 percent less likely to start using drugs, 33 percent less likely to exhibit aggressive behavior, and 27 percent less likely to start using alcohol than their peers (Grossman & Garry, 1997; Ingersoll, 1997). Schools, as sites where juveniles spend a majority of their weekday time, also offer primary opportunities for prevention and intervention efforts, but not in isolation from concerned citizens, communities, and other agencies.

Objective #5. The fifth objective deals with breaking the cycle of violence by addressing youth victimization, abuse, and neglect. Considerable evidence has accumulated suggesting that childhood victimization experiences are related to subsequent delinquency and adult criminality. For example, Thornberry (1994) found that children who had been victims of violence were 24 percent more likely to report engaging in violent behavior as adolescents than those who had not been maltreated earlier. Widom (1992) reported that child abuse increased the risk of future delinquency and adult criminality by almost 40 percent. Many have begun to ask how such "cycles of violence" can be broken.

The *Safe Kids/Safe Streets* initiative by OJJDP is designed to help youth at risk for abuse and neglect; to encourage communities to strengthen the response of their criminal and juvenile justice systems to child abuse and neglect; and to enhance system coordination with child and family service agencies (Ingersoll, 1997). One site funded through this recent initiative is Burlington, Vermont, where a communitywide stakeholder collaborative was organized to address specific needs previously identified by a community survey. Intervention activities include providing additional resources to new and existing primary and secondary prevention efforts targeting at-risk families and child and adolescent victims of abuse; strengthening interagency protocols and collaboration; training the police, courts, and juvenile providers in effective means of supporting families affected by child abuse, neglect, or both; and involving stakeholders in a community governance structure (OJJDP, 1998). Implementation and evaluation of such initiatives are underway, but outcome data are not yet available.

Nurse Home Visitation is a promising new primary prevention effort, although evaluation data as of yet are scarce. The *David Olds' Nurse Home Visitation Program* in six U.S. sites has been supported by several federal agencies (Ingersoll, 1997). Six hundred at-risk, low-income, first-time mothers (including drug-addicted mothers) and their babies were served through a prenatal and early childhood home-visitation program. Through frequent home visits during the first 2 years of life, program nurses work intensively with new mothers to strengthen the mothers' parenting and vocational skills and improve early childhood development and health. The *Healthy Start Program* in Hawaii is an ongoing project that attempts to prevent child abuse and neglect by reducing the risks of poor family management and academic failure, and enhancing the protective factor of parent-child bonding (Howell, 1995, p. 58). The program screens mothers who are admitted to hospitals for childbirth, examining 15 at-risk factors. Families determined to be at risk are offered comprehensive services to aid child health and development from birth to age 5. Ninety-five percent of families accept the offer. Preventive health care is emphasized, including home visits to provide parent training and family counseling. Trained paraprofessional workers assist parents to enhance parent-child interaction, stimulate child development activities, provide health and social service linkage and coordination, and provide emotional and social support. The intensity of services varies according to the family's assessed level of need. Howell (1995) reports that three major controlled studies of early childhood education and home visitation (the *Perry Preschool Program* in Ypsilanti, Michigan; the *Houston Parent-Child Development Center;* and the *Syracuse Family Development Research Project*) have tracked participants well into adolescence and have shown that these interventions predict lower rates of violence and crime.

Similar partnerships attempt to enlist the cooperation of justice and human service agencies. The Yale/New Haven Child Development-Community Policing Program (CD-CP) engages community policing officials and mental health professionals in addressing child victimization and family violence (Marans & Berkman, 1997). Through federal support, nearly 300 communities now have Children's Advocacy Centers, which act as information clearinghouses, provide training and technical assistance, and coordinate the response of judicial and social service systems to child abuse (Ingersoll, 1997).

Curtis (1985) provides further evidence for the effectiveness of strategies to enhance community opportunities and reduce risk factors. Community-based approaches refer to programs located in specific neighborhoods, designed and implemented mainly by nonprofit community groups rather than justice or social service agencies. Community-based interventions may target individuals, families, and structural conditions in specific locales (Welsh et al., 1996; Welsh et al., 1999). *House of Umoja* (West Philadelphia) and *El Centro* (Puerto Rico) are examples of two long-standing, stable, residential programs that provide an extended family for minority juveniles in trouble with the law. Programs emphasize character building, mediation, self-responsibility, self-respect, community service (e.g., rehabilitation of old houses for low-income families), education, and employment. Although rigorous evaluations are lacking, reported recidivism results have been impressive (Curtis, 1985).

Several large-scale efforts aimed at strengthening minority families were implemented in the 1970s, including federally funded Child and Family Resource Centers located in different communities across the country. These centers provided a wide range of services to families (e.g., day care, tutoring, parenting skills, family counseling, etc.). A review by the U.S. General Accounting Office suggested that the centers enhanced family functioning at very low cost, and they may have reduced delinquency indirectly by improving parent-child relations and school performance (Curtis, 1985).

Other programs have targeted minority youth unemployment in high-crime communities (Curtis, 1985). Many of the better federal job-training programs of the 1960s and 1970s were successful at reducing crime, improving earnings, and reducing long-term costs. Training for adequate jobs, unfortunately, was only rarely provided. If job training leads to dead-end jobs, illegal opportunities may become even more attractive to youths. Youths' decisions to remain in legitimate jobs depended not only on money, but on intrinsic job satisfaction and gaining respect from their peers.

Long-term community economic and social development must also be addressed (Curtis, 1985). For example, capable community organizations have become increasingly involved in crime prevention through programs aimed at strengthening community involvement, employment and economic development, family supports and services, and a host of other activities (e.g., block watches, escort services, home security, etc.). Economic development is a necessary goal to improve the quality of residents' lives in many areas, including but not limited to crime. Creating financial self-sufficiency is at least as important as reducing illegal opportunities or addressing other causes of crime (Curtis, 1985).

When Violent Crime Goes Down, Do We Know Why?

How can we explain recent decreases in violent crime since 1993, the largest in over 30 years? Significant decreases in homicide have been recorded every year since 1991, when a peak rate of 10.5 per 100,000 was recorded. The homicide rate of 7.4 per 100,000 in 1998 was the lowest recorded since 1968. Drops in other violent crimes (e.g., robbery, rape, and aggravated assault) have been recorded every year since 1994 (U.S. Department of Justice, 2000). How much is this downward trend related to criminal justice policies, prevention strategies, economic or social conditions, or other factors (e.g., changes in age distributions, drug markets, and weapon availability)?

Experts generally agree that changes in the use of weapons are important in understanding recent peaks and valleys in homicide, particularly juvenile homicide (Blumstein & Rosenfeld, 1998). The growth in homicides by young people from 1985 to 1993 was entirely due to homicides committed with handguns. Recent decreases are similarly due to decreases in handgun-related homicides. These trends are most pronounced for large cities and appear to be related to the rise and fall of crack markets and violent competition in large cities.

Recent decreases in violent crime may also be partially due to economic upturn (e.g., reduced unemployment rates), police crackdowns on illegal markets, increased incarceration rates, and increased youth involvement in legitimate labor markets. However, it is extremely difficult to parcel out specific causes for the decrease (Blumstein & Rosenfeld, 1998). Probably all played some role in interaction with one another.

Social institutions (i.e., mutually shared and reinforced patterns of norms, rules, and laws) provide another potential explanation for recent decreases in violence (LaFree, 1998). In the peaceful post-World War II years, social institutions (e.g., political, economic, and family) were strong. In the 1970s, public trust in political institutions plummeted; economic inequality, inflation, and decline of labor unions all reduced confidence. The traditional family of the 1950s was severely weakened in the 1970s (e.g., both parents working, more single parents, higher divorce rates). Violent crime rates increased dramatically from 1963 to 1974. American society fought back against institutional decline by investing heavily in other institutions, especially criminal justice, education, and welfare. All three put downward pressure on crime rates, LaFree suggests.

Curtis (1998) suggests that many people had written off inner cities at the peak of the crack problem in the late 1980s and early 1990s. But how do we explain the sudden decline in violent crime in these neighborhoods, especially in New York City? Curtis cites ethnographic research in two New York City neighborhoods to suggest that many youths began to withdraw from public life as violence around them increased. He further suggests that community activism against violence played a role, even though economic vitality can hardly be said to have increased markedly. At the same time, aggressive policing against drug gangs and long prison sentences helped reduce the influence of large drug gangs because many downsized and many disbanded. Remaining distributors became more discreet and moved indoors, and turf battles were eliminated.

Fagan, Zimring, and Kim (1998) argue that those who would give credit to police strategies for recent declines in crime in New York City have little evidence for their claims. Why was there a steady decline in nongun homicides long before Mayor Rudolph Giuliani and former Police Commissioner William Bratton took office and began their multifaceted war on crime? As Fagan and colleagues note,

> The trend in nongun homicide for more than a decade remains a pleasant mystery that shrouds the whole explanation of variations in New York City homicide in fog. Even the best statistical data on incidence will not yield easy answers on causation. (1998, p. 13)

Conclusions

We have reviewed diverse prevention and intervention efforts throughout this book. These examples serve to illustrate the broad, interdisciplinary nature of prevention and intervention required to successfully reduce unacceptably high rates of violence in our society. Violence prevention must strive for an appropriate balance between punishment and prevention, between reactive and proactive approaches, between legal and educational interventions, between social development and social control.

Much further research on risk factors and causes contributing to violence is desirable, and more rigorous, valid evaluations of program effects are needed. Valid analyses of risk factors and causes are critical prerequisites for designing effective violence reduction strategies (Welsh & Harris, 1999). In the absence of such information, untested assumptions and hunches will continue to drive critical policy decisions, and unacceptably high rates of injuries and deaths will persist.

In spite of perceptions by many that violence in the United States is out of control and beyond control, careful examination indicates that violence is more prevalent among some groups than others, occurs more in some places than others, and involves certain types of situations and participants more often than others. There is reason for optimism as researchers and practitioners work together to explore and evaluate rational approaches to reducing violence.

Significant challenges remain, however. Successful interventions cost money and a significant investment of human resources. It is not yet clear that local, state, or federal government officials are prepared to sustain a commitment to approaches based upon valid research and knowledge, rather than policies calculated to win votes at election time. Nor is it clear that government officials will fund evaluation studies at the level necessary to determine what works. A dearth of valid evaluations has hindered progress in our knowledge about what works. Everyone seems to agree that better coordination and cooperation among government, private, and nonprofit agencies is needed, but little attention is devoted to exploring how to make such relationships work given the diverse backgrounds and agendas of participants (Welsh, 1995; Welsh & Harris, 1999).

Perhaps the best that can be said for now is that violence prevention in the United States has a promising but unpredictable future. To the degree that interventions can reasonably balance punishment and prevention, and take a rational approach based upon existing and emerging knowledge, that promise may yet be realized.

Endnote

1. Special issues of journals addressing relationships between race, crime, and punishment include the following: *Crime and Delinquency, 33*(2), 1987, edited by Barry Krisberg; *Journal of Research in Crime and Delinquency, 31*(2), 1994, edited by Carl Pope and Todd Clear; and *Justice Quarterly, 9*(4), 1992, edited by Julius Debro, Darnell Hawkins, and Coramae Richey Mann.

References

Andrews, D., Zinger, I., Hoge, R., Bonta, J., Gendreau, P., & Cullen, F. (1990). Does correctional treatment work? A clinically relevant and psychologically informed meta-analysis. *Criminology, 28*, 369–404.

Applegate, B., Cullen, F., Turner, M., & Sundt, J. (1996). Assessing public support for three-strikes-and-you're-out laws: Global versus specific attitudes. *Crime and Delinquency, 42*, 517–534.

Baldus, D. C., Woodworth, G., & Pulaski, C. A., Jr. (1994). *Equal justice and the death penalty: A legal and empirical analysis.* Boston: Northeastern University Press.

Bilchik, S. (1998). *A juvenile justice system for the 21st century* (NCJ-169276). Washington, DC: Department of Justice, Office of Justice Programs, Office of Juvenile Justice and Delinquency Prevention.

Blumstein, A., Cohen, J., & Nagin, D. (Eds.). (1978). *Deterrence and incapacitation: Estimating the effects of criminal sanctions on crime rates.* Washington, DC: National Academy of Sciences.

Blumstein, A., Cohen, J., Roth, J. A., & Visher, C. (Eds.). (1986). *Criminal careers and career criminals* (2 vols.). Washington, DC: National Academy of Sciences.

Blumstein, A., & Rosenfeld, R. (1998). Assessing the recent ups and downs in U.S. homicide rates. *National Institute of Justice Journal, 237*, 9–11.

Bohm, R. M. (1989). Humanism and the death penalty, with special emphasis on the post-Furman experience. *Justice Quarterly, 6*, 173–195.

———. (1999). *Deathquest: An introduction to the theory and practice of capital punishment in the United States.* Cincinnati, OH: Anderson.

Bowers, W. J. (1974). *Executions in America.* Lexington, MA: Lexington Books, D.C. Heath.

Burch, J. H., III, & Chemers, B. M. (1997). *A comprehensive response to America's youth gang problem* (Fact Sheet #40). Washington, DC: Department of Justice, Office of Justice Programs, Office of Juvenile Justice and Delinquency Prevention.

Catalano, R. F., & Hawkins, J. D. (1996). The social development model: A theory of antisocial behavior. In J. D. Hawkins (Ed.), *Delinquency and crime: Current theories.* New York: Cambridge University Press.

Chaiken, J. M., Lawless, M., & Stevenson, K. A. (1974). *The impact of police activity on crime: Robberies on the New York City subway system* (R-1424-NYC). Santa Monica, CA: Rand Corporation.

Clarke, R. V. (1992). *Situational crime prevention: Successful case studies.* New York: Harrow & Heston.

Clarke, R. V., & Cornish, D. B. (1985). Modeling offenders' decisions: A framework for policy and research. In M. Tonry & N. Morris (Eds.), *Crime and justice: An annual review of research* (Vol. 6, pp. 147–185). Chicago: University of Chicago Press.

Cole, G. F., & Smith, C. E. (1998). *The American system of criminal justice* (8th ed.). Belmont, CA: West/Wadsworth.

Conrad, J. P., & van den Haag, E. (1983). *The death penalty: A debate.* New York: Plenum.

Curtis, L. A. (1985). Neighborhood, family and employment: Toward a new public policy against violence. In L. A. Curtis (Ed.), *American violence and public policy: An update of the national commission on the causes and prevention of violence.* New Haven, CT: Yale University Press.

Curtis, R. (1998). The improbable transformation of inner-city neighborhoods: Crime, violence, drugs, and youths in the 1990s. *National Institute of Justice Journal, 237,* 16–17.

Ehrlich, I. (1975). The deterrent effect of capital punishment: A question of life or death. *American Economic Review, 65,* 397–417.

Fagan, J., Zimring, F., & Kim, J. (1998). Declining homicide in New York City: A tale of two trends. *National Institute of Justice Journal, 237,* 12–13.

Feyerherm, W. H. (1995). The DMC initiative: The convergence of policy and research themes. In K. K. Leonard, C. E. Pope, & W. H. Feyerherm (Eds.), *Minorities in juvenile justice* (pp. 1–15). Thousand Oaks, CA: Sage.

Foucault, M. (1977). *Discipline and punish.* New York: Pantheon.

Furman v. Georgia, 408 U.S. 238 (1972).

Gendreau, P. (1996). The principles of effective intervention with offenders. In A. T. Harland (Ed.), *Choosing correctional options that work: Defining the demand and evaluating the supply.* Thousand Oaks, CA: Sage.

Greenwood, P. W. (1982). The violent offender in the criminal justice system. In M. E. Wolfgang & N. A. Weiner (Eds.), *Criminal violence* (pp. 320–346). Beverly Hills, CA: Sage.

———. (1992). Substance abuse problems among high-risk youth and potential interventions. *Crime and Delinquency, 38,* 444–458.

Greenwood, P. W., Rydell, C. P., Abrahamse, A. F., Caulkins, J. P., Chiesa, J., Model, K. E., & Klein, S. P. (1994). *Three strikes and you're out: Estimated benefits and costs of California's new mandatory-sentencing law.* Santa Monica, CA: Rand.

Gregg v. Georgia, 428 U.S. 153 (1976).

Grossman, J. B., & Garry, E. M. (1997). *Mentoring—A proven delinquency prevention strategy* (NCJ 164834). U.S. Department of Justice, Office of Justice Programs, Office of Juvenile Justice and Delinquency Prevention.

Hagan, J., & Peterson, R. D. (1995). Criminal inequality in America: Patterns and consequences. In J. Hagan & R. D. Peterson (Eds.), *Crime and inequality* (pp. 14–36). Stanford, CA: Stanford University Press.

Harris, P. W., Welsh, W. N., & Butler, F. (2000). A century of juvenile justice. In G. LaFree, R. Taylor, R. Bursik, & J. Short (Eds.), *Criminal justice 2000: Vol. 1. The changing nature of crime.* Washington, DC: U.S. Department of Justice, National Institute of Justice.

Hawkins, J. D., Arthur, M. W., & Catalano, R. F. (1995). In M. Tonry (Ed.), *Crime and justice, A review of research* (pp. 343–427). Chicago: University of Chicago Press.

Hawkins, J. D., & Catalano, R. F. (1992). *Communities that care: Action for drug abuse prevention.* San Francisco: Jossey-Bass.

Howell, J. C. (Ed.). (1995). *Guide for implementing the comprehensive strategy for serious, violent, and chronic juvenile offenders* (NCJ 153681). Washington, DC: U.S. Department of Justice, Office of Justice Programs, Office of Juvenile Justice and Delinquency Prevention.

Ingersoll, S. (1997). The national juvenile justice action plan: A comprehensive response to a critical challenge. *Juvenile Justice, Journal of the Office of Juvenile Justice and Delinquency Prevention, 3*(2), 11–20. (NCJ-165925). Washington, DC: U.S. Department of Justice, Office of Justice Programs, Office of Juvenile Justice and Delinquency Prevention.

Kelling, G. L., Pate, T., Dieckman, D., & Brown, C. E. (1974). *The Kansas City preventive patrol experiment: A summary report.* Washington, DC: Police Foundation.

Kennedy, D. M. (1997). *Juvenile gun violence and gun markets in Boston.* Research Preview. Washington, DC: Department of Justice, Office of Justice Programs, National Institute of Justice.

Kracke, K., & Special Emphasis Division Staff. (1996). *Safe futures: Partnerships to reduce youth violence and delinquency.* Fact Sheet #38. Washington, DC: Department of Justice, Office of Justice Programs, Office of Juvenile Justice and Delinquency Prevention.

LaFree, G. (1998). *Losing legitimacy: Street crime and the decline of social institutions in America.* Boulder, CO: Westview Press.

Loeber, R., & Farrington, D. F. (Eds.). (1998). *Serious and violent juvenile offenders: Risk factors and successful interventions.* Thousand Oaks, CA: Sage.

Maguire, K., & Pastore, A. L. (Eds.). (1999a). *Sourcebook of criminal justice statistics* [On-line], Table 4.19. Available: <http://www.albany.edu/sourcebook> [January 30, 2000].

——— (Eds.) (1999b). *Sourcebook of criminal justice statistics* [On-line], Table 2.58. Available: <http://www.albany.edu/sourcebook> [January 25, 2000].

Marans, S., & M. Berkman. (1997). *Child development community policing: Partnership in a climate of violence.* Bulletin. Washington, DC: U.S. Department of Justice, Office of Justice Programs, Office of Juvenile Justice and Delinquency Prevention.

McCleskey v. Kemp, 478 U.S. 1019 (1987).

McDonald, D. C., & Carlson, K. E. (1993). *Sentencing in the courts: Does race matter? The transition to sentencing guidelines, 1986–1990.* Washington, DC: Department of Justice, Bureau of Justice Statistics.

Nagin, D. (1998). Criminal deterrence research at the outset of the twenty-first century. In M. Tonry (Ed.), *Crime and justice: An annual review of research* (Vol. 23, pp. 1–42). Chicago: University of Chicago Press.

National Prison Project. (1990). Juvenile justice: Is there a better way? *National Prison Project Journal, 5*(2), 1.

Office of Juvenile Justice and Delinquency Prevention (OJJDP). *Safe kids, safe streets project: Burlington, VT.* Available: <http://www.ncjrs.org/ojjdp/safekids/burlin.htm>.

Packer, H. L. (1968). *The limits of the criminal sanction.* Stanford, CA: Stanford University Press.

Pope, C. E. (1995). Equity within the juvenile justice system: Directions for the future. In L. K. Kempf, C. E. Pope, & W. H. Feyerherm (Eds.), *Minorities in juvenile justice* (pp. 201–216). Thousand Oaks, CA: Sage.

Pope, C. E., & Feyerherm, W. H. (1992). *Minorities and the juvenile justice system: Final report.* Washington, DC: Office of Juvenile Justice and Delinquency Prevention.

Reiss, A. J., Jr., & Roth, J. A. (Eds.). (1993). *Understanding and preventing violence* (Vol. 1). Washington, DC: National Academy Press.

Roth, J. (1994). *Understanding and preventing violence.* NIJ Research in Brief (NCJ-145645). Washington, DC: U.S. Department of Justice, National Institute of Justice.

Sechrest, L., White, S. O., & Brown, E. D. (1979). *The rehabilitation of criminal offenders: Problems and prospects.* Washington, DC: National Academy of Sciences.

Shichor, D., & Sechrest, D. K. (Eds.). (1996). *Three strikes and you're out: Vengeance as public policy.* Thousand Oaks, CA: Sage.

Snell, T. L. (1999, December). *Capital Punishment 1998* (NCJ-179012). Washington, DC: U.S. Department of Justice, Bureau of Justice Statistics.

Thornberry, T. (1994). *Violent families and youth violence.* Fact Sheet. Washington, DC: U.S. Department of Justice, Office of Justice Programs, Office of Juvenile Justice and Delinquency Prevention.

Tonry, M. (1987). *Sentencing reform impacts.* Washington, D.C.: U.S. Department of Justice, National Institute of Justice.

Torbet, P., Gable, R., Hurst, H., IV, Montgomery, I., Szymanski, L., & Thomas, D. (1996). *State responses to serious and violent juvenile crime.* Washington, DC: Department of Justice, Office of Justice Programs, Office of Juvenile Justice and Delinquency Prevention.

Tyler, T., & Boeckmann, R. (1997). Three strikes and you are out, but why? The psychology of public support for punishing rule breakers. *Law and Society Review, 31,* 237–265.

U.S. Department of Justice, Bureau of Justice Statistics. (1999). *Crime facts at a glance* [On-line]. Available: <http://www.ojp.usdoj.gov/bjs/glance/viotrd.txt> [January 30, 2000].

Vandaele, W. (1978). Participation in illegitimate activities: Ehrlich revisited. In A. Blumstein, J. Cohen, & D. Nagin (Eds.), *Deterrence and incapacitation: Estimating the effects of criminal sanctions on crime rates* (pp. 319–335). Washington, DC: National Academy of Sciences.

Walker, S., Spohn, C., & DeLeone, M. (1996). *The color of justice.* Belmont, CA: Wadsworth.

Welsh, W. (1995). *Counties in court: Jail overcrowding and court-ordered reform.* Philadelphia: Temple University Press.

Welsh, W., & Harris, P. (1999). *Criminal justice policy and planning.* Cincinnati, OH: Anderson Publishing Co.

Welsh, W., Harris, P., & Jenkins, P. (1996). Reducing overrepresentation of minorities in juvenile justice: Development of community-based programs in Pennsylvania. *Crime and Delinquency, 42*(1), 76–98.

Welsh, W., Jenkins, P., & Harris, P. (1999). Reducing minority over-representation in juvenile justice: Results of community-based delinquency prevention in Harrisburg. *Journal of Research in Crime and Delinquency, 36*(1), 87–110.

Widom, C. S. (1992). *The cycle of violence*. Research in Brief. Washington, DC: Department of Justice, Office of Justice Programs, National Institute of Justice.

Zahn, M. (1990). Intervention strategies to reduce homicide. In N. A. Weiner, M. A. Zahn, & R. J. Sagi (Eds.), *Violence: Patterns, causes, public policy* (pp. 379–390). New York: Harcourt, Brace, Jovanovich.

Zimring, F., & Hawkins, G. (1986). *Capital punishment and the American agenda.* Cambridge, MA: Cambridge University Press. ✦

Author Index

Skogan, W. G., 18
Sloane, J., 306
Smith, C. E., 358
Smith, M. D., 143, 144
Snell, T. L., 351, 352, 353, 354, 355
Snipes, J. B., 21, 82
Snyder, H. N., 187, 300
Sorenson, S. B., 159
Spector, M., 4, 19
Spelman, W., 125
Spergel, Irving A., 147, 365
Spohn, C., 357
Steadman, H. J., 132
Stevenson, K. A., 198, 348
Straits, B. C., 49
Straus, M. A., 17, 153
Sutherland, Edwin, 83, 87, 88, 89, 90, 110, 281
Swartz, J., 3
Sykes, 192, 120, 282

T

Tajfel, H., 279
Tarde, Gabriel, 87
Thoennes, N., 155, 157, 159, 160
Thommeny, J., 133
Thornberry, T., 367
Tims, F. M., 338
Tjaden, P., 155, 157, 159, 160
Tobler, N. S., 339
Toch, H., 241, 247
Tomsen, S., 133
Tonry, M., 356
Torbet, P., 360
Toupin, J., 175
Turk, A., 262, 263

U, V

Useem, B., 244, 245, 246
Vandaele, W., 353
van den Haag, 353, 354
Visher, C., 350
Vold, G. B., 21, 82, 89

W

Wald, 338
Walinsky, A., 128
Walker, L. E., 164
Walker, S., 19, 359
Walters, G., 320
Weiland, D., 333, 334
Weinberg, L., 252, 260
Weiner, N. A., 1
Weinrott, M., 229
Weis, K., 220
Wellford, C. F., 164
Welch, Danny, 280
Welch, W. M., 249, 280
Welsh, W., 10, 19, 84, 199, 300, 313, 350, 355, 356, 358, 360, 366, 369, 372
Wexler, H., 321, 336, 337
White, B. J., 278
White, S. O., 349
Widom, C. S., 367
Wiersema, B., 30, 40, 41, 51, 312, 313
Williams, J. S., 102
Williams, K. R., 154
Wilson, M. I., 157
Wilson, W. J., 243
Wintemute, G., 126
Wish, E. D., 320
Wisiniewski, N., 221
Woestendiek, J., 240

Wolfgang, Marvin E., 33, 83, 93,
  101–102, 146
Woodworth, G., 351
Wright, J. D., 126, 177, 186, 193,
  300, 301, 305
Wright, Q., 239
Wright, R. T., 192, 194, 195, 198,
  199, 313

X, Y, Z

Yant, M., 249, 250
Zahn, M. A., 1, 129, 130, 143,
  144, 353, 354
Zawitz, M. W., 155
Zimbardo, P. G., 247
Zimring, F. E., 299, 312, 353,
  354, 371 ✦

Subject Index